SOCIOLOGY OF MEDICINE

SOCIOLOGY OF MEDICINE:
Diversity, Conflict, and Change

William R. Rosengren
University of Rhode Island

HARPER & ROW, PUBLISHERS

New York   Hagerstown   Philadelphia   San Francisco   London

Sponsoring Editor: Dale Tharp
Project Editor: Pamela Landau
Production Manager: Jeanie Berke
Compositor: Maryland Linotype Composition Co., Inc.
Printer and Binder: The Maple Press Company
Art Studio: Allyn-Mason, Inc.

Sociology of Medicine: Diversity, Conflict, and Change

Library of Congress Cataloging in Publication Data

Rosengren, William R   1929–
    Sociology of medicine.

    Includes index.
    1. Social medicine.   2.   Social medicine—United
States.   I.   Title.
RA418.R68   362.1   79–13486
ISBN 0–06–045582–9

To my mother and the memory of my father

Contents

recruitment of physicians; The moral socialization of the physician;
The contexts of medical training; Elite education and
colleagueship; State education and staff-student conflict in medical
school; Urban medical education and alienation between faculty
and students; Securing a practice

construct; The medical-social model dispute—The case of
hyperkinesis; Mental illness and psychiatry—whither and
whence?; The rise of the therapeutic milieu; Psychomedications
and deinstitutionalization

Preface

This book is addressed primarily to undergraduate students and mainly to those who intend neither to "major" in sociology nor to go on to advanced study to become professional sociologists. It is certainly hoped, however, that the book will be of use to those two latter groups. It is written as a general introduction to the field of medical sociology for students from all around the college or university, and who take such courses out of general interest in the subject matter rather than as a necessary constraint of either a liberal arts or a preprofessional curriculum. It is perhaps most usefully read by students who have had at least an introduction to sociology, although an effort has been made to avoid special jargon wherever possible so that any college student of reasonable intelligence, whatever his or her concentration, can understand it and benefit from it. Thus, the book is addressed to students in their capacities as citizens and as people who are on the way to becoming educated, informed, and interested participants in their society.

A basic premise underlies this book, namely, that the institutions of medicine are a public resource and not the private property of those who practice it. It is in this sense that both the patient and the social scientist who approach the medical establishment do so in their multiple roles as contributor, creator, and sustainer of the very institutions to which they may be temporarily compliant. As such, the *rights* of citizens can never be fully separated from the *obligations* of patients. And in this sense, the sociology of medicine is as much a political science and a moral philosophy as it is a technical-social science. It is this complex posture this book aims to nurture in the minds of students.

Toward this end, the content and organization of this book is designed to set it apart from other textbooks in medical sociology while retaining its anchor in the mainstream of general sociology. First, each chapter deals with a basic dimension of health and society that most such courses at the undergraduate level cover, each emphasizing the dilemmas and contradictions in attempting to view medicine as a public resource. Second, the moral and ethical choices faced by citizens vis-à-vis the structure of medicine is emphasized throughout. In addition, reference is made to current trends and studies in medical sociology as well as retaining the threads of developments in the field as they have taken place over the past 15 to 20 years. Fourth, each chapter is *preceded* and *closed* with a brief *scenario,* each of which is intended to dramatize the main theme or themes within each chapter. Some of these are fictional, some are drawn from the author's own experiences, still others are brief excerpts from previously published works. They intend to focus the students' thinking as they move from chapter to chapter. Each chapter is followed by a brief listing of basic readings dealing with the topic at hand. Students may find these lists helpful in preparing term papers, in class discussion, or in organizing book reports.

In addition, as medical sociology courses continue to come into increasing demand, more and more faculty members are called up to organize such courses, perhaps for the first time. Under the assumption that many such instructors will not have a ready-made syllabus from which to work, a pedagogical aim of this book is to offer a content and a format that will not "get in their way," but will serve as a framework within which their own particular organization of the field can be set forth without creating serious conflicts and dilemmas in the minds of their students.

So in this context, this book, although it aims to be comprehensive in scope, does not cover *in depth* all of the topics instructors might wish to include or expand upon. It does not, moreover, contain an extensive bibliography, because other very good and comprehensive ones are currently available. These are excellent sources for collateral readings in depth, as are the citations and readings listed for each chapter in this book.

ACKNOWLEDGMENTS

As is customary, the publication of a book of this nature is an invitation for the author to indulge in some nostalgia about where it all came from. Actually, the publication of this book comes on the twentieth anniversary of my first publication in medical sociology, and that calls for some thanksgiving, especially to the members of the medical profession who suffered my presence and publications over the years: To the staff and patients of the Emma Pendleton Bradley Hospital, the Rhode Island State Department of Health, the Providence Lying-In Hospital, the Butler Health Center, the Rhode Island Hospital, the Rhode Island Institute of Mental Health, the Highland View Rehabilitation Hospital, the Cleveland Rehabilitation Center, the Rhode Island Division of Mental Retardation, the many individual members of the medical profession, and the American Medical Association.

Individually, I wish to thank Betty Jones and Marilyn Damon for their fine typing work, to David Lyons for bibliographic assistance, to Thomas Grzebien for some legal help, to Louis Brinsky for help in keeping me up to date on some matters in Chicago, and to Richard O'Toole, Clifton Bryant, and Judith Lorber for helpful comments on earlier drafts. In addition, I want to express a more general thanks to Eliot Freidson for being such an excellent role model over the years. He has constantly set the standard to which all medical sociologists aspire.

Again, to my wife and son who were not even a part of my life when this all started 20 years ago, but who are now the most important part of it.

Finally, I wish to thank my mother, whose love and support have helped sustain me over these 50 years, and the memory of my father, which has always been with me. Although he did not live to see his sons grow to adulthood or to become old with his wife, I believe that if he had, he would not have been disappointed with the way it has all turned out.

W.R.R.

SOCIOLOGY OF MEDICINE

The "medicalization" of nearly everything?

The emergence of a conglomerate health profession has rendered the patient role infinitely elastic. The doctor's certification of the sick has been replaced by the bureaucratic presumption of the health manager who arranges people according to degrees and categories of therapeutic need, and medical authority now extends to supervised health care, early detection, preventive therapies, and increasingly, treatment of the incurable. Previously, modern medicine controlled only a limited market; now this market has lost all boundaries. Unsick people have come to depend on professional care for the sake of their future health. The result is a morbid society that demands universal medicalization and a medical establishment that certifies universal morbidity.

In a morbid society the belief prevails that defined and diagnosed ill health is infinitely preferable to any other form of negative label or to no label at all. It is better than criminal or political deviance, better than laziness, better than self-chosen absence from work. More and more people subconsciously know that they are sick and tired of their jobs and of their leisure passivities, but they want to hear the lie that physical illness relieves them of social and political responsibilities. They want their doctor to act as lawyer and priest. As a lawyer, the doctor exempts the patient from his normal duties and enables him to cash in on the insurance fund he was forced to build. As a priest, he becomes the patient's accomplice in creating the myth that he is an innocent victim of biological mechanisms rather than a lazy, greedy, or envious deserter of a social struggle for control over the tools of production. Social life becomes a giving and receiving of therapy: medical, psychiatric, pedagogic, or geriatric. Claiming access to treatment becomes a political duty, and medical certification a powerful device for social control.

With the development of the therapeutic service sector of the economy, an increasing proportion of all people come to be

Ivan Illich, Ph.D.
From Ivan Illich, *Medical Nemesis*. New York: Pantheon, 1976.

perceived as deviating from some desirable norm, and therefore as clients who can now either be submitted to therapy to bring them closer to the established standard of health or concentrated into some special environment built to cater to their deviance.

CHAPTER 1

Health care and the sociology of medicine: diversity, conflict, and change

In commenting recently on the state of health in the United States, Stephen R. Graubard said[1]:

> Medicine touches intimately on the physical and emotional lives of most Americans, eliciting strong reactions, whether of approval or disapproval. It provides an almost infallible measure of public sentiment about the efficiency of government, the vitality of the medical professions, and the justice of new moral perceptions and demands that modern medical practices have elicited, . . . in a labor intensive industry such as health care, the views and opinions of both professionals and workers weigh heavily. So, also, do the opinions of those who seek medical help, who, in one way or another, express concern about its availability, quality, humanity, and cost.

An underlying theme in this textbook is the conviction that it is only in very recent times that the voice of the nonmedical professional has been heard at all strongly in the debate over the struggle for a public policy in regard to health. And it is the diversity of these opinions that is largely responsible for the degree of conflict and incipient change now clearly discernible on the health scene.

HEALTH AS UNSTABLE EQUILIBRIUM

The idea of "balance" seems to be an ancient one in the development of what we now know as Western medicine, and this notion has its roots as far back as the time of Hippocrates. Health, as Henry Sigerist has pointed out, ". . . appears as a condition of perfect equilibrium. When we are in good health we breathe freely, digest our food, excrete urine, move and think as a matter of course, without being aware of it. But this equilibrium can be upset by atmospheric factors, faulty diet, wrong mode of living or other conditions. And this upset balance manifests itself in pain, fever, swellings, disturbed functions and other symptoms of disease."[2]

The logic of Greek scientific thought led to the conclusion that inasmuch as illness represented an imbalance in this ideal state of equilibrium, the task of medicine was to seek the sources of these imbalances and return them to a condition of equilibrium. This approach undoubtedly led to the body intervention form of medical treatment that predominates today. There is an inescapable duality in these age-old notions about the nature of disease and health in that even the Greeks recognized that illness-producing imbalances could be found in sources outside the human body. Therefore the central problem with which medicine continues to grapple after centuries is how to resolve an *intraorganism* orientation to health and illness, as against an extraorganism point of view. The pursuit of the first has resulted in the incredible elaboration of the laboratory sciences and has come to dominate the medical scene, at least for the past century. Alongside this avenue of development has been another route—one that does not view illness as simply an internal phenomenon and health as brought about by mechanical interventions to reestablish internal balances. Rather, illness is considered to be traceable to external sources, and medicine to be a social science par excellence. As Sigerist put it:[3]

> . . . when a man falls ill he ceases to be a useful member of society. He drops out, so to say, and may even become a burden to his fellow men. The more differentiated a society becomes, the more it is affected by the ill health of its members. . . . I have seen blind people (in the Soviet Union) performing skilled work in many factories, and other plants have special workshops for the physically handicapped where the speed of the conveyor belt is adjusted to their capacity. Cripples are organized in Craftsmen's cooperatives. All this is very uneconomical from our point of view because the productivity of such individuals is obviously reduced below the normal. It is only possible in a society which is itself the employer. . . . The goal of medicine is not merely to cure diseases; it is rather to keep men adjusted to their environment as useful members of society, or to readjust them when illness has taken hold of them. The task is not fulfilled simply by a physical restoration but must be continued until the individual has again found his place in society, his old place if possible, or if necessary a new one. This is why medicine is basically a social science.

One can hardly pick a quarrel with a lofty goal as "returning men to their old place"—or a new one, if necessary—in society. The debate, rather, hinges around who shall bring about such physical restoration, social preservation, personal adaptation, and social readjustment. Shall it be the physician (Illich says medicine already has too much influence in our lives), whose expertise seems better grounded in the "internal" imbalance sources of illness and health, or shall it be invested in citizens or their representatives who, in a constitutional democracy, are vested with the right and power to alter their own social circumstances?

If the layman is not expert in the laboratory sciences, it is equally true that the physician possesses no expertise in the social sciences or in social policy.[4] It is this duality and "antagonistic cooperation" between the medical and social philosophies concerning health and medicine that constitute the theme of this book.

By way of beginning, it should be made clear at the outset that this is a textbook in the sociology of medicine, not in medical sociology. The importance of this seemingly trivial distinction is underscored by the fact that medical sociology, as commonly understood, is in fact a pantheon of subject matters; it includes far-reaching conceptual issues that relate social phenomena to health and illness matters. It is perhaps for this reason that most textbooks in *medical sociology* take the form of long review articles, under the heading of chapters, containing long compendia of research findings centering around some collection of topics. These serve students best as guides to the literature and as a way of organizing their thoughts about certain topical subject matters in the field. These are enormously useful books and they will continue to be written and used.

Recently, however, more thematically organized texts have emerged. They do not pretend to "cover all of the literature." Instead they have limited themselves to reviewing and evaluating the state of some selected issue or policy matter in the field of health: race and ethnic relations, medicine in rural areas, the matter of dying, economic constraints on health delivery, current issues in medicine and social change, and others with a similarly limited and selective focus. This thematic focus came about basically because of needs. First, there has been a need to untangle the bewildering amount of data on social science–health related research, that has accumulated, especially over the past 20 years. Second, there has been a growing need to provide students with course textbooks that in some way are responsive to current social trends rather than being simply summaries of professional research.

With respect to the first need, the astounding expansion of medical sociology as a field of study and the difficulties encountered in expecting undergraduate students to "master the field" by digesting a single long compendium of research reports has to be set down as a prime limiting factor. In this context, the membership of the Medical Sociology Section of the American Sociological Association now numbers well over 1200 individuals.[5] A recently published, selective bibliography in medical sociology contains nearly 500 separate books, book chapters, and journal articles. This growth has occurred almost entirely during the past 20 years.

It is now virtually impossible for the professional sociologist—not to speak of students—to comprehend this backlog of writing, let alone place it in some meaningful and responsible thematic scheme; there is simply too much there. Merely glancing at random at a recent bibliography under the umbrella category of medical sociology turns up the following kinds of topics calling for brief summarization and inclusion in a contemporary text: "social psychological factors in the development of rheumatoid arthritis," "the effects of social isolation on schizophrenia," "symptom manifestations and situational press," "the story of modern preventive medicine," "the public drinking house and society," "patient responsibility in the delay of cancer treatment," "hospital-community relations in the South," "friendship patterns in a state hospital," "attitudes of youth toward mental health problems," "relatives' attitudes and mental hospitalization," "change in a traditional attitude resulting from modern health problems," "determinants of the role image of the patient in a psychiatric hospital," "medical development in a Maori community," "medicine and pharmacy of the New England Indians," "a longitudinal view of patient conduct," "acceptance of the Salk polio vaccine," "reference groups and loyalties in the outpatient department," "social responsibility of the physician," ad infinitum.

The list is virtually endless and the range and variety of topics dealt with are mind-boggling. Its contents defy manageable and meaningful categorization and interpretation, let alone comprehension by beginning students. Indeed, if the effort were to be made, and assuming that judicious selection and pruning of the list would yield about one-third of the publications deserving comment and inclusion in such an opus and assuming also that each item included deserved a one-page summary and commentary, this would result in a textbook of at least 2000 pages—not likely to be read, and certainly not understood, by many students.

In short, the field literally cries for organization. The present book is an attempt to offer one such organization while admittedly sacrificing the comprehensive synopticon approach.

MEDICINE AS A POLICY SCIENCE

The second need is for a textbook for undergraduates that makes an effort to be responsive and traceable to a recognizable set of social values and policy directions to which many people can subscribe and with regard to which members of this society are going to be exposed, for good or for ill.

In this connection, therefore, the assumptions throughout this book are that health—in terms of physical integrity, a feeling of personal well-being, and capacity for satisfying and appreciated social membership and participation—is a desirable condition and that its benefits, especially in a democratic society, should be extended to as many of its members as possible. Among the corollaries of this assumption are the following: Sometimes a state of physical integrity brought about by medical technology is not accompanied by feelings of personal well-being. On the other hand, sometimes feelings of personal ill-being and social incapacitation are not accompanied by a breakdown of physical integrity, and this may represent as undesirable a condition as in the previous situation. Whether the last-mentioned cases ought to be counted as "illnesses" is a moot question, which could involve long-range implications for the power of the medical establishment to control and oversee "nonmedical" manifestations of undesirable personal circumstances.

A further corollary is that a commitment to widespread good health among the citizenry may lead to threats to the very constructs of democracy that have been instrumental in raising good health to its present level of preeminence among the values we embrace. It leads to the question of whether coercion of one form or another by whatever group is justified if done so in the name of the extension of health. Moreover, it leads to the overarching question of whether the widespread diffusion of good health is so inherently desirable that it should be pursued whatever the costs, both monetary and nonmonetary. At present the further elaboration of medical technology may no longer be the problematic issue that it once was. Rising to preeminence are questions rooted in the larger arenas of social-political policy on the one hand and in issues of professional and social organization on the other.

The astounding accomplishments of medical technology are evidenced all around us. So great are they, in fact, that they loom so large in our consciousness as to cloud the underlying issues and problems of policy and social organization concerning the use and distribution of these accomplishments. The matter of the social organization of medicine—including its professional framework and the accompanying policy issues—constitutes an underlying theme throughout this book.

TECHNOLOGY AND PROFESSIONAL AND SOCIAL ORGANIZATION

A related premise is that medical care is a function of the interaction between the three basic factors of (1) medical technology, (2) professional organization, and (3) the more encompassing social and cultural milieu to which the first two are related.

By technology is meant the capacity of medicine to predict and create outcomes. It does not refer merely to implements and drugs, but rather to the entire intellectual edifice in which contemporary modern Western medicine is housed and out of which it operates. That is, the predominating microanalytic approach to illness generally is as much a technology as are the somewhat less precise conceptualizations falling under the umbrella of emotional or mental disorder or illness. The transactions between practitioners and patients are but specific manifestations of these global medical technologies and ideologies.

Moreover, the capacity of medicine to identify, define, and create its own monopoly over illnesses and instabilities is as much a function of technology as it is of professional organization. Hence, what diseases are given diagnostic and treatment priority are not self-evident. Such disease eminence is a socially produced phenomenon, assisted in its rise by the accepted power and influence of "technical" definitions and sustained through the professional organization of medicine.

Included in technology as well as in professional organization are the relationships between patients and illness and between patients and the professional setting of diagnosis and care. That is, only under rare circumstances can the patient be regarded as a passive "agent" who happens to carry a disease and is uninvolved in the health-illness process. That is, persons who are ill live in a situation of "antagonistic cooperation" with the professional organization and in most cases are participants both in creating the disease and defining process as well as in treatment. And we do not always mean patients in the *literal* sense either. This term is used in the sense that the social and cultural constraints, norms, expectations, and institutional complexes of society are as critical to the disease-making process as they are to the professional organization-treatment complex.

The patient therefore is usefully regarded as a participant—sometimes an antagonistic or unwitting one—in the illness-health process. Sometimes a patient's participation is conscious and goal-directed; more frequently it is a function of institutional patterns, role expectations, and cultural constraints over which he or she has little direct personal control.

By "professional organization" is meant the patterns and content of the occupational division of labor in medicine and its above-mentioned extensions to include the reciprocal roles into which laymen —as patients—are channeled. Thus the social organization of medicine includes its place in the major economic and political structures of society, political, its patterns of member recruitment, and the almost infinite variety of ways by which it incorporates its technologies and distributes them to patient groups.

Finally, we come to broader considerations involving the place of medical technology and medical social organization in the larger and historically given major institutions of society, including the cultural beliefs and ethos surrounding the medical complex.

The student is enjoined to consider that the "sociology of medicine" set forth in this book is a consideration of the constant interplay between these factors—technology, professional organization, and social cultural milieu.

PLAN OF THE BOOK

Hence, the substantive chapters contained in this book address this interplay by considering first the shifting patterns of illness and its reciprocal of health occurring in this society over the past several decades (Chapter 2). Chapter 3 deals with some critical aspects of health care costs, how they are changing, and to what professional and organizational factors such changes may be attributable. Chapter 4 explores some basic methodological problems in developing a sociology of medicine, some special difficulties encountered in conducting research in medical contexts, and particularly the primary distinction between the prevailing *medical model of illness* and its chief contemporary competitor, a *social model of illness*.

Chapter 5 concerns the process by which persons are differentially drawn from the population to enter this prototypical profession, as well as some of the patterns that appear to exist in the moral as compared with the technical socialization of physicians. There is also some discussion of the manner by which entrance into the profession may be affected by prevailing patterns of professional organization.

Chapter 6 is concerned with the hospital as a range of organizational types and in which both the technology and professional organization of medicine finds its most dramatic expression. At the same time it is recognized that the hospital, like other complex organizations, is a creature of the culture in which it is grounded.

Chapter 7 examines some elements of the occupational division of labor in medicine, including the proliferation of specialist medical technicians, and the uncertain role of the so-called physician's assistant and a variety of other paraprofessionals who are something more than technician but less than doctor, yet who both are a function of and contributors to the present complexity of the medical establishment. Of special interest here is the reappearance of the midwife, heretofore a folk practitioner nearly eradicated by organized medicine but now drawn into the orbit of influence of the medical establishment.

Chapter 8 deals with the social organization of medical practice, with particular reference to the role of patient participation in this institution of patterned antagonism-cooperation.

Chapter 9 discusses some of the principal marginal systems of medical practice—ranged along a pair of intersecting continua, from "credible" to "incredible" practices and from those that are accepted as "authentic" to those that are not.

Chapter 10 is concerned with a broad overview of the major issues —historical and contemporary—surrounding the definition and management of what is commonly understood to be the "functional" illness-behavior disorders, emotional disturbance, and so forth.

Chapter 11 explores a range and variety of recent attempts to go beyond "standard" forms of medical care delivery organization and reach for the goal of "comprehensive care"—from neighborhood health centers to regional medical centers.

Finally, Chapter 12 considers medical care from a "whither and whence" perspective—what the future might hold in terms of the issues and problems taken up in the previous chapters of the text.

A RECURRING THEME: DIVERSITY, CONFLICT, AND CHANGE

Except by resorting to a high level of abstraction, it is not judicious to make sweeping generalizations about the contemporary medical system. Indeed, one may easily argue that in a strict and literal sense, there is no medical "system" at all if we use that term to mean a functionally interrelated and interdependent complex of subunits within which modifications of one sort or another taking place in one subunit can be understood to have functional consequences for all the other subunits. In the terminology of Loomis:

> Any level of interaction furnishes examples of social systems: the direct, fact-to-face, personal interaction of two actors, or the indirect, enormously interlinked, impersonal interaction of a society. The concept of the social system enables the analytic observer to move from a given subsystem to the larger societal system and back again. It is equally legitimate to examine American society and the relations of the doctor and his patient, since both constitute social systems exhibiting an orderly uniformity of interaction.[6]

It is a difficult task to square that contention with the range and variation of form and activity we can observe in the medical scene. The problem of dealing with the concept of "system" in relation to the sociology of medicine is further exacerbated by the structural-functional dictum, also given by Lommis, that "At any given moment the structure of a given social system may be described and analyzed in terms of [these] elements."[7]

The elements referred to by Loomis are (1) belief, (2) sentiment;

(3) end, goal, or objective; (4) norm; (5) status-role; (6) rank; (7) power; (8) sanction; and (9) facility. When challenged to do so, a reasonably intelligent person will not find it too difficult to reflect on affairs medical and come up with some examples, observations, and examples to fit reasonably well under these nine highly generalized "elements" in the medical "social system." The rub comes very quickly when it becomes apparent that a wide range of cases and examples seem to fit logically under each rubric, and even more quickly when one is challenged to see or infer functional interrelationships between factors representing these systemic "elements." Part of this difficulty lies in the fact that the concept of a system—generally when applied to a society and more specifically to the social organization of medicine —implies stability, uniformity, predictability, pattern, coordination, routinization, and organized arrangement, method, or plan.

In fact, what comes to our consciousness as we observe and reflect on medicine is more often instability, variability, unpredictability, multiplicity of patterns, lack of coordinatation, disorganization, disorder, and so on. In short, the social system perspective implies that the medical social complex is monolithic. But a commonsense view teaches us that it is more tessellated. To use a geological metaphor, the social system approach finds the earth of medicine to be a monolith, but casual observation leads us to believe that it is more like a conglomerate.

Thus, as this book proceeds from a consideration of "changing health patterns" at the beginning to an attempt to glimpse into the future, we shall be especially sensitive to the special properties of conglomerates: *diversity, conflict,* and *change.* It is assumed, therefore, as well as substantiated by the accumulation of social science research, that the pluralism and diversity typifying most major institutional forms in American society is no less true of the social forms and conduct that make up the subject matter of the sociology of medicine. That is, processes such as disease discovery and awareness to major contemporary politics concerning the social and economic structures of health care are riddled through with a diversity of form, content, and purpose, as well as with conflict, dispute, opposing presuppositions, and other competing forces that make change not only ubiquitous but inevitable. Some of the flavor of this systematic diversity is, by way of introduction, exemplified by the remainder of this first chapter.

THE SOCIAL CHARACTER OF ILLNESS

Illness, in lay perspective, is commonly understood to be something out in the environment that "happens" to people almost in a random fashion. We may of course understand, if exposed to a sufficient amount of media influence, that there are certain "risk factors" involved in some diseases. We know, for example, that the chances of heart attack and stroke are increased by smoking and by poor dietary habits both in kind and amount. We know also that certain living conditions and life-styles are likely to increase the chance of one's contracting tuberculosis. By the same token there is clear evidence that smoking is a major contributing factor in lung cancer and emphysema, and that extended exposure to the rays of the sun increases the chance of developing skin cancer. Yet we take consolation in the fact that many people smoke all their lives and then die of unrelated causes. And many people living on the margins of society never "catch" tuberculosis, and many members of numerous occupational groups work and live all their lives in the sun and never develop skin cancer. These "commonsense" observations of departures from the "scientific norms" concerning illness both reassure and frighten us. They tell on the one hand that we may behave with impunity and have a chance of dodging illness. On the other hand, they serve as archangels warning us that at any moment, and without warning, either the doors of the hospital or the gates of the cemetery may be opened to us.

Thus, just as illness can be easily understood as the random interplay between the human body and "external" pathogenic agents, so too can the efforts of the medical establishment be mistakenly understood to be the application of value-free therapeutic "agents" by technologically sophisticated and justified practitioners in order to exorcise the offending foreign disease entity.

Hence, by this reasoning, we have a simple model of illness and medical care: behave pretty much as you wish and take your chances. If you are unlucky and "catch" something, go to the medical establishment and receive a rationally and technically applied cure.

Contrariwise, another view is that illness is socially produced as well as socially managed by the behavior patterns and cultural constraints in which people engage and to which they have become acculturated.

By this same token, medical technology as well as medical care can be understood to be a social science par excellence in the sence that definitions of illness, inventions of medical technologies, differential diagnosis, types of medical care organization, and their varied and *differential application* to populations is a function not of the technology itself, but of social and cultural forces that play upon the medical establishment itself.

The links between culture, social organization, behavior and illness are never better illustrated than by the classic case of the high incidence of cancer of the scrotum among English chimney sweeps in the eighteenth century. During the process of collecting morbidity data at that time it came to the attention of the public health officials that there was an unduly high rate of this cancer, especially in the industrial North of England. Using the model here sketched, the problem was to entertain the hypothesis that the disease did not strike randomly, but was socially and culturally patterned. The mode of investigation is deceptively simple: what do victims of the same disease have in common socially? The answer in this case was occupational group. Chimney sweeps fell victim to the disease far more frequently than did other members of the society. Now the question is "why?" The answer seems obvious: Coal is a carcogenic agent and the work of a chimney sweep differentially exposes him (particularly with the one sweeper's uniform most possessed at that time) to this agent. And, as was typical throughout most of Britain at the time, bathing was a rare luxury. Nevertheless, with a strong educational program the sweeps were encouraged to bathe more frequently, and shortly thereafter the number of new cases of this cancer declined sharply. Would that all illnesses were that simple.

Not dissimilar is the case of the high rate of throat cancer among black immigrants from South Africa to London discovered only a few years ago. The web of social-behavioral factors in illness is somewhat more complex here. While living in South Africa these persons were subject to the discriminatory apartheid laws, one of which was the prohibition against the consumption of alcohol. But indigenous to their culture was a potent brew that they bottlegged in order to satisfy their thirst. When arriving as immigrants in London they, as is true of most immigrants to metropolitan centers, were subject to the ecology and politics of the city and were forced to make their homes in the least desirable sections of London. This happened to be the upper reaches of the Thames estuary, the berthing and distribution center for crude oil tankers. Carrying with them as they did their culturally acquired taste for their native liquor, they cooked it in discarded petroleum drums. Petroleum being a carcogenic agent, we have a neat link between culture, behavior, and illness.

A further illustrative case involves the excessively high infant mortality rate occurring among infants in the Gambia in West Africa. The rate was found to be much higher than that suffered by babies in other parts of Africa at a similar level of social-technological development. Again, the question posed by the point of view that illness as well as its treatment is brought about by social factors had to do with what was occurring socially and culturally in this community to produce the high infant mortality rate. First, after extensive record keeping, it was determined that the vast majority of infants were dying during the rainy season from a lung disease, the physical etiology of which involved undue exposure to dampness and moisture. Moreover, it was discovered that most of the dying infants were of ages within two or three months of one another. Hence, in comparison with the remainder of the year there were an excessive number of infants of dying age at this time of the year. So the question became, knowing the physical cause of the deaths, what was it that produced such large number of babies "at risk" during the dangerous rainy season? Simple extrapolation meant that these risky infants were all conceived within two or three months of each other—also in statistically high numbers. As the epidemiologist subsequently uncovered, there was a prohibition in the Gambia (one of the major peanut producers in the world) against sexual intercourse during the planting season. Following the close of the planting season there tended to be an exceedingly high rate of sexual activity resulting in pregnancy and birth at a time of the year coinciding just prior to the beginning of the rainy season. Thus we have a coincidence of culture, climate, and economy that produced a major health problem.

A case in a children's psychiatric hospital illustrates not only the effects of *individual* behavior in producing disease, but also the effects of the social organization of medicine in failing to discern it. (It should be pointed out that this hospital served 56 patients with a staff of 120 at a cost of medical and psychiatric care of approximately $14,000 per year.) One of the patients, age 11, suddenly became unexplainably ill. He had nausea, loss of appetite, generalized weakness, and a slight fever. The hospital turned its battery of technologies to him without success. After a week or ten days he was sent to the major general hospital in the community for a diagnostic workup. Nothing definitive was uncovered, so his tonsils were removed and he was returned to the psychiatric treatment center. The identical symptoms reappeared and he was transferred to the state communicable disease hospital where an effort was made to isolate the problem. Again, nothing was found. So his adenoids were removed and he was returned once again to the institution and there the symptoms persisted. After some three months of this fruitless technical search, the psychiatric hospital interns were rotated, and an intern trained in India joined the staff. He examined the patient quickly and immediately announced, "This boy has typhoid fever." This diagnosis proved to be correct, and the condition was corrected. Now, two questions arise: Why typhoid fever in a patient at a high-technology hospital? And why was the medical establishment unable to diagnose it? Now, the State Epidemiology Division began its work on the question of what *behavior* this individual engaged in to contract such a "rare" disease. The answer is as bizarre as it is both social and psychological.

One of the behavioral aberrations to which this boy was prone was to consider himself a dog. He would drop down on all fours, hop around barking, refuse to eat unless a plate of food were placed on the floor, and occasionally nip at staff members' heels. How did he "catch" typhoid? A group of child patients had, in the early part of the summer, been taken on an overnight trip to a well-known resort area. During this outing the patient at issue "became a dog" and lapped water from a polluted mud puddle!

Why the inability of three high technology hospitals correctly to diagnose a simple case of typhoid fever? The answer is simple but important; physicians and medical institutions generally, when confronting patients, tend to entertain a limited number of hypotheses concerning what may conceivably be "wrong" with the patient.[8] The hypotheses entertained are usually generated out of the individual practitioner's prior experience with cases handled in the past that have exhibited similar symptoms. That is, most medical institutions encounter and recognize those diseases and illnesses that are common to their practices. This, however, is deceptive because of the twin processes of "differential diagnosis" on the one hand, and "treatment of choice" on the other.

With the possible exception of diagnosis by means of X rays, exploratory surgery, and a handful of other visual means of inspection, physicians often make a diagnosis on the basis of the utterances that patients make about their body sensations. People report symptoms verbally and the physician makes a judgment as to what these mean in terms of body lesion. The problem with this is that reported symptom A may in fact reflect either condition 1, 2, 3, or 4. However that might be, the doctor—like a baseball umpire—*does* make a diagnosis. This is differential diagnosis. Following that, a curative or palliative prescription is made. If diagnosis 1 has been made, the doctor may prescribe treatment a, b, c, or d, each of which may be remembered to have had some effect on lesion A, if that is what in fact ails the patient. This is known as the "treatment of choice." In short, in the vast number of cases with which physicians deal, they rely upon their *recollection* of similar symptoms reported by patients in the past, their further recollection of what diagnosis they made in most such cases, their additional recollection of what the prescribed intervention was, and their memory about its effects.

Finally, the exceedingly high tuberculosis rate found until recently among islanders on the Isle of Lewis-Harris in the Outer Hebrides illustrates a most complete relationship between social structure and illness.

Lewis-Harris is a narrow island some 40 miles long with a main population of some 6000 persons living in the harbor town of Stornoway, and otherwise sparsely populated over the tundralike, peatmosscovered, saline land. The main industry is the weaving of Harris tweed. The technology of this industry is as follows: sheared sheep wool is imported from the mainland and the mills in Stornoway dye and spin it into skeins. The cloth, however, is not woven in the mills, but rather by crofters, who live in small dirt-floor thatched-roof cottages scattered throughout the hinterlands of the island. The term "croft" has four separate meanings. First, it refers to the small plot of land (usually no more than 3/4 of an acre) occupied by the crofter. It refers also not only to the crofter but to the building occupied. Finally, it refers to the *legal* relationship of the crofter to the land the croft sits upon. Legally, the crofter owns the building but not the land. One may pass the building on to one's heirs, but not the land; the latter is occupied as a matter of *noblesse oblige*. The croft, in winter-time, is heated by peat moss, and by tradition each crofter has rights to cut peat moss in the bogs of the landed lords each spring—hopefully enough to permit survival through the bitter cold winter months.

Small as the croft is, and saline as the land is, with a short growing season, the crofter cannot raise enough crops to survive. To supplement his income he places himself in debt for the "hire purchase" of a loom from a mill in Stornoway. This is placed directly in the one-room craft and there the crofter looms bolts of Harris tweed for a fee of approximately 5 pounds each. Thus, the crofter works in bitter cold conditions from early morning until late at night—often in a dirt-floor hut heated only meagerly by a pile of smoldering peat moss. Hence we see the beginnings of the man-made conditions likely to produce the seeds of tuberculosis.

More than that, however, the island is dominated institutionally by the conservative wing of the Church of Scotland, of the fire and brimstone variety, which prohibits, among other pleasures of the flesh, the consumption of alcohol. The crofters, for their part, engaged in an active bootlegging activity and large quantities of whiskey are consumed to fill the empty hours alone on the moors.

There we now have the ideal conditions, many the work of man himself, to create fertile ground for TB: an icy climate with inadequate housing and heating, a poor diet, and the overconsumption of alcohol.

What aggravates the situation even further is that the Church teaches that blood in one's sputum is the "mark of the devil," and the crofter who discovers it does not go immediately to the castle in Stornoway, which has been transformed over the years into a TB hospital. Rather, he hides from his neighbors while his health deteriorates. Finally, because of his "selling" his bolts of tweed he is legally defined as an entrepreneur and therefore is excluded from numerous social welfare benefits to which he might otherwise be entitled.

In sum, law, custom, living habits, religion, and socioeconomic macrostructures combine on Lewis-Harris in a rare mix to produce tuberculosis of near epidemic proportions.

Illness therefore is not something that merely "happens" to people. In the vast number of instances it is brought about by the socially and culturally patterned behavior of persons. This book rests upon the implications of this assumption.

Now these transactions between the social aspects of illness and the social behavior of medical practitioners take place within the context of organizational settings that can be as highly varied as may patient and practitioner response to illness.

PROFESSIONAL ORGANIZATION

In addition to differential patient behavior, the kind and quality of health care received is a function not only of medical technology but also of the social organization of that technology and the nature of the patient role that ill persons are expected to enact. That is, health care received at a large metropolitan medical center is not the same as that in a small rural community. And even within that category the nature of health care received at a teaching hospital can be very different from that delivered at even a prestigious general hospital, but one without medical school affiliations. By the same token, the nature of care received at a neighborhood mental health clinic is in no way similar to that received at an elite psychoanalytically oriented psychiatric hospital.

By the same token, treatment in the office of a solo fee-for-service physician can in no way be compared with treatment received at a Health Maintenance Organization. And treatment in a surgical ward is organizationally very different from treatment in a medical ward, and care received in the "typical" state psychiatric hospital bears little resemblance to that received in most private psychiatric facilities. In short, medical care is received in the nexus of *some* kind of organizational setting, the nature of which is a prime determinant of the care received.

In general, the health care received is a joint function of available technology and complexity of medical organization; that is, the more complex the organization, the more complex the technology, and therefore the greater the *potential* for higher-quality medical care. The caveat in this formula is, however, an important one. As Eliot Freidson has pointed out: The greater the complexity of the social organization of medicine (and therefore the more sophisticated and available the viable technology) the lower the patient satisfaction and, by logic, the more reluctant is the client to enact the appropriate reciprocal role.[9]

Even the ostensible autonomous physician in solo fee-for-service practice does in fact have some degree of organization and cooperation with other physicians, if only on an informal basis. At minimum he or she has reciprocal arrangements with one or more other physicians in the local community who "cover" each others' practices on days off and other occasions. Thus, inadvertently, a patient may fall under the purview of more than one doctor. Such informal covering arrangements are, however, inherently unstable because to perpetuate them means that the exchange of overload work must be more or less equal and reciprocal. If a doctor calls upon a collaborating colleague's time too often, the colleague may withdraw from the arrangement. More important, however, if a physician sends patients to another doctor too frequently, the referring doctor is in danger of losing patients to the practice of the collaborating physician. Nevertheless, some degree of organization and collaboration typifies even the work of the solo fee-for-service doctor, if only through informal discussions of "cases."

In dentistry, for example, it is becoming increasingly common for dentists in general practice to refer their patients for consulation with dental specialists, and for this informal network to meet together to formulate a cross-specialty treatment program for clients; from general dental maintainance, to periodontal work, to orthodontics, to root canal work, to oral surgery, and self-administered oral hygiene.

A further step toward formally organized cooperative practice is what Freidson has termed the "informal partnership." This typically involves two physicians; one an older doctor who wishes to ease off on his or her work load and a younger beginning physician who is interested in avoiding the problems involved in developing a practice and clientele and who joins the older doctor to help share the work and the income on some informally but mutually agreed upon basis. Here, the patient may or may not have a choice of physician when coming to the office for care. Most important, however, is that both the older physician and the younger one are constantly under one another's scrutiny during the daily round of work; hence the quality of care provided is at least partially subject to peer review and control rather than merely self-control, which is more typically the case in solo practice.

A final step in the direction of bureaucratic medical practice is the association. This widespread form of cooperation in the United States is typified by the numerous "medical centers," "doctors' buildings," and others in which usually three or more physicians, either of the same or different speciality, share a common physical facility and overhead costs but *not* patients, except insofar as they may "cover" for one another. Hence, participants in this kind of an organized arrangement share the costs of building rental and operating expenses, secretarial and perhaps nursing salaries, and the purchase and maintenance of technical equipment that they may use in common. Still each physician is his or her own economic agent in this arrangement, although there is easy access to the knowledge and advice of colleagues if only on an informal basis.

Beyond that is the legal partnership, which resembles the association but differs from it in two fundamental respects. First, income generated is distributed among the members according to some legally binding formulas, and patients are shared. Thus, a patient may not know which physician will be attending at any given visit. This is a common form of organization among pediatricians as well as internists. It has the distinct advantage of calculability of income and avoids the problems engendered by the inherently unstable informal colleague relationship outlined earlier.

A sharp break occurs here and large-scale cooperative complex medical organization begins. Typical of the bureaucratic form are group practice on the one hand (which may include the operation of proprietary hospitals), and various forms of health maintenance organizations. In group practice, five or six or even more physicians, representing different medical specialties, enter into a legally based cooperative practice resembling a general clinic setting. Patients are referred from specialist to specialist *within the practice*, as deemed necessary, and costs as well as profits are shared.

Finally, the health maintenance organization involves the legally established participation of the full range of specialists in a prepaid practice. That is, client members of the health maintenance organization pay an annual fee in return for which they are guaranteed comprehensive medical care of whatever kind and for as long as is needed. The emphasis here is of course upon preventive medicine, for it is only through prevention and early detection that such comprehensive and potentially long-term care can be provided at modest cost. Membership is usually of a group nature, so income may be secured from a large number of clients with the rationally based expectation that only a few will require costly care. Some HMOs even reinsure through standard Blue Cross programs in order to benefit from special actuarial tables.

But in terms of organization and complexity, the hospital represents the zenith. It can best be described as a technical bureaucracy containing within it a complex division of labor with the physician as superordinate over all and the patient as compliant and powerless. The importance of the modern hospital can be underscored by the fact that the physician is hardly able to survive professionally without a hospital affiliation, and that hospital can be a prime determinant of his or her place in the local power structure of medicine as well as determine the technologies to which the physician and the physician's patients shall have access. Here the patient falls not only under the dominance of the profession of medicine (awesome in itself) but also under bureaucratic rules and their dominance. Indeed, much of what patients complain about with regard to hospital treatment are the rules of the bureaucracy as well as those of the physician—although they both may stem from one and the same individual. In fact, when doctors function in hospitals, their power over patients is increased rather than diminished.

But sociologically, the most distinguishing difference, as far as patients are concerned, between the hospital and other forms of cooperative care is the fact that the patient enters into residential status in hospitals. Care in an outpatient clinic or in the doctor's office allows the physician to handle "cases" on a serial basis, and he or she need not orient toward them as members of a collectivity. That is, the time between visits belongs strictly to each patient. But in residential hospitalization the patients are a presence on a round-the-clock basis, and "free time" has to be filled with some collectively defined social definition of hospitalization. The hospital, on its side, is constrained under residential circumstances to provide a definition of illness that takes into account the round-the-clock residence of patients. The patients, on their side, can be in continuous contact with one another —sometimes over quite long periods of time. As a result of this kind of patient contact and interaction, the hospital is likely to develop a patient subculture, part of which is a second or alternate social definition of illness and hospitals. In other words, there is one set of definitions created by the staff and another created by the patients.

Thus each hospital, though similar to others in some basic structural dimensions, contains a distinctive ethos, which is a blend of the staff conception and the conceptions of the patients—as to what is involved in free time.

If the staff and patient definitions coincide, the technical work can be expected to proceed more or less smoothly. But if in their interaction the patients create a different social definition of their hospitalization, then a counterculture is likely to emerge that will cause the hospital officialdom considerable difficulty.

General hospitals, especially those containing primarily single- or double-occupancy rooms can effectively neutralize the potentially disruptive fact of free time, first by the relatively short period of time most patients spend in such hospitals, second by the segregation of patients from one another, and third by the fact that free time in such a hospital is spent in relative isolation of one patient from the other. Hence, patients eat alone in their rooms, read or watch television in isolation from other patients, and complain to their "civilian" visitors rather than to the staff. There is also the mechanism of medication, which serves further to nullify the potential problems generated by blank free time. This nullification is less easily accomplished in open wards.

But free time, as an important sociological element in the technical treatment process, is exacerbated in other kinds of hospitals—specialty hospitals and psychiatric hospitals especially. In fact, psychiatric hospitals are archetypes in this regard. Even in the most elite of private psychiatric hospitals, the typical patient is in direct contact with a *formal* therapeutic agent for no more than an hour a day; the remainder is free time spent in the company of other patients and other staff members. How shall this time be spent and what shall it mean?

There can be, at one extreme, the situation found in many state hospitals in which free time is effectively without *any* meaning. At the other extreme is the "therapeutic milieu," in which every moment is imbued with potentially therapeutic or pathogenic consequences.

As one strolls through the corridors and past the rooms in a typical state hospital one is immediately struck by the silence and lack of activity there. Patients are found sitting or reclining in attitudes of lassitude, waiting in isolation and solitude form one meal to the next, and then until bedtime. There is little conversation taking place, little physical mobility; the patients are in fact "doing time." The staff spend as little time as possible with patients, and what little social interaction takes place is likely to occur at a minimal level of stimulation in the coffee shop or during meals. In most such institutions there are sporadic efforts, usually instigated by new staff members, to create some kind of meaningful social milieu during the deadening free time: dances, arts and crafts, religious lectures and services, sports and other "busywork" activities. Usually there is a flood of patients into such activities initially. Then attendance wanes after a short period of time—a fact that demoralizes staff and patients alike.

By comparison, in hospitals that embrace the ideology of a therapeutic milieu a different view of the uses of free time is held. In such institutions the entire 24 hours of the day are regarded as critical in either enhancing or eroding the patients' emotional health. This can range from highly elaborate psychoanalytic conceptions of patient-staff interaction to those that enunciate a rather simple work or activity ethic. The hospital that is successful in imprinting its free-time definition on patients *is* successful to the extent that patients accept and internalize such a definition. Hence, in such instances of hospitalization the definition of the illnesses involved are transformed by the social definition given to free time. An example or two will illustrate.

The author worked for some period of years in a children's psychiatric hospital in which an overarching Freudian-based psychoanalytic definition of free time was held. In terms of activities, much free time was spent in boys' athletic games; games were defined not as fun but as ways of "letting off steam," and thus a great deal of hyperactivity among the patients was encountered. In the game of softball, the rules, in line with Freudian deductions, were changed to allow five rather than three strikes. An 11-year-old was at bat and struck at but missed the first five balls from the pitcher. He was told by the supervising adult to relinquish his bat to the next player. The boy relied, "Aw, give me another chance, I've got a weak ego."

In another example, a collective pattern of misbehavior in which the patients frequently engaged (it was called "contagion" by the staff) in the dining room during mealtime was to flip pats of butter onto the ceiling. Each time this happened it became an object of analytic probing during later formal therapy sessions. Once each year the owner of a local amusement park and clambake dining room invited all the patients for free rides and a free lunch. One boy, diagnosed as schizophrenic, announced that he didn't want to go. When asked why, he said, "Because you can't throw your butter on the ceiling down there."

The general point to be made, however, is that illness, when taken into an organizational setting, acquires a wholly different set of social definitions that importantly affect the kind of "treatment technology" to be applied by medical experts. This same problem of using and defining free time is found in specialty hospitals of all kinds: rehabilitation hospitals, tuberculosis hospitals, research hospitals, chronic illness hospitals, and others involving residential treatment. In spite of these interorganizational differences in treatment settings, hospitals themselves are the creatures of even more fundamental social processes that determine what kinds of hospitals shall be available and therefore the technologies to which doctors and patients shall have access.

SOCIAL ORGANIZATION

Perhaps the central fact, pursued in detail in Chapter 3, involved in the social organization of medicine in the United States is that health care is a market commodity consumed by persons in relation to their location in the socio-economic structures of society. In virtually every other modernized society of which we know, health care is defined as a right of citizenship and distributed to persons simply on the strength of their possessing membership in the society. Such other societies, therefore, make the assumption that inasmuch as health care is a citizen's right, the health care of persons who cannot pay for it themselves ought to be subsidized by heavier taxation rates levied on those with the capacity to pay. It is often the opposite in the United States. With the exception of Medicaid and Medicare—catering respectively to the abject poor and the elderly, such an assumption is not made in American society. An individual's health is his or her own affair both, in terms of sustaining it and paying for it. This obviously causes problems for poorer people who share much the same high health hopes as those who are well off, because health care costs are relatively inelastic —a hospital room for a poor person costs about the same as one for a rich person. Combine cost inelasticity with high health expectations and the outcome is the fact that the poor expend a higher proportion of their total income for health care, and in some cases spend quite similar amounts in terms of absolute costs. What they often must forgo are dental care, pharmaceuticals, optical care, and so on.

This problem of the market commodity character of health care is exacerbated by the fact that U.S. culture is woven through with two opposing norms in conflict, which importantly affect the structure of health care. We are faced with the paradoxical conflict between the twin norms of "equality" on the one hand and "achievement" on the other. That is, we believe people in a democratic society should be treated equally. At the same time, we believe that people who achieve differentially should receive differential rewards. These dual themes run through all of our major social institutions. There is obviously a problem in both treating people equally and differentially rewarding differential achievers. You cannot treat people equally and at the same time treat them unequally, except insofar as the operation of each of the two norms is organizationally segregated from that of the other. And this is what has occurred in American medical organization. Thus, we have a public sector of medicine that answers to the norm of equality, and a private sector which answers to the norm of achievement. The former is in response to the rights of citizenship and the other to the forces of the market. As a result we have dual medical systems in American society—a public sector and a private sector— each with separate funding sources, with separate facilities and capital resources, with separate medical staffs, and with separate clienteles. We shall turn to the issue of the slow erosion of this distinction in the last chapter of this book.

A further sociopolitical factor that importantly affects the nature of health organization in American society is our tradition of political pluralism. That is to say, at both the local and national level the development of health-related social policy and acting can be characterized as what Norton Long has called an ecology of games in which the interests of pluralistic constituencies compete for attention as well as for short resources,[10] leading usually to attitudes of compromise and accommodation. For example, there are at the present time some 7400 general community hospitals in the country, with an average bed capacity of approximately 125. It is generally conceded that hospitals of this size have neither the staff nor the capital to provide the kind of medical care that modern technology has made possible. But given the pattern of staffing that such hospitals practice and the manner by which they are created, we continue to rely on local community processes to produce more and more small general hospitals. Part of this has to do with the fact that the possession of a general hospital is almost a requisite for the maintenance of community self-esteem in most local communities of any size. Horeover, hospitals tend to emerge close to where doctors who can staff it live, not the other way around. Thus, many small general hospitals do not arise as a response to a market; rather, they serve to create a market once they have been established.

But the effects of political pluralism is no more evident than in the political process by which national legislation effects changes on the medical scene—the impact of local constituencies on the one hand and lobbying effects on the other. For example, the Comprehensive Health Planning Act passed by Congress in 1966 aimed "to make available the highest quality health care for all Americans through cooperative efforts at the National, State and Local levels," but "*without interference with existing patterns of health care delivery.*" (italics mine) Thus, our health care system is a mosaic of institutions and organizations, each operating under *relative* autonomy and under the support and partial control of *multiple sponsors.*

Two final elements are crucial to the diverse manner by which ill persons are handled by the medical establishment, and they are the twin facts that illness represents a special form of deviancy (a departure from basic norms of conduct), whereas the medical establishment must therefore be regarded as an agent of social control. In order to get at the implication of this it is essential to draw a distinction between being ill and being sick.

Illness involves a lesion or morphological abnormality in the body that can be observed either directly or indirectly. Sickness involves a special and temporary social role that exempts persons from normal social responsibilities until such time as they can resume normal social-role performances. Thus the special and contingent role of the sick is reserved exclusively for persons who have an illness that, in the view of the medical establishment, is likely to impede adequate social-role performance. Hence it is possible for one to be ill but not accorded the contingency role of the sick. These we call minor illnesses, but in many cases this may depend upon the social definition and cultural evaluation of any number of social and cultural intervening variables, such as age, sex, and occupation, among others. On the other hand, it is possible for persons to embrace the role of the sick when they are not ill; this we call either malingering or hypochondria. But in the typical cases, role performance for men in modern American society means the capability of pursuing gainful employment; and up until now, role performance for adult females implies the ability to handle the role of family integrator. A major contemporary problem with this view, however, as discussed in the following chapter, is the fact that acute illnesses are generally on the decline, whereas chronic illnesses are on the increase.

The conception of a *temporary* social role for the ill is no longer as useful a conception as it once was in the light of the fact that while technological society demands higher and higher levels of social-role performance, partially generated out of the now mythological character of medical technology, we have more and more "semi-ill" people, who are only *marginally* capable of adequate role performance but are cast more or less *permanently* into the role of the "half-sick." Patient attitudes and the professional organization are only now beginning to address and adapt to this new trend, on the one hand by diverse forms of partial hospitalization and on the other by various forms of "self-help."

Thus, by way of introduction, a sociology of health and medicine must take into account the triple factors of patient attitude and behavior, the organization of the medical establishment, and the surrounding sociocultural environment. A final matter has to do with the growing pressures for a reassessment of medical ethics and medical social policy, an issue treated in the last chapter of this book.

SUMMARY

The search for health is like reaching for the stars—seemingly just within our grasp, but not quite. Health is like a gossamer, once it is firmly in our hand, it disintegrates and is lost. This is attributable in no small part to the inherent nature of life itself as well as to the problem of how difficult it is in a complex society to reach any workable consensus as to good health is in more than the most platitudinous of statements. And even if some minimax of agreement in specific cases could be reached, it is not long lasting as a guideline for medical organization or medical policy because of its lack of permanence. What we were willing to settle for twenty years ago is no longer acceptable.

Given, therefore, the illusive nature of health, it is little wonder that the complex of institutions surrounding the medical industry continues to grow more complex and diverse, with repeated patterns of conflicting elements seeking for attention, resources, and dominance.

Given, finally, the character of the links, especially in the Western world, between science, technology, and medical practice, it should come as no surprise that the elements in making up the medical establishment are in continual processes of change. If we combine this with democratic traditions and the current sense of urgency, we have the final themes of diversity and conflict combining with ubiquitous change.

SCENARIO II

The "other side" of health

Illness is the night-side of life, a more onerous citizenship. Everyone who is born holds dual citizenship, in the kingdom of the well and in the kingdom of the sick. Although we all prefer to use only the good passport, sooner or later each of us is obliged, at least for a spell, to identify ourselves as citizens of that other place. . . . I want to describe not what it's really like to emigrate to the kingdom of the ill and live there, but the punitive or sentimental fantasies concocted about that situation; not real geography but stereotypes of national character. My subject is not physical illness itself but the uses of illness as a figure or metaphor. My point is that illness is *not* a metaphor, and that the most truthful way of regarding illness—and the healthiest way of being ill—is one most purified of, most resistant to, metaphoric thinking. Yet it is hardly possible to take up one's residence in the kingdom of the ill unprejudiced by the lurid metaphors with which it has been landscaped. . . .

TB is thought to provide an easy death, while cancer is the spectacularly awful one. For over a hundred years TB remained the

Susan Sontag
Reprinted with the permission of Farrar, Straus, & Giroux, Inc. from *Illness as Metaphor* by Susan Sontag. Copyright © 1977, 1978 by Susan Sontag.

preferred, edifying way of willing off a character in a novel or play—a spiritualizing, refined disease. Nineteenth-century literature is stocked with descriptions of painless, unfrightened, beatific deaths from TB, particularly of young people: of Little Eva in *Uncle Tom's Cabin* and of Dombey's son Paul in *Dombey and Son* and of Smike in *Nicholas Nickleby*, where Dickens describes TB as the "dread disease" which "refines" death. . . .

Contrast these sentimental, ennobling TB deaths with the slow, agonizing cancer deaths of Eugene Gant's father in Thomas Wolfe's *Of Time and the River* and of the sister in Bergman's film *Cries and Whispers*. The dying tubercular is pictured as made more beautiful and more soulful; the person dying of cancer is portrayed as robbed of all capacities of self-transcendence, humiliated by fear and agony.

NOTES

1 Stephen R. Graubard, *Doing Better and Feeling Worse*, John H. Knowles, Ed. New York: Norton, 1977, p. viii.

2 Henry Sigerist, *Civilization and Disease*. Chicago: University of Chicago Press, 1962, p. 150.

3 Ibid., pp. 65–66:

4 Eliot Freidson, *Profession of Medicine*. New York: Dodd, Mead Company, 1970.

5 William R. Rosengren, "Institutional Types and Sociological Research: An Hypothesis in Role Systems and Research Models," *Human Organization*, 20 (Spring 1961), 42–48; William R. Rosengren, "Sociologists in Medicine: Contexts and Careers." *Professional in the Organization*, M. Abrahamson, Ed. Chicago: Rand McNally, 1967, pp. 143–155.

6 Charles E. Loomis, *The Social System: Essays on Their Persistence and Change*. New York: Van Nostrand, 1960, p. 4.

7 Ibid., p. 5.

8 Thomas Scheff, "Typification in the Diagnostic Practices of Rehabilitation Agencies." *Sociology & Rehabilitation*, Marvin B. Sussman, Ed. Washington, D.C.: American Sociological Association, 1966.

9 Eliot Freidson, "The Organization of Medical Practice." *Handbook of Medical Sociology*, Howard E. Freeman, Sol Levine, Leo G. Reeder, Eds. Englewood Cliffs, N.J.: Prentice-Hall, 1963, pp. 273–295.

10 Norton Long, "The Local Community as an Ecology of Games," *American Journal of Sociology*, 64 (Nov. 1958), pp. 251–261.

SUGGESTED READINGS

Rene Dubos, *The Mirage of Health*. New York: Harper & Row, 1959. *A general statement of the links between social life, illness, and death.*

Ivan Illich, *Medical Nemesis: The Expropriation of Illness.* New York: Pantheon, 1976.
A polemic attack on modern medicine that sets commonsense assumptions "on their heads."

John H. Knowles, Ed., *Doing Better and Feeling Worse.* New York: Norton, 1977.
A series of statements on the current status of health in America focusing on contemporary issues and problems.

"Life and Death and Medicine," *A Scientific American Book.* San Francisco: Freeman, 1973.
Selections from Scientific American *on aspects of the medical system.*

"Medicine and Society," *Annals of the American Academy of Political and Social Science* (March 1963).
Thirteen articles delineating the newly developing field of medical sociology. A dated but basic reference.

David D. Rutstein, *The Coming Revolution of Medicine.* Cambridge: Massachusetts Institute of Technology Press, 1967.
A doctor outlines the shortcomings of current medical organization.

Henry E. Sigerist, *Civilization and Disease.* Chicago: University of Chicago Press, 1943.
The relations between health, illness, medical practice and the growth of Western civilization. A classic book.

―――――――――

The limits of technology

It is the year 1900. A young man, age 19, is cleaning the horse stalls on his father's farm located a short distance from a medium-size city. A horse kicks with his rear legs and strikes the young man a heavy blow with a hoof, directly beneath the chin. A "crack" like a rifle shot can be heard, and the man sprawls unconscious on the floor of the stall. He is found shortly thereafter by his father, who, not having a telephone, lifts his son onto his horse-drawn carriage and takes him the few miles into town to the office of his doctor. With no X-ray equipment the physician can only indirectly discover what has happened: sharp pinpoints applied to the extremities and the uppor torso indicate that the young man has suffered a break in his spinal column sufficiently close to the brain to produce paralysis from the neck down.

With the help of the father, the patient is carried to the horse-drawn carriage and taken to the local hospital where he is placed, unconscious, in a bed. He remains unconscious and his breathing is labored and shallow. The parents conduct a vigil throughout the night and the following day, during which time the patient's breathing becomes more and more shallow and infrequent. Toward mid-morning of the next day, breathing stops altogether and the patient is pronounced dead. The body is returned to the parents' home to be prepared for burial. From accident to death is less than 24 hours. Why did the patient die? The answer is that in cases of high spinal-column severance patients frequently lose their capacity for autonomic breathing. Being unconscious, the patient could not deliberately try to breathe, so the autonomic stimulus and response pattern was slowed and finally terminated, and the patient died—not unlike what is not thought to occur in the case of so-called crib death.

A slight modification of this scenario of 1900 is that the patient survives the first critical days of endangered breathing, although his paralysis remains unchanged. He can neither move nor feel from the neck down and must be fed, dressed, and cleaned by others and must be mechanically assisted in his excretory functions. He lives, but only for a short period of weeks or months. Eventually massive bedsores develop over his body, out of which develop a series of infections with which the pharmacology of the day cannot cope. In due time the young man dies of generalized staph infection, pneumonia, heart failure, or other more specific organ infections. As best (or worst), the patient lives for a period of months following the accident.

CHAPTER 2

The changing health scene

By way of introduction, and in order to approach a comprehensive understanding of the social factors involved in the emergence, definition, and etiology of illnesses, and of the manner by which medical technology, professional organization, and social organization interrelate to produce particular kinds of health outcomes for people, it is essential to take into account a number of recent historical drifts on the health scene. The overview presented in this chapter is intended to present the student with some of the recent critical and sweeping changes in health, illness, and medical organization. To provide a better appreciation of the fact that while our interest in this book will be primarily on the sociology of medicine in contemporary American society, we shall continually remind the reader that medical technology, professional organization, and the overarching social organization are in continuous processes of change and evolution in all of their dimensions.

SINCE 1900

A useful point in history is the turn of the century. Any date at which to begin is necessarily arbitrary. But to see ourselves in relation to what was unfolding in the world of medicine at that time is to catch medicine and medical organization in transition to the modern. Further, the year 1900 is not so far in the distant past that it must be viewed as strictly out of date with us now. It was the time during which the author's grandparents, parents, and their contemporaries were falling ill, seeking medical care, and dying in large numbers, even though many innovations in technical and organizational changes, and conditions of patient attitudes had either already been launched or were "just around the corner." That is, many of what are now mainstays of medical technology had already appeared on the scene: Obstetrical forceps had existed since 1670; there already existed basic clinical understanding of maladies such as pneumonia, cancer, diabetes, and others; the stethoscope was invented in the early 1800s; surgery with the use of anesthesia had been practiced since the mid-1800s, and the ophthalmoscope had been in use since about the same period; the importance of the use of antiseptics had been known since shortly after the Civil War, though not necessarily widely practiced, the discovery of the principal life-threatening bacilli (tubercle, cholera, staphylococcus, malaria, yellow fever, diphtheria, and others) all had taken place prior to the turn of the century.

Many of these innovations, though known, had not yet diffused throughout the medical profession—a commentary on the state of the organization of the profession at large, and the paucity of medical journals by which to distribute knowledge of the burgeoning changes. Still in all, while the clinical nature of syphilis was known, its cure had not yet appeared. By the same token, insulin was still a quarter of a century away—and diabetics, children especially, could expect a debilitating and relatively short life. The electrocardiogram was not to be invented until the early 1920s, and heart disease—not nearly so widespread then as it is at the present time—could be monitored and treated in only the most superficial way. Even the risk fatcors of obesity, diet, and smoking were largely ignored at the time. By the same token, while the first human kidney removal is reported to have taken place as early as 1869, it was to be nearly a hundred years until the term "end-state renal" disease did *not* necessarily mean that the victim faced certain death. There was to be a wait of 30 years until the fabrication of penicillin, and later the more sophisticated antibiotics that were to play so crucial a role in avoiding in World War II the widespread death of soldiers wounded in the field as occurred during the three previous wars in which the United States had been involved. And of course poliomyelitis was largely untreatable until the discovery of polio vaccine in the early 1950s and its widespread use in mass inoculation programs in the early 1960s.

At that time the trauma-producing quadraplegia was still a certain killer, as was leukemia and other forms of cancer that are now at least somewhat tractable to either surgery or chemotherapy. The whole field of preventive medicine was still largely unheard of, as were the now widely known forms of treatment for mental and emotional illness, psychomedication especially. In short, medical technology in 1900 was on the springboard of change. But while many of the now standard implementations and technologies had been discovered or created, they were neither widely known nor widely practiced by doctors at the time.

Part of the problem of lack of diffusion of such innovations, and their effective application to patients, had to do with the relative primitive nature of medical education at the time as well as the social cohesion of the profession at large. That is, while sweeping changes were on the horizon in both of these respects, medical education at the time can best be described as haphazard, nonuniform, and uncoordinated. Many training institutions that passed as "medical schools" were in fact degree mills operated on a profit basis with minimal standards of student admission and faculty appointment. Many, for example, allowed students to enter into training following the completion of high school and provided only two years of classroom training, with no supportive clinical experience either in supervised home treatment settings or in hospitals. Most such "medical schools" operated without state or professional licensure procedures and without any connection whatsoever either with a hospital that could provide clinical learning experiences or a university that could provide adequate preclinical education. As might be expected, therefore, curriculums were unstandardized, as were the conditions of achievement justifying the awarding of the "M.D." degree. The two major instruments bringing uniformity of standards of admission and training brought about by the Osler and Flexner report were both still nearly a decade away.

In any event, as the nineteenth century turned to the twentieth, medical education bore little or no resemblance to what we now have. As a result, and as Freidson has pointed out, at this time in history a person in 1900 who perceived himself to be ill and gave himself to the care of a physician stood about a 50-50 chance of benefiting from the encounter. Much of the technology was on line, but the system of medical education was not prepared to accommodate and integrate it into the practice of medicine.

An additional part of this cultural lag had to do with the relatively simple professional organization at the time. Practice was limited largely to general medicine, the burgeoning of medical specialties had yet to take place. The vast number of physicians practiced in classic solo fee-for-service form—one doctor, perhaps with one nurse, operating more or less in isolation from other physicians. The hospital had not yet emerged as the key institution for medical care. It did not hold, as it does now, preeminence in the diagnostic and treatment process; nor did it serve as the common reserve of medical technology and colleague contact. No technical innovation, however revolutionary, in any field of endeavor can make a significant societal impact unless it is diffused to and assimilated by the practitioners of that technology. And a basic prerequisite of that diffusion and assimilation is a uniform and monitored system of training and a professional organization that allows for professional contact and diffusion and public control. Neither of these conditions existed at all at the turn of the century. It is true that technical changes were well advanced toward the modern, and critical organizational changes were in the wind. But it must also be mentioned at this point that little attention was paid to the importance of life-style in sustaining health or to general conditions of hygiene and nutrition. Even today, it has been estimated that one in five persons who enter a hospital for treatment leave with a disease or an illness they did not have when they entered the hospital.

However that might be, in 1900, and to a lesser extent today, there was a considerable cultural lag between changes in the technology of medicine and changes in the professional and social organization that could bring those technological benefits to people. For even as this is being written, medical researchers report the creation of what is said to be an effective vaccine against meningitis—a dreaded killer of children in particular. One wonders how many years it might be before the professional system is mobilized to bring that vaccine to the millions of persons who might benefit from it?

CHANGES IN POPULATION BASE

An additional way of grasping a basic dimension of the health scene in the early 1900s is to consider the members of the population who were the recipients of the care that was available. A useful way of looking at the population in 1900 is its age-sex composition. This refers simply to the percentage of males and females who were alive—and therefore subject to illness, disease, and possible death—at the time. Both age and sex differentiations are important for health patterns and treatment organization, because young people tend to fall victim to certain

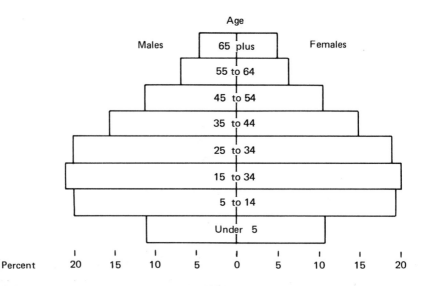

FIGURE 2.1 American age-sex pyramid, 1900.

Source: U.S. Bureau of the Census, various reports.

groups of illness and older persons to others. Furthermore, depending upon the nature of family, economic structure, and prevailing attitudes, large numbers of potentially ill women tend to produce different kinds of health problems than do large numbers of men who might fall ill.

The nature of the population in 1900 deserves comment: Of first importance is the fact that the proportion of males and females who were alive in any ten-year age category tended to decline rather steadily and evenly starting at the 25-to-34 age group. What this means, stated in yet another way, is that both males and females tended to die at roughly the same rate, with a small but noticeably larger number of females surviving into their late 60s and older. The effects of medical intervention in the process of population attrition was yet to take place.

As a result, we can draw something of a portrait of life and death at this point in our history. First, disease and death was more or less an accepted part of life. People did not expect to live very long; nor did they necessarily expect all of their children to survive to adulthood. Families were relatively large, not counting those who had died. Most dying took place in the home rather than in the hospital, and what are now called "extraordinary" measures to prolong life did not exist. Family members "managed" the process of dying, typically in the home setting. The bodies of family members who died were washed, dressed for burial, often by family members, and funerals were conducted in the home. As shall be displayed, infant and maternal mortality rates were far higher than they are now. This means, among other consequences, that many children were lost to disease early in life, and many mothers died in childbirth, leaving behind their widowed husbands—who typically were left with several small children requiring care. The state of family technology at the time, as well as working conditions, made it virtually impossible for the family to survive without the presence of a hard-working female. Hence, remarriage after the death of a wife was a common occurrence.

It is also to be remembered that this was an era preceding by many years the benefits to older people of Social Security. Health insurance plans were virtually nonexistent, as were industrial retirement plans. A final fact to be noted in the age-sex composition of the population in 1900 is the relatively small percentage of males and females alike who survived beyond the age of 55. That is, only about 6 percent of the live males and females were between the ages of 55 and 64, and only about 5 percent of both sexes were 65 or older.

Hence, only a small proportion of the population were in the economically unproductive phase of life requiring economic subsidy and support, or perhaps neglect.

In sum, it was a population for whom most growing medical advances were beyond reach, economically as well as organizationally.

It was also a population for whom the explosion in popular medical knowledge had not yet taken place. It was a population for whom illness, debilitation, and death were common companions. It was a population that did not have to face the twin problems of elevated health expectations on the one hand and skyrocketing medical care costs on the other. And the highly sophisticated medical technologies for dealing with what was then certain death were to be reserved for a later generation of citizens.

It is important for the student to understand that this population pattern (and its associated health-related matters) remained *largely unchanged* through the 1920s. It is the decade of the 1930s, moreover, that constitutes something of a watershed in this regard as evidenced by the fact that by 1940 the percentage of females who were 65 or over had more than doubled, a figure only signaling dramatic changes yet to come. We shall return to the assertion that the 1930s represent something of a medical watershed in both a technical and organizational sense.

Nevertheless, it is helpful to compare this portrayal of the year 1900 with the age sex pyramid as it existed in 1970. This is shown in Figure 2.2. As can be noted, the percentage of males and females surviving remain substantially unchanged. It would be wrong, however, to conclude that the health situation of young persons was the same in 1970 as in 1900. In fact, what is happening in 1970 is a sharp

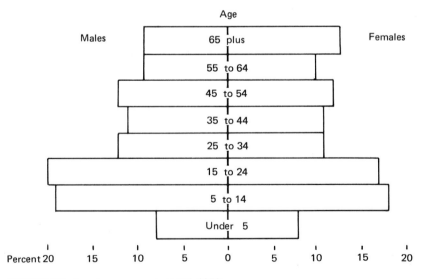

FIGURE 2.2 American age-sex pyramid, 1970.

Source: U.S. Bureau of the Census, various reports.

decline in the birthrate, along with an *increase* in the survival rate. That is, a large number of babies were born in 1900 and many of them were dying. This is as compared with 1970 in which *fewer* babies were being born but *larger* numbers of them were living through infancy and childhood, as were their mothers.

How do we account for the fact that in 1900 larger percentages of males and females were alive in the 25-to-44 age categories than in 1970? One need merely to reflect on the fact that as more and more people survive through the adult years of economic productivity, it necessarily means that the percentages are then more or less *equally distributed* along a greater span of years. In fact, it is between the age of 25 and up that we see the beginnings of the effects of modern medical technology and medical organization. More and more people are living through adulthood and into old age. But the future that we wish to draw special attention to is the percentages of males and females who, in 1970, lived to be 65 and older: some 10 percent in the case of males, and nearly 15 percent in the case of females. Looked at in terms of long-term trends, we are slowly but inexorably becoming a nation of older people—widowed women especially, who are beyond the economically productive years. The U.S. Bureau of Census, for example, estimates that in 1977 the percentage of the population over the age of 65 was approximately 20 percent of the total. And if present birth, mortality, and morbidity trends continue, by the year 2020 we can expect the elderly population to constitute slightly more than 50 percent of the total population. Given the present occupational and economic structure of the society, such a proportion of economically unproductive persons will impose burdens on the under-65 working population of unthinkable proportions. These larger numbers of older people will not only be expected to be a monumental economic burden on the working members of the society, but also are likely to present new health problems and social problems as well. Thus the advances in medical technology and medical care delivery that have brought about the changes in the age-sex pyramid just enumerated have brought about a situation in which we can expect larger numbers of people to live into old age, but only with some kind of chronic or disabling impairment. At the same time, American culture is generally not particularly well equipped to deal with unproductive older people. In spite of widespread protestations to the contrary, it seems that most people would prefer not to be troubled by the presence of older people. Our life-style has little place for them, and this accounts partially for the large number of old people who find themselves in nursing homes in which little nursing is done and in most instances are not very home-like.

In any event, we are speaking of a population in the 1970s very different from that of 1900. Health expectations continue to rise even to the point that persons *with* some kind of health insurance pay *more* dollars out of pocket for health than do people without health insurance. Although health insurance is now edging beyond the reach of many people, we have a population of families prepared to mortgage themselves for life in the interests of receiving medical care. And in spite of that fact we do not have solid figures as to actually how many families on the edge of personal bankruptcy would in fact vote *against* some form of national health insurance, we feel sure that a large number would.

Perhaps most important is that it is a population in which infant, childhood, and maternal death are the exception rather than the rule, and it is a population of increasing numbers of elderly people, with the special problems engendered, paradoxically, by *advances* in medicine and public health over the past half-century—the full impact of which is not likely to be known for another half-century.

CHANGING DEATH RATES

A next step is to examine some of the important changes which have taken place in the mortality picture during this period. Trends in the crude mortality rate are shown in Figure 2.3.

As can be seen, a rather profound change has taken place in the American death rate over the past few decades. In fact, it has been nearly cut in half—from approximately 17 deaths per 1000 people at the turn of the century to just under 9.0 per 1000 in 1975, with the

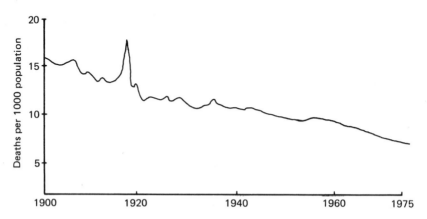

FIGURE 2.3 Crude mortality rates from all causes, United States.

Source: Adapted from various reports of the U.S. Office of Vital Statistics, and Odin Anderson and Monroe Lerner, Health Progress in the United States, 1900-1960. Chicago: University of Chicago Press, 1963.

decline being rather more precipitous during the first 40 years of this century in comparison with the second "40" years. The single dramatic exception to this pattern is of course the influenza epidemic (pandemic, really) of 1919–1920, during which time the death rate jumped to well above what it was in 1900.

A fact worth mentioning about this influenza epidemic is that its causes remain largely unknown, as are the reasons for its decline. Parenthetically, the same appears to be true for most of the major epidemics that devastated Europe in an earlier era. They came out of no known cause, killed hundreds of thousands of people, and then as mysteriously disappeared. The facts, buried as they are without a history, will probably never be known.

The American death rate experienced a steady and significant decline between the turn of the century and the decade of the 1930s. Following those latter years, the decline has been slower and slower— declining only by two persons per thousand in the 20-year period, 1940–1960 and then only by about 1.5 persons in the 15-year period between 1960 and 1975. What accounts for the rapid decline in the earlier period and the much slower decline in the later period? Can we necessarily conclude that this dramatic drop in the death rate is directly attributable to treatment transactions taking place between individual doctors and individual patients? Probably not, although the diffusion of medical innovations within the practicing profession un- doubtedly accounts for some of this decline. But this was an era of rapid advances in standards of hygiene and cleanliness both in the public sphere and in the practice of medicine. Improvements in nutri- tion, general levels of economic affluence, and increasing awareness of health matters among the population itself were, together, probably more responsible for this decline than were the clinical efforts of individual physicians.

Gersuny, for example, has described the general conditions of public health tolerated in industrial settings at the turn of the century:[1]

> To those living in a time and place where getting a drink of clean water on the job is taken for granted the problems attendant upon this simple need in the Fall River cotton mills around 1910 must seem incredible. Yet at hearings in that year on the inspection of factories, testimony was given indicating that city water was unavailable in many textile plants except in the mill yard. The reason for lack of running water on the upper floors was "because it is an expensive operation for the mill. If they provide drinking water, the law does not say where it shall be provided," testified Dr. MacKnight.
>
> Q. *Do I understand that the mills are exempt from this new law that requires the disuse of the public drinking cup?*
> A. *Yes.*

In addition to the hazard embodied by the communal cup, the condition of the barrels into which these cups were dipped speaks for itself. Not only were they repositories of the airborne cotton fibers, dust and dried sputum that contaminated the atmosphere, but according to the physican cited above,

> . . . the man who carries the water is the man who scrubs the water closets, and a great many times he scrubs out the water closet before he cleans the barrel, and often with the same mop. That has been proven more than once. . . . A great many times the mops after they have been used to clean out the water closet are set mop end up and drip into the barrel. . . . The ice carried to the top floor is sometimes carried in the same pail that is used to clean the water closets.

The ice had to be paid for by "voluntary" subscription of the employees collected by a supervisor, but no guarantees as to its purity were involved.

Not only were hazards to health and safety countenanced by the mill management, but employee complaints were discouraged, according to Dr. MacKnight, who testified that five to ten workers visited his office nightly to report about mill conditions, and labor unions sent reports as well, but under the law complaints had to be in writing, signed by the worker. This stopped complaints for two reasons, he testified. First, mill workers were "unwilling to put their signatures to anything for fear of discharge." Second, many more mill workers had difficulty expressing themselves in writing than the 23.2 percent of foreign-born illiterates enumerated in the 1910 census for the city.

The general impact of working conditions on life expectancy was documented by the positive correlation between length of service and mortality rates. While the pattern was not consistent, Perry concluded that

> . . . among cotton-mill operatives of similar age the factor of mill work as a contributory cause of death is active commonly according to the length of the period of employment in the mill.

The hazards deriving from conditions in the mill were compounded by the level of living to which the prevailing wage rates subjected the mill operatives and their families.

So these were years that saw the relatively rapid decline of the major infectious diseases, through improvements in antiseptic practices and general standards of hygiene that heretofore had devastating effects upon members of the population who were "at risk": pregnant women, infants and young children, and older persons suffering from other health complications. But the pattern of more contemporary interest is the relatively slow decline in the death rate between the years 1960 and 1975—only from about 10 to about 8.9 per thousand. Why, in the face of modern technology have we been unable to reduce the latter figure? There are two principal factors at work. First, as technology sustains life for longer and longer periods of years, the members of the increasingly aged population eventually and inexorably succumb to the ravages of the years. The second, and not unrelated factor, is that as disease after disease is overcome by medical science, the remaining causes of death (heart disease, cancer, and stroke as exceptions) increasingly become the exotic and rare disease. Thus, as we become an increasingly healthy population, medicine turns much of its attention to the diseases that strike only a tiny proportion of the population. For example, as renal disease becomes less of a certain killer, only about 25 persons in a million may be affected—hardly a figure to make much of an inroad on the overall death rate, though of the utmost importance to the unfortunate 25. The same can be said of many of the other seemingly intransigent diseases and illnesses that now confront medical science.

DECLINE IN COMMUNICABLE DISEASES

This trend away from the principal communicable diseases over the years is indirectly underscored by Figures 2.4 and 2.5, which depict the decline in the maternal and infant mortality rates over the past several decades.

As can be seen in Figure 2.4, the decline in the maternal mortality rate parallels almost exactly the general decline in death rates, at least since 1915. It is not difficult to pinpoint the factors responsible for this decline, namely improvements in hygienic practices and the general

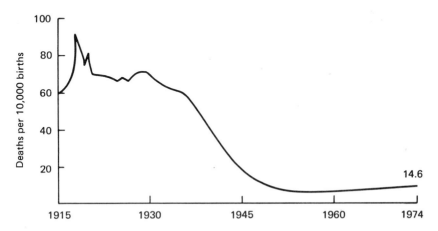

FIGURE 2.4 Maternal mortality, United States.

Source: Adapted from various reports of the U.S. Office of Vital Statistics, and Odin Anderson and Monroe Lerner, Health Progress in the United States, 1900-1960. Chicago: University of Chicago Press, 1963.

elimination of the widespread communicable diseases that heretofore had rendered large groups of women poor obstetric risks. During this period more and more women were having their babies in hospitals and more and more were undoubtedly seeking earlier prenatal care. But whatever the specific reasons for the decline in maternal mortality, this surely stands as a dramatic example of what improved medical technology can accomplish, on a broad base, and its interdependency with a changing social organization. In any event, it is accurate to say that having a child 50 or 60 years ago was by no means the rather routine undertaking that it is today, when death during pregnancy is not widely regarded as a proximate threat.

Much the same can be said for the decline in the infant mortality rate, which is shown in Figure 2.5. As in the case of maternal mortality, infant death both during pregnancy and during the first year of life has undergone a remarkable decline, unquestionably because of the same factors of hygiene, antisepsis, and the prior elimination of many poor risks from the child-bearing population. Thus, as communicable diseases are eradicated, one cannot escape from witnessing a decline in both maternal and infant mortality rates, which has assisted in producing the kind of age-sex pyramid we now have. Although it is true that the infant mortality rate underwent a decline from about 100 deaths per thousand (10 percent of all live births) 60 years ago to under 17 per thousand (less than 2 percent of all live births) today, these figures take on added import when placed in a comparative con-

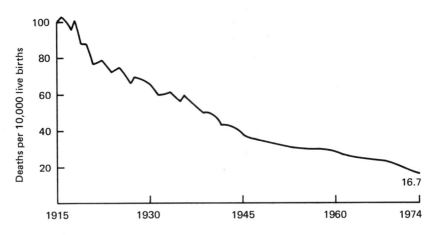

FIGURE 2.5 Infant mortality, United States.

Source: Adapted from various reports of the U.S. Office of Vital Statistics, and Odin Anderson and Monroe Lerner, <u>Health Progress in the United States, 1900-1960</u>. Chicago: University of Chicago Press, 1963.

text. That is, as late as 1935, among the countries with which we normally compare ourselves in both a political and economic sense, only Norway, Sweden, and the Netherlands exhibited infant mortality rates lower than our own, while England and Wales, Scotland, and Denmark had rates of infant deaths that *exceeded* our own. But by 1965 our infant mortality rate *exceeded* that of all of these six Northern European countries.

In point of fact, by 1974 the following countries report infant mortality rates lower than our own: Japan, Sweden, the United Kingdom, France, Finland, Denmark, Belgium, Austria, Italy, Poland, and Norway, among others. What is the reason for this? What do these countries have in common—different as they otherwise are—that might account for their remarkably low infant mortality rates? First, all of these are relatively small countries, both in terms of population and geography. Second, all of them have some kind of nationwide health plan that virtually assures the availability of uniform health care to all members of the population. Third, and not unrelated to the last factor, all of these countries are relatively homogeneous in terms of the social and cultural composition of the population. This latter makes it far more easy than it is in our own large and heterogeneous society to devise and administer a health care program of uniform scope and depth. But surely of utmost importance is the absence, in these other nations, of profound racial differentiations, the consequences of which reverberate throughout the American health care picture. However, when the infant mortality rate (35.1) for nonwhites—that is blacks—is eliminated from the American computations, then the U.S. infant mortality rate compares favorably with that of these other six nations. This is not to say that the black-white differentiation is capable of explaining the full range or mortality differences, but its impact is surely profound.

Although maternal and infant mortality data are an indirect measure of the effects of the elimination of the killer communicable diseases, this factor is addressed more directly in Figure 2.6. As can be seen, deaths from the major communicable diseases were widespread at the turn of the century, being reduced to about 30 per 100,000 in the late 1950s—reaching a plateau at about that level to the present time. Thus, as an indicator of the decline of communicable diseases in general, pneumonia, influenza, and tuberculosis as special cases dramatize what has taken place over the decades. The failure to push this rate below its present, relatively sustained level is also largely accounted for in the age-sex pyramid, and this will be discussed shortly. Now tuberculosis represents something of a prototype of communicable disease in the sense that in 1900 the death rate from this disease was almost exactly that of the two big killers—pneumonia and influenza.

Yet it has experienced a steady decline until in 1974 less than 1 person in 100,000 died of this disease. Does this mean that people do not contract tuberculosis any more? Of course not; it simply means that the disease can now be managed in ways that were neither possible nor even thought of a relatively short time ago: Patients must be placed on a strict regimen of life-style and chemical therapy so as to arrest the disease. Tuberculosis is now a *chronic illness*, the maintenance of which requires the constant and continuous cooperation of the patient. Like all other chronic illnesses, the tuberculosis patient must become his or her own physician in order to avoid relapse and rehospitalization. That is, the chronically ill person must become a full participant with the medical establishment in ministering to the illness, with full recognition that the burden of health rests as heavily on the shoulders of the patient as it does on the shoulders of the physician, a matter taken up in detail in Chapter 8.

Tuberculosis is prototypical in yet another sense in that treatment for tuberculosis is now a citizen's right. That is, persons suffering from the disease—probably more so in the future—may receive medical care provided for and paid for by the state. As in the case of other services that come to be regarded as rights of citizenship, they have a way of becoming a citizen's obligations as well. That is, not only may a citizen be treated for tuberculosis without financial charge, it is also true that one *will not* choose to avoid treatment once the disease is detected. How widely this reciprocal between rights on the one hand and obligations on the other will be carried remains a moot question,

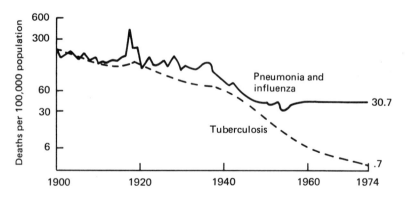

FIGURE 2.6 Mortality from major communicable diseases, United States.

Source: Adapted from various reports of the U.S. Office of Vital Statistics, and Odin Anderson and Monroe Lerner, Health Progress in the United States, 1900-1960. Chicago: University of Chicago Press, 1963.

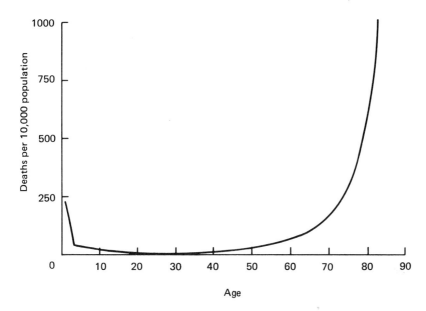

FIGURE 2.7 Mortality from pneumonia and influenza, by age, United States, 1958.

Source: Adapted from various reports of the U.S. Office of Vital Statistics, and Odin Anderson and Monroe Lerner, Health Progress in the United States, 1900-1960. Chicago: University of Chicago Press, 1963.

but it is surely a facet of health care in America that deserves careful scrutiny.

In spite of remarkable advances in medical technology and increased complexity, if not uniform efficiency, in the social organization of medical care delivery, the specter that haunts the changing medical scene is the fact that in spite of all, the human body is finally given to disease, debilitation, and death. The aging process—though it can be delayed and prolonged, as evidenced by trends in the age-sex pyramid—cannot be forestalled indefinitely. This is no more evident than in the pattern of mortality by age for influenza and pneumonia, the rates for which are shown in Figure 2.7.

Although death from these diseases is no longer the scourge of the population that it once was, it still deserves the appellation "the old man's blessing," inasmuch as no one accurately knows the state of chronic ill health plaguing the large number of elderly people who finally and officially succumb to these illnesses.

The point of the drift toward chronic illness and disability is perhaps no better illustrated than in the data and trends found in Figures 2.8 through 2.10. The first deals with deaths from diabetes, the second with trends in the combined rates for heart disease, cancer, and stroke, and the third with heart disease.

We see an apparent unusual pattern of increase and then a slowly decreasing rate of death from diabetes. Perhaps it is surprising that there was a relatively low rate of death at the turn of the century, then an increase peaking at about 1940, and then a slow and gradual decline in the rate to just under 19 in 1975. This is all the more curious in that insulin was fabricated in 1922, and yet we observe a quite rapid rise in the mortality rate from this disease for the next quarter-century.

How is such a pattern to be explained? First, one must remember the distinction between childhood diabetes and the form that occurs later in life. What appears to have been happening in the early years of the current century is the gradual increase in the number of older diabetics, along with the increased proportion of the population surviving to the older years. It is undoubtedly the case that the comparatively small number of deaths noted at the turn of the century may be attributed to the early death of diabetic children for whom no effective control existed. Even in those years, the manipulation of diet was at least partially effective in managing many cases of diabetes setting in during the adult years. Nevertheless, we have the problem of an *increase* in the rate of death *following* the introduction of insulin. At least three factors account for this. One is that the assimilation of *any* medical innovation takes at least some time before it diffuses within the medical profession. That fact can be relied upon to account for at least part of this "postinnovation" increase. The second is that by that time the increase in general life expectancy will have produced larger

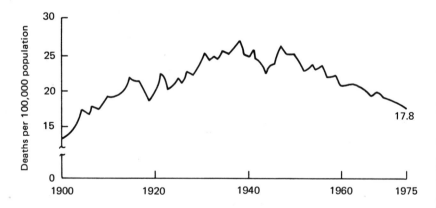

FIGURE 2.8 Mortality from diabetes, United States.

Source: Adapted from various reports of the U.S. Office of Vital Statistics, and Odin Anderson and Monroe Lerner, Health Progress in the United States, 1900-1960. Chicago: University of Chicago Press, 1963.

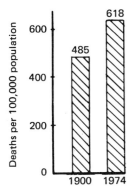

FIGURE 2.9 Mortality from heart disease, cancer, and strokes, United States, 1900 and 1974.

Source: Adapted from various reports of the U.S. Office of Vital Statistics, and Odin Anderson and Monroe Lerner, Health Progress in the United States, 1900-1960. Chicago: University of Chicago Press, 1963.

numbers of partially managed diabetics for whom the late introduction of insulin was unable to take effect. In short, the mere discovery of a control or cure agent does not necessarily assure the immediate decline in either morbidity or mortality for both technical and organizational reasons. Third is the increase in the proportion of older people who are at risk during this span of time. And it is to be remembered that the control of diabetes lies almost exclusively in the hands of the afflicted; a strict pattern of self-monitoring is required, as is a continually shifting medication requirement, as well as *constant* attention to dietary intake. Thus we have a situation at the present in which, in spite of technical knowledge and the availability of insulin and oral medication, diabetes is now the *fifth* leading cause of death. And with the increasing numbers of older persons so afflicted, this illness is likely to advance its position in that regard.

But by far the most prevalent causes of death today are those depicted in Figure 2.9: heart disease, cancer and stroke. As is seen, these three had a combined death rate of approximately 485 per 100,000 in 1900 but *rose* to well over 600 in 1974. Heart disease, cancer, and stroke are now the three leading causes of death in this country. More important, these leading three, unlike most other illnesses and diseases, have *increased* markedly over the past few decades rather than decreased. Although it is true that deaths from some specific forms of cancer have decreased during this period of time, the general trend has been toward an increase. Moreover, there is even sharper prevalence of death from these causes with increasing age. Thus as we look to the future, and unless there is some as yet unforeseen and unanticipated technical breakthrough, we can anticipate death from these three major illnesses to increase rather than decrease in prevalence. Increasing age, however, does not have a *direct* relationship to death rates, especially if sex is taken into account when considering death from heart disease. The rates for males as compared with females is shown in Figure 2.10.

The factors producing these dramatic differences in fatal heart disease between the sexes is far too complex to be discussed at length here. There are, however, two principal arguments, both of which carry with them both reason and plausibility.

First, one may take the position that women are constitutionally better endowed with respect to their resistance to heart disease. The argument is bolstered by some evidence that the female hormone estrogen seems to act as a counteragent against many forms of heart disease. However, there is also the argument that stress, and its associated risk factors of hypertension, obesity, smoking, and others, are more typical of the life-style of males in American society than of females. The argument goes further to say that occupational stress is more typical of males than of females, and even *more* typical of males as one *ascends* the system of social stratification. Again some evidence is available to underscore such an argument: There is generally a higher rate of heart disease as the system of stratification is ascended;

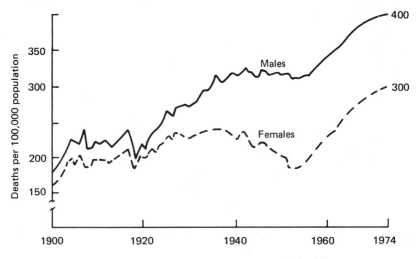

FIGURE 2.10 Mortality from diseases of the heart, by sex, United States.

Source: Adapted from various reports of the U.S. Office of Vital Statistics, and Odin Anderson and Monroe Lerner, Health Progress in the United States, 1900-1960. Chicago: University of Chicago Press, 1963.

TABLE 2.1
Leading causes of death in the United States

1900	1967	1974
Influenza and pneumonia	Heart disease	Heart disease
Tuberculosis	Cancer	Cancer
Gastroenteritis	Strokes	Stroke
Heart disease	Accidents	Accidents
Strokes	Influenza and pneumonia	Pneumonia
Chronic nephritis	Diseases of early infancy	Diabetes
(renal diseases)	Arteriosclerosis	Cirrhosis of the
Accidents	Diabetes	liver
Cancer	Other circulatory diseases	Suicide
Diseases of early infancy	Other bronchopulmonic	Homocide
Diphtheria	diseases	Emphysema

that is, higher-status males have higher rates of death from heart disease than do high-status women. And this evidence holds for British males as well as American males. The two arguments, however, are not necessarily mutually exclusive; note the sharp increase in death from heart disease among females between 1960 and 1974. Whether the women's liberation movement and Equal Opportunity Affirmative Action have now had sufficient "bite" in the American occupational structure so as to diffuse women more equitably among more higher-stress occupations remains a moot question. What is indisputable, however, is that males still suffer from heart disease far more frequently than women, but that women—Americans anyway—are beginning to catch up. But it remains true that the *discrepancy* between the male and female rates of heart disease is today substantially what it was 30 years ago.

THE LEADING CAUSES OF DEATH AND THE HALF-SICK

In broad outline, perhaps the most convenient way to grasp the changing health scene is simply to enumerate shifts in the leading causes of death over the period of years we have considered in this chapter. Thus, the ten leading causes of death among the American population for 1900, 1967, and 1974 are listed in Table 2.1, in descending order of prevalence.

In looking over these three lists, some major differences become immediately apparent. First, there has been a dramatic shift *away* from the major infectious diseases and a shift in the direction of illnesses that in many instances are of a *chronic* nature. That is, those that kill do so in many cases only following a relatively long period of medical treatment and management. Second, we are witness to an increasing shift in the direction of more and more deaths from those illnesses and disease the onset of which is in large number of cases directly attributable to the life-style and social behavior patterns of the victim. That is, consistent with the original premise of this book, illness and disease are no longer usually regarded as maladies that strike persons in a random fashion without regard to the direct participation of victims in assisting in the creation of their own illnesses. Hence, just as modern patients are in many ways responsible for their own troubles, so too, as chronic illnesses become more common, do they hold a major responsibility in the management and cure of their various debilitations.

Indeed, if it is agreed that suicide is the prototype of those forms of death in which the dead person has directly participated in his or her own demise, much the same can be said for at least seven of the ten leading causes of death in American society: heart disease, cancer, stroke, homocide, suicide, diabetes, cirrhosis of the liver, and emphysema.

The situation with regard to patient participation in producing illness, and the general trend away from acute infectious diseases to chronic diseases, is shown in Figure 2.11.

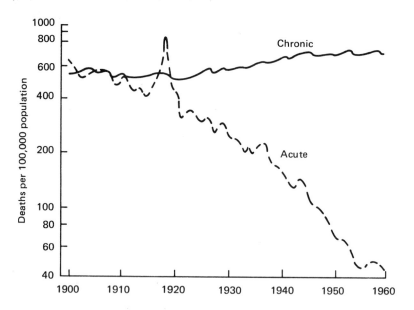

FIGURE 2.11 Mortality from chronic versus acute diseases, United States.

Source: Adapted from various reports of the U.S. Office of Vital Statistics, and Odin Anderson and Monroe Lerner, Health Progress in the United States, 1900-1960. Chicago: University of Chicago Press, 1963.

By definition, persons who suffer from acute illness are ill for a relatively short period of time, while those who suffer from chronic illness, also by definition, continue to be ill—in varying degrees—for a comparatively long period of time. Our society now is populated by larger and larger numbers of persons who are chronically ill, or potentially so. Not only has this historical trend dramatically altered the medical scene in this society, but it has been accompanied by radical changes in the technologies of medicine, by stresses upon the capacity of the medical establishment to organize itself to cope with the new problems confronting it, and by important consequences for the structure of medical economics. What is the nature of the system of personnel and facilities geared to deal with modern health problems, and how is all of this paid for? We turn our attention to these matters in the chapter to follow.

SCENARIO II

The technological explosion

It is the year 1978. A young man is riding his motorcycle too fast on a coming curve, goes off the road, and smashes into a tree and falls unconscious to the ground. A nearby resident sees the accident and calls the rescue squad, which arrives in a matter of minutes. The paramedics suspect a broken neck and call the emergency service on the telephone to report their observations. The attending physicians instruct the paramedics to check for paralysis, monitor breathing, and rush the patient to the emergency room. The paramedics find no sensation in the extremities and shallow breathing. They supply oxygen during the trip to the hospital, whereupon the patient is placed in an intensive care unit and immediately in an iron lung. Life support systems are on hand if they should be needed. The patient is kept in the iron lung for shorter and shorter periods of time until the medical team is confident that the patient will not die of pulmonary collapse.

Following this initial lifesaving period, the patient is transferred to a rehabilitation hospital and into the quadraplegic ward where he joins eight other young men who have suffered a similar tragedy; severance of the spinal cord has been confirmed. Now starts the long endless road to some plateau of rehabilitation. The rehabilitation team is headed by a neurologist and a physiatrist (a specialist in physical medicine skilled in retraining atrophied muscle for which the neural system is no longer functioning). The patient is slowly weaned from the iron lung and the extent of muscle capability is carefully assessed.

Typically, it is now known that quadraplegics with a cord break no higher than the seventh vertebrae retain some motility in the shoulder muscle and with physical therapy are able to hunch their shoulders and even squeeze the arm against the armpit. Thus, following surgery in order to lock the fingers into a "hooked" position, it is possible for the physical therapy team to teach the paralyzed person to move objects with the hands by hooking with the fingers and hunching the back. The victim is now on the road to what may be maximum rehabilitation.

What about the bedsore problem? This has been solved by the invention of the Stryker bed, a framelike structure with one canvas cotlike bed contoured to the patient's torso. The other, which rests on a frame above the torso cot, is contoured to the patient's back. The patient lies on his torso gazing at the floor for a period of time. By and by a nurse comes, cranks the back-contoured bed down onto the patient's back, after which the patient is rotated onto his back and the torso half of the bed raised. By this means the patient now rests on his back for the prescribed period of time. Thus has the bedsore problem been solved, and the patient can now look forward to a relatively normal life span.

But this is not all. A technician in the hospital is now fashioning a light metal frame, not unlike an external skeleton, which will fit the patient from the shoulders down to the fingertips, hinged at the appropriate places. This contrivance is attached to a pneumatic air bag, which is suspended in the patient's armpit. With proper instruction and motivated self-will, the patient can learn to move his arms and hands by applying pressure with his armpit to the pneumatic bag. Indeed, the fingertips of the metal skeleton can be fitted with various implements so that in due time the patient will be able to turn the pages of a book and even eat soft food. Moreover, properly motivated and under a long-term program of training, some quadraplegics will learn to move from a bed to a wheelchair, and even to an automobile especially fitted so that he will be able to drive. Science has here conquered death, and perhaps even the will to die.

A modification of this scenario reads as follows: A young man in his early 20s suffers a high spinal cord break in a diving accident. After initial recovery of breathing capacity, he realizes what has happened to him. His younger brother visits him in the hospital daily, during which time the victim begs to die. The brother, in anguish, smuggles a gun into the hospital and kills his brother with one shot to the head. The young man who pulled the trigger is indicted for first-degree murder and is found not guilty.

NOTES

1 Carl Gersuny, "Health and Mortality of Fall River Mill Workers, 1908–1912," unpublished manuscript, 1978, pp. 2–4; adapted from Massachusetts Commission to Investigate the Inspection of Factories, Workshops, Mercantile Establishments and Other Buildings, 1910. Hearings, July 1–Nov. 5, 1910. Typescript, State House Library, Boston, Mass., pp. 270 et passim.

SUGGESTED READINGS

Ronald Andersen and Odin W. Anderson, *A Decade of Health Services.* Chicago: University of Chicago Press, 1973.
A national survey of the utilization of health services in the United States.

Odin Anderson and Monroe Lener, *Health Progress in the United States, 1900–1960.* Chicago: University of Chicago Press, 1963.
A detailed compilation of changing health patterns and economic indicators in the field of health over a half century.

Lawrence Corey et al. *Medicine in a Changing Society.* St. Louis: Mosby, 1972.
A series of articles by physicians and social scientists on a range of "upfront" change elements in American medicine.

Milton I. Roemer, *Rural Health Care.* St. Louis: Mosby, 1976.
Special health problems and needs of rural populations.

Howard D. Schwartz and Cary S. Kart, Eds., *Dominant Issues in Medical Sociology.* Reading, Mass.: Addison-Wesley, 1978.
An up-to-date and critical "reader" in medical sociology dealing with current issues in medicine.

Anselm Strauss, Ed., *Where Medicine Fails.* New Brunswick, N.J.: TransAction Books, 1972.
Essays on some seemingly intractible modern health problems.

Howard B. Waitzkin and Barbara Waterman, *The Exploitation of Illness in Capitalist Society.* Indianapolis: Bobbs-Merrill, 1974.

A sociopolitical critique of the contemporary medical scene, primarily from a Marxist perspective.

Jerry L. Weaver, *National Health Policy and the Underserved: Ethnic Minorities, Women, and the Elderly.* St. Louis: Mosby, 1976.

Special health care needs and problems of the socially and culturally disadvantaged.

———————————

Medical care and cost in the pretechnological era

Before Charles II died of uremia in 1685, the royal physicians subjected him to the following treatment:

> A pint of blood was extracted from his right arm; then eight ounces from the left shoulder; next an emetic, two physics, and an enema consisting of 15 substances. Then his head was shaved and a blister raised on the scalp. To purge the brain a sneezing powder was given; then cowslip powder to strengthen it. Meanwhile more emetics, soothing drinks, and more bleeding; also a plaster of pitch and pigeon dung applied to the royal feet. Not to leave anything undone, the following substances were taken internally; melon seeds, manna, slippery elm, black cherry water, extract of lily of the valley, peony, lavender, pearls dissolved in vinegar, gentian root, nutmeg, and finally 40 drops of extract of human skull. As a last resort bezoar stone was employed, but the royal patient died.

Thus ended the reign of Britain's Merry Monarch.

Although history leaves no accurate record of costs, such was the care for royalty prior to the great technological breakthroughs. The substances, of course, had to be purchased and the royal household surely had a physician on retainer. But by whatever standards one wishes to apply, the costs of Charles' care and death were very low indeed; surely no one expected him to survive, and he didn't.

CHAPTER 3

The structure of medical economics

It would be neither particularly useful nor even realistic to examine in any great detail the structure and function of medical institutions in any society without taking into account the broad outlines of what medical care costs. What kinds of resources, monetary as well as non-monetary, are being devoted to medical care? How are these aggregate costs distributed among the various components of the health industry, and how are these costs met? Is it possible to forecast, on the basis of past experiences, what the future is likely to hold with regard to health care costs?

As far as the individual consumer is concerned, an instructive figure of costs is simply to consider the total personal expenditures for medical care, and its change, over the past several years. These figures are shown in Figure 3.1.

These figures include all out-of-pocket payments for health care of all kinds, including physicians' fees, hospital expenses, fees paid to dentists, pharmaceutical costs, premiums paid for medical insurance, and other direct payment costs. They do not include publicly supported payments, which shall be mentioned in another connection. In any event, the increases shown in Figure 3.1 can only be described as astronomical, particularly the sharp increases occurring since 1960. Although some of these increases must be at least partially attributed to increased costs of living generally throughout this period, much of it must be traced to inflation within the medical establishment itself.

In fact, if one considers the percentage increase by decade over this period of time, one can observe the relatively sluggish growth during the depression decade of the 1930s, amounting to less than 1.5 percent each year, as compared with the 12.5 percent per year increases in the decades of the 1950s and the 1960s, followed by the climb to $63 billion in 1975. In other words, the growth since 1940 in private medical care expenditures has outstripped the general rate of inflation in the United States. Indeed, in 1965 medical care costs of this type consumed only 5.9 percent of the gross national product. But by 1975, these health care costs accounted for more than 8 percent of the gross national product.

Now, it is true that population growth may account for some of this increase, though even when population size is taken into account, the per capita expenditure for health care in 1930 (still a reasonably good year economically) was $28.00. By 1975, however, per capita costs had risen to $256.00.

By whatever measure, Americans are being parted from their dol-

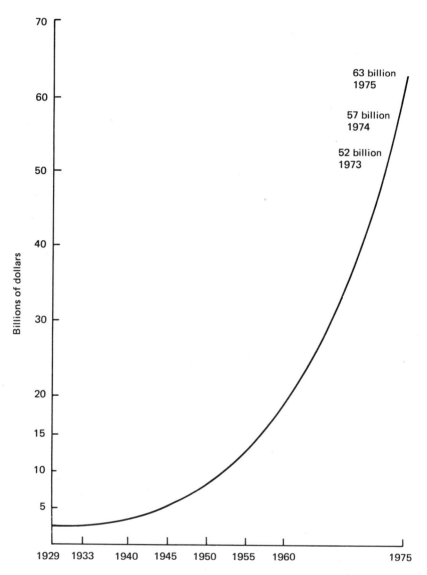

FIGURE 3.1 Total personal expenditures for medical care in the United States.

Source: Adapted from various reports of the U.S. Office of Vital Statistics, and Odin Anderson and Monroe Lerner, Health Progress in the United States, 1900-1960. Chicago: University of Chicago Press, 1963. By permission.

lars in larger and larger amounts for medical care costs. When total *public* expenditures are added to the already high $63 billion figure from the private sector, we have a grand total expenditure in 1975 of over $103 billion—greater than the total cash flow in the entire automobile industry. Placed in the context of the more recent years, the average cost of a hospital stay (this does not include physican's and anesthesiologist's fees) came to $311 in 1965, but had risen to $547 just a decade later.

In fact, the per capita costs of medical care increased just slightly over 10 percent in the decade 1930 to 1940, 87 percent during the 1950s, 88 percent during the 1960s, and 135 percent in the years between 1960 and 1973, a total percentage increase of over 80 percent during the overall period. What factors may be pointed to which have brought about these dramatic increases?

THE STRUCTURE OF MEDICAL SERVICES AND THE ESCALATION OF COSTS

A strategic point at which to begin a probe into the astounding figures cited above is first to consider the place and status of the working hospital in the American health care system. While the high costs presently surrounding the delivery of medical care cannot be attributed exclusively to the institution of the hospital, it is certainly of crucial importance.

In this context, factors specific to the medical establishment may be pointed to as helping to account for bringing about increases of this magnitude.

A prime factor has to do with the sheer magnitude of the value of the physical plant of the more than 7000 hospitals presently existing in the United States. Figure 3.2 presents these figures in billions of dollars.

As the country entered and passed through the decade of the 1930s—even well into the 1940s—the assessed value of the hospital system grew only very slowly, and by the end of the 1940s totaled less than 6 billion dollars. In fact, the growth rate during the depression years of the 1930s was practically nil, with only a modest absolute growth until just about 25 years ago. This means that the hospital plant during these years was an aging one—and one that had not yet faced the technological explosion that was to increase plant costs drastically in the years to come. In any event, rapid growth began to take place in the early 1950s, spurred on in no small measure by the passage of the Hill-Burton Act. This act made federal funds available for the construction and expansion of community oriented, relatively small general hospitals throughout the country. What local communities were unable to do for themselves was made possible through the Hill-

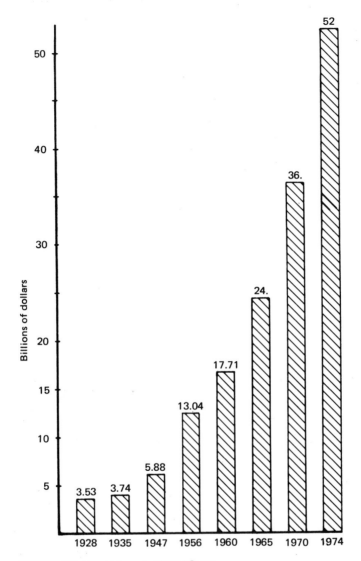

FIGURE 3.2 Hospital assets, United States.

Source: Adapted from various reports of the U.S. Office of Vital Statistics, and Odin Anderson and Monroe Lerner, <u>Health Progress in the United States, 1900-1960</u>. Chicago: University of Chicago Press, 1963. By permission.

Burton Act. The only single overriding constraint in the acceptance of such funds was that the receiving institutions would allocate a specific percentage of staff time and resources for the free treatment of the indigent. This was probably one of the first federal incursions into the heretofore relatively autonomous operation of the local community general hospital.

The effects of the operation of the Hill-Burton Act have rippled through the medical system to the present day in that it has been largely responsible for the current average size of American general hospitals at around 100 beds. A plant this size is avowedly much too small to be able to benefit in any effective way from the advances in medical technology and the medical occupational division of labor that have taken place since the advent of Hill-Burton. This is to say that the idea underlying Hill-Burton was consistent with the political pluralism and local community autonomy that has been so pronounced in the American experience. Simply stated, it rested upon the assumption that community hospitals were precisely that—responsive to the presumed needs of the individual units in the mosaic of relatively small communities scattered throughout the nation, each capable of serving the needs of its own identifiable clientele constituency, and more important, each capable in spite of its small size of containing within its walls the staff and technologies needed to provide up-to-date medical care to the members of its local constituency.

Such a view may well have been consistent with the nature and content of medical technology at the time of the bill's debate and passage, and most certainly it rested upon an ideological foundation with which no vote-conscious congressman or senator could easily argue. The ideological local autonomy and pluralism that was the foundation of the Hill-Burton Act was utterly consistent with the political realities of the American scene. And it was certainly consistent with the ideological and philosophical tenets of the American Medical Association, which took as a major point of departure the principle of local autonomy in matters of health care. All that was relinquished was the right to set fees for certain patients, or in effect agreeing to provide *some* health care free of charge. Parenthetically, it must be pointed out that no adequate figures are available to document just how much free care was already being given, not on a contractual basis with the federal government but rather on the basis of the tradition-bound concept of *noblesse oblige*, which had served so long as the justification for physician autonomy in the matter of setting sliding fee scales.

A second major funding program that helped to produce the astronomical value of the American hospital plant was the Regional Medical Program. As *its* service point of departure this program advanced the idea that rather than construct a nationwide array of small general hospitals, what was actually needed was a relatively small number of strategically located complex medical centers that would contain large-scale and comprehensive organization of the best, most modern, and most sophisticated medical technologies. Each component part would be located contiguous to the others, including research facilities and personnel and various kinds of specialty hospitals. All of these would be arranged in some meaningful pattern with relation to important centers of medical education and training. Thus, rather than provide numerous small general hospitals providing primary care to local constituencies, the regional medical center concept was to provide a limited number of centers-in-depth with comprehensive training, research, and treatment capabilities. Here concepts of excellence and specialization could hardly be denied as appealing motives for creating such a system, just in the same sense that localism and pluralism were strong appeals for supporting the idea underlying the Hill-Burton concept. But the two were essentially in conflict with one another, and were competing for the lion's share of the limited, and less than ideal, level of funding the federal appropriation process normally permits.

The success of the mobilization of these greatly increased medical service resources can only be regarded as flawed in one basic respect, namely the inability to bring about a workable interorganizational set of mechanisms by which sufficient numbers of patients in need could be efficiently and appropriately moved from the site of no longer effective primary care (the local community general hospital) to the needed technical expertise of the regional medical center. The organization of the American medical profession—bifurcated as it is into primary general practice on the one hand (located mainly in the kinds of general hospitals created by the Hill-Burton Act) and academic-scientific medicine on the other (to be found primarily in and around the relatively small number of regional medical complexes)—is poorly equipped to handle the problem of interhospital cooperation. Excellent as both organizations may be when considered in vacuo, they inevitably miss the service mark if patients are not shifted, as needed, from one to the other under circumstances of medical need.

FAILURE OF INTERHOSPITAL LINKAGES

Thus a central problem that continues to plague the American hospital system is the lack of any working organizational mechanism to link primary care settings with those possessing the most sophisticated and advanced technologies. A prevailing pattern is for the hospital setting, at whatever level, to exhaust its technologies and capabilities before undertaking to refer, by whatever means do exist, to the next level of service provider. Cost effectiveness, therefore, is of crucial importance in the sense that local resources may well be exhausted before patients are located in the proper tier of medical service.

It is by processes such as these that the value of the hospital system in this country has been estimated in 1974 to be worth approximately 52 billion dollars—nearly *10 times* what it was a mere 30 years ago. These costs must be borne somewhere.

In a very strong sense, and perhaps paradoxically, processes of interhospital competition appear not to have brought about a *lowering* of costs, but rather have contributed to an *increase* in costs. That is, hospitals operating under the established norms of local autonomy compete for scarce resources. This makes such resources increasingly scarce and therefore more valuable. This leads to increases in costs not only because of competition for dollar resources but also because of competition for technical advantages in physical plant and equipment. For example, a cobalt machine for the treatment of cancer may cost as much as half a million dollars. By a similar token the installation and operation of even a moderate-sized hemodialysis unit can cost a million dollars or more, while the addition of a kidney transplantation capability will add very measurably to that figure. So long as this process continues we can expect plant value to increase and therefore expect costs to increase as well.

One way for this growth in technical plant to take place is through the addition of more beds to a hospital. This expansion of the potential catchment area of a hospital has the potential for justifying the addition of new medical specialties to the staff as well as new sources of revenue. In the long run, it also provides a basis for justifying the creation of new technologically distinct services—all of which become more costly to equip, staff, and operate.

For example, recent estimates are that it costs approximately $30,000 to provide each additional one-bed room to a hospital. This cost must be borne whether or not the room is producing revenue for the hospital or not. By existing architectural guidelines, this means that to construct a hospital room can be expected to cost $150 or more per square foot. This compares with less than half that figure for the construction of other institutional facilities. While it is true that over 50 percent of all hospital assets are in the category of private nonproprietary hospitals, even these institutions cannot operate at a deficit forever lest they irreparably deplete their reserve funds and dip too deeply into their endowment. Nor can they necessarily depend upon the reliability of the vagaries of the stock market to balance their income and expenditures.

SPECIALIZATION AND HIGHER COSTS

With all of these aforementioned forces at work, one must also take into account increased hospital size and specialization and their attendent cost escalations. As Figure 3.3 suggests, the larger the number of beds in a hospital, the greater is the number of specialty departments included in the service repertoire.

It is to be kept in mind that all of these facilities are costly, and their investments must be amortized, whether they are generating revenue on a continuous basis or not. For example, the following shows

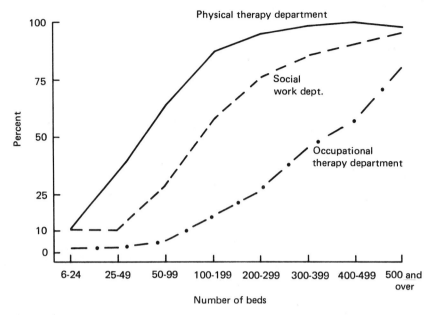

FIGURE 3.3 Percent of hospitals with selected services, by hospital size, 1973.

Source: Adapted from American Hospital Association, Hospital Statistics. Chicago: AHA, 1974. By permission.

the degree of medical specialization contained by two hospitals—one large and one small—located in the same metropolitan community.

The importance of this for cost is underscored not only by the special equipment required and its maintenance in the larger, more specialized facility, but also by the fact that the small unspecialized hospital employs just 2.5 persons per bed. The larger, more specialized institution employs nearly 5 persons per bed. Hence, in terms of the available bed services, the more specialized medical institutions become, the most *costly* they become in terms both of staff and material. There seems every reason to believe that as population density increases, so too will the catchment areas of hospitals, and so will the temptation to add more beds to individual hospitals—thereby creating the conditions under which specialization with its associated increase in costs will also increase.

PROPRIETARY HOSPITALS AS A SPECIAL CASE FOR COST EFFICIENCY

In terms of sponsorship, hospitals are customarily classified into one of four major categories, each of which is distinctive in terms of cost and revenue structures, and their presence in our society must be taken into account in any consideration of medical care costs. These categories are as follows: (1) *federal* institutions, which include army and navy hospitals and a few others supported out of the national reservoir; (2) *nonfederal* government institutions, which include all that are supported at the state, county, and municipal levels—the largest subtype of which are long-term state-supported psychiatric facilities, of which more shall be said later; (3) *private nonproprietary hospitals,* which are financed at least partially out of interest from endowment investments and philanthropic funds; and (4) the now growing number of *private proprietary hospitals,* the economics of which hinge upon the magnitude of patients' fees. It is these last two that are of principal concern here.

Part of the lore surrounding hospitals, rooted in their early histories in Western societies, is that medical care is probably better left to hospitals that are nonprofit in their motives. The assumption has been widely held that considerations of money ought not interfere with the

TABLE 3.1
Typical facilities in small and large hospitals

Small hospital (70 beds)	*Large hospital (700 beds)*
Postoperative recovery room	Intensive care unit
Premature nursery	Open-heart surgery facilities
Blood bank	Postoperative recovery room
Physical therapy department	X-ray therapy
Occupational therapy department	Cobalt therapy
Full-time registered pharmacist	Radium therapy
Dental services	Radioisotope facility
Emergency department	Histopathology laboratory
Psychiatric emergency services	Blood bank
Social work department	Electroencephalography
Family planning service	Physical therapy department
Total Services: 11	Inhalation therapy department
	Full-time registered pharmacist
	Dental services
	Renal dialysis
	Inpatient
	Emergency department
	Psychiatric emergency services
	Social work department
	Rehabilitation services
	Outpatient unit
	Home care program
	Hospital auxiliary
	Organized outpatient department
	Total Services: 24

structure and operation of hospitals. Such a view stems at least partially from an era in which hospital and medical care costs were inexpensive and in which the elaborate and costly technologies of the present day simply did not exist. Even the treatment of Charles II could not have cost more than a shilling or two. Hence, history has left us with the message that economic rationality, especially a view to realizing a reasonable profit over costs, was somehow alien to the medical enterprise.

The corollary to this has been that hospitals organized "for profit" are somehow anomalies on the medical scene and ought to be eliminated where possible. The argument has been roughly as follows: Inasmuch as such hospitals must pay their bills out of patient fees and show a profit as well, their professional staffing patterns should not be contaminated by intrusion of crass economic considerations. One could expect, so it was thought, that physicians would be appointed to the staffs of such institutions on the basis of the number of paying patients they could bring into the institution rather than on the basis of objective professional expertise. Further, so the argument goes, persons appointed in such institutions to positions of chief of services would receive their appointments on the strength of the efficiency of their patient referral capabilities rather than their medical competence.

On the other hand, nonproprietary hospitals have been understood to be institutions in which "cost is no consideration." And inasmuch as monetary matters need not be considered, medical care in such places would harbor no such base influences and could therefore provide medical care of the highest quality and kind. However appealing such widespread assumptions might be, they are flawed in two ways: First, neither set of assumptions has been placed to empirical test; and second, these assumptions do not necessarily fit in with the principal threats that hospitals now face.

As has been stated:[1]

> As proprietary hospitals increase in size and incorporate multiple units, they increase in efficiency since they do not add to the scope of services provided. By comparison, the individual-unit voluntary nonprofit hospital typically adds to the comprehensiveness of its services, which leads to an increased cost per patient date.

And further:[2]

> How are the proprietary hospitals able to give quality care, charge lower fees than other hospitals in the same community, pay taxes, and still pay dividends to their shareholders? It would appear that the free enterprise system is operable in the hospital field, as illustrated by some of the proprietary "chains" that are organized around a corporate structure. The for-profit hospital in some cases has to be more innova-

tive and use business efficiency, as it provides an element of competition for health services. The for-profit hospital chains seem to utilize more sophisticated, centralized management systems in order to meet their defined goals. The mass approach to monetary savings and controls is more businesslike in operation, as it utilizes centralized purchasing, standardization of procedures, systematized record keeping, and computerized accounting procedures, among others. These hospital chains also provide a greater opportunity for upward mobility because of their multi-unit corporate structure, especially in their administrative section.

Furthermore, the nonproprietary hospital may feel itself free of economic considerations and may be lured into the economic morass of overspecialization and overexpansion exacerbated to some extent by the availability of widespread third-party payments, which in turn encourage rapid expansion of costs and facilities that ultimately must be passed on to clients in one way or another. It is in this sense that specialization, costs, and size are dimensions of hospital change which intertwine one another. For example, the small 70-bed hospital mentioned earlier in this chapter expends an average of $25,000 per year per bed, while its sister 700-bed hospital expends nearly $41,000 per year per bed. Illustrated in yet another way, the per-employee payroll costs in the small hospital are $15,714 per year per bed, while the payroll costs of the larger hospital are $25,600 per year per bed.

There is some reason to believe, therefore, that nonproprietary hospitals may have become far too sanguine in their neglect of simple economics while viewing the "organized for profit" hospital in far too pejorative terms. Some of this is evidenced by the fact that whereas in 1960 proprietary hospitals represented less than 2 percent of all hospital assets in the country, by 1974 they accounted for over 8 percent of hospital assets.

However much modest growth might signal some coming change in attitude toward the proprietary hospital, it is still true that nonprofit hospitals in 1960 and 1970, respectively, accounted for 50 and 57 percent of all hospital expenditures, while profit hospitals expended only 3 and 4 percent, respectively, during those years. Each type maintained its relative position.

But as far as present trends indicate, our hospital system is still dominated by the private nonproprietary hospital, prone as it is to increasing size, increasing specialization, and therefore increased costs.

As to the distribution of overall costs within the hospital system itself, Figure 3.4 indicates how the hospital dollar is allocated, first in community general hospitals, and second in teaching hospitals.

Quite aside from fees paid directly to physicians over and above the costs of hospital operation, it is clear that the key to hospital costs lies in the personnel column. Again, the actual allocation of these costs

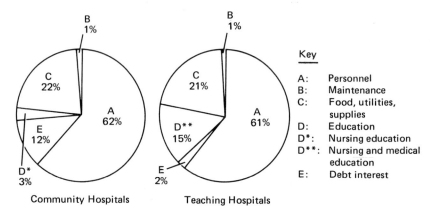

FIGURE 3.4 Allocation of "medical dollar" by community hospitals and teaching hospitals.

Source: Adapted from James Hepner and Donna Hepner, The Health Strategy Game. St. Louis: The C. V. Mosby Company, 1973. By permission.

is not immediately visible or apparent to the paying patient who does not directly transfer money from his wallet into the hands of hospital personnel. Rather they are subsumed under other fee categories (room and operating theater rentals primarily). Nevertheless, costs of paying hospital employees consume in both the typical community general hospital and in the teaching hospital over 60 percent of all costs. Equipment and construction costs—widely appreciated to be very high— can be amortized over the long run, and therefore account for but 2 percent of costs in the teaching hospital and 12 percent in the community hospital.

That increased costs appear to be rooted in higher personnel expenditures is evidenced by the fact that in 1960 hospitals employed some 114 persons for every 100 patients cared for, but in 1974 it required no less than 250 employees to aid in the treatment of every 100 patients. In the latter years, these personnel-employed figures ranged from a low of 100 employees per 100 patients in psychiatric hospitals to a high of 323 employees per 100 patients in private non-proprietary hospitals. And in connection with what has already been said about possible differences in cost effectiveness, in 1974 proprietary hospitals employed 283 persons per 100 patients as compared with the 323 employees in nonproprietary institutions.

ALLOCATION OF THE HEALTH DOLLAR

A further vantage point from which to consider health care costs is the differential allocation of the health dollar with respect to a comparison of the variety of medical services that can lay claim to at least a portion of it. The percentage changes in these allocations are shown in Figure 3.5 from 1929 to 1960, and then to 1970.

As is displayed, the proportion of the health dollar spent for hospital fees has steadily increased over the past four decades, from less than 14 percent in 1929 to over 26 percent in 1960, then jumping in ten years to 38 percent in 1970. Correspondingly, the proportion paid directly to physicians has *decreased* from nearly one-third in the first year, to 25 percent in 1960, and then to 20 percent in 1970. The conclusion is inescapable that our rising health care costs are in the main attributable to the expansion and increased use of the hospital as the focal treatment setting in American medicine.

Before discussing some of the implications of this in more detail, other figures are worth mentioning that are not unrelated to hospital

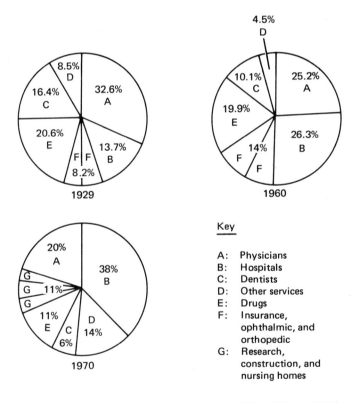

FIGURE 3.5 Composition of the U.S. medical dollar for 1929, 1960, and 1970.

Source: Adapted from James Hepner and Donna Hepner, <u>The Health Strategy Game.</u> St. Louis: The C. V. Mosby Company, 1973; and Odin Anderson and Monroe Lerner, <u>Health Progress in the United States, 1900-1960.</u> Chicago: University of Chicago Press, 1963. By permission.

costs: First is the fact that the percentage of the health dollar spent for dental care has *decreased* from over 16 percent in 1929 to just 6 percent in 1970. Similarly, relative expenditures for drugs has decreased over this period by about 50 percent—from about 20 percent in the earlier year to about 11 percent in the latter year. In the case of the latter figures, it is not implausible to assume that as hospitalization as a first step in treatment increased, so too does the proportion of total money spent for drugs expended in the hospital context and added to the "hospital care" column, rather than for prescriptions written by the private physician and filled by the patient at the independent pharmacy. So that decline may be more illusory than real.

In the case of dental fees, two forces seem to arise as preeminent in explaining that decrease. One is that as the total funds available to the spender for medical care are increasingly eroded by the rising costs of general medical care and hospital fees, the amounts left over for "discretionary" medical expenditures, such as dental care and ophthalmic care, shrinks. This in no way means that dental care has become "cheaper" in any sense of the word at all. Quite the opposite is indicated by the number of discrete dental specialties that have become increasingly ubiquitous over the years—the cosmetic practice of teeth straightening, oral surgery to correct a variety of morphological anomalies in the mouth, root canal excavations so as to avoid tooth extraction, and extensive periodontal procedures in order to retain the natural teeth until the remainder of the body succumbs in some other way. All of these specialties do, in one way or another, reflect the effectiveness of the dental community—both teaching and practice—in devising and implementing at both the individual and community level various aspects of *preventive* dentistry, producing together a situation in which we have a potentially large and relatively poor population that simply cannot afford modern dentistry and another, more affluent group that is able to avail itself of the high-quality dental technology regardless of the cost. For many people, therefore, dental health care is an all-or-nothing game.

INVOLUNTARY NATURE OF HOSPITALIZATION

Let us now return to the growing proportion of the health care dollar that is spent for services provided by hospitals. It is important to realize that consulting a practicing physician about a perceived health problem is strictly discretionary on the part of the lay patient. One need not attend to one's bodily sensations to an extent that leads one continuously to the office of the doctor. In fact, there is some evidence to suggest that the vast number of persons tend to define their symptoms in familiar and benign ways for a considerable period of time.

Except in the case of special categories of persons (some employees of some firms, military personnel, and a limited number of others), one is not *ordered* to go to the physician for observation and diagnosis; it is a voluntary act. On the other hand, the doctor typically *orders* a patient to enter the hospital in ways that do not resemble an invitation. That is, there is an element of compulsion in hospitalization that is absent in the context of the original coming together of patient and doctor. This has at least something to do with the asymmetry existing between the physician and the layman. The physician is in possession of esoteric knowledge—and the mystique surrounding that knowledge-ability—that is beyond the grasp of the patient. Hence, it is only in exceptional cases (religious commitments prohibiting hospitalization being the typical case) that patients refuse to accept the "doctor's orders" to enter the hospital.

And because of the asymmetry between the medical specialist and the ignorant layman, it is possible for a number of forces to become activated to *increase* hospitalization and therefore to drive medical care costs up.

Certainly the increased possibility of becoming the target of a malpractice (better stated as "underpractice") suit serves as an incentive for the physician to "tilt" in the direction of hospitalization and to engage in wide-ranging and expensive batteries of diagnostic procedures and monitoring. It should also be said, however, that this tendency to increased "medicalization" of the health scene is countered by the recently developing patterns of "demedicalization" within the ranks of the lay population. Nevertheless, however widespread the self-help movement might be, all indications seem to be that hospitalization is going to continue to be the principal treatment modality in American medicine, brought about at least in part by the increased specialization in medicine. The growth of medical specialties in the medical profession creates a need on the part of larger and larger numbers of physicians for expensive mechanical and back-up staff that the physician is unable to provide in his or her own practice; hence, increased reliance on the hospital. Further, the declining proportion of general practitioners in the profession makes it more and more imperative that patients short-circuit the general practitioner route to specialists referral and go directly to a specialist. The latter, in turn, can usually be relied upon to charge higher fees than the typical general practitioner.

In 1974–1975, for example, it was estimated that the number of medical students in the general practice stream was estimated to be smaller than the number required merely to replace the number of retiring general practitioners, even without taking into account population growth. The percentage of physicians in various forms of practice over the past four decades is shown in Figure 3.6.

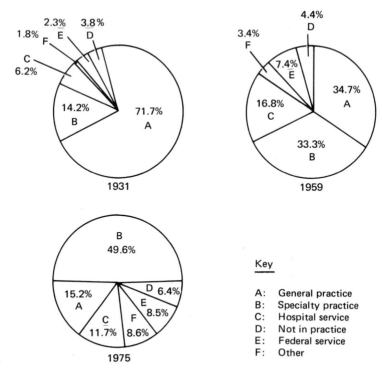

FIGURE 3.6 Physicians in the United States by type of practice for 1931, 1959, and 1975.

Source: Adapted from James Hepner and Donna Hepner, The Health Strategy Game. St. Louis: The C. V. Mosby Company, 1973; Odin Anderson and Monroe Lerner, Health Progress in the United States, 1900-1960. Chicago: University of Chicago Press, 1963; and various reports of the Statistical Abstracts of the United States. By permission.

CHANGES IN LABOR FORCE

It should come as no surprise that the proportion of specialists within the total American physician pool has steadily increased over the past four decades. There are several reasons for this: One has been the increased technological sophistication of contemporary medicine, which in turn cannot be viewed in isolation from the growing distinction between medical practice and scientific medicine. That is, when larger and larger numbers of physicians devote virtually full time to the scientific boundaries and temporary limits of the science of medicine, one is bound to *observe* increasing technical sophistication, followed in turn by increasing specialization in the medical education scene and ultimately in the division of labor of medicine. And this is precisely what we have witnessed over the course of the modern era in Western medicine. Yet a second element has to do with the composition of the faculties of medical schools. That is, being mostly specialists themselves, the members of the medical faculties serve as role models for medical students and however much a beginning medical student may originally aspire to general practice, the pressures to specialize are very considerable up through the internship and residency structures.

It would be unrealistic to ignore the very genuine intrinsic and extrinsic rewards that accompany specialty practice. Access to staff appointment to top-flight hospitals and medical school faculties is increased, as is the freedom to pursue one's special interests in medicine, with a greater probability of having the necessary resources to do so. Over and above that, however, is the expanding opportunity for enriched financial rewards that come from specialized practice. As for example, while it may be true that the average income of all physicians in 1972 was $42,000 per year, it is also true that the average income of board-certified specialists in obstetrics/gynecology even a decade earlier was $63,000. It is this latter figure to which the discussion will later turn so as to dramatize the economic structure of the American medical system.

In spite of the astounding advances in medical technology, health care is one of the few remaining highly labor intensive industries, far in excess of the other main divisions of human service that lay a claim to client particularism—education, social welfare, and the law. To illustrate, the number of persons employed in the health industry since 1940 are shown in Figure 3.7.

The increase in the number of medical employees from approximately 1 million in 1940 to 4 million three decades later represents a growth of more than 250 percent during that period. In the earlier year M.D.s constituted some 12½ percent of the total, while in the later year physicians made up about 8½ percent of the total number of health employees. These figures reflect not only the magnitude of the human resources now devoted to the health care professions, but also the increasing complexity of the medical division of labor in the sense that while in 1972 the total employees in health was approximately 4 million, only 25 percent of that 4 million occupy the traditional professions of physician and nurse. The remaining 3 million consist of administrators, housekeepers, and a growing variety of paraprofessionals and medical technicians whose members perform increasingly specialized tasks in the medical treatment setting and all of whom contribute to the aggregate costs of medical care. All receive their salaries regardless of the frequency with which their skills are applied to the needs of patients.

With regard to the increases in the personnel pool of physicians and nurses only, reference is made to Figure 3.8. As can be noted, the rate of increase in the number of nurses has far exceeded that of

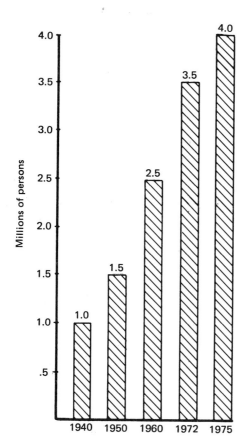

FIGURE 3.7 Persons employed in the U.S. health industry.

Source: Adapted from various reports of the U.S. Office of Vital Statistics, and Odin Anderson and Monroe Lerner, <u>Health Progress in the United States, 1900-1960</u>. Chicago: University of Chicago Press, 1963. By permission.

physicians from the turn of the century until about 1960. Then the supply of physicians began the catch-up phase, and this has continued to the present. Again, these trends not only reflect increased complexity in the medical division of labor, but also indicate the contributions that increased technological sophistication makes to increased costs.

MEDICINE AS A "SPECIAL" ECONOMY

Traditional laissez-faire economics would have it that increases in the supply of a commodity should result in decreased costs. But this does not appear to hold with regard to the special market activities of medical care: As the supply of physicians, nurses, and other medical specialists has increased, so too has the demand. And as the demand has increased, so too has the cost. At least until very recent estimates, there has been in this country an untapped, and heretofore unanswered, demand for health care that even now appears to outstrip the present number of suppliers.

With regard to physicians in particular, both licensure restraints and restrictions on medical school admissions resulted in only modest increases in the number of physicians through the 1930s and up to the early 1960s, a date that corresponded to the twin concerns with growing medical care costs on the one hand and an announced shortage of doctors on the other. At that time, there was considerable hope that if the pool of physicians was sharply increased, what this would have some dampening effect upon the then documented rise in health care costs. As a result of that expectation, the American Medical Association Council on Medical Education dropped its opposition to federal subsidy of medical student training. Moreover, if a severe shortage of doctors was to be avoided, at least 20 new medical schools would have to be constructed in the decade to come, and the output of medical schools would have to double so as to avoid this crisis shortage by the late 1970s or early 1980s. In response to this, enrollments in medical schools

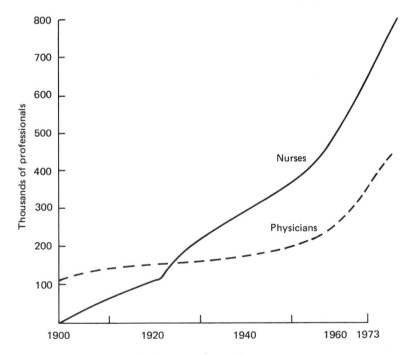

FIGURE 3.8 Physicians and nurses in the United States.

Source: Adapted from various reports of the U.S. Office of Vital Statistics, and Odin Anderson and Monroe Lerner, Health Progress in the United States, 1900-1960. Chicago: University of Chicago Press, 1963. By permission.

increased, as did the number of graduate physicians. Correspondingly, the ratio of physicians to population has steadily increased to the point in 1970 at which the American doctor-to-population ratio is exceeded only by that obtaining in West Germany and Austria. But medical care costs did not, as hoped, go down. Rather, they went *up*, and at such a pace that it is now thought that in the aggregate we now have *not too few* physicians but too *many*. In fact, the presumed relationship between an increase in suppliers and a corresponding reduction in costs has now been rejected, and replaced with the assumption that the addition of each new physician now *adds* approximately one-quarter of a million dollars annually to medical costs; it *does not* result in a reduction.

Thus, while medical care in some ways resembles a market commodity, it is clearly one that does not follow the laws of the market in a slavish fashion.

THE EFFECT OF FEDERAL MONEY

The recent intrusion of large amounts of public money in the sphere of medical care is further illustrative of this generalization. Thus far, we have dealt with medical care costs largely as effected within the private sector. But the governmental role through the allocation of tax money has greatly expanded in recent years, contributing to special costs paid for by this means.

While direct government payments for health care costs on any large-scale basis are relatively new, there have been marked increases over the past decade alone. Figures 3.9 and 3.10 show the portion of

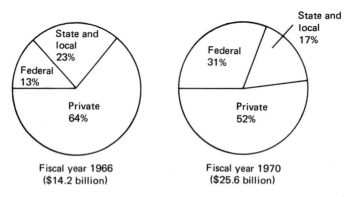

Fiscal year 1966
($14.2 billion)

Fiscal year 1970
($25.6 billion)

FIGURE 3.9 Public and private payments of total hospital costs in the United States, 1966 and 1970.

Source: Adapted from James Hepner and Donna Hepner, The Health Strategy Game. St. Louis: The C. V. Mosby Company, 1973. By permission.

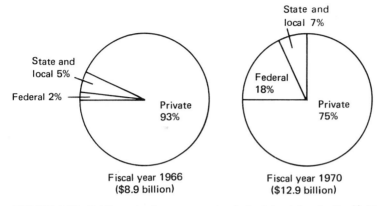

FIGURE 3.10 Public and private payments of physicians' fees in the United States, 1966 and 1970.

Source: Adapted from James Hepner and Donna Hepner, The Health Strategy Game. St. Louis: The C. V. Mosby Company, 1973. By permission.

hospital costs and physicians' fees paid for out of public funds in 1970 as compared with 1966.

In 1961 the federal government paid for only 13 percent of all hospital bills, a figure that reached over 30 percent less than four years later, largely because of Medicare expenditures. And there seems to be every probability that this proportion is likely to continue to increase as the predicted changes in the age-sex pyramid continue to be borne out and the increase in chronic illnesses continues to expand the scope and extent of hospitalization for the handicapped.

But it is the expenditures for physicians' fees that is of paramount importance in attempting to understand the principal dynamics of medical care costs. In this regard we observe that private sources still account for 75 percent of all money paid to physicians in the context of the billing routines of their private practice. Although it is true that this percentage is down somewhat from earlier years, the special market position occupied by the practicing physician remains substantially unchanged.

A somewhat different perspective toward public expenditures is displayed in Table 3.2. Not only have medical expenditures under public assistance programs increased by 188 percent between 1969 and 1975, the noteworthy fact is that the number of specific programs underwriting such expenditures has grown from 6 in the earlier years to no less than 13 programs just 6 years later. What has brought this about, quite aside from conceding that such programs may in fact meet a heretofore unmet set of needs? One must look for an explanation in the funds appropriation mechanism as it operates within the Federal

TABLE 3.2

Medical expenditures under public assistance programs, 1969 and 1975

A. 1969: Total expenditures	B. 1975: Total expenditures
$4,273,439	$12,318,468
Physicians' services	Physicians' services
Dental services	Nursing home care
Nursing home care	Intermediate care services
Indigent hospital care	Hospital services
Prescribed drugs	Dental services
	Lab and radiological services
	Home health services
	Family planning services
	Clinic services
	Prescribed drugs

SOURCE: Adapted from various reports of the U.S. Office of Vital Statistics.

bureaucracy. Here it is useful to turn to Norton Long's concept of the "ecology of games." That is, each administrative unit within the overall administrative structure operates in a competitive relationship with all other units, in spite of the fact that in a putative sense all share a common purpose or legal mandate. The successful program, therefore is one that is funded, and the larger the appropriation secured the more 'successful' is the program and therefore the more likely to survive. This cannot help but lead to a situation in which funding may and will be sought after for its own sake as a device for administrative survival and leading to the "additive" character of the Federal system of service programming. That is, over time agencies and units tend toward self-aggrandizement, regardless of what contribution that aggrandizing may or may not make to the achievement of overall agency mandates.

For example, proposed authorizing legislation (asking budgets) under the Health Services Extension Act of 1977—merely one asking category—for fiscal year 1978 would exceed by *115 percent* the actual appropriations made for fiscal 1977. If the requesting agencies are to be judged as successful they must succeed in acquiring a good share of that asking figure. The appropriations called for are in the magnitude of millions of dollars and would be expended for such purposes as state comprehensive health services, hypertension, the establishment of migrant health centers, community health centers, family planning centers, research into sudden infant death syndrome, hemophilia treatment centers, home health services, services for crippled children, and others.

Thus, by whatever standard one wishes to apply, medical care costs represent the most inflationary industry in contemporary society. The critical question is why?

THE MEDICAL ECONOMY AS A FLAWED "SYSTEM"

The crucial role played by the hospital in escalating costs is clear from what has already been said. Beyond that, the special place occupied by the privately practicing physician is strategic in any attempt to expand an explanation of contemporary medical care costs.

As has already been mentioned, the median income (after expenses have been deducted) of board-certified American obstetricians was estimated at about $63,000. Adding only a modest cumulative inflation of 6 percent annually to this figure yields a current income considerably in excess of $100,000 per year. By way of contrast, in the earlier year a practicing British midwife could anticipate an increase of approximately 5000 pounds sterling annually, which at the then existing rate of exchange added up to about $12,000 per year. This contrast is made even more striking when reflecting on the fact that the fetal and infant mortality rate in Great Britain is actually *lower* than in the United States. The question is not whether the American obstetrician is making too much money and the British midwife too little; rather, the question is how to account for the fact that the American doctor earns a truly handsome income, allowing for a life of considerable luxury, while the British counterpart who performs the same work earns a comfortable but modest living.

In the American case, some 95 percent of all births—including those following the first child—take place in a hospital and under the supervision of a medical team headed by an M.D. who in most cases has monitored the course of the pregnancy since it became known. This is in contrast to the British situation in which about 95 percent of all *first* births take place in a hospital, while over 90 percent of all *subsequent* births take place in nursing homes under the direction and supervision of a trained midwife and not a doctor. The use of paraprofessionals in this single case is illustrative of how costs can be dramatically reduced, and how on the contrary the American reliance of the twin instruments of the physician and the hospital can contribute to high costs on both the practitioner and organizational setting sides.

How may American physicians explain and justify their high income? First, they may with some truth assert that they, in comparison with other medical specialists in particular and other professionals in general, work very hard at what they do, but then so do British physicians and midwives.

A second justification is that high incomes are certainly not out of line with the long period of schooling doctors must undergo before they can benefit from the fruits of their labor. But the same argument—though less true for British midwives—is certainly true for British doctors.

A more cogent argument is simply to disavow any excessive avarice or greed and say merely that the money just "rolls in," seemingly without effort, once a practice has been established. This is more to the point.

The issue has basically to do with the fee-setting structures in the two countries. In the American case, and in spite of a wide range of cooperative practices involving two or more practitioners, the American physician sets his own fees partially in relation to the socioeconomic composition of his clientele. Thus, fees for the same medical services can range very widely from doctor to doctor, and especially so in those common situations in which the nature of professional morality reduces the likelihood that one practitioner will discuss the nature and magnitude of his fees with other physicians. And given the nature and content of possible medical regimens, the size of one's practice need not be an indicator of one's income; physicans who are less busy are in a very easy position to fill free time merely by prescribing more treatment to the patients they have. And as T. H. Marshall has said in relation to this same problem in Britain before the advent of Nation Health Service in that country:[3]

> He [the physician] is unable to go in for mass production and is forbidden to offer cheap lines for slender purses. Since he works for a limited market it is not surprising that he should choose one which is solvent and concentrate on the wealthier individual client. In other words, he must find an employer, and the general public [was] not organized for his employment.

In the British case, the public is the doctor's (and the midwife's) employer and each is paid on the basis of a capitation rate—so much salary is paid by the government to each, depending upon the number of patients they have assigned to their rolls. Thus, aside from whatever private practice in which they choose to engage, the British doctor's income is more or less fixed at a level designed to guarantee an adequate, but not opulent, standard of living. Hence, he need not seek out a wealthy clientele because his income remains substantially the same whether his patients are rich or poor. Of course in the case of the obstetrician, the fact that a vast number of babies are delivered by midwives outside a standard medical hospital contributes further to lower *aggregate* cost.

There is one final difference that deserves mention, and that is the distinction between the general practitioner and the consultant (or specialist) in British medicine. General practitioners do not practice within a medical specialty, not even minor surgery. Moreover, they do not hold appointments to hospitals. Each sees the patients on his or her roll on a per capita basis. If in the GP's judgment a patient requires hospitalization, he or she refers the patient to a hospital, which is staffed exclusively by consultants (specialists), who then take over the case. The GP may not treat the patient in the hospital; the patient has now become the client of the hospital collectively and not the patient of a particular specialist employed by the relevant hospital board. The patient does not pay the hospital, or the specialists, both of whom are supported out of tax funds. Perhaps more important, the legal responsibility of the patient has under these circumstances been transferred from the shoulders of an individual doctor to the hospital as a corporate body. As a result, individual doctors need not increase their fees as "insurance" against the specter of possible malpractice suits.

In any event, the medical system in Britain has been removed rather completely from the special market situation that in the United States helps to generate high costs.

A fundamental element creating this situation is the fact that the vast majority of physicians in the United States practice outside of any organizational context and are therefore free of the bureaucratic rules that help to militate against other professionals' attaining the same freedom from market forces that the physician enjoys. The student is asked in this regard to compare the median incomes of the occupations listed in Table 3.3.

In spite of numerous differences, a central feature distinguishing the work situation of physicians from that of *most* other professions is

TABLE 3.3
Median incomes of selected professionals, 1971[a]

Profession	Income
Physicians	$42,000
Attorneys	21,396
Accountants	19,800
Engineers	17,880
Professors	16,799
Teachers	9,269

[a] After deductions.
SOURCE: Adapted from Howard Waitzkin and Barbara Waterman, *The Exploitation of Illness in Capitalist Society.* Indianapolis: The Bobbs-Merrill Company, Inc., 1976. By permission.

that they are not constrained by organizational employment. As a result, they are free to determine the level of service they will provide and, within broad limits, its price as well.

In light of the changing patterns of health and illness outlined in the previous chapter, and the complexities of medical economics suggested in this chapter, attention now turns to some special problems and choices faced by the social scientist who ventures, as researcher, into the world of medicine. What shall the social scientist study in medicine and where shall his or her scientific bias be found?

SCENARIO II

Medical care cost in a technological era

The typical patient with advanced uremia or other forms of chronic kidney failure face a different future than in 1685. The so-called "artificial kidney machine" had been invented and placed into fairly widespread use by the early 1950s. In order to maintain life, the patient must be dialyzed; that is, the destroyed capacity of the kidneys to clean the blood must be replaced by artificial means. The blood must be removed from the circulatory system, circulated on one side of a series of layers of cellophane membranes while a salt solution circulates throughout the other side of the cellophane. By this means, waste products in the blood diffuse through the membrane into the bath solution and the purified blood returned to the patient's circulation. This is accomplished by attaching a tube to a vein from which the blood is withdrawn, and another attached to an artery into which the cleansed blood is returned.

The process takes from three to eight hours and must be undergone under very special clinical conditions two to three times each week. Failure to dialyze will bring death in a short time. Prior to the 1960s patients on long-term dialysis had a quite short life expectancy, due largely to the trauma caused by repeatedly gaining access to the circulatory system; vascular collapse was common. In 1960, however, the cannula (or "shunt") was invented. This plastic connector is permanently implanted in a vein and an artery. This can then be attached repeatedly to the kidney machine, and the blood cleansed over and over again. Barring the incursion of other complications (by no means infrequent), carefully selected patients can be maintained for a period of years by such means. The long-term prognosis for many such patients is not yet very good, and transplantation continues to be the preferred modality, although this too has a number of physical, psychological, technical, and even legal-ethical impediments. Nevertheless, the modern patient does not face King Charles' imminent death.

The average cost of a year's dialysis for one patient is approximately $30,000. Under some special selection circumstances, dialysis can be performed in a specially prepared room in the home with a family member or visiting specialist nurse attending. This procedure generally results in a savings of approximately $5000 per year.

NOTES

1   James O. Hepner and Donna M. Hepner, *The Health Strategy Game*. St. Louis: Mosby, 1973, p. 60.
2   Ibid., p. 60.
3   T. H. Marshall, *Class, Citizenship, and Social Development*. Garden City: Doubleday, 1965, p. 174.

SUGGESTED READINGS

Edgar Berman, *The Solid Gold Stethoscope*. New York: Macmillan, 1976. *Subtitled "Warning: Your Doctor May Be Hazardous to Your Health," this book by a physician "exposes" the monetary exploitation by doctors.*

Victor R. Fuchs, *Who Shall Live? Health, Economics, and Social Choice*. New York: Basic Books, 1974. *An important book dealing with medical economics and its impact upon society and individual life chance.*

James O. Hepner and Donna M. Hepner, *The Health Strategy Game*. St. Louis: Mosby, 1973. *A book aiming "to examine strategies and forces used by selected health occupations to resist change in the health care delivery system."*

Elton Rayack, *Professional Power and American Medicine*. Cleveland: World Publishing, 1967. *An analysis of the political and economic power of the American Medical Association.*

Anne Somers, *Health Care in Transition: Direction for the Future*. Chicago: Hospital Research and Education Trust, 1971.

The probable uneconomical consequences of the addition of new occupations to the medical division of labor.

Herman M. Somers and Anne R. Somers, *Medicare and the Hospitals*. Washington, D.C.: Brookings, 1967.

A study of the social and economic impacts of the Medicare program.

Richard A. Ward, *The Economics of Health Resources*. Reading, Mass.: Addison-Wesley, 1975.

An overview of the economic structures and processes peculiar to the health industry.

SCENARIO I

The social model of illness

. . . It is not exact laboratory science that has provided modern man with the best substitute for the instinct of health postulated by Virey. The most effective techniques to avoid disease came out of the attempts to correct by social measures the injustices and the ugliness brought about by industrialization . . . the huge populations suddenly crowded into the factories and tenements of the mushrooming cities lived in squalor and were exposed to great physical and emotional hardships. . . . Their privations and physiological misery created everywhere social and health problems so acute that they became an obsession for the European conscience. . . . We shall consider in a later chapter how the concern with social reforms rapidly evolved into the public health practices that brought about spectacular improvements in the sanitary and nutritional state of the Western world. Suffice it to state here that this achievement *cannot be credited to the type of laboratory science with which we are familiar today.* . . . Although the laboratory scientist was only the laborer of the eleventh hour in the campaign against disease that began a century ago, he occupies now the center of the stage everywhere. . . . Their success [the nineteenth-century reformers] had been due more to zeal in the correction of social evils than understanding of medical problems.

From Rene Dubos, M.D., *Mirage of Health.* Garden City: Doubleday, 1959, p. 29 passim.

CHAPTER 4

Problems of method in medical sociology

However sharp a sociologist's conceptual and methodological skills may be, when it comes to conducting research in the world of medicine, the sociologist enters as an alien, and is generally so regarded by those who populate that special world. As the anthropologist Robert Redfield would have it, medicine is one of the "Great" cultures of modern civilization to which the uninitiated must always remain outsiders occupying positions of relative asymmetry, even with respect to the lower-level members of the medical community. This is to say that the sociologist who wishes to cast an analytic eye upon affairs medical finds it is essential to understand some of the sources of that asymmetry and some of their consequence for what we understand to be the sociology of medicine.

The term *Great culture* refers simply to those realms of special knowledge and relatively insulated social organization that we commonly know as the "professions." Without undergoing that long period of technical socialization that typifies training for the professions of medicine, the physician being the prototype, the outsider is necessarily at a disadvantage when the sociological task centers around questions of problem definition as well as of understanding causative processes. This problem of understanding is even further exacerbated when it comes to grasping the content and significance of the *moral* community of medicine—the system of cognitions and values that differentiates the views and attitudes of the medical establishment from those common to individuals who are "on the outside looking in."

SOCIOLOGISTS AS "OUTSIDERS"

It is a commonplace though nonetheless important assertion that the sociologist is *always* a guest in the quest for knowledge through research. This is to say that neither the discipline of sociology nor the vast number of its practitioners has an empirical, organizational, or problem domain that is understood to be exclusively its own. By the same token it is also true that a handful of sociologists do come to be regarded as friendly sojourners in the domain of others and live nearly all of their working lives as accepted long-term boarders in the houses of others. A few, for example, over a long period of work develop an expertise (which really means domain acceptance) in the world of the military and become military sociologists. Others make a similar colonization in the world of law and build careers in that community. Some are even able to achieve such status in some special neighborhood in the medical society and move in permanently; the mere mention of their name will open the doors of doctor's offices and special hospitals of one sort or another. A handful of others gain prominence in their pursuit of the social foundations and correlates of particular kinds of diseases. For the most part, however, medical sociologists penetrate the borders of medicine only periodically and do so strictly under the sufferance of those whose domain it is.

Thus, just as there is a special sort of tentativeness about whatever it is that sociologists say about medicine and the medical establishment, so too is the acceptance of the migrant sociologist in the world of medicine typically of a highly tentative nature. Although all physicians do not come from Missouri, most do say "show me."

As the student may have already surmised, there are some rather special methodological problems that the sociologist must try to recognize and deal with in any effort to conduct sociological research in any of several realms of medicine.

Perhaps at the root of this series of special methodological problems lies the fact that with the exception of studies evolving from the use of secondary data (such as the health statistics reported in the previous two chapters), the sociologist who aspires to examine some facet of medicine from a sociological point of view must engage the approval and cooperation of a physician, or of someone who works under the direction of a physician, in order to carry such a study through to completion.

Overcoming this initial obstacle can be far more difficult than one might imagine, and for a number of reasons. First of all is the asymmetry prevailing between the physician and the sociologist (the latter is typically also a college or university professor). Simply put, entree to a vast number of research sites is made possible merely by uttering the word "professor" or "sociologist"; merely declaring one's status as a member of the academic community is often enough to open both doors and mouths. Very often, in fact, persons and organizations tucked away in the seldom-traveled corners of society may often be flattered to be "taken account of" by someone of such presumed eminence. Such persons will often welcome any kind of relief from the boredom of their workaday world (the "human relations" school of industrial relations, which evolved serendipitously from the Hawthorne Electric Studies is illustrative) and take considerable pains to make the sojourning social scientist welcome and at home in the alien scene. In such cases, the sociologist need only to express an interest and imply compliancy, and open cooperation is normally forthcoming.

Not so in the case of medicine, partly because of the greater generalized authority and prestige that emanates from the core of medicine. Unlike the situation in so many other research sites, the physician is likely to ask "why?" when asked to lend support to a research problem that intrigues a sociologist. Sometimes the mere answer "because I am interested" is sufficient to open the door, but more often than not sociologists are asked to justify their work in ways that make some kind of sense to the medical practitioner.

It must be remembered that the initiated in medicine tend to operate within a well-circumscribed set of understandings concerning their work and their work situation, both of which are often highly problematic to the social science observer. Whereas modern physicians and those who work with and under them have the weight of a century of biochemical reductionism bearing down upon their view of the world, the sociologist is more likely to suggest a holistic and macrophenomena explanation far different from the "taken-for-granted" world of the physician. Thus in a strictly intellectual sense the sociologist is viewed with considerable suspicion, as one who is in some vague way some kind of threat to the established order of things in the medical world as they are.

Given the highly scientific and technical character of medical education (and the earlier scientific tilt of the previously undergone college and secondary school experience) the social sciences in general and sociology in particular are likely to be remembered in a number of lights, none of which are particularly flattering or conducive to moving physicians to open their hearts, practices, files, or hospitals to sociological scrutiny. These abiding memories may include some mix of the social sciences as "fuzzy" in their thinking and therefore of little practical use, as prone to overgeneralization without sufficient evidence, as neglecting the contingencies surrounding special cases as departures from general propositions, as deficient in careful scientific procedures, or as essentially radical in nature and hypercritical of the status quo. Such views of the social sciences on the part of many medical practitioners erect formidable barriers to easy entree into the medical community. At the very least, the approaching sociologist is easily regarded either as an "outsider" who carries some generalized kind of "threat," or as a relatively benign bungler who has little to offer with the possible exception of some acknowledgement of skills in the area of constructing questionnaires for the gathering of information that medical practitioners are able to collect on their own.

In this regard, Mary Goss and George Reader have distinguished four social types of physicians as they are understood to view the traveling sociologist. First are the "benevolent skeptics," who are likely to see the research sociologist as a relatively harmless figure who has little to offer by way of added understanding but whose presence is suffered so long as he or she doesn't get in the way.[1] Second are the so-called "overly expectants," not infrequently found in the technology-barren realm of institutional psychiatry, who optimistically hope that the sociologist is capable of bringing about some special magic so as to do for the medical institution what it cannot do for itself. Third are the "convinced skeptics," more often found in high-technology medical organizations, whose attitude is precisely what the label implies: The sociologist is seen as having little to offer and therefore is to be put off wherever and whenever possible. Fourth, and finally, are the "indifferent bystanders," probably constituting a plurality, who take a wait-and-see attitude and are likely to extend qualified acceptance to the sociologist on a trial basis. These exude a "show me" attitude.

Absent from the Goss and Reader list is what may be termed the ideal research host—the "no-strings-attached welcomer," who is open to whatever it is the research sociologist wishes to investigate and by whatever means for whatever purpose. That these are few and far between is evidenced not only by their not being mentioned by Goss and Reader, but also by the fact that research sociologists in medicine are seldom invited back for a second look at whatever level they may have traveled in the affairs of medicine. Unfortunately, it is true that replication of research is rare in sociology generally and virtually nonexistent when it comes to medical sociology. A particular hospital is studied *once* only; a given patient population is interviewed just *once*, seldom for a second time; a particular group of physicians or nurses are studied on a one-shot basis and not for a second time. Why this sad fact?

The answer lies somewhere in the web of factors that produce the outcome that from the point of view of the medical establishment, the sociologist seldom offers much that is regarded as of value to the ongoing concerns of the medical enterprise.

DIFFERENT POINTS OF VIEW

The toilers in the vineyards of health are first of all people of practical affairs. They deal with individual cases in which they seek for some kind of improvement. This is to say that they have little interest in patients in general but great interest in individuals. They have a profound interest in "their hospital" but not very much in hospitals as a general category of social organization. They exhibit great curiosity about the unknowns and uncertainties that surround them, but only if the unknowns are approached from an applicable medical paradigm.

They are interested in their profession, but not in professional organization in general.

In light of these perspectives, sociologists come into medicine with a different cognitive set. They have little interest in special cases whether they be persons or organizations; they care little about the ubiquitous reductionist medical model that pervades virtually every facet of modern medicine; their paradigm is systemic rather than intracellular. Sociologists are likely to be interested in the factors that impede health, but not in those that may accelerate and promote health. Whereas the medical practitioner is inclined to accept the social organization as it exists in the here and now, the sociologist is likely to be skeptical in both an historical and contemporary sense.

Given these differences, sociologists have but a limited number of options. For example, they can take their chances and openly state their research and theoretical biases in the hope that complete honesty will lead to a cooperative welcome. Alternatively, they can assume skepticism on the part of the medical practitioner and reveal only half-truths as to what is really being researched, suggesting however subtly that perhaps the research will prove useful. At a more deceptive level, they can deliberately mislead the medical hosts and do something quite different from what was claimed. As will be pointed out, these two broadly different ethical points of departure are often found in association with the use of widely contrasting kinds of research strategies and followed by different kinds of conclusions.

As a research strategy, moreover, it is useful to distinguish between the approaches and work of the "involved interviewer," "unobtrusive observer," and the "secondary data" analyst.

Whether he or she tells the medical participant the truth or elects to employ the strategy of deception, the "involved interviewer" must negotiate rough terrain that the other two types may be able to circumvent.

Of prime importance is that involved interviewers must confront their subjects at the verbal level and ask them probing questions. There are at least two very difficult problems that arise in this connection. First, the interviewer takes up time—often for no good or apparent reason. Second, in the field of medicine especially, the interviewer is in danger of blundering onto taboo turf and asking questions that no reasonable person can be expected to answer and may attempt to interview in circumstances that no thoughtful person would even consider encroaching upon. As a result, many potentially interesting studies in medical sociology are clumsily aborted, potential interviewees are offended and research doors slammed permanently, and areas of interest remain unexplored.

As to using up valuable time, the workday routines of the organizations of medicine are tightly organized, leaving little or no time for frivolous detours from the medically relevant and the case-related. In the case of trying to interview physicians, for example, it is essential that sociologists understand and express their appreciation of the fact that the physician is relinquishing his or her time (valuable in a monetary sense if during working hours, and personally valuable if during off-hours) to give information virtually invaluable to the sociologist, for which the physician often receives in return little more than a "thank you," if that.

In addition, interviewers have a great difficulty working effectively and with thoughtfulness in especially critical areas of medical care and activity: the surgical arena, the inner quarters of the local medical society, the emergency room, the intensive care unit, the terminal and quadraplegic wards, the hemodialysis unit, the weekly case conference, the post mortem conferences between the physician and the next of kin, and others that may in fact highlight aspects of social structure and dynamics of high interest to the medical sociologist. Nevertheless, sensitive researchers must respect the sanctity of such places and of such events, lest they offend and actually do harm. The "hardened" sociologist, however, may sometimes storm ahead, thereby risking ruining it for others still to come.

Further than that, effective interviewing requires the presence of the researcher in a setting for relatively long periods of time. And when involved in research in a complex social organization—a hospital especially—the sociologist is confronted with the problem arising from the fact that medical practitioners are accustomed to locating persons meaningfully within some kind of rational division of labor. Unfortunately, in most medical establishments sociological researchers have no such legitimate place in the scheme of things. As a result, they are likely to be "given a place" in terms of the prevailing medical definition, which can importantly affect whom they talk to and what they see.

Related to this is the common practice of medical establishments to be operated on a more or less authoritarian basis. This is to say that physicians are generally *in command* and they are accustomed to giving "orders" and having them obeyed. This can often flood over into the research enterprise, which is diametrically opposed to such a hierarchy of authority. In more specific terms, the sociologist is typically ill equipped to "do what he or she is told," especially in those frequent circumstances in which there is no contractual obligation or commitment to the host institution.

Thus, involved interviewers are in very considerable danger of being coopted, by those they are ostensibly studying, into a technician role serving strictly at the will of the medical leaders, or by withdrawing into a detached and alienated posture of criticism and debunking that can do little more than make real the worst fears and stereotypical view that the members of the medical world had of sociologists in the first place.

Properly formulated and conducted, however, the informed interview can reveal social facts with profound analytical power from a sociological point of view. It can be responsive to the felt needs of the medical establishment while leaving the door open to other social scientists who may follow. Some of the best of medical sociology stems from work rooted in this style. Other studies turn out to be hack work that should have been done by members of the medical community themselves, if at all. Others can be vitriolic and scathing attacks on the medical status quo. Neither of the latter two types make worthy contributions to medicine or even to social science in the long run.

The unobtrusive observer encounters special difficulties of a rather different kind. In the case of the involved interview, the persons studied are active and willing participants in the research enterprise and are very much in a position to influence the course of the study and ultimately its conclusions. Thus the coparticipation role can have undesirable results.

The unobtrusive observer attempts to avoid these pitfalls by making his or her presence and intentions as unobtrusive and innocuous as possible. While direct deception may not be involved here, those persons under the scrutiny of the researcher are presumably unaware of the purposes of the research and what its final content is likely to be. In the involved interview situation, the subjects of the studies undergo a gradual revelation process by which their understanding of the research enterprise is gradually enriched and deepened, and it is hoped that their cooperation will be increased. On the other hand, unobtrusive observers gather around themselves the cloak and mystique of outsiders, who are presumably able to see and fathom underlying meanings thought to be neither understandable nor appreciated by those being examined. Thus sociologists who opt for such a research strategy place themselves and their discipline in the unenviable and somewhat indefensible position of being accused of "seeing things" that are declared not to be there or out of order by those who are in the medical world and therefore regard themselves in a position to "know." Whereas the involved interview leads to an unfolding of gradual revelation, the unobtrusive observer skates in the direction of debunking the research site. The ethical problems in such an endeavor are patently obvious.

The researcher who chooses to employ and analyze so-called secondary data has yet a different prime difficulty with which to contend. The use of secondary data refers to the analysis of information previously collected and compiled for purposes other than those which may inform the intentions of the secondary analyst. Census data first come to mind, as do such materials that are gathered by the numerous other federal agencies which make available the kind of materials presented in the chapter in this book dealing with the changing American health scene and the following chapter on medical economics.

Such data have the virtue of institutional legitimacy about them, as, to some extent, does the material collected in the normal course of events in patient case records, nurses' notes, commission reports, and other such information that has normally been collected *directly by* or under the *supervision* of the key figure in the medical community, the physician.

A problem central to the secondary data approach is that it is exceedingly difficult for the researcher to get beyond the established, cognitive, and conceptual categories organized and set forth by others.

In sum, there is a very strong set of pressures to assume both reliability and validity of research categories as well as their epistemological truth. In other words, it is hard to organize, collate, represent, and recodify the established metaphysical presumption of empirical imperativeness about "medical data." Diagnostic categories can be relied upon to reflect objective reality, conceptions of medical causes ought to be taken for granted, and thus interpretations of meaning must link in reasonable ways with presumed reality. Under such circumstances, the sociological researcher is in danger of becoming an organizer and formal presenter of a *medical* rather than a *sociological* point of view.

A FALSE DISTINCTION

This question of the variant roles that may be played by the medical sociologist has been approached in the past by referring to the broad distinction between the sociology *of* medicine as contrasted with sociology *in* medicine. The distinction is worth repeating now, and related to what has been said thus far in this chapter. The distinction has to do with the degree to which any particular piece of research into social aspects of health or medicine *accepts* and works with the assumptions, definitions of reality, research paradigms, and value premises of the institutions of medicine as an ongoing system or, on the other hand, the degree to which these are rejected while a different and often conflicting set of assumptions, definitions, paradigms, and value premises are substituted for those of the medical establishment. The former conditions constitute a sociology *in* medicine and customarily attempts to make some *direct* contribution to the world of medicine *on its own terms*. The latter circumstances are related to the sociology *of* medicine, and usually make the effort to address a non-medical audience in its entirety, thereby making only an indirect contribution to medicine while standing aside from that community of thought.

In a sense, then, the distinction is *not* between "practical" and "theoretical" medical sciences. That distinction is a false one when applied to medical sociology. The difference is more subtle than that and includes, in addition, whether or not the medical establishment is or is not willing to accept and assimilate the *implications* of any particular social science statement. So that, in a truly pragmatic sense, the definition of what is sociology "of" or "in" medicine is located fundamentally in the hands of the members of the medical establishment itself.

As has already been intimated, and as Eliot Freidson has written convincingly and at length, the medical profession is "dominant" in that it possesses a monopoly over matters of health in contemporary society and as such exercises its autonomy in determining what information and implications shall be allowed to enter into and alter this domain dominance. Hence, in many instances, sociologists who wish to make a practical impact on the subjects of their endeavors must be not only correct but persuasive as well. Much more could be said about the special methodological problems surrounding the medical sociology enterprise, but it is worth attempting to synthesize what has already been said concerning the strategies, problems, and issues which lead to the very broad distinction between the sociology *of* medicine versus sociology *in* medicine, and these are summarized in Table 4.1.

In a general sense, the sociologist *of* medicine is regarded as a critic of the medical perspective and the medical establishment, while the sociologist *in* medicine is regarded as a contributing—and largely a compliant—member of the medical world, including its system of meanings and its division of labor. The former tends to reject the broad implications of the established medical model, while the latter integrates it into his or her perspective. How, basically, do these two perspectives—the medical and the sociological models—differ? Given the fact that they differ at virtually every level of the scientific exercise, it is a matter of some wonder that the proponents of each are able to tolerate one another at all, at least when they are embodied in two different persons.

THE MEDICAL MODEL

The prevailing and dominant medical view of illness and the social organization appropriate to its practice differs sharply from the view typically espoused by sociologists. These different views have deep

TABLE 4.1

Issues, problems, and cases in the sociology in and the sociology of medicine

	RESOLUTION AND CONSEQUENCES	
Issue	*Sociology in*	*Sociology of*
Focus of attention	Explanation of "cases"	Interpretation and generalizations
Level of analysis	Reductionist	Recourse to macro-explanations
Purpose	Health promotion	Impediments to health
Results of findings	Integrated into medicine as "practical"	Rejected by medicine as "irrelevant" and "critical"
Relation to medical authority	Accepts authority of medical world	Rejects authority of medical world
Relation to medical values	Coopted by medical ethos	Alienated from medical ethos
Typical research "strategy"	Secondary data analyst	Unobtrusive observer

historical roots and tend to be sustained by the relatively long periods of training and socialization to which members of the medical profession and the sociological community are exposed. Whatever the specific roots and contemporary sustaining structure might happen to be, it is primarily these differences that produce the special research problems that are the main attention of this chapter.

In terms of the medical model of illness, the more specialized the practice of medicine, the more reductionistic is the view of medicine. As shall be pointed out in more detail in the chapter dealing with medical education, this tilt toward increasingly discriminating biochemical explanations and the resulting world view probably has its start in the emphasis on the physical sciences even in secondary school, continues through the undergraduate college years, and is given a jogging importance in the amount of effort and attention devoted to the study of gross anatomy in the preclinical years in medical school, followed up by an even more microscopic and intracellular search for disease-causing foreign substances, or alien processes, in the human mechanism. From such a point of departure it is only one short step between this mechanistic view of the human person and the development of regimens of treatment that involve some kind of mechanistic intervention so as to exorcise and correct the defective organ tissue or chemical imbalance found therein.

This "microbe" approach to human illness has proved to have enormous power (evidence the changing health statistics enumerated in Chapter 2) and has led to the type of social organization of medical practice with which we are so familiar, which constitutes much of the hallowed mythology of the contemporary medical scene. That is, if it is accepted dogma that the biomechanical nature of illness demands biomechanical interventions and that the most microscopic of such determinations are of a higher order of scientific reality and potency than are other conceptions, then it is easily accepted that the skilled physician is the most authoritative scientifically and therefore must be in command of the health enterprise. This is not at all inconsistent with the medical professions's customary posture of omnipotence, with practitioner's reliance on their "science" as irrefutable and compelling, the autonomous exercise of medical judgment (and usually its irreversibility), and the authoritarian attitudes normally found within practice settings. Hence, founded as it is upon the empirical analysis of disease as manifest at the *microlevel*, the entire edifice of the medical community's dominance rests upon its claims of technical expertise and the need for compliance by others. That is, while physicians may often have to settle for verbally reported "symptoms," they are much more comfortable with the detection of "signs," which are normally assigned a higher level of reality than are symptoms.

Thus, the medical model of disease and its management can be understood as flowing along the chain as in Figure 4.1. It cannot be emphasized too strongly that the medical and social models depicted here represent the metaassumptions of the medical world and the community of social science, respectively, and not the kind of everyday self-consciousness that directs specific clinical work in the first instance or informs specific steps in the sociological research enterprise in the second. Rather, they represent how each tends to approach their work in an *implicit* sense, and it is because of this implicitness that the difficulties often encountered between medical personnel and sociologists are clouded by the profundity of their different points of view and attributed to the minor disputes that crop up periodically in any cooperative work effort. That is, I am emphasizing the way in which the world view of the *mainstreams* of medicine and the *mainstreams* of social science depart at crucial points of philosophy and social values.

Now in terms of the schemata presented in Figure 4.1, the medical mind starts with the assumption (increasingly including conditions under the umbrella term of "mental illness") that some form of biochemical or cellular anomaly, instability, or insult occurs in the human body in either a functional or structural respect. Thus, the medical focus is both literally and figuratively on "organic" matters. Student physicians receive their first useful introduction to this model in the study of gross anatomy, in which they learn the structure of the healthy body organs and the "signs" of their pathology. Later, more

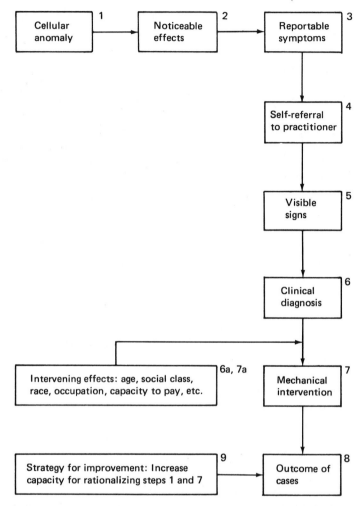

FIGURE 4.1 The medical model: disease detection and case outcome.

microscopic clinical studies provide a closer-up literal look at the finer structural defects that one may note in the diseased organ. Thus in a general sense the medical model calls for greater and greater precision in detecting anomalies in the organic system.

Troublesome anomalies produce in the host body noticeable effects such as pain, "unexplained" weight loss or gain, nervousness, change in body tone, changes in eliminatory or digestive patterns, and so on. The "rational" person who experiences these troublesome signs translates these into reportable symptoms, consults a medical practitioner of certified competence, takes time off from work, and goes to the doctor. The physician listens to symptoms and looks for recognizable signs.

Signs, it should be said, are preferred over symptoms because they lend themselves more easily to the empirical verification sought for, as implied in the previous paragraph. Indeed, the point at which Sigmund Freud first entered into his separate route in Western medicine was to assert that people could in fact be ill in the absence of visible signs, and that the verbal complaints of people ought to be taken as serious indicators of debilitating illnesses that lacked signs. I hurry to reassure the reader that it is not implied that the physician does not believe what his or her patients say; it is merely that words uttered by patients are not necessarily taken for granted.

Thus, based upon a consideration of signs along with symptoms, the physician executes as specific a diagnosis as possible, consistent with his or her focus, prescribes a mechanical intervention (usually either in the form of a chemically acting pharmaceutical substance or surgery), and then awaits the outcome. Should this not be effective, an alternate diagnosis might be made following further laboratory testing of blood and other body substances, and further interventions may be undertaken. It is at the point between clinical diagnosis and mechanical intervention that "intervening effects" may enter onto the medical scene. By this is meant the fact that in the analysis and management of the patient, the doctor may well take note of subsidiary social characteristics surrounding the patient such as age, sex, rough guesses as to social class, and so forth, as well as the patient's capacity to pay. But these are seen, from the point of view of the medical model, not as potential causative agents, but merely as possible impediments to securing the patient's compliance to a treatment regimen. In short, from the perspective of the medical model, steps 1, 2, 3, and 5 (*the assumption of cellular anomaly, noticeable effects, the appearance of reportable symptoms,* and *the detection of visible signs*) are the objects of "search" and "attention," whereas steps 4, 6, 7, and 8 are the "taken for granteds" that flow logically from the initial first steps.

The remaining elements in the health configuration possess equally strong mechanical components: First, there is the presumed automatic nature of professional dominance and the flat emotionality which is assumed to be the ideal in the doctor-patient relationship. There is also the authoritarian relations between the several levels of authority in a medical organization and the presumed finality of the status quo. This mechanical view also makes it difficult, if not impossible, for a patient to be accepted as a whole person. This, in turn, makes it difficult for medical practitioners genuinely to take account of what are here called "intervening effects" in illness. Finally, at the policy level, the mechanical model implies that the eradication of disease can best be achieved by technically increasing the physician's cognitive powers so as to detect more and more health-threatening anomalies, and to increase the number of health workers in the existing division of labor in medicine. In contrast, the social and cultural conditions which may have given rise to the recognized patterns of poor health do not, from a mechanical point of view, commonly play a prominent role in such program assessments and policy formulations.

The social model that most sociologists carry into their research contrasts sharply with the one just depicted. This is shown in Figure 4.2.

THE SOCIAL MODEL: FROM SOCIAL STRUCTURE TO TREATMENT ARBITRATION AND NEGOTIATION

While not denying the reality of body lesions, the metaassumptions underlying the social model of the medical community and constituting the substructure of most research that leans in the direction of sociology *of* medicine include the commonplace that human beings live within and against the backdrop of a holistically conceived environment. This environment is, though is not limited to, the history of the society of which the individual is but a contemporary and temporary member, the physical environment, and its technical resources of both specific and general kinds. Also included are the main institutional patterns of politics, religion, and philosophy, systems of wealth accumulation and patterns of distribution, and the system of stratification by which resources, power, and influence are generated, allocated, and used in the society. It is this holistic environment in which medical institutions are found and within which they must and do function and in which illness arises, is noted, and dealt with in various ways.

However small and undifferentiated a society might be, individual members are located differently in the places the social structure makes available to them. These status differentials of age, sex, occupation, life-style, socioeconomic level, and racial and ethnic positions expose people to different elements in the holistic environment and impose upon them differing norms for conduct. This combination of environment, social structure, and conduct norms in the aggregate produce differential behavior patterns on the part of members. These in turn expose persons differentially to illness risks and permit differential resistance to those illness insults.

Parenthetically, it is at this point (4a in the social model) that step 1 in the medical model is envisioned. However that might be, different people perceive and conceptualize their symptoms in different ways; some are disposed to think in classic medical terms, while others are inclined to think in folk or lay terms. However, automatic self-referral to a "regular" physician practicing standard medicine in the standard

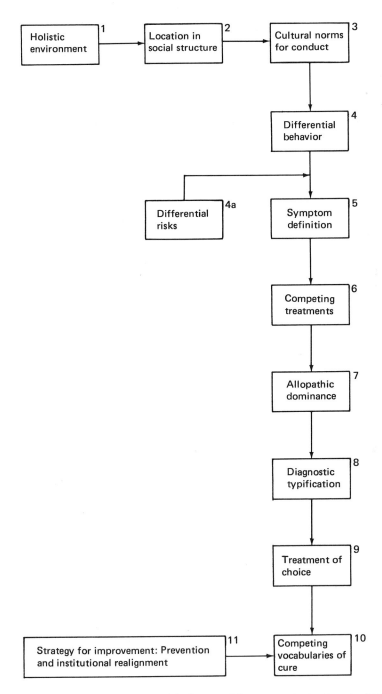

FIGURE 4.2 The social model: from social structure to treatment arbitration and negotiation.

way, cannot, from the social model, be taken for granted. This is because differential symptom definition elicits the entrance of competing coping strategies and institutions in the symptom scene. That is, some persons may route to quacks, some to lay or folk advisers within their interactional realm, others to parapractitioners, and still others to agents of self-help, and so on. Nevertheless, the vast majority in the modern Western world are routed, either directly or more slowly, to some component of the allopathic medical community where a "differential diagnosis" is made, as sketched in Chapter 1. In the absence of "clear signs," the social model leans in the direction of concluding that many diagnoses are in fact judgments based upon a practitioner's limited scope of practice and professional contacts and perpetuated as a result of the reliability of the practitioner's memory as to the outcome of "similar cases" in his or her experience. We may call this "diagnostic typification," which constitutes step 8 in the social model. Following that, a "treatment of choice" judgment is made and an intervention selected in much the same manner and on a basis similar to that which informed the diagnostic typification process.

The "end of the case" in the social model is termed "competing vocabularies of cure" in the sense that a determination of "being cured" is as much a function of personal and social reaction as is the definition of illness itself. Is the blind person who has been supplied with a white cane and dog "cured"? Is the person who has survived a massive coronary attack and had a heart pacer implanted to be assigned the "cured" category? Is the "reformed" alcoholic cured? The medical model seeks for palliation of the lesion; the social model suspects that stigmata attach to more troubles than syphilis or leprosy.

The last, and perhaps most important, step constitutes the predominating strategies for "health improvement" that flow from the medical and social models, respectively.

In the first instance, health improvement is seen as involving increased and expanded precision and capabilities in discerning cellular anomalies and dealing with them in a more intense and in-depth manner than heretofore may have been the case. Hence the logic of the medical model leads inescapably to the conclusion that greater strides in medical scientific reductionism will lead to the discovery of the Holy Grail, especially if the number of health care workers continues to increase. Technology and health personnel hold the key to the ideal conditions of more widespread health among the population. And this is precisely what the mainstream of modern medicine has been promoting, at least since the turn of the century.

On the other hand, the social model of the illness-treatment chain leads to a very different set of conclusions concerning improvement strategies. The logic of such a model is rather as follows: Inasmuch as illness has its roots in inadequacies in sociobiologic patterns (represented in their fullest blossom in established institutional arrangements), and given also that the prevailing modes of referral, professional organization, and treatment styles are in fact mere extensions of these macrolevel institutional formats, there can be very little improvement expected so long as those major institutional arrangements and forms of practice remain unchanged—perhaps even to the point of making major and primary institutional changes. In fact, from such a point of view desired changes are likely to be profound in their impact and lasting in their staying power if changes are not merely superficial or cosmetic as optional "add-ons" to the prevailing care structure, but are in-depth and broad-scope changes in entrenched sociocultural patterns.

In this sense, then, the social model of medicine, whether espoused and practiced by a sociologist *or* by a recognized member of the medical establishment, *always* represents something of a threat to the status quo. The extensions and ramifications of the medical model are essentially conservative in outlook and lean toward "improving" existing elements in the prevailing medical system. By contrast, the extensions of the social model are fundamentally radical in their approach (as seen, that is, by the proponents of the continuing state of affairs). And this major difference constitutes the primary stumbling block to widespread, ongoing, and effective collaboration between *most* social scientists and *most* members of the medical establishment.

In summary, then, the central and ongoing "special" problem encountered in medical sociology is the profound difference in the ways in which the world is perceived and assessed by social scientists on the one hand and by medical personnel on the other. And these differences pervade every link in the chain from conception of causes of illness, to its treatment, management, and economic foundations, to the broad dimensions of social and professional policy in the medical realm.

In order to concretize the argument on methods that is here being set forth, perhaps some specific examples and cases will be of some utility.

KURU: MADNESS AND DEATH IN OCEANIA

Anthropologists had, for many years, been intrigued by the phenomenon of *kuru*, observed among certain nonliterate people living in the South Pacific. The *kuru* condition exhibited behavioral manifestations remarkably similar to what most practitioners in the modern Western world would call schizophrenia: apparent hallucinations, inappropriate behavior in the context of social interaction, and appearance of being detached from the surrounding social and physical environment, and other classic "signs" of schizophrenia.[2]

Carefully controlled clinical investigation reveals a picture of an acutely onset, progressive, degenerative disease of the central nervous system that appears to begin with minor symptoms not immediately apparent to the Western observer, followed by visible changes in gait and posture to the stage where the victim can no longer walk. Death usually occurs some nine months after symptoms first become apparent. Although some males are observed to have the disease, most victims are females, especially during the age of childbearing. And whereas this clinical picture had been known for quite a long time, the medical model was unable to specify an etiological agent until very recently, when a close and careful look at cellular materials obtained from autopsied cadavers revealed that those who died of kuru suffered from a viral infection in the brain that eventually destroyed life. *It is at this point of cellular discovery* that the "medical model" is satisfied; its practitioners can now proceed to step 2 and those that follow.

The proponents of the "social model" persisted largely because of the predominance of cases found among women. Further anthropological field research revealed that the peoples among whom kuru was found were endocannibalistic, which is to say that under certain circumstances the flesh of dead members is eaten, principally the brains of dead parents, presumably as a magical effort to sustain and perpetuate the souls of diseased loved ones. In any event, the *practice* is for the women to prepare the flesh by cooking the brains prior to eating. The virus, of course, is carried in the brain (often in those who have died of kuru) and the women frequently "sample" the uncooked flesh prior to the killing of the virus through the cooking process and thereby inadvertently infect themselves with the deadly virus. A triumph for the explanatory power of the social model? Not necessarily, because further pursuit from the point of view of the medical model revealed that the "original" appearance of the virus appeared to have a genetic basis in that it was "caused" by a single gene pair which was sex-linked and recessive in the male while dominant in the female. Hence, an end to *that* argument! Again not so, because it was also shown that the extent to which the kuru gene appeared was highly dependent upon the prevailing marriage patterns in the community (the social model). But then it was also shown that the appearance of the gene itself seemed to be linked to nutritional differences (the medical model). But differential nutritional intact was not unrelated to whether or not the afflicted individual, and her offspring, had been *bewitched* (the social model) prior to the onset of the disease. And so the debate continues, with further knowledge of the sociobiogenetic character of this strange disease being increasingly uncovered. The pedagogical point, however, in the chain of intervention, treatment, and explanation stems from whatever point in the *regressive* chain it is able to negotiate with its intellectual competitors "agreement" that the "real" causes have been found.

Perhaps a more contemporary and Western example will be more convincing of the argument that medical reality is not immediately apparent from *either* the medical or the social model; there are important differentiations *within* each that stem from contrasting ideological roots and in their own right lead to debate and decisions within even the ranks both medical and social science colleagues. Let us present a further illustration to make the point.

BIRTH DEFECTS AND THE MARXIAN TOUR DE FORCE

In the early 1950s a major investigation of the life course was begun by means of the close interdisciplinary, and longitudinal, study of an entire year's cohort of first-time pregnant women in a major city in Great Britain. Inasmuch as some 95 percent of all births, and prenatal care taking place prior to birth, took place within a single hospital in which the obstetrical research unit was located, it was not a difficult task to secure access to the 3600 women and their families.[3] A vast amount of data—medical, psychiatric, physiological, social, psychological, nutritional, and obstetric—were gathered. The primary research question had to do with identifying and explaining birth defects (and subsequent later child growth and development) including spontaneous abortion, measurable abnormalities, and anomalies during pregnancy and childbirth, pre- and postnatal infant mortality and morbidity, including stillbirths and instances of severe and profound mental retardation (or learning backwardness as British idiom would have it).

The principal independent variable in the study was *social class*, and the cluster of dependent variables included birth abnormalities as well as pre- and postnatal deaths. Thus, the study represents a classic example of the social model with the social variable locatable at step 2 in the social model, with the medical analysis beginning at steps 5 and 6 in the medical model. Operationally, social class was determined on the basis of husband's occupation as classified I, II, III(a), III(b), IV, and V in the publications of Her Majesty's Stationery Office. This is the standard mode of assigning social class position in British sociological circles. This classification system and specific case assignments are made by social scientists. Birth anomalies, defects, and actual pre- and postnatal deaths were identified and recorded by highly trained medical personnel during the *normal course* of obstetric care during pregnancy.

The fundamental conclusions of this study are quite straightforward and not particularly surprising. It is their *interpretation* that throws the medical model in bold relief and distinguishes these conclusions sharply from others that are derived just as directly from the social model but do not make that final regression to exploring the specific institutional content of step 1, the "holistic environment."

The analysis began by empirically documenting the *status and stature* hypothesis first enunciated many years ago by Sorokin—namely, that women of short stature tended to exhibit more birth anomalies and natal deaths than did taller women. Although the correlation was not impressively high, nevertheless it was there: the shorter the woman, the greater the probability of defects cropping up during pregnancy and the early months of life. This empirical discovery led to the so-called "poor birth risk" category, into which were classified women who had exhibited such defects as compared with those who did not. It was then shown that there were larger numbers of women of lower social class origins in the "poor birth risk" category than in the "no risk" group.

Hence, the explanatory regress proceeds as follows: The lower the social class, the shorter the woman; the shorter the woman, the greater the probability of birth anomalies. Hence, the lower the social class, the higher the rate of birth defects. Now begins the search for the links between the identified "location in the social structure" and "Differential Risks." That is, what is there about social class that helps to produce short women, who become poor obstetric risks? The case has been summed up by Richardson and Guttmacher:[4]

> . . . studies show that there is greater risk of pregnancy and delivery room complications and premature births among women of lower social class than among those of upper social class. The findings, however, do not mean that social class causes differences in reproductive risk but, rather *point the way to further research* on such factors as poor nutrition, stunting of physical growth, poor hygiene, prevalence of infectious diseases, large numbers of pregnancies, and close spacing of children, which may contribute to reproductive disturbance. (Italics mine)

Thus the argument is that social class position produces different ways of life, which in the case of lower-class women includes more often than in the case of women of higher social status poor dietary intake and poor hygienic practices, lack of access to birth control information and implements, histories of poor health and frequent infectious diseases, and other cultural norms and differential behaviors that create large numbers of women who, in addition to small stature, are found to exhibit the kind of physical anomalies that lead to birth defects.

The *interpretive* step is then not far away: Inasmuch as the prevailing occupational division of labor is traceable to developments taking place in Great Britain during and after the industrial revolution, the class structure represents the most pernicious consequences and is a vestige of the landed British aristocratic tradition operating in concert with modern industrial capitalism. Finally, if industrial capitalism constitutes the central holistic environment out of which differential rates of birth defects are traceable, anything short of a major reconstruction of the political and economic structures of societies are merely cosmetic palliations. In fact, the class conflict perspective towards social phenomena in the British Isles can be pushed as far back as the fourth century A.D. and into the brief reign of Arthur, the first British king to precede the rebellion by the English:[5]

> The rise of Ausonius and the proliferation of country mansions in Britain were symptoms of a general trend, the concentration of property in the hands of fewer and mightier magnates, at the expense of the poor and middling free holders. Ausonius managed the numerous ˌestates on which he did not live through his inefficient agent Philo, "The image of his class, Grey, shock-haired, unkempt, a blustering bully. . . . Visiting peasants, farms, towns and villages." Increasingly, the great men passed the crippling burden of taxation on the poor, and the Treasury found it cheaper to acquiesce. The law kept pace with economic change, reinforcing the authority of the *dominus*, master over the dependents distinguishing between *honestiores*, gentlemen, whom it condemned to fines, exile, or execution by the sword, and *humiliores*, small freeholders, tenants, peasants, who expiated the same offenses by torture, mutilation or burning at the stake. Starved by excessive taxation, bullied by blustering agents, denied justice in a landlord's court, the poor of farm, town and village were impelled to standing discontent and occasional rebellion.

So much for life in Camelot; but brutish as British life must have been, the father of Ausonius, Professor of Latin at the University of Bourdeaux at around A.D. 350, "studied medicine and practiced as a doctor, attending the poor without fee; . . . these were the men whose code enjoined a paternal responsibility toward their social inferiors, and a duty of public service to the city of their birth and to the empire."

This history notwithstanding, the Marxian analysis of the Scottish birth defect study tends to falter at the issue of how it is that Britain, the chief architect of corporate capitalism, gave rise in 1948 to the National Health Service, which guaranteed uniform health care to all citizens regardless of class position. More to the point of this account, however, is that the substance and content of medical sociology from the point of view of a social model is not necessarily self-evident, but merely that the conception of "holistic" environment usually invites a radical reconstructionist position. This is in marked contrast to the economic and political extension of the medical model, which often is disguised as "value-free."

THE SOCIAL APPLICATION OF THE MEDICAL MODEL: THE PRESUMPTION OF "VALUE-FREE" IN THE MIDTOWN MANHATTAN STUDY

The first, and still the most comprehensive, interdisciplinary study of the prevalence of mental illness was published by a team of sociologists, anthropologists, and physicians beginning in 1962. The aim of the investigation was to determine the extent of treated *and* untreated mental illness in a modern urban population. The kinds of questions informing the study in fact anticipated its conclusions:[6]

> How many people in the United States actually are mentally ill? How many mental health clinics do we need? How many psychiatrists? How many psychiatric nurses? All of these questions are responsible and important. . . . It may be argued that, since *the deficiencies in service personnel* [italics mine] are so great, why bother collecting data to prove what is already known. . . . Our great need is for facts . . . many facts, accurate facts. . . .

With this anticipatory point of departure, an extensive and meticulously executed study was done of the prevalence of mental illness symptoms among a population sample in New York City. In terms of findings, of first importance is that in New York at the time a mere 5 out of every 1000 persons (or 0.5 percent) were institutionalized for mental illness, and just less than 17 percent were under treatment at a clinic.

In conducting carefully patterned assessments of the members of the study sample, the investigators conclude that the prevalence of mental illness is in fact much higher, as shown in Table 4.2. And while the findings are far more complex than can be summarized briefly here, symptoms and impairment increased with age, as did lack of treatment. In addition, symptoms and impairment were somewhat lower among married persons than among single individuals, while "wellness" increased with an increase in socioeconomic status. Similarly, being "well" seemed to be associated with having experienced upward social mobility, while impairment was more prevalent among those who

TABLE 4.2

Symptom manifestations in the Midtown Manhattan study; prevalence of illness in the untreated population

Degree of illness	Percent of population
Mild symptoms	36.3
Moderate	21.8
Marked	13.2
Severe	7.5
Incapacitated	2.7
Total percent of population who are "impaired"	23.4
Percent of "impaired" who never received treatment	73.3

SOURCE: Adapted from Leo Srole et al., *Mental Health in the Metropolis.* New York: McGraw-Hill Book Company, Inc., 1962. By permission.

had suffered downward social mobility. Significantly, not a great deal is made about these latter two class-related findings.

What is important for present purposes is the nature of the research strategy itself, which in an implicit manner assumes that the nature of "anomaly" of mental illness is so difficult to detect that even in the case of severely impaired persons, *nearly 75 percent* never move from step 1 to step 4 in the medical model, and hence do not fall under the purview of the proper practitioner; they remain as functioning members of the community.

As the authors of the Midtown Manhattan Study admit, detection and referral required extraordinary and admittedly exhaustive effort and skill on the part of the detectors:[7]

> As in a clinic, the psychiatrist's task was one of evaluating in its entirety the sizeable body of relevant evidence gathered about each sample respondent. Representing one variant in a universe of permutations and combinations, each individual cluster of information items called upon the psychiatrist to weave an extremely complex set of discriminations into a single net judgment. Operating doubtless in this subjective process were some idiosyncratic elements related to the psychiatrist's own combination of professional training, clinical experience, theoretical learnings, personal sensitivities, selective inattention, and the like— some rooted in levels of perception and cognitive synthesis probably beyond his own reach for explication. Thus, the series of mental health categories used to devise the Study's dependent variable, far from being a firmly delineated yardstick, was essentially a crude heuristic scale devised to structure the psychiatrist's refracted judgment in an ordinal manner.

One can only conclude that the writer is conveying the message that *only* the highly skilled, experienced, and professionally certified "expert," supplied with virtually unlimited skills and staff, is able to detect large number of hidden ill people heretofore buried in the population and functioning without benefit of professional assistance.

Indeed, the social action implications of this study are even more strongly suggested to focus on more elaborate and costly applications of existing psychiatric categories and judgments with an expansion of existing diagnostic and treatment facilities:[8]

> Large sample surveys provide a scanning overview of the community landscape for detection of intergroup differences in mental health. However, their extensive coverage is bought at a price of loss in intensity of individual examination. . . . Resonant in these questions are tones of objective self-appraisal (willingness on the part of large numbers of people to accept their faults as professionally detected) of openness to change. . . . Discernible here, we believe, is a kernel of the professional helping role that operates in the knowledgeable light of what Bettelheim has succinctly and felicitously called the "informed heart."

Assuming this widespread willingness to accept their hidden defects as pointed out to them by members of the psychiatric cadre, then it is not far to go from there to the authors' final conclusion that the medical view has gone to superseding other explanatory schemes and modes of human morality, assessment, and control:[9]

> Here is a veritable theological transformation acquiring momentum on a scale probably unprecedented in the centuries since the Reformation. As fathers of Protestant thought, Luther and Calvin at important points have given way to the dynamic insights of Freud. Parallel developments are under way in the sanctuaries of both Judaism and Catholicism. These are all facets of a larger development gathering momentum that [foreshadows] a "new era of scientific humanism."

The student is enjoined to reflect on the very different implications of the British birth defect study on the one hand, and the Midtown Manhattan Study on the other. The first, dealing with presumably irrefutable biological 'facts' leads to conclusions of a highly radical kind with regard to the super-structures of contemporary modern society. The latter, documenting in meticulous detail the extent of 'illness' in New York City, merely prescribes a more widespread and intensive application of the prevailing medical technologies with expanded numbers of personnel and facilities. Skilled and reputable sociologists and physicians collaborated in both studies.

THE PROBLEMS OF MEDICAL SOCIOLOGY: METATHEORETICAL AND ORGANIZATIONAL, NOT TECHNICAL OR STRATEGIC

As the student may have surmised, conducting research in the fields of medicine is seldom easy, but it can be nonetheless stimulating, rewarding, and productive if care is taken along the way. It is a mistake, however, to assume that the problems are merely technical or strategic —for example, that responsible research in this area is achieved merely by selecting the correct research technique and applying it with skill and accuracy (although that approach is certainly useful). The issue is to recognize the fact that medicine and social science differ in profound organizational and metatheoretical ways that can lead to insoluble conflict and dissession (as in the case of the Scottish birth defect study), to cooptation (as in the Midtown Manhattan Study), or to healthful ongoing dialogue and interstimulation (as in the case of the Kuru mystery).

In general, however, in pursuing what is said, reported, and referred to in this book the student would be well advised to keep these basic points in mind:

1. Medicine possesses a technical and organizational domain into which sociologists can be only partially inducted and into which they must enter as guests, often with severe constrictions as to their role.

2. Medicine is a "moral" community that even the most skilled of social scientists can only partially penetrate.

3. Medicine is but one among numerous audiences the sociologist might choose to address, and the content depends in large part on the audience. Fellow sociologists may constitute a friendly audience to some messages and the medical establishment a rejecting and hostile one.

4. Sociologists entering medicine must provide an acceptable justification for their work, and that need can be self-defeating if justification leads to cooptation.

5. The roots of the medical model extend deeply into Western history, and the pressures are very great for sociologists to accept it as the only viable view. In fact, however, the social view or model is far more congruent with the world view of most contemporary social scientists.

6. The increasing power of the social model is partially reflected in the recent trends toward the "demedicalization" of society, following a period of roughly 50 years of increasing "medicalization," and this is evidenced in a variety of countermedicine drifts, which shall be elaborated in a later chapter of this book. That is, there is some scattered, though persuasive, evidence that the medical model may be nearing its peak, to be followed first by a decline in the monopoly over matters of health presently held by the medical establishment and later by an

overall realignment of other "interested parties" with regard to matters of health and illness.

The student should be advised to keep the criticisms and tentativeness suggested in this chapter in mind as the remainder of this book is read.

SCENARIO II

The medical model of illness

Or if we're going to have laws, I'll make up two of my own. The first is that we really don't comprehend the underlying mechanisms of that list of today's diseases, and we have an enormous amount still to learn. The second is also a guess: *for every disease there is a single, central, causative mechanism* that dominates all the rest, and if you are looking for effective treatment or prevention you have to *find that mechanism first, and start from there.* For tuberculosis it was the tubercle baccillus; for syphilis the spirochete; for pellagra and pernicious anemia it was a single vitamin deficiency . . . when the dominant cause at the center—the bacillus or spirochete or nutritional lack was identified and got rid of, the whole bewildering array of disease in all the affected organs could be switched off, all at once. This approach succeeded spectacularly for the infectious disease, and it is succeeding today in other major disorders. I believe that cancer will turn out to have a single switch gone wrong, somewhere at the deep interior of the cell. I agree that there are numberless environmental carcinogens, all capable of launching cancer, but at the center is that switch, common to all forms of cancer, waiting to be found. . . . I believe that schizophrenia will turn out to be a neurochemical disorder with some single, central, chemical event gone awry. I believe that stroke and coronary occlusion are centrally caused by abnormal mechanisms affecting blood vessel walls, still to be discovered. I believe that the span of human life is set by a kind of genetic clock and cannot be altered. . . . In short, I am an optimist, and a true believer in the effectiveness and indispensability of the science of medicine.

From Lewis Thomas, M.D., "Medicine in America," *TV Guide,* December 31, 1977, pp. 25–26.

NOTES

1 Richard H. Williams, "The Strategy of Sociomedical Research," in *Handbook of Medical Sociology*, Howard W. Freeman, et al., Eds. Englewood Cliffs, N.J.: Prentice-Hall, 1963, pp. 423–447.
2 V. Vigas, 'Kuru in New Guinea: Discovery and Epidemiology," *American Journal of Tropical Medicine and Hygiene*, 199 (1970), 13–132.
3 D. Baird, "The Influence of Social and Economic Factors on Stillbirths and Neonatal Deaths," *Journal of Obstetrical Gynaecologia British Empire*, 52 (1945), 217–234, 339–366; D. Baird, "Variations in Reproductive Patterns According to Social Class," *Lancet*, 2 (1946), 41–44; D. Baird and A. M. Thompson, "The Epidemiological Approach to Obstetrics," *Gynaecologia*, 138 (1954), 226–245; D. Baird, A. M. Thompson, and E. H. L. Duncun, "Causes and Preventions of Stillbirths and First Week Deaths: II. Evidence from Aberdeen Clinical Records," *Journal of Obstetrical Gynaecologia British Empire*, 60 (1953), 17–30; Raymond Illsley, "The Sociological Study of Reproduction and Its Outcome," in *Social and Psychological Aspects*. Stephan A. Richardson and Alan F. Guttmacher, Eds. Baltimore: Williams & Wilkins, 1967.
4 Stephen A. Richardson and Alan F. Guttmacher, op. cit., pp. 36–37.
5 John Morris, *The Age of Arthur*. New York: Scribner, 1973, p. 4.
6 Leo Srole et al., *Mental Health in the Metropolis*. New York: McGraw-Hill, 1962, p. 9.
7 Ibid., p. 341.
8 Ibid., p. 364.
9 Ibid., p. 367.

SUGGESTED READINGS

Jane E. Chapman and Harry H. Chapman, *Behavior and Health Care: A Humanistic Helping Process*. St. Louis: Mosby, 1975.
A "holistic" view of the promotion of health, similar to the social model, reduced to the specific patient-helper relationship; rejects the standard "professional" model.

Diana Crane, *The Sanctity of Social Life: Physicians' Treatment of Critically Ill Patients*. New Brunswick, N.J.: Transaction Books, 1977.
From the Hastings Report: Crane's findings are sure to be essential reference points for the continuing discussion of the social and moral problems surrounding dying in America.

Sidney H. Croog and Sol Levine, *The Heart Patient Recovers: Social and Psychological Factors*. New York: Human Sciences Press, 1977.
A social view of the rehabilitation of heart patients.

William A. Glaser, *Social Settings and Medical Organization*. New York: Atherton, 1970.
A cross-national study of the differential effects of religion, the family, economics, and urbanism on hospital structure and function in Western Europe, the Middle East, and the Soviet Union.

J. Kosa et al., Eds., *Poverty and Health: A Sociological Analysis*. Cambridge: Harvard University Press, 1969.

A series of essays and articles on the relationship of poverty to various aspects of health and illness.

Marcia Millman, *The Unkindest Cut: Life in the Backrooms of Medicine.* New York: Morrow, 1977.

A informally written book dealing with the problems of peer regulation and control in the application of the medical model.

Robert A. Scott, *The Making of Blind Men.* New Brunswick, N.J.: Transaction Books, 1979.

A study of several hundred agencies for the blind and how they help to create blindness as a social role and status position.

SCENARIO I

Student perspectives favoring specialization

The second criterion students use in thinking about general as opposed to specialty practice addresses itself to the question of the relative broadness of each of the styles of practice. The student says to himself: "As a general practitioner I will be called on to treat every disease that anyone ever gets while as a specialist I will deal only with a small fraction of all diseases. I can know just about everything there is to know about the specialty I take up but no one can ever know enough to be prepared for everything a G.P. might be faced with. On the other hand, a specialty practice will be narrow and limited while a general practice will be infinitely varied and interesting." A senior looking forward to what lay beyond graduation expressed the criterion this way:

> I asked Jack Crown, "What kind of medicine do you intend to practice when you get out?" He said, "Well, I intend to go into general practice in some small town." I said, having spoken to him about this and gotten the same answer a year ago, "You haven't changed your mind very much about that, have you?" He said, "No, I haven't. I guess that's probably what I'll still end up doing, although I have been thinking a little bit about going into a specialty maybe." This surprised me. (We talked for a while about possible specialties.) Then Crown said, "Actually, the reason I am thinking about a specialty is that the idea of going to general practice kind of scares me." I said, "It does?" He said, "Yes. When you think about all those people just walking in off the street and they might have anything under the sun, from a brain tumor to diabetes to cancer—and you might not recognize it. It's kind of frightening and I just don't think I know enough to handle it. I really don't. So that worries me. I sometimes think it would be a lot better to learn one field pretty well and be able to deal with that, rather than trying to do it all. I think you have to know an awful lot to be a good general practitioner, but it would be easier to be a good specialist, I think."
> Two other seniors, Heston and Pound, agreed. Pound said, "Boy,

From H. S. Becker et al. *Boys in White*. Chicago: University of Chicago Press, 1961, pp. 372–373.

I sure agree with you there, Jack. General practice would scare me too. I would never go into general practice, not me. I don't think anybody knows enough to do that, to tell you the truth." Heston said, "Well, the idea of it doesn't make me very happy either, but I don't know whether I could last through a long residency or not."

(*Senior Surgical Specialties,* September 1956)

In another mood, students will speak about the tremendous challenge of general practice, about the great variety of patients and diseases one will see and the continuing interest one will be able to maintain in it.

CHAPTER 5

Becoming a physician

By whatever standard one wishes to apply, the medical community—its physician cadre especially—is probably exceeded in its impact on the lives of people, as well as upon the general shape and contours of society, only by the activities of our economic-financial leadership on the one hand and our central political and military circles on the other. In a very literal sense both the quality of our lives, and much of the contents of our pocketbooks are in the hands of those who populate these three institutional complexes.

How is membership in this special sphere brought about? What are the considerations that come into the minds of those who wish to become doctors? What are the special motivations of those who presume to become one of those who shepherd us from the womb to the tomb? How are physicians drawn from the population? What special skills and moral outlooks, if any, do they possess? How, in short, is a person transformed from a mere member of the "lay" culture of our society into a knowledgeable, powerful, prestigious, financially well off, and consequential member of the "great" culture of medicine? Who are these some 400,000 persons who in the aggregate helped to consume over $63 billion dollars in 1975 and who alone have the discretion and freedom to "pull the plug" or to sustain us in conditions of semilife? What is the nature of the process by which one "becomes a physician," not only in the technical sense of acquiring certifiable skills and objectively assessable knowledge but in the moral and organizational senses as well?

Medicine has long been regarded as a prototype of the modern profession not only because of its monopoly over its technical content, but on social organization grounds as well. Carr-Saunders and later William Goode,[1] for example, delineated many years ago the central distinguishing features of the "professions": A profession may be understood to be an occupation (1) involving extended periods of training having to do with the acquisition of a body of specialized knowledge of a "service-oriented" nature, (2) which sets its own standards and methods of training, (3) is typically a lifetime commitment on the part of its members, (4) in which the right to apply acquired knowledge is granted only after licensure and certification, (5) with sufficient political influence to shape in important ways the legislation which affects it, and (6) is relatively free of external controls.

Whichever of these criteria one may choose to select as the most important and decisive, medicine stands head and shoulders above all other professional aspirants, particularly in its relative lack of *external accountability* and its *internal organizational autonomy.*

Yet, in spite of the obvious "pull" factors involved in becoming a physician, a surprisingly small number of individuals actually take the steps necessary to join this elite corps. In 1976 only slightly more than 42,000 persons made formal application for admission to medical school—a tiny fraction of the total that might in fact count themselves as eligible.[2] While some information is available about the social origins and characteristics of these 42,000, little is in actual fact known as to how the "applicants" might differ from the "eligibles."

THE PROBLEM OF DIFFERENTIAL SELECTION

Although we have a very substantial body of information as to how the medical profession as a social organization functions and exerts itself, there is somewhat less known about the sociological dimensions of the medical education process, and even less about what features distinguish the medical school aspirant.

The aim of this chapter is to examine some of the sociological aspects of the long process of becoming a physician. It is unfortunate that much of what we might like to know must be inferred. The work that has thus far been done must also struggle with the fact that the forces that may importantly affect the becoming process may come and go with the tides of history and social change. Thus, what is said here may not be totally up to date and may somewhat inaccurately reflect what is taking place here and now.

We know that applying to medical school is a highly competitive situation, evidenced first by the fact that a very considerable amount of original self-screening undoubtedly takes place, leading to the relatively small pool of applicants from which medical schools must select. And even at that, only about one out of every three applicants is actually granted admission to the portals of the medical profession. But not only is the application process itself very competitive, there is also a very considerable competition among medical schools to secure the "best" students it can possibly obtain.

Applicants typically seek for admission to the best possible medical school, meaning a highly reputed school that is presumed to have a distinguished teaching and research faculty, up-to-date clinical training facilities, heightened probability of securing an internship in a hospital of comparable status, and ultimately somewhat easier access to the more rewarding sectors of the practicing profession. More of this later.

Which schools are the chosen few? In a recent survey, Paxton asked the deans of graduate schools to name the universities that possessed the "top" medical schools in the country. The answer, in rank order of *generalized* prestige, was as reported in Table 5.1.

Given this kind of general prestige level of these medical schools, it is of some interest that only two of these high-prestige schools, the University of Chicago and Washington University (St. Louis), succeeded in securing a place among the top ten schools in terms of the number of applications they processed in 1975. Furthermore, only two in the top-ranked five (Chicago and Stanford) were among the top ten in terms of the number of applicants per available *openings;* both had approximately 50 applicants for each seat. The State University of New York at Stony Brook was far and away the leader in this regard, with nearly 150 applicants per available space. Further, just two top-ranked schools (Harvard and Columbia) were in the top ten when it came to the number of recent graduates who had succeeded in becoming board-certified specialists. But only one (Johns Hopkins) succeeded in being among the top ten medical schools on the basis of having 100 percent of their graduates pass licensure examinations (ranging from Albert Einstein, of which 100 percent passed and 100 percent took out-of-state examinations, to the University of California–Irvine, which graduated 100 percent successful graduates, only 4 percent of whom took out-of-state examinations.

On a somewhat different basis for comparison, four of the top ten (Harvard, Columbia, Johns Hopkins, and Chicago) reached the top ten list in the number of alumni who were themselves on the faculties of medical schools, with Harvard far and away in the lead with nearly

TABLE 5.1

Prestige ranking of American medical schools by medical school deans

Medical school	Percentage of deans placing school in "Top Five"
Harvard University	96
Johns Hopkins University	58
Duke University	40
Stanford University	40
Yale University	36
University of Chicago	30
Washington University (St. Louis)	24
University of California (San Francisco)	20
University of Washington	20
Columbia University	16

SOURCE: Adapted from Harry Paxton, "The Ten Best Medical Schools—or Are They?" *Journal of Medical Economics,* 53 (February 1976), 91.

TABLE 5.2
The 'best' medical schools

School	Number of times in "Top Ten" lists
Harvard University	6
University of Chicago	5
Columbia University	5
Johns Hopkins University	5
New York University	5
University of Pennsylvania	5
Cornell University	4
Washington University (St. Louis)	4
Albert Einstein College of Medicine (Yeshiva University)	3
University of Michigan	3
State University of New York (Brooklyn)	3

SOURCE: Adapted from Harry Paxton, "The Ten Best Medical Schools—or Are They?" *Journal of Medical Economics,* 53 (February 1976), 91.

13,000 such graduates. Further, Harvard, Chicago, and Washington (St. Louis) each found a place in the top ten schools that have produced alumni who have become deans of medical schools, while the University of Washington, Columbia, Johns Hopkins, Duke, Harvard, Stanford, and Washington (St. Louis) all are among the top ten in the dollar value of research grants received from the National Institutes of Health. Combining these several criteria, Table 5.2 indicates the *overall best* ten medical schools in the country.

Obviously, the competition for student places in these highly regarded medical schools is very keen and can serve only to heighten the competition to secure places here and others of similar renown that stand some chance of offering their graduates a measure of "sponsored" mobility within the profession. Given the rigors of the process of merely preparing to apply to medical school, it is reasonable to infer that those who do apply possess very considerable *self-confidence,* which may in fact be congruent with the manner by which medicine is in fact practiced. What seems to be the process that activates this self-confidence in the would-be physician? Rogoff has supplied some answers in her study of students' decision to enter medicine.[3]

THE DECISION TO ENTER MEDICINE

In a very large number of cases, it seems that the decision to try to become a doctor has its roots early in childhood, although this seems to be *somewhat* less true now than in the recent past. However, both cases, *early* and *late* deciders, undoubtedly present their own special problems for medical educators, and they probably carry with them into the practice situation the soil for the flowering of quite different perspectives toward the profession itself. As Table 5.3 shows, a large number of the students Rogoff studied *first considered* becoming a doctor when they were very young.

In spite of the recognized limitations of such "retrospective" data, these findings lend themselves to important interpretation. Why do so many young people think about becoming a doctor so early in life (and subsequently actually become medical students), and what may this portend for later school training and professional socialization? First, the job of "doctor" is one of the very few boys and girls of young age conceive of as being "out there" in the division of labor. And the conception children have of this handful of "visible" occupations is likely to be both romanticized and unrealistic. This is likely to be in contrast to the growing numbers of late deciders, whose conception of occupational roles generally is more tentative, less romanticized, and more realistic.

It is to be remembered that the "early deciders" (those in their early teens and even younger) have yet to experience the rigors of high school and college sciences required for the premedical programs and generally have had only the most casual contact with any knowledge of the physician's actual status and role. This represents not only a challenge but an opportunity for the socializing agents in medical education: On the one hand the process of "revelation" must be such as to nurture the commitment of these early deciders, while disclosing the realities of the medical role without disaffecting the neophytes. On the other hand; the early deciders have probably only half-formed ideological conceptions of the world of medicine and their proper place in

TABLE 5.3
Age at which medical career was first considered

Age	Number of students	Percentage
Younger than 10	178	24%
10–13	200	27
14 or 15	134	18
16 or 17	123	17
18 or older	106	14
	741	100%

SOURCE: Adapted from Natalie Rogoff, "The Decision to Study Medicine," in *The Student Physician*, Robert Merton et al., Eds. Cambridge: Harvard University Press, 1957. By permission.

it, and therefore can be molded in such a fashion as to modulate the strains of intergeneralization change in the profession itself. The late deciders present quite a different mix of challenge and opportunity. It is this broad distinction between the "technical" versus the "moral" socialization of new physicians that seems especially critical at the present juncture in the development of Western medicine, and we shall pursue this theme in greater depth in the latter half of the present chapter.

In a very critical sense, it would appear that the age of decision is of decisive importance in the structure of motives and orientations that medical students bring to their professional socialization. In this connection, that the possibility of influence stemming from a medical source of a very special kind is probably involved to a considerable degree is shown in Figure 5.1.

In general, the earlier the age of deciding, the greater is the exposure to possible *medical* influence—particularly parental in the case of those young persons contemplating this career at a very early age. It is not unreasonable to inquire as to exactly what exposure such people have to the medical world, which may in fact form the substructure of later, more rationalized reasons for entering the profession? If the father, or another close relative, happens to be a physician, little more than the following may impinge on the aspirant's consciousness: The young person whose parent is a doctor knows that somehow father or mother "helps" sick people in some unknown way; that the parent

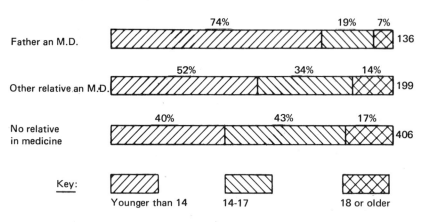

FIGURE 5.1 Age at first contemplating a career in medicine, according to relationship to physician.

Source: Adapted from Natalie Rogoff, "The Decision to Study Medicine," in The Student Physician, Robert Merton et al., Eds. Cambridge: Harvard University Press, 1957; By permission.

goes off to work each morning dressed neatly and driving a nice car. The child knows that they live in a nice house in a nice neighborhood and generally want for nothing. He or she has every expectation of growing up to be comfortable and successful like his or her parent, and also knows that somehow this parent is important. Beyond that little is known at this age of decision making. In yet a more specific sense, Rogoff found that the actual final decision to become a physician was, in the aggregate, made very early in life. Table 5.4 shows this.

Again, the fact of early decision making is evident. But in addition to reaffirming what has just been said about the decision to become a physician, it is worth noting that in this late 1950s sample about 20 percent of the students came to a final decision after the age of 20. This compares with a more recent study reported in 1977 in the *Journal of Medical Education,* in which it was shown that more than 50 percent of the students who became surgeons made the decision to enter medical school *before they entered undergraduate college.* Over 50 percent of the students who became committed to general and family medicine made their career decisions *during* or *after* entrance into undergraduate college. These data are shown in Table 5.5.

More to the point, however, is that Rogoff found nearly 20 years ago that only 15 percent made their final career decision after the age of 20, whereas the more recent sampling found that figure reduced to about 11 percent, with 8 percent of the surgeons making the late decision and nearly 18 percent in the general and family medicine category.[4]

Finally, it would appear from the evidence in Figure 5.2 that the decision to become a physician is not an easy or quick one, with the

TABLE 5.4

Age at which definite decision to study medicine was reached

Age	Number of students	Percentage
Younger than 10	58	8
14 or 15	73	10
16 or 17	191	26
18–20	310	41
21 or 22	77	10
23 or older	38	5
	747	100

SOURCE: Adapted from Natalie Rogoff, "The Decision to Study Medicine," in *The Student Physician,* Robert Merton et al., Eds. Cambridge: Harvard University Press, 1957. By permission.

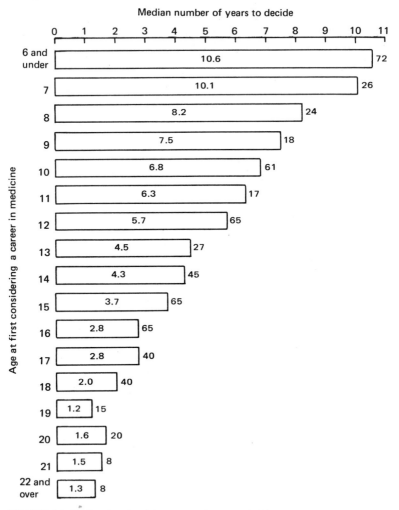

FIGURE 5.2 Median length of time to reach career decision.

Source: Adapted from Natalie Rogoff, "The Decision to Study Medicine," in The Student Physician, Robert Merton et al., Eds. Cambridge: Harvard University Press, 1957. By permission.

length of time involved in making the decision increasing significantly as the age of first considering it is younger.

We may reasonably conclude from all of this that a vast number of physicians think about becoming a physician at a very early age when their conception of the work of the doctor is probably framed in stereotypic and unrealistic terms. For many students there is a considerable amount of family influence, and the age of final decision making

TABLE 5.5

Premedical years in which physicians decided to study medicine, according to field of medicine selected

	FIELD OF STUDY SELECTED			
Time of decision	Medical	Surgical	Other specialties	General and family practice
Before high school	11.4%	12.5%	7.9%	6.0%
First 2 years of high school	9.4	9.4	5.2	6.7
Last 2 years of high school	18.8	20.5	17.2	15.1
Between high school and college	8.0	8.6	7.6	11.4
First year of college	9.9	10.5	9.8	13.0
Second year of college	11.0	13.8	15.9	13.0
Third year of college	15.7	12.1	16.6	11.4
Fourth year of college	6.6	4.1	6.9	5.7
After college	9.5	8.8	12.9	17.7

SOURCE: Adapted from "Time of Decision to Study Medicine: Its Relation to Specialty Choice," *Journal of Medical Education,* 52:1 (January 1977), 78–81. By permission.

seems to be forced by the structure of the curricula of junior high school and high school and certainly by the first year or two of the college experience. So, on the one hand, the scientism of the educational system and parental influence works to encourage an early and unrealistic decision. On the other hand, the rationalization and popularization of medicine, and particularly the discernible trend toward family medicine and so-called "humanistic" medicine, seems to encourage later and possibly more considered and realistic decision making. It would appear that the specialty structure of the medical world may leaven the conflict between these two opposing forces, with the more community- and family-oriented specialties attracting many late deciders, and with the "glamour" specialties serving as the training stream for more of the early deciders.

The data supporting such a conjecture, however, are not at all conclusive, and one can only say that medicine is unique not only in its stature as the prototype of the professions but apparently also in the strength of the motivations carried by those who determine to enter its ranks.

Beyond this, however, what do we know about differential recruitment to the medical profession and its possible impact upon the course of medical training and ultimately to the practice of medicine?

DIFFERENTIAL SELECTION FROM THE APPLICANT POOL

Although the number of student places in medical schools has increased over the past few years, the number of students applying to medical school has increased even more. As seen in Table 5.6, the total number of applicants among whom medical colleges can choose has increased markedly. Has the composition of this population changed? What effects may these changes in numbers and in kind be shown to have had on the vital question of who becomes a doctor?

   Why is it important to raise a question such as this in a text on medical sociology? The answer is that the composition of any professional group should not be considered in vacuo but rather in the context of the sociopolitical times in which its composition is examined. In this connection we are now living witnesses to an overwhelming conflict in American society that is just now beginning to make itself felt in the hallways of medicine: namely meritocracy versus democratization and even populism. That is, we now live with high exposure to two predominating themes in American society, which has been dubbed the norms in conflict or "achievement versus equality." The first set of norms answers to the criteria of scientific objectivity, rationalism, and achievement. The other responds to standards of democratization and equalitarianism. The first is an agent of competency as indicated by the exercises of science; the other works on behalf of equality of opportunity and of status. More plainly, shall persons become physicians strictly as a consequence of demonstrated skills and technical expertise, or shall we select our physicians-to-be on the strength of a dispersion of other secondary social characteristics?

   The debate is not an exercise in sophistry, because it reaches to

TABLE 5.6

Number of medical college application test examinees

Year	Number of applicants
1968	26,539
1969	28,880
1970	33,869
1971	45,324
1972	51,695

SOURCE: Compiled from *Journal of Medical Education* (various issues).

the core of the institutions of democracy as well as calling to task medicine's claims of scientific exclusiveness. It brings into the limelight the issue as to whether medicine shall retain its insulation from the lines of accountability that are attached to most service activities taking place in the public arena. If, for example, it can be demonstrated persuasively that the adequate performance of the tasks of the physician can be undertaken by a wide range of the citizenry rather than by merely a limited slice of it, then the present physician selection system takes an entirely different tone—one that demands an examination of the extent to which presumed meritocratic selection processes shield the operation of nonmeritocratic standards, which do not fit with an equalitarian conception.

A second major theme in medicine generally and medical education in particular has to do with the proper mix between technical socialization of the student physician on the one hand and moral socialization on the other. More important, what connection is there between what is *presumed* to be a meritocratic selection process on the one side and the *presumed* exclusive emphasis on *technical* socialization in the medical education process on the other side?

In short, is the citizenry of our society fairly represented in the applicant pool to medicine schools, and are the chosen few fairly selected, and on what grounds? Finally, how does the content of medical education reflect these two prior processes? These are elusive but important questions, but only indirect and inconclusive answers are presently available.

We know, for example, that over the past decade the number of female applicants to medical schools has nearly doubled, but the percentage of women who actually make up the student population in medical training, while it has increased somewhat, has not experienced that kind of growth. Nevertheless, a 1976 forecast predicts that by 1980 females will make up approximately 30 percent of all medical school enrollees.[5] If such a forecast is borne out, it raises a number of issues concerning the flexibility of medical education in developing role models in medical practice that go beyond making a female physician more "malelike," in the specialties that heretofore seemed to lend themselves to this kind of partial accommodation: obstetrics, pediatrics, psychiatry, and pathology. As it stands, the surgical theater, like the squash court, still retains its male middle-class tone.

In fact, the question of female and minority group representation in the medical training groups is part of a large issue as to whether the present basis upon which admission decisions are made are optimal in terms of providing the best possible kind of health care, whether seen purely in technical terms, humanistic terms, or some combination of both.

The admission system as it presently operates tends to place heavy emphasis on formal test scores, such as the Medical College Aptitude Test, high school and college grades, and the distillation of the results of the still present "personal interview" of applicants. As of this date, neither of these primary methods of admission and exclusion appear to be strong indicators of either successful performance in medical school or subsequent qualitative performance as a physician.[6] In fact, the traditionally relied-upon formal measures are less adequate as predictors of being admitted to medical school than are a number of subsidiary social characteristics that are not easily fitted into a meritocratic model of student selection.

MEDICINE AS MIDDLE CLASS?

Folklore has long held that medicine is a middle-class profession, both in terms of the social origins of its members and its ideological posture. Much of this lore has been substantiated by social research into the question, even in the light of the present-day emphasis upon affirmative action and equal opportunity. For example, the impact of the social class origins of recent medical school applicants is shown in Table 5.7. A persisting middle-class bias is shown in relation both to parental income (as shown in Table 5.7) and to father's occupation (as reported in Table 5.8).

With only minor deviations, the percentage of students who apply to medical school *increases* as one ascends the income ladder, as does the percentage of students accepted into medical training. By the same token, the average college grade-point average increases with increasing family income, as do average scores on the Medical School Aptitude Test. However, lest it be concluded that the formal and meritocratic criteria for acceptance are natural concomitants of social class position, it is to be noted that the percent of students admitted to school from families with incomes under $10,000 is approximately 35 percent while the acceptance figure rises to only 48 percent in the case of students with family incomes between $25,000 and $50,000. The problem appears not to be the inability of lower-income applicants to measure up to reasonable and acceptable standards on such measures, but rather the *small pool of applicants* from low-income families. That is, the social class bias appears to be set in motion far earlier than the time for actual admission decisions. Much the same can be said for the occupational social origins of these applicants. This is shown in Table 5.8, where it can be seen that the difference between the grade-point average of the applicants whose fathers were physicians and those whose fathers were unskilled workers was a mere 0.11—that is, 3.19 as com-

TABLE 5.7

Medical college admission test scores, undergraduate grade-point averages, and acceptance rates of applicants by parental income, 1975–1976 first-year class

Parental income	APPLICANT POOL		MEAN TEST SCORES					Percent accepted
	Total no.	Percent	VA	QA	GI	SCI	GPA	
Less than $5,000	1652	5.3	501	540	489	514	3.09	33.8
$5,000–$9,999	3156	10.2	523	562	511	543	3.20	36.3
$10,000–$11,999	2981	9.6	535	576	518	559	3.25	38.5
$12,000–$14,999	4059	13.1	539	582	525	566	3.28	38.4
$15,000–$19,999	5024	16.2	546	592	530	578	3.31	41.5
$20,000–$24,999	4640	15.6	553	597	535	585	3.31	43.5
$25,000–$49,999	6063	19.6	560	601	540	588	3.29	46.0
$50,000 or more	2997	9.7	557	596	538	582	3.25	47.9

SOURCE: Adapted from W. F. Dube and T. Gordon, "Study of U.S. Medical School Applicants, 1975–76," *Journal of Medical Education* (September 1977), p. 727.

TABLE 5.8

MCAT scores and undergraduate grade-point averages, by father's occupation, 1975–1976

Father's occupation	APPLICANT POOL		VA	QA	GI	SCI	GPA
	Total no.	Percent					
Physician	4887	11.6	552	586	535	573	3.19
Other health occupation	1917	4.5	543	582	528	568	3.25
Other profession	9267	21.9	556	697	538	581	3.30
Manager, administrator	10394	24.6	547	593	532	577	3.26
Clerical, sales worker	2433	5.8	541	586	530	565	3.24
Craftsman, skilled	4009	9.5	528	566	515	551	3.20
Unskilled worker, laborer	1712	4.0	498	542	493	520	3.08
Farmer	1334	3.2	509	556	497	536	3.23
Homemaker	133	.3	503	528	499	508	2.95

SOURCE: Adapted from "Study of U.S. Medical School Applicants, 1975–76," p. 729.

pared with 3.08. Similarly, the difference in MCAT scores was equally small, but the pool of middle-class applicants was far greater than was the pool of lower- and working-class medical school aspirants.

One observer attributes this to inadequacies in the premedical counseling services available to high school and college students, and argues that medical schools and their sources of applicants are "worlds apart" in communication and that career choices tend to be made by trial and error rather than by rational deliberation.[7] However true this might be, it remains the case that the vast majority of workers in a modern division of labor "drift" into their jobs, with only a small number taking the early and deliberate steps typical of those who enter medicine.[8]

Whatever the truth of this might be, it seems clear that parental influence—direct or indirect—is of very considerable import in motivating persons to become physicians. And so long as this remains the prime motivator, two subsequent factors are likely to remain substantially unchanged: one is the perpetuation of medicine as a middle-class occupation with intergenerational links; the other is intergenerational continuity in the basic conservatism of the members of the profession at large. That is, so long as women and racial-ethnic minorities do not become physicians, they cannot become the parents or close relatives of the next younger generation of possible physicians, hence making it exceedingly difficult to break the white middle-class conservatism in the chain of events and experiences that together help to sustain the status quo of medical profession.

In this connection, how in fact do applicants from medical families and nonmedical families differ if they are very much like one another when it comes to objective measures of social class? One study compared two such groups of students in terms of the factors listed in Tables 5.9 and 5.10.

In general, one is forced to the conclusion that students entering medical schools and coming from families with a physician possess intellectual aptitudes and display academic performance levels not very different from those of other "nonmedical family" applicants. Of note is the fact that students from medical families tend to come from more prestigious undergraduate colleges and universities than is the case with their nonmedical family cohorts, reinforcing the view of medicine as having middle-class conservative roots.

A minor counterpoint to this is the highly limited study of medical student "activists" undertaken by Maxmen and reported in 1972. In his report of 13 student activists at Yale Medical School he found that although all came from middle-class families, they rated their parents as being from "liberal" to "radical" in their politics. He suggests that such students may have the potential for becoming innovators in medi-

TABLE 5.9
Students from medical and nonmedical families

Criteria	Medical families, mean	Nonmedical families, mean
Premedical GPA		
Overall	3.24	3.28
Scientific subjects	3.31	3.35
Last two terms	3.31	3.24
Admission interviewer's ratings	2.85	2.86
Medical college admission test		
Verbal ability	572	567
Quantitative ability	577	571
General information	568	565
Age	21.62	22.38
Prestige rating of under-		
graduate college	3.52	3.25

SOURCE: Adapted from H. Gough and W. Hall, "A Comparison of Medical Students from Medical and Nonmedical Families," *Journal of Medical Education,* 52 (July 1977), 543. By permission.

cine, with the caveat that such radical tendencies are likely to be "educated out of them" during the long training process.[9]

In spite of what Maxmen says of his 13 radical students, Cliff and Cliff's study of 630 beginning medical school enrollees tended to rate the future economic aspects of their careers considerably higher in importance than the social value of their careers. This tendency to rate economic values higher than others was even more pronounced among those students who were aiming for careers as surgeons.[10]

Thus, although we may pride ourselves on having open avenues of mobility through our occupational division of labor, medicine remains *primarily* a profession of the comfortable to well-to-do, white, male, urban, middle class, and especially in the case of those who have been favored in terms of having undergone preferential educational experiences at the collegiate level. In spite of the rigors of medical school application procedures, which *appear* to embody meritocratic criteria par excellence, evidences of "sponsored" mobility far outweigh the evidence pointing to "contest" mobility as the road to success in entering the portals to this choice profession.[11]

And what of those whose life experiences and social origins do not lead them into the sponsored mobility stream that leads most easily into the mainstream of medical education? What of women, blacks, ruralists, and others who are underrepresented?

WOMEN AND MINORITIES

Assuming that all persons should have equal access to a career in medicine, in terms of either evenly applied universalistic or ascribed standards, the avenue to such equity is neither clearly marked or without obstacles. There is a remarkable paradox in the fact that while the American medical system takes very considerable pride in its diversity in terms both of training contexts and schemes and forms for the practice of medicine, and even modes of payment, there is a persisting *lack of diversity* in the social origins of physicians.

In connection with the enrollment of females, for example, data on the years 1971 through 1976 are instructive (see Tables 5.11, 5.12, and 5.13).

During this five-year period, the number of applications (by males and females) to medical school increased by a whopping 48 percent, but the percent of applicants admitted *decreased* from 42 to 36 percent—a decline of 6 percent.[12] The pressures to take account of the secondary social characteristics of those applying and admitted to medical schools seems to be occurring at a point in American history when the application-and-admission process is becoming increasing competitive. This can only be expected to perpetuate the traditional bases for selection of which we have already spoken.

Within this aggregate, however, applications from women in-

TABLE 5.10
Performance of students from medical and nonmedical families

Indicators of performance	Medical mean	Nonmedical mean
Medical school grade point averages		
Year 1	49.1	50.0
Year 2	50.0	49.8
Year 3	50.9	49.9
Year 4	50.0	49.9
Cumulative	50.0	49.9
Faculty ratings		
General effectiveness	50.99	50.11
Clinical performance	51.23	50.09
Factorial criteria		
Clinical factor	191.9	188.1
Academic factor	139.3	138.7

SOURCE: Adapted from H. Gough and W. Hall, "A Comparison of Medical Students from Medical and Nonmedical Families," *Journal of Medical Education*, 52 (July 1977), 544. By permission.

TABLE 5.11
Summary of application activity, 1971–1976

Class	No. of medical schools	No. of applicants	No. of applications	Applications per individual	First-year enrollments	Percent of applicants accepted
1971–72	108	29,172	210,943	7.23	12,361	42.3
1972–73	112	36,135	267,306	7.40	13,677	38.1
1973–74	114	40,506	328,275	8.10	14,159	35.4
1974–75	114	42,624	362,376	8.51	14,763	35.3
1975–76	114	42,306	366,040	8.65	15,295	36.3

SOURCE: Adapted from W. F. Dube and T. Gordon, "Applicants for 1975–76 First Year Medical School Class," *Journal of Medical Education,* 51:7 (July 1976), 867–869. By permission.

creased by nearly 100 percent during that period, and while the total number of women accepted into medical school increased from 1685 in 1971 to nearly 3700 in 1976, the percent of women applicants who were accepted into training decreased from 45 percent to 38 percent.

In terms of minorities such as black Americans, American Indians, Mexican Americans, and mainland Puerto Ricans, a somewhat different picture is to be noted; see Table 5.13. Looking at a two-year period only, applicants from these minorities constituted only a very small proportion of the total applications, and although between 40 and 50 percent of all such applicants were accepted, they still accounted for less than 10 percent of all medical school admissions.

Now, assuming that women and minorities are likely to suffer

TABLE 5.12

Women applicants to U.S. medical schools and first-year women students, 1971–1976

Years	Percent of all applicants who are women	Percent of women applicants accepted	Percent of first-year class who are women
1971–72	12.8	45.1	13.7
1972–73	15.2	43.0	16.8
1973–74	17.8	39.5	19.7
1974–75	20.4	38.9	22.2
1975–76	22.6	38.0	23.8

SOURCE: Adapted from W. F. Dube and T. Gordon, "Applicants for 1975–76 First Year Medical School Class," *Journal of Medical Education*, 51:7 (July 1976), 867–869. By permission.

TABLE 5.13

Minority applicants[a] to U.S. medical schools, 1974–1976

	MINORITY APPLICANTS		MINORITY ACCEPTEES		
First-year class	Total applicants	Percent of all applicants	Number	Percent of all acceptees	Percent of minority applicants accepted
1974–75	3174	7.4	1406	9.3	44.3
1975–76	3049	7.2	1308	8.5	42.9

SOURCE: Adapted from W. F. Dube and T. Gordon, "Applicants for 1975–76 First Year Medical School Class," *Journal of Medical Education*, 51:7 (July 1976), 867–869. By permission.
[a] Data reflect minorities that are underrepresented in U.S. medical schools (black American, American Indian, Mexican American, and mainland Puerto Rican).

TABLE 5.14

MCAT scores of accepted and nonaccepted applicants, 1971–1976

First-year class	MEAN MCAT SCORES			
	Verbal	*Quant.*	*Gen. info.*	*Science*
	ACCEPTED APPLICANTS			
1971–72	560	606	556	565
1972–73	562	614	555	575
1973–74	567	609	563	592
1974–75	563	611	559	603
1975–76	575	620	550	615
Second-year class	NONACCEPTED APPLICANTS			
1971–72	519	549	517	510
1972–73	512	551	514	510
1973–74	518	550	521	524
1974–75	518	555	518	532
1975–76	522	562	513	539

SOURCE: Adapted from W. F. Dube, "Women Enrollment and Its Minority Component in U.S. Medical Schools," *Journal of Medical Education* (August 1967), 691.

greater disadvantages in the educational springboards from which they make their effort at medical school admission, it is important to consider the data in Table 5.14, which indicate that the meritocratic criteria for admission has very noticeably increased, among both accepted and nonaccepted applicants, over this five-year period.

The fundamental question still persists, however, as to whether or not the selection of physicians on these basis in fact produces better physicians. One can argue that the principal problem in medicine today does not lie in not a lack of qualified talent but in the organization of the medical system itself. If this is in fact the case, then it would appear that the present emphasis upon objective simulators of individual technical competence (which presumably is what college grades and scores on the MCAT actually measure) may serve as impediments to overcoming these organizational obstacles.

As far as females and ethnic minorities are concerned, however, the root of the problem lies not so much in differential selection of white male urbanites of European ethnic extraction, or lack of the required technical talent among other groups, but rather the relatively small numbers of others who are motivated to make the effort.[13] And in fairness, it must be said that the relative absence of females or ethnic minorities as positive medical role models is an issue that is far out of the control of the medical establishment, however powerful it might be in other spheres of human affairs.

THE 'INFORMAL' RECRUITMENT OF PHYSICIANS

Let us venture a little further into the vineyards for physicians and review once again here Oswald Hall's now classic study of the community level selection and sponsorship process. Hall's work, published in the mid-1940s, must now be considered dated. Still he points out deeply rooted elements of special power and privilege that many suspect still operate in the student selection process.[14]

In this early study of the social organization of the medical profession in a medium-size New England urban center, Hall came upon a town with a highly visible system of ethnic stratification that permeated through the secondary and higher educational systems and extended through the ranks of the medical profession, to the several avenues for medical training, and back once again into the structure of medical practice, including the hospital system in the community.

More specifically, the community's educational system was sharply divided into an elite stream, which included private preparatory school education for the very young, which led in most cases to collegiate education at the one prestigious "Ivy League" college in the community. This tract of training was followed by the prestigious, influential, and mainly Anglo-Saxon members of the local medical community who had themselves moved on to medical training at one of the prestigious Ivy League medical schools in the region, only to return to find a place in the medical system. This system included easy access to the establishment of a lucrative practice and appointment at the single large-scale hospital that dominated the community. Newcomers with the "right" family background secured a sponsor in medicine, who helped all the way along the route from prep school, to Ivy League college, to prestige medical school, and back to the local community power structure of medicine, and a practice centering around the dominating "Anglo-Saxon" hospital.

A second slice of the ethnic composition of the community included the members of the Southern European Catholic community, whose medical school aspirants tended to be educated in the local parochial schools, to attend the single Catholic college in the area, and to be sponsored as an applicant to one of the less prestigious medical schools in the area or to a foreign medical school, and then to return to the community as an "outsider" to the mainstream of medical politics in the community, and to a practice that included appointment at one of the two Catholic-chartered hospitals in the community. A third group contained the members of the Jewish community who wished to become physicians. Again, informal sponsorship seemed to be the rule, in this case by an established Jewish physician (who may or may not have been the student's father). The progression was from either a public or private secondary school to a local or distant college of considerable repute, and then to one of a wide-ranging group of medical schools, to return to a "ghettolike" practice of medicine, including appointment at the one Jewish hospital in the community. Indeed, up until the early 1950s the "Anglo-Saxon" hospital here referred to did not have a single Jew on its staff, nor did the Jewish hospital extend staff privileges to a single Gentile in those days. Thus, the inclusion of so-called secondary social characteristics in the selection process—however informal—can be a double-edged sword and work to exclude rather than include.

These *hard* ethnic barriers have since been very much eroded, although whether they have been completely eradicated, and with what result, remains a moot point in this one community—not to speak of the many others having a similarly complex ethnic composition.

But whatever the future might hold, the medical school seems to be critical in forming long-lasting orientations toward the profession, and ultimately affecting the future shape and pattern of the organization of medicine might be.

THE MORAL SOCIALIZATION OF THE PHYSICIAN

The technical content of medical education is remarkably uniform from school to school and is divided into the preclinical years, which primarily involve classroom instruction in the basic sciences, and the clinical years, which involve increasing exposure to actual diagnostic and treatment procedures. Yet in spite of this uniformity, a hallmark of the American medical system is its diversity combined with its slow rate of change. In short, the American medical system is not a monolithic structure about which easy generalization can be made. The range and variety of medical schools—at least by reputation and prestige—is enormous as is the number of specialties among which students may choose. The clinical settings in which actual practical learning can take place are also highly diversified. Finally, the structure of medical practice is highly variable in its form and in the kind of incentives that induce persons to undertake one form of practice rather than another. Perhaps most important, it is not easy to find, even within the corridors of the American Medical Association, any generally *consistent* political stance other than to *oppose* change or—if that seems impossible—to direct and control change in such a manner as to minimize the erosion of autonomy enjoyed by the profession. Paradoxically, perhaps, the American Medical Association is as vocal, if not more so, at a policy pronouncement level on nonmedical matters as it is on matters directly associated with its sphere of technical expertise. For as Perrow has pointed out, the American Medical Association has flexed its muscles on numerous issues:[15]

> The House of Delegates of the American Medical Association passed a resolution stating that it shall not take a position on legislation not bearing directly on medicine, yet they opposed daylight saving time, federal housing for indigents, favored limitations on federal taxation powers, and the Bricker amendment, opposed collectivism in schools, minimum wage standards, and compulsory social security coverage.

Does this mean that medical students typically are exposed to a regimen of socialization and value inculcation during the training period so as to instill the "right" social and economic orientations toward their work and toward their careers? Is there, in short, a self-conscious social-political content to medical education? It must be said that there is no strong evidence to support such a conjecture. As near as can be determined, the education of the physician is so highly loaded by its technical components that little time is left over for there to be very much concern with the moral elements in the practice of medicine or in the conduct of professional affairs; these are left mainly to local medical societies. In short, there is no discernible *moral* curriculum in medical education—only nuances of moral tone and ethical climate, some of which are more conducive to one set of precepts in the practice of medicine than to others. In this context, there is perhaps an understandable "tilt" toward the "medical model," and a corresponding thinness of factors that would incline toward the "social model." Indeed, Coe, Pepper, and Mattis[16] in a study published in 1977 support the long-standing supposition that the vast majority of students who enter medical school do so with essentially conservative outlooks and that these are reinforced in the medical education process. And in this context it is instructive to take note of the attempt at the University of Kansas Medical School to alter the admission procedures so as to deliberately admit students with a philosophy of action-orientation and problem solving.[17] To do so, admission was based upon the content of personal interviews directed in this way with only a minimum cutoff point in high school grades and admission tests. Prior to this experiment medical school admission had positive correlation with admission test scores (.59) and a negative correlation with race (−.30). After interviewing, however, these correlations with formal scores and race were almost completely washed out, although the evidence that "innovators" were in fact being admitted was not at all convincing. In fact, there is no reason to reject the proposition that most applicants to medical school are generally conservative in their attitudes before they enter medical school and that the medical school experience does little to change that fundamental point of view.

Numerous facets of the medical role may be counted as crucial in determining the shape and future direction of medicine in modern society, and a critical question has to do with what effects medical education may have in shaping those facets. That is, let us assume that the formal measures of medical school admission and pedagogical procedures are sufficiently polished to assure—within acceptable limits at least—a minimax of technical competence/incompetence.

Beyond that, however, how does a student physician learn to behave like a doctor when he or she doesn't feel like one? How, at what point, and to what extent do student physicians begin to grasp the complexity of the medical enterprise, its options, and its problems? When and under what circumstances do young physicians acquire and exercise priorities in the exercise of their judgments and talents? At what level are health standards set—the points at which the physician is satisfied to concede that "enough has been done"? What are the conditions and circumstances under which a physician develops and begins to exercise his or her own professional economy: How many patients should be served? What ancillary costs will be attached to the treatment provided? What extraordinary procedures should be used, and for whom? What will his or her attitude be toward thirty-party payments and to national plans such as Medicare, Medicaid, and that will-o'-the-wisp, National Health Insurance? What choice should be made with regard to type of specialty on the one hand, and type of practice on the other? Should he or she try to maximize the realization of the stereotypical solo fee-for-service form of entrepreneurship, or should one of the more elaborate forms of cooperation be considered? What should be his or her role in and attitude toward the politics of the medical profession at the local, state, and national level?

What should the individual's posture be toward academic and scientific medicine as distinguished from the practice of medicine? Should he or she follow in the footsteps of the vast majority and reject public health as a career and opt for the traditional physician role in one or the other of its manifestations? Perhaps the most crucial turning point of all is whether he or she embraces the predominating "technocratic" model of the physician or the flirtatious but as yet ill-defined "humanistic" model, with all of the career uncertainties that the latter choice presently holds? It is not without reason to argue that the political atmosphere favors the encouragement of innovative, humanistic, and comprehensive modes of medical practice, while the recruitment, educational, and practice structure stack the deck in favor of traditional, technologically oriented, and specialized modes of practice. How will the questions be answered and what will be the resolution of the aforementioned conflict? What role does medical education play in favoring one view as against the other?

THE CONTEXTS OF MEDICAL TRAINING

Coombs and Vincent correctly point out that medical education ought not to be viewed, at least initially, aside from the basic trends in higher education generally.[18] Toward this end, they delineate three basic "eras" in higher education over the past 170 years or so: first, the "Liberal Arts" era (preceded by the "Classical" era), lasting from the early part of the 1800s until about the mid-1950s; second, the "Graduate Training and Research Era," beginning in the mid-1950s and lasting until the late 1960s or the very early 1970s; and finally, the "Community Era," beginning around 1970 and yet to unfold into a coherent overall education philosophy and form.

Not out of line with these phases of development, Coombs and Vincent identify four periods in medical education: (1) *General Practice,* emerging in the early part of the twentieth century and lasting until about 1940; (2) the *Specialty Era,* between 1940 and 1960; (3) the *Scientific Era,* during the decade of the 1960s; and (4) the *Community Era,* since the beginning of the 1970s. According to the authors, critical to the movement from science to community involvement is a fundamental generation gap between establishment members who tend to be traditional and authoritarian in their orientation toward practice and the profession, and the newer students who lean in the direction of the expression of existential interests in medicine. How widespread this difference in fact is remains a moot point. And even if it is widespread in the medical education scene, how much impact the "newer" students are likely to have on the structure and function of medical institutions remains to be seen. In support of their hypothesis concerning the shift from a scientific to a community orientation, the authors offer the material shown in Figure 5.3 concerning the non–natural science concentration recently selected by students at Harvard Medical School.

It is true enough that the presence of the social sciences increased noticeably over this short period of time (largely, and perhaps regretably, at the expense of programs in the humanities), but this is hardly acceptable as irrefutable evidence of the preeminence of a "community orientation" in medical education. In fact, reluctance to accept such a proposition on the strength of evidence of this sort is only deepened by the data given in Figure 5.4, having to do with the percentage of Harvard students concentrated in various fields during the undergraduate years. Summarizing the 1971 (Scientific Era) and 1973 (Community Era) student concentrations in rank order of frequency of selection, the points on page 143 are revealed:

In spite of the designation of recent years as the "Community Era" it seems clear enough that the physical and organic sciences retain

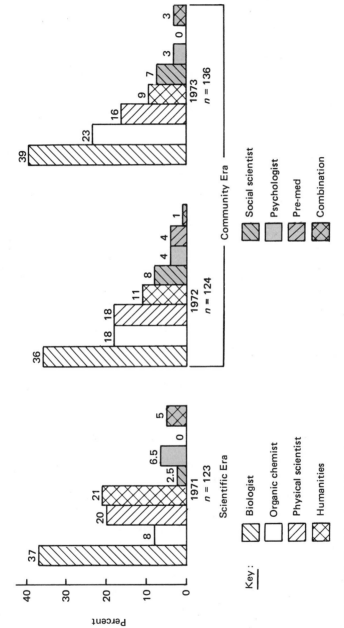

FIGURE 5.3 Classification of Harvard medical students by field of concentration.

Source: Adapted from Robert H. Coombs and Clark F. Vincent, Psychosocial Aspects of Medical Training, Springfield, Ill.: Charles C Thomas, Publisher, 1971. By permission.

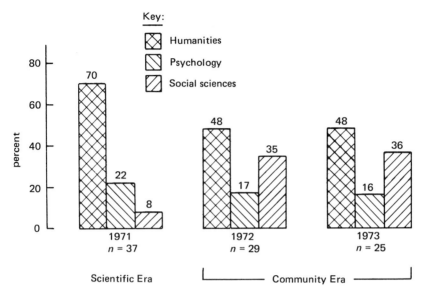

FIGURE 5.4 Classification of Harvard medical students by non-science fields of concentration.

Source: Adapted from Robert H. Coombs and Clark F. Vincent, Psychosocial Aspects of Medical Training. Springfield, Ill.: Charles C Thomas, Publisher, 1971. By permission.

1971 (scientific era)		1973 (community era)	
Biologist	(37%)	Biologist	(39%)
Humanities		Organic chemist	
Physical scientist		Physical scientist	
Organic chemist		Humanities	
Psychologist		*Social scientist*	*(7%)*
Combination		Combination	
Social scientist	*(2.5%)*		

their supremacy in the educational experience of medical students, while that field which most easily lends itself to a "community" posture and point of view remains only thinly represented in the training experiences of medical students, and of minimal consequence in their own ranking of importance. In fact, the presumed drift away from scientism in medical education may be more wish than reality. Indeed, the prevailing "one-on-one" nature of the typical patient-practitioner diagnostic-treatment situation (both in training simulation and realities of practice) goes far to mitigate the more elaborate organizational conceptions that stem logically from the premises of a "community" educational philosophy or a social model of illness and its treatment.

In general, the emphasis on formal measures of medical "competence" and the process of admission to medical school appears to be loaded in favor of a continuation of the specialization drift, which in turn is the primary substructure of the present institutionalized practice of medicine and perpetuates the "medical model" as the predominating force within the political sphere of medicine. In this connection it has been shown that there is a very strong relationship between scores on the Medical College Aptitude Test and the probability that a student will select specialty practice rather than general practice,[19] and more likely to enter into the practice scene via rotating specialized internships particularly in nonsectarian hospitals. These in turn are more likely to emphasize specialist services and, in their own right, have important effects upon the structure of medical politics at the local community level and ultimately in the continued preeminence of the "medical model."

And what of students' motives in entering the medical profession? The answer may seem obvious in the question, in the sense that the spontaneous reply is "Why not?" The financial rewards are very considerable, and in spite of occasional public expression of dissatisfaction, the physician is a person of consequence—respected, admired, and allowed to do pretty much as he or she wishes. Nevertheless, one study of medical students' motives is worth mentioning if only for the reason that it does not seem to address the central issue now at stake, namely, how flexible and responsive to future contingencies in the social organization of medicine will the next generation of physicians likely be?

In a study of junior and senior medical students, it was found that the vast majority of beginning students enter with predominantly "humanitarian" motives, with "professional" and "scientific" interests as strictly secondary. Following the period of training, although humanitarian motives continue to predominate in the minds of senior students, scientific and professional interests play a somewhat more important role in their outlook on the profession. The differences that do emerge during the course of training are, however, not impressive in their magnitude, suggesting either that the moral socialization undergone during medical training tends to reinforce the original humanitarian motives while providing more balance in the scientific and professional spheres or, contrariwise, that the moral socialization component in medical education is in fact not very strong at all. That there may well be a strong link between the original motivations of medical students, the emergence of role models while in medical school, and toward later practice types and the perpetuation of the "medical model" is indirectly supported by Korman and Stubblefield's study of freshmen and senior medical students.[20]

Korman and Stubblefield found that the medical training climate seemed to contain two distinctly different role models for students: First was the practicing "patient-oriented physician," who is invested with many desirable characteristics by these students. He is attentive to people and interested in their troubles. He is good-natured and easygoing. He is conscientious, ready to cooperate, and socially poised. ". . . Both freshmen and seniors see this complete physician as being skilled in establishing a good physician-patient relationship, as well as in recognizing and managing the social problems of his practice. He is also more likely to be *interested in the total patient* (italics mine) than in the disease entity. . . ."[21]

This second role is that of the "research-oriented physician-teacher" for whom students predict success in experimental medicine and as a researcher, and likely to be stronger in the diagnosis of disease than its treatment. "In contrast to the plethora of warm, endearing traits showered on the patient-oriented (role model) doctor, he (the researcher-teacher) is viewed as a rather colorless individual who knows the answers to medical problems."[22]

The authors' own concluding words are the best summary: "What is striking is the relative *fixation* (italics mine) of these ideas, despite the experiences over 4 years including the specific experience of being involved in the medical education process."[23]

Although there are exceptions, one is led to the conclusion that the motivations of medical students are remarkably stable over the period of formal training and that medical education is either considerably weaker in moral impact than is often thought or merely serves to perpetuate the motives and interests that serve to stabilize the profession as an ongoing institutional network in society. The question seems not to be "What moral impact does medical education have?" but rather, "What prior moral forces help to make medical education primarily a technological experience?" While the rise of "academic medicine" and increased prestige of careers in public health may have led to subtle changes in this regard, it still seems to be the case that the practice of scientific medicine remains *strongly* influential in medical education.

Still, if the moral socialization component of medical education is not adequately captured by the approaches summarized above, it is prima facie the case that the experience of medical experience is lasting in its impact. Is nothing more than technical information conveyed and original motives reinforced? That does not square with our intuitions about long-term institutional socialization. Perhaps the wrong questions have been addressed. The three major studies of medical students summarized below take somewhat different approaches and find their way to different conclusions. Each, however, argues that the social relationship between students and teachers is of critical importance in forming the professional posture of physicians.

ELITE EDUCATION AND COLLEAGUESHIP IN MEDICAL SCHOOL

The famous, though admittedly somewhat dated, study of Cornell, University of Pennsylvania, and Western Reserve medical schools by Robert Merton and his associates generally concluded that the relationship between students and teachers in these prestigious schools was characterized by a spirit of cooperation, consensus, and colleagueship. Specifically, teachers were seen by students as primarily helping persons assisting neophytes to adopt the preferred attitudes of poise and detached concern for patients and to leaven basically humanitarian interests with the required element of cynicism and personal distance that would allow the maximum degree of technical efficiency in later professional performance with an acceptable blend of personal satisfaction and social concern.

In all, education at these three schools was conceived as a parent-child relationship with growing self-confidence, increased awareness of the limitations of medical science and its frontiers, and an introduction to the complexity of the medical division of labor as well as to the variety of career avenues soon to open to the graduates of these highly rated schools. The theme throughout this look at medical education in the elite sector is one of gradual, and basically unhindered, acquisition by the student of the role set and professional attitude configuration that will permit a smooth absorption into the prevailing institutional network of medicine. Unfortunately, the data that substantiate this view are largely inferential. But in spite of this, Merton says:[24]

> From this standpoint, medical students are engaged in learning the professional role of the physician by so combining its component knowledge and skills, attitudes, and values, as to be motivated and able to perform this role in a professionally and socially acceptable fashion . . . it would seem particularly useful to attend systematically to the less conspicuous and more easily neglected processes of indirect learning. . . . Students learn not only from precept, or even from deliberate example; they also learn—and it may often be, most enduringly learn—from sustained involvement in that society of medical staff, fellow students, and patients which makes up the medical school as a social organization.

And while the authors of this study are cautious not to overgeneralize, the overriding conclusion is that the central values and attitudes students carry away from medical school are attitudes that have been nurtured in the nexus of helping relationships among students, teachers, and patients. Quite a different conclusion is reached by Howard S. Becker and his research team at the medical school of the University of Kansas.[25]

STATE EDUCATION AND STAFF-STUDENT CONFLICT IN MEDICAL SCHOOL

In contrasting their conclusions with those of the "elite" school study, Becker et al. write:[26]

> . . . we felt it not fruitful to think of the student's training as providing him with the attitudes and values necessary for professional practice. We do not feel that we know what attitudes and values will help the student adjust most easily and adequately to the professional role he is going to play, for we do not know what that role consists of. Furthermore, the argument that certain things are learned latently which will have an effect on the student's behavior in the distant future strikes us as quite speculative. . . .

In general, Becker and his colleagues unearth a predominating mood of cynicism and opportunism prevailing in the minds of medical students, brought about largely by the structure of medical education on the one hand and the "gatekeeping" function of medical school faculty on the other. They say:[27]

> Two sets of ideas characteristic of medical students seem particularly cynical to other people. As a result of their experience in school students acquire a point of view and terminology of a technical kind, which allow them to talk and think about patients and diseases in a way quite different from the layman. They look upon death and disabling disease, not with horror and sense of tragedy the layman finds appropriate, but as problems in medical responsibility. The technical attitude which prevents the student from becoming emotionally involved in the tragedy of patients' diseases seems to the layman cruel, heartless, and cynical. . . . Similarly our finding that freshmen decide it is necessary to select some of the material they are presented with for intensive study while ignoring other material will seem to some people an unjustifiably cynical approach to the study of medicine.

What brings about this cynical frame of mind in medical students, and does it persist into the practice years? According to the Kansas study, cynicism is a necessary ingredient for survival in the medical school. Emotionally distant faculty members, seemingly unsurmountable barriers to successfully completing the curriculum, a hardened view toward health matters on the part of senior staff members, an apparent attempt to place hurdle after hurdle in front of students during their training, the seeming impossibility of absorbing all of the information said to be essential to obtaining the M.D. degree—all of these foster an unavoidable relation of conflict between students and faculty, with the students resorting to whatever processes of subculture formation may help them in their struggle for survival. Unlike the Merton study, which revealed consensus in the medical school, the Kansas study uncovered conflict. Which attitudes persist in the years following training? No one really knows for sure. But Bloom's study of the Downstate Medical Center in Brooklyn offers yet a third formula for the social context of medical education: alienation.[28]

URBAN MEDICAL EDUCATION AND ALIENATION BETWEEN FACULTY AND STUDENTS

In his study of a metropolitan New York "streetcar" medical school, Bloom found a training situation about to be disrupted by a wave of student protest and militancy heretofore unheard of in a professional school. The smoldering powder keg is explained by Bloom as follows:[29]

> The growth and development of the medical school, however, has been handicapped by ambivalence of purpose and an ambiguous value climate. On the one hand, a strong consensus exists among the full-time faculty and administration that the medical school should be dominated by "academic" values, and that the value of knowledge for its own sake should be transmitted by "education" and not "training." Blocking this goal, they believe, is student motivation toward practical goals more than academic goals. The students, in turn, are disappointed in their expectations of an advanced and adult educational experience. The most important consequence of the resulting situation is the reaction by both faculty and students in a *defensive type of withdrawal behavior.*
>
> For the faculty, the retreat is mainly to a pathway in which they have assured security, into research activity where achievement can be rooted in the clear standards of one's own discipline and not, as in the different tasks of teaching, subject to the vagaries of an unclear set of institutional standards. The teaching responsibility is accordingly narrowed to a focus on one aspect of its potential function; i.e., the fostering of competence, defined in the limited essentially technical sense of that term. The students similarly withdraw, but into a different form of behavior characterized by "a passion for anonymity," or a philosophy of "don't make waves."

This rift in major perspective and purpose (the medical model from the point of view of the faculty, and the social model from that of the students) resulted in a breakdown in interaction—even of a conflict kind—between the two groups, followed by the emergence of major areas of misunderstanding and confusion with their resulting malaise of confusion, ambiguity, and alienation among the students.

The students thought the faculty members were interested only in their private practices and not in teaching (the reverse was in fact true). The faculty thought of the students as medical school rejects (in fact the students compared very favorably with all other medical students). The faculty thought the students were motivated to become doctors strictly out of greed (this was not the case). The students thought the faculty was out to flunk them (in actual fact the faculty was very concerned that students successfully complete their training). There was a host of other misunderstanding feeding the flames of alienation.

Bloom concludes by saying that:[30]

> The primary goal of medical education, in the minds of both students and faculty, is to integrate as effectively as possible the roles of *"healer"* and *"scientist"* in the future physician. Yet, at the same time, each group sees the other as important obstacle to the achievement of these goals.

What is medical education, a situation of consensus, conflict, or alienation? And what attitudes do medical students actually carry with them into their careers as physicians? The answer to the first part of this question is somewhat more easily managed than the second.

All the evidence—from the ranking of medical schools pointed out at the beginning of this chapter, from the variable emphasis placed upon specialty versus general practice training, from the multiple criteria on which admission is granted, and from the wide variation in learning climates in schools—leads one to conclude that there is enormous diversity in American medical education in spite of the very considerable uniformity in the technical content of training. In any event, the three sets of medical schools described here probably do not exhaust the types of social milieu found in medical schools throughout the country, nor do we know for certain that the elite status of the schools studied by the Merton group is at the root of the consensus model they appear to foster. Nor do we know that a somewhat parochial state practice orientation fostered by the school investigated by Becker and his associates accounts for the conflict model revealed there. And of course we are not certain that the metropolitan setting and lack of history and tradition are responsible for the patterns of alienation found there.

There is even greater uncertainty about what career-related social attitudes and orientations are in fact fostered in medical education and—if they are—how much staying power they have. Certainly, it is not unreasonable to suspect that as in many professional careers, post-training socialization and attitude formulation merely begin with the end of training and are not finished by it. Just as diversity typifies medical training, so too diversity and change seem to be endemic to the American medical career.

But it seems certain that the context of medical education constitutes the predominant bridge spanning the worlds of training and the worlds of practice.

SECURING A PRACTICE

Selecting and establishing a practice is probably the most personally consequential career decision (after the specialty decision has been made) that a physician is likely to make. While the choice is objectively highly varied, we know that the actual decision and subsequent action is constrained by a number of factors—economic, technical, and social. We know that most medical students come from urban communities and return to them to practice. Most students seek to practice with an affluent rather than an impoverished clientele, and their office locations and hospital affiliations reflect that. Rural areas have fewer practicing physicians than their population size and health problems would justify. The same is true of some specialties in medicine—some are oversubscribed by members and others underprescribed. This means that for some populations some treatment opportunities are abundant while others are scarce. Beyond this a closer scrutiny is called for.

Table 5.15 shows the distribution of practicing physicians in various types of practice in 1968 and 1974. As has already been noted, there was a considerable increase in the supply of working physicians

TABLE 5.15
Physicians by type of practice, 1968 and 1974

Type of practice	1968	1974	Change
Active physicians	296,312	350,609	+54,237
	100.00%	100.00%	+18.2%
Nonfederal practice	96.3%	98.5%	+ 2.2%
Patient care	80.4%	79.4%	− 1.0%
Office-based practice	61.1%	57.4%	− 3.7%
General practice	18.6%	12.3%	− 4.3%
Other specialty	42.6%	44.1%	+ 1.5%
Hospital-based practice	19.6%	21.4%	+ 1.8%
Training programs	14.2%	15.7%	+ 1.5%
Full-time hospital staff	5.4%	5.7%	+ 0.3%
Other professional activity	9.5%	7.0%	− 2.5%

SOURCE: Various reports of the U.S. Office of Vital Statistics.

(more than 18 percent in less than a decade), but the distribution of them in various forms of practice remains substantially unchanged over this period. That is, federal employment (in either armed forces medical facilities, U.S. Public Health Service, or federal nonmilitary research and treatment facilities) remains a career choice for only a small proportion of doctors, while office-based practice is the principal choice. But some form of practice involving full- or part-time employment in a hospital is a growing choice for larger and larger number of physicians, with the numerous technical perquisites such a choice carries with it. Although there may be at least an apparent decline in one's hallowed professional autonomy and lower financial rewards, these are balanced with greater economic security. There is the additional factor of not having to deal with a "clientele" as is the case in office-based practice—although somewhat less so for specialists than for general practitioners. Insofar as one may equate hospital-based specialty practice with favoring a medical model of illness, and office-based general practice with something of a tilt toward a social model, the latter appears to be losing ground rather than gaining it.

But in spite of the overall increase in the number of physicians, and in spite of a growing concern, even within some quarters of medical education itself, it is important to note that the most pronounced change is the decline by over 4 percent in the number of office-based general practitioners. By implication, as well as by rough mathematical calculation, the loss of some 20,000 general practitioners means that approximately 2 million persons—heretofore turning to the office-based general practitioner for primary care—must now look elsewhere. Again, we can infer the erosion of the career choice likely to foster the adoption of a social model of illness, and the growing primacy of those forms of practice learning more in the direction of the medical model.

In general, however, it is worth noting that although the supply of physicians has increased by nearly one-fifth over this period, the career choices among the major alternatives remains fundamentally unchanged. Thus whatever diversity may exist in the motivational structures of persons entering medicine and whatever the hopes and intentions of segments of the medical education community, the career choices remain basically unchanged—again the decline of general practice, along with some noticeable increases in hospital-based practice, which have to be noted as possible exceptions. What is suggested, of course, is that career and practice selection may be effects not so much of the socializing effects of medical school, but of prior motives and career contingencies that arise at the close of and following the formal period of training.

A recent overview of the practice choices is reported in Table 5.16.

TABLE 5.16
Types of practice, 1974[a]

	Type of practice	Office based	Hospital based	Other
Total	100.00%	62.4%	28.8%	8.8%
General practice	69,445	73.9%	14.6%	11.5%
Specialty	260,821	59.6%	31.2%	9.2%
Medical specialties	89,919	55.6%	23.7%	10.7%
Surgical specialties	105,890	69.8%	26.4%	3.8%
Psychiatry and neurology	29,552	50.0%	34.5%	15.5%
Other specialties	35,480	45.7%	37.1%	17.2%

[a] Includes federal and nonfederal physicians.
SOURCE: Various reports of the U.S. Office of Vital Statistics.

As can be seen, general practice now is a career choice followed by a minority of doctors. Specialties are absorbing more and more of the available medical personnel, and *surgical* specialties are predominating over medical specialties. And consistent with what might be expected, hospital-based practice of one form or another is the preferred line for about 25 percent of both medical and surgical specialists. The pattern is clear: Specialties are predominant, and although office practice is still the primary form of work, hospital practice is growing, and as we shall see, so is the range and variety of forms of practice that depart from the stereotypical solo fee-for-service form.

With this as background, what other factors assist or impede in establishing a practice? It is often thought that the M.D. is a totally free and independent entrepreneur, who is free to set up a practice wherever and however he or she chooses. That may be true in a general and ideal sense, but there are numerous constraints upon that—whether it be hospital-based practice or one of the office forms.

Probably of first importance is the need for a hospital staff appointment. Even the general practitioner providing only baseline primary care can hardly succeed without a hospital appointment—if only for consultation purposes, use of laboratory facilities, and so forth. To bring this about, the fledgling doctor has to display at least one of three essential elements: a supply of patients that a hospital needs, a specialty that the institution needs, or a strong sponsorship stemming from the existing members of the local community professional network. The beginning doctor has, by definition, no patients and so must rely upon one or more of the other two ingredients. Inasmuch as we know that most career planning—even that by medical students—is seldom sufficiently rationalized to meet a needed market, it is unlikely that many persons take medical training specifically geared to the future needs of a hospital. It may be the case, however, that the interhospital competition in a community may be so intense that one or more hospitals may extend staff privileges with considerable impunity inasmuch as the added costs extending to the hospital as a result of the special needs that new staff members may have can often be buried in third-party payments or in the expansion of external funds. Such appointments are likely to be more often the case in periods of relatively easy money but more rare when hospitals are attempting to reduce inter-hospital competition and to cut costs. Thus, in the absence of economic abundance, the "old boy" network, which Hall argued long ago was essential to the medical school admission process, may be equally vital in a young doctor's securing the endorsement of existing staff members in the search for a hospital appointment, which is the first line of attack in establishing a reliable and ongoing practice and source of patients.

But as specialty practice becomes more and more the case, a hospital staff appointment is more and more essential because it enhances one's position in the intercolleague referral of patients who are referred back and forth from specialist to specialist in the growing absence of a "home base" in the form of a community-based general practitioner.

Given, therefore, the drift toward a kind of "mechanical" solidarity in the medical division of labor, reliance upon the goodwill of the "old boy" network is likely to fade in importance, while objective economic and technical considerations may play a more and more important role in determining who practices what kind of medicine and where.

What of the hospital as the primary location for the practice of modern medicine? A look at diversity, conflict, and change in that sector is the theme of the chapter to follow.

SCENARIO II

Faculty pressures favoring broad-scope moral education

That seems to be the nub of the problem in applying scientific research as well as in the broader field of education. Teaching has generally been approached as though the presentation of information, documentation with soundly derived data, and logical analysis leading to solid conclusions would elicit new or different behavior. (And many times it does, if the new learning is not inconsistent with basic values that guide the life of the individual or institution.) How to translate into behavior new facts, new principles, new guidelines that are at odds with currently held values is really the issue posed by this research. How, in John Gardner's words, to accomplish continuing organizational (or individual) self-renewal more profound than a mere operational facelifting.

In an age in which rapid communication and transportation have reduced the globe nearly to the size of a neighborhood, major problems no longer stem from inadequate or incomplete information but from a conflict of values. As E. B. White wrote, with penetrating perception: ". . . clubs, fraternities, nations, these are the beloved barriers in the way of a workable world." In microcosm, the medical school as a social system reflects the turmoil of the time: the willingness to look at hard questions but the reluctance to respond to hard answers; the desire to reach for a brighter future but the need to cling to a comfortable present.

Medical educators alone cannot be expected to change the course of the world, but they might contribute significantly to that necessary change if they learn how to deal more perceptively with the institutions over which they do have control. As scientists they will recognize in this volume, as well as in their own experience, evidence that feelings must be as important as facts in determining their behavior. When they accept this evidence at the level of the heart as well as the mind, and begin to act upon it, then real institutional change may begin to occur.

G. Miller, in Samuel Bloom, *Power and Dissent in the Medical School.* New York: Free Press, 1973, p. v. passim.

NOTES

1 E. M. Carr-Saunders and P. A. Wilson, *The Professions.* New York: Oxford, 1933; William J. Goode, "Community within a Community: The Professions," *American Sociological Review,* 22 (April 1957), 194–200.
2 Ralph Gancher, "Turn 18 Medical School Rejections into an Admission," *Journal of Medical Economics,* 53 (September 1976), 173.
3 Natalie Rogoff, "The Decision to Study Medicine," in *The Student Physician,* Robert K. Merton, George Reader, Patricia L. Kendall, Eds. Cambridge: Harvard University Press, 1957.
4 Ibid.
5 Elaine Crovitz. "Comparison of Male and Female Physicians Association Program Applicants," *Journal of Medical Education* (July 1975).

6 Virginia Calkins, "Impact on Admission to a School of Medicine of an Innovation in Selection Procedures," *Psychological Reports,* 35 (1974), 1135–1142.

7 John G. Bruhn, 'The Ills of Premedical Advising," *Journal of Medical Education,* 52:8 (August 1977), 676.

8 "Time of Decision to Study Medicine: Its Relation to Specialty Choice," *Journal of Medical Education* 52:1 (January 1977), 78–81.

9 J. S. Maxmen, "Parental Influences on Medical Student Activities," *Journal of Medical Education,* 47 (May 1972), 351–353.

10 May M. Cliff and T. Menzie Cliff, "Attitudes of Medical Students toward Medical School and Their Future Careers," *Journal of Medical Education* 47 (1972), 534–537.

11 Ralph Turner, "Sponsored and Contest Mobility and the School System," *American Sociological Review,* 25 (December 1960), 855–867.

12 "Applicants for 1975–76 First Year Medical School Class," Editors, *Journal of Medical Education,* 51:7 (July 1976), 867–869.

13 Ibid.

14 Oswald Hall, "The Informal Organization of the Medical Profession," *Canadian Journal of Economics and Political Science,* 12 (1946), 30–41.

15 Charles Perrow, "Members as Resources in Voluntary Organizations," in *Organizations and Clients,* William R. Rosengren and Mark Lefton, Eds. Columbus, Ohio: Merrill, 1970, p. 109.

16 Rodney Coe, Max Pepper, Mary Mattis, "The New Medical Student: Another View," *Journal of Medical Education.* 52:2 (February 1977), 89.

17 Calkins, op. cit.

18 Robert H. Coombs and Clark F. Vincent, *Psychosocial Aspects of Medical Training.* Springfield, Ill.: Charles C Thomas, 1971.

19 Harry Perlstadt, "Goal Implementation and Outcome in Medical Schools," *American Sociological Review,* 37 (February 1972), 73–82.

20 Maurice Korman and Robert L. Stubblefield, "Role Perceptions in Freshmen and Senior Medical Students," *Journal of the American Medical Association,* 184:4 (1963), 287–289.

21 Ibid., 288.

22 Ibid., 289

23 Ibid.

24 Robert Merton et al., *The Student Physician.* Cambridge: Harvard University Press, 1957, pp. 41–42.

25 Howard S. Becker, Blanche Greer, and Everett Hughes. *Boys in White: Student Culture in Medical School.* Chicago: University of Chicago Press, 1961.

26 Ibid., p. 420.

27 Ibid., pp. 421–422.

28 Samuel W. Bloom, *Power and Dissent in the Medical School.* New York: Free Press, 1973.

29 Ibid., p. 3.

30 Ibid., p. 142.

SUGGESTED READINGS

Howard S. Becker, Blanche Greer, and Everett Hughes, *Boys in White: Student Culture in Medical School.* Chicago: University of Chicago Press, 1961.

*An important analysis, from a symbolic interaction point of view, of social-
ization toward disenchantment in medical school.*

Samuel W. Bloom, *Power and Dissent in the Medical School.* New York:
Free Press, 1973.
*A survey research analysis of what went wrong in a medical school that
seemed to have all the resources to "do it right."*

Eliot Freidson, *Profession of Medicine.* New York: Dodd, Mead, 1970.
The definitive analysis of the social organization of the medical profession.

Eliot Freidson and Judith Lorber, Eds., *Medical Men and Their Work.* New
York: Aldine-Atherton, 1972.
*A reader on the sociology of the professional work and organization of
doctors.*

Robert K. Merton, George Reader, and Patricia L. Kendall, Eds., *The Student Physician.* Cambridge: Harvard University Press, 1957.
*A collection of studies, from a functional perspective, of the sociology of
medical education in three elite schools.*

Neil B. Shulman, *Finally I'm a Doctor.* Washington, D.C.: Hemisphere Publishing Company, 1978.
*A doctor's novelized account of going through medical school, "from losing
his first patient to misplacing a cadaver's gallbladder."*

David S. Viscount, *The Making of a Psychiatrist.* Greenwich, Conn.: Faw-
cett, 1972.
*A practicing psychiatrist discusses the acquisition of the psychiatric per-
spective.*

———————～～～———————

*The search for authority in the broadly
oriented "social model" hospital*

Some years ago I visited a small psychiatric hospital for children
with a view to taking a job as a research sociologist there, and
that did happen. This hospital had 56 patients between the ages of
7 and 11, for which some 110 full-time staff members were
provided, along with a large number of part-time consultants and
community and college volunteers. The aim was to provide a
social milieu of "total" treatment, which would harness the
insights and technologies of a wide range of medical and
social-psychiatric resources in order to effect useful change in
these difficult children.

During my visit I tried to get some insight into how the
hospital was organized and how it ran. Thus, when interviewed by
the director (a psychiatrist), I asked him, "Who runs this place?"
and he said, "I do." Later that morning I put the same question to
the head of the Clinical Psychology Department, and he said
that "We psychologists do." Just before lunch I spoke with the
chief psychiatric social worker, and asked her who ran the place
and she said that she did. After lunch I talked with the head of
the School Department and asked her the same question and,
not unpredictably, she said that she did. In mid-afternoon I chatted
with the ranking child care supervisor (chief attendant) and
asked him who ran the hospital and he said that he did. Then I
turned to a small boy about 9 years old and asked, "Hey, who
really runs this place?" He turned and pointed to a larger and
older boy and said, "He does."

I left that afternoon feeling that I had learned quite a bit about
that hospital.

CHAPTER 6

The structure and dynamics of hospitals

It is customary for a textbook on the sociology of medicine to include a few paragraphs on the historial development of the modern hospital. The point of this exercise is not to "teach" history in the sense that it may lead us either to the induction of some general laws which seem to guide the structure and dynamics of hospitals, or to an "artifact" approach to events long since past.

Historian-philosophers Spengler and Toynbee stand eminent in scholarship among those who regard history as repetitive and therefore of interest because it makes possible the understanding of the present as well as the forecasting of the future. Such a view is normally reducable to a cyclical model of historical change, not dissimilar to the grand civilization theories which are reflected even in the extensions of Marxist philosophers. Others regard the study of history as worthwhile in its own right, quite irrespective of lessons which might be drawn from it. The view adopted here owes allegiance to the thinking of the English historian, Edward Hallet Carr, who says:[1]

> My difference with Toynbee is that he regards history as repetitive, whereas I think of it as continuous. For him (Toynbee) history consists of the same things happening over and over again with minor variations in different contexts; for me history is a procession of events about which almost the only thing that can be said with certainty is that it moves constantly on and never returns to the same place. And this difference naturally affects one's view of the lessons that history can teach.
>
> The difference turns on fundamental conceptions of the nature of history. Toynbee's view, like Spengler's, rests on the analogy between history and science in which historical thought has been enmeshed for nearly two centuries. *The analogy is false* (italics mine). In science the drama repeats itself over and over again because the *dramatis personae* are creatures of the past or inanimate objects. In history the drama cannot repeat itself because the *dramatis personae* at the second performance are already conscious of the prospective denouement; the essential condition of the first performance can never be reconstituted. . . . All analogies between history and science, all cyclical theories of history, are tainted with the fundamental error of neglecting human consciousness of the past. You cannot look forward intelligently into the

future unless you also are prepared to look back attentively into the past.

I would add at this point that although history may not be repetitive in the grand-cycles sense of a Toynbee or a Spengler, neither is it completely random and episodic as suggested by the stance taken by Carr. It might be safe to assert that history is at least *additive* or *cumulative*. The present is not a sheer repeat of the past, nor is it unrelated to the past. And in this sense the history of the hospital is of consequential importance for understanding some of the contemporary complexities of the present social organization of the hospital, expressing as it does so many of the facets then, when written large, may in fact have typified Western hospitals during particular times in the past. Thus much of the diversity now characterizing the hospital as a social organization may be traceable not only to its current external linkages and internal complexities but also to the remnants of tradition of which even the most rationalized of social institutions are never fully rid. In this light, the themes of diversity, conflict, and change can be found woven through the sociology of the hospital, a situation probably more characteristic of the past than what is reflected in standard accounts of the history of the hospital.

Given the assumption of adversity and conflict within and between hospitals—both as types and as specific entities—a further point of departure for this chapter lies in the fact that hospitals, at whatever point in history, constitute a highly regarded and exceedingly valuable resource for a society. Therefore, competition for its control can be expected to be intense, and dependent on the strains and lines and opposition found in the society at large.

Perhaps partially for this reason, hospitals hold a special fascination for most people, held as they are in some combination of awe, curiosity, fear, forbearance, and hope. So much so are we both drawn and repelled by hospitals that they have often been the butt of much humor, with the physician as prime target. Mark Twain, for example, when offering advice for the correct attitude to take when having a surgical operation said, "Console yourself with the reflection that you are giving the doctor pleasure, and that he is getting paid for it." Or the quip, " 'The medical profession, because of the public attitude, is made up largely of troubleshooters and repairmen when maintenance men are what are most needed.' " However, partially because of the pervading laissez-faire theme in the social organization of medical care and partially because of the widespread reluctance of persons to incorporate total rationality into personal planning for health needs, hospitals remain basically crisis-oriented institutions engaged in post hoc repair and troubleshooting.

It must be kept in mind that no complex organization—however esoteric or commonplace its technology might happen to be—can be usefully understood by considering it in vacuo, as if it existed apart from the surrounding social organization that has given rise to it and makes it possible to be sustained. The rather simple lines of connectedness between hospital and social order are perhaps more easily seen with regard to ancient forms of hospitals than in the case of the diverse institutions we now call "hospitals." This simplicity, however, may be a function of the myopia brought about by the passage of time rather than being inherently true of old as compared with new health organizations.

In making this argument that hospitals must be viewed in the context of the key threads in the fabric of social life, a helpful point of departure and empirical example is still Solomon's study of the Chicago of the 1950s and the chain of associations between recruitment to medicine at the start, and the context of subsequent practice.[2]

URBAN DIFFERENTIATION, MEDICAL TRAINING, AND MEDICAL PRACTICE

Solomon's interest lay in the structure of the modern urban population, its differentiation on the one hand, and patterns of medical training and practice on the other. His question was an important one: How far and in what way do nonmedically related social phenomena influence the important process by which the division of medical service in a modern urban center is brought about? And, especially, how might different forms of hospital sponsorship lie at the root of the kinds of differentiations found?

In order to get at this thorny problem, Solomon first classified a random sample of physicians then practicing in Chicago in terms of their *ethnic* background, and then once again according to the medical school from which they had graduated. The results of this exercise are summarized in Table 6.1.

The first point to be made is that the medical schools are listed roughly according to the degree of prestige they possess, ranging from the Medical School of the University of Chicago (listed consistently, you will recall, as among the top ten in the country) and Rush Medical College with the highest rank, down through the State School, the two principal Catholic-affiliated schools, to those not recognized by the AMA. That is, students who attend the higher-ranked medical colleges can expect to be exposed to the most elaborate teaching hospital affiliations, to occupy favored positions when it comes to internships and residencies, and to have contact with a distinguished teaching faculty and therefore have the enhanced possibility of establishing a favored

TABLE 6.1

Ethnic identity of Chicago physicians and origin of medical training

	ETHNIC GROUP				
	Anglo-Saxon	Irish	Italian	Polish	Jewish
Number of physicians	164	135	126	108	155
Medical school attended:					
University of Chicago and Rush	21.3	8.8	5.6	6.4	17.4
Northwestern	21.3	13.4	2.4	3.7	3.8
University of Illinois	14.1	15.5	20.6	17.6	38.1
Chicago Medical School	0.6	3.0	1.6	2.8	1.9
Stritch School of Medicine of Loyola	10.3	43.0	34.1	38.9	7.1
Medical School purchased by Loyola in 1917	4.9	2.9	1.6	4.6	3.9
Schools not recognized by AMA	6.1	2.2	19.8	14.8	12.3

SOURCE: Adapted from Stanley Lieberson, "Ethnic Groups and the Practice of Medicine," *American Sociological Review*, 23 (October 1958), 547. By permission.

link to the next step to the actual practice of medicine. Just the reverse can be expected to be the fate of those who, for whatever reason, secure admission to a less prestigious school. On the face of it, the relationship between the ethnic origins of physicians and their educational origins is remarkable: A very large plurality of the Anglo-Saxon physicians had attended the three high-prestige Protestant-sponsored medical schools in the Chicago area (Chicago, Rush, and Northwestern), with these figures declining systematically among those ethnic groups having experienced more recent migration to this country: Irish, Italian, and Polish. (The Jewish doctors constitute something of a special case and will be commented on later.) One can reasonably exhibit curiosity as to whether the capability to undertake successfully a program of high prestige medical training is found disproportionately among Anglo-Saxon young people, whereas ethnically distinct applicants are found disproportionately wanting in these abilities. Or perhaps whether the putative meritocratic admission criteria are in fact contaminated by the effects of secondary social characteristics which go beyond sheer race and sex differentiations.

A next step taken in the study by Solomon was to examine the relationship between the ethnicity of the physician on the one hand,

and the nature of the physicians' hospital affiliation on the other. Solomon's results are summarized in Table 6.2.

With regard to Table 6.2, while the fit is not exact, it is fair to assume that the vast majority of staff appointments in "elite Protestant" hospitals (over 90 percent) were held by doctors in the "unidentified" category. It is a reasonable assumption that the vast majority of Anglo-Saxon physicians are to be found in that category; Jewish doctors make up less than 7 percent of the staff appointments in the elite Protestant category. By the same token, Jewish doctors comprise 98 percent of the total appointments in the hospitals operating under Jewish sponsorship. Finally, the ethnic staffing patterns in the Catholic hospitals is somewhat less unequivocal in that over 60 percent of their physicians are "unidentified" in terms of ethnic origins, but yet 25 percent are either Polish, Italian, or Czechoslovakian.

A similar ethnic twist is to be noted in Table 6.3 in relation to the proportion of physicians working in each type of hospital who are board certified in a specialty. Greater specialization is to be found among the staff in the elite Protestant hospitals, the next highest in the Jewish hospitals, and the lowest in the Catholic and "other" categories of hospitals.

Thus, the linkages between ethnicity and medical practice are revealed to be quite strong indeed in these two studies. But in the case of Chicago, and by implications those in other large urban centers, the spatial or ecological distribution of physicians in the city is equally

TABLE 6.2
Ethnic identity of Chicago physicians and hospital sponsorship

	HOSPITAL AFFILIATION					
Ethnic identification	Elite Protestant	Other	Catholic	Jewish	None	Total
Unidentified	93.8	60.4	60.2	0.9	60.6	55.2
Jewish	6.2	37.1	14.8	98.2	21.1	33.3
Polish, Italian, Czechoslovakian	—	2.5	25.0	0.9	18.3	11.5
Total	100.0	100.0	100.0	100.0	100.0	100.0
Number in sample	64	202	88	112	388	854

SOURCE: Adapted from David Solomon, "Ethnic and Class Differences among Hospitals as Contingencies in Medical Careers," *American Journal of Sociology*, 65 (March 1961), 463–471. By permission.

TABLE 6.3

Hospital affiliation and degree of specialization

Degree of specialization	HOSPITAL AFFILIATION					
	Elite Protestant	Other	Catholic	Jewish	None	Total
No specialty	6.3%	32.7%	42.0%	46.4%	74.2%	52.3%
Partial	6.3	28.2	21.6	3.6	16.0	17.1
Full-time	23.4	16.8	13.6	13.4	8.8	12.9
Certified	64.0	22.3	22.8	36.6	1.0	17.7
Total	100.0%	100.0%	100.0%	100.0%	100.0%	100.0%
Number in sample	64	202	88	112	388	854

$$\chi^2 = 290 \qquad \text{d.f.} = 12 \qquad p < .001$$

SOURCE: Adapted from David Solomon, "Ethnic and Class Differences among Hospitals as Contingencies in Medical Careers," *American Journal of Sociology*, 65 (March 1961), 463–471. By permission.

interesting. Specifically, where in the city do most doctors practice, and where does this differential place them in the context of the informal and formal social organization of the profession on the one hand, and in relation to delivery of services to patients on the other? Some insights into this matter are suggested by the data contained in Table 6.4 and 6.5.

The top half of Table 6.4 shows clearly that Anglo-Saxon physicians *and* Jewish physicians show a much greater chance of being engaged in specialty practice. The second half shows also that members of these two ethnic groups have a greater chance of conducting their practices in the downtown (so-called "Loop") area of the city of Chicago. With what we can surmise about the nature of medical technology, medical costs, client selectivity, and interphysician referral of patients, it is safe to assume that the doctors practicing in a specialty possess at least a higher potentiality for delivering, or making available, to patients a more sophisticated and broad level of care.

Again the Anglo-Saxon and Jewish doctors are strongly favored in this regard.

The Loop is the economic center of Chicago. It is where the professional network is most tightly woven. It is the headquarters of the American Medical Association. Here, too, is the impressive Medical Society Library. Within walking distance of most physicians' offices in the Loop is the Northwestern Medical School as well as several of the largest and most technically sophisticated hospitals in the area. Here too are the private men's clubs where the elites and the would-be elites meet for lunch, drinks, squash, and conversation. Here, in colloquial phraseology, is "where the action is." Again, it is the Anglo-Saxon and Jewish physicians who dominate the practice of medicine in this place, with the Italian, Irish, and Polish groups falling far behind in their access to the centers of formal and informal power and prestige in the medical community.

But perhaps of more telling importance are the data in Table 6.5, which indicates the degree of *ethnic similarity between physicians and their patients.*

A word about the statistical measure, the index of dissimilarity, will be helpful. In any given intersecting cell, (Anglo-Saxon physician and Anglo-Saxon ethnic population, for example) if the figure reported were "zero" this would indicate that virtually *all* patients of all Anglo-Saxon physicians were themselves Anglo-Saxons. If, on the other hand, this figure were 100.00 it would mean that virtually *no* patients of

TABLE 6.4

Percent of physicians who are full-time specialists and percent practicing in Loop, by ethnic membership

Characteristics and basis of comparison	ETHNIC GROUP					
	Anglo-Saxon	Irish	Italian	Jewish	Polish	Random sample
Percent specialized						
Actual	43.3	32.6	19.0	48.4	20.4	40.3
Expected on basis of medical school	43.3	35.8	31.3	40.6	30.9	40.3
Actual minus expected	0.0	− 3.2	−12.3	7.8	−10.5	—
Percent with office in loop						
All physicians	30.4	20.3	11.5	37.8	8.9	26.5
General practitioners	14.0	12.0	3.9	14.3	5.6	8.5
Specialists:						
Actual	50.7	37.0	39.3	62.5	21.7	52.5
Expected on basis of specialty	50.9	49.6	51.1	52.9	53.6	52.5
Actual minus expected	− 0.2	−12.6	−11.8	9.6	−31.9	—

SOURCE: Adapted from Stanley Lieberson, "Ethnic Groups and the Practice of Medicine," *American Sociological Review,* 23 (October 1958), p. 548. By permission.

TABLE 6.5

Index of dissimilarity between physicians and their patients

Physicians' classification		SELECTED ETHNIC POPULATIONS				
		Anglo-Saxon	Irish	Italian	Jewish	Polish
Anglo-Saxon	(N112)	38.8	45.5	57.1	51.8	73.1
Irish	(N110)	43.0	40.2	59.7	60.2	73.4
Italian	(N116)	53.6	52.4	30.6	70.0	69.9
Jewish	(N102)	34.1	49.3	55.1	31.4	64.4
Polish	(N102)	72.2	76.1	65.3	76.2	29.9

SOURCE: Adapted from Stanley Lieberson, "Ethnic Groups and the Practice of Medicine," *American Sociological Review,* 23 (October 1958), 545. By permission.

Anglo-Saxon physicians were of Anglo-Saxon origin. It means, therefore, that if the figure is *below 50* it would be safe to conclude that Anglo-Saxon doctors treat *more* Anglo-Saxon patients than mere statistical probability would lead us to expect. If, on the other hand, the figure is *higher than 50* we may be satisfied that Anglo-Saxon doctors take care of *fewer* Anglo-Saxon persons than mere chance would lead us to expect. A low number means that doctors and patients tend to be *similar* to one another in terms of ethnicity. A high figure means that they tend to be *dissimilar.*

There are a number of interpretations to be made of this table, but only two principal points are to be made here: (1) Across all ethnic classifications physicians and patients tend to be ethnically more similar than they are dissimilar; that is, Anglo-Saxon doctors tend to have Anglo-Saxon patients, Polish doctors tend to have Polish patients, and so forth. (2) Where the social distance between ethnic groups (as well as the time elapsed between their respective migrations into this land) is greater, less is the likelihood that doctors and patients will share ethnic identity; that is, Anglo-Saxon physicians tend to have very few Polish patients and by the same token Polish doctors tend to have few Anglo-Saxon patients. In Lieberson's concluding words:[3]

> . . . the data strongly suggest that the ethnic identification of physicians significantly influences their pattern of medical practice. Both the spatial distribution and the functional differentiation of physicians reported here suggest that medicine may be viewed as a system resulting from and concordant with the more specialized and segregated services performed by each component of the medical profession.

This pattern—linking the social origins of physicians to the stature and prestige of the medical school they attend, then to the type of practice in which they engage, to their hospital affiliations, to their location in the social ecology of the medical system, and finally to the social composition of their patients—is of more than merely passing interest. It highlights the important *extramedical* factors that strongly influence these important processes and structures, and it also details the effects of historical developments on these facets of the contemporary medical scene. That is, the history of the city, including its divisiveness and changing institutional differentiation, must be taken into account in making sense out of these ecological differentiations. So too is it in trying to map out the extra hospital linkages of hospitals in an earlier era.

FROM THE CITADEL TO VOLUNTARY TECHNICAL BUREAUCRACY[4]

It matters little if one chooses to regard the Greek health spas as "hospitals," catering as they did primarily to people from the ancient cities who were already more or less in good health and could otherwise afford to travel what was then long distances to enjoy the salubrious breezes and invigorating pools of coastal Greece. What does matter is that even at this early time special activities and places were set aside for the promotion of good health and made available to those who could afford them. It is noteworthy, however, that in the past sick people were not taken to special places for care by medical specialists; it was quite the other way around. Instead of large numbers of sick people collected in one place to be cared for by small number of specialists, it was more likely that one or more medical specialists gathered around single individuals—usually rich ones, in their homes or palaces—to await and watch over their deaths.

We have thought of the hospital, from Roman times till the present, as a *segregated* place for the tending of the sick (as distinguished from catering to the leisurely well). However, although the Greek spa may have been considered as a place for retreat and rejuvenation for the wealthy and propertied class, it ought not be regarded as a hospital. Still and all, as a place for the promotion of well-being (as distinguished from a place for the tending of the sick) these precursors to the hospital were like their modern counterparts if only to the extent that they were responsive only to those members of the society so dictated by the larger social order. And it is not really important to know whether the Temples of Asclepius preceded or followed the spas, but only that their links to the prevailing religious-philosophical tenets of the time were strong. For just as Lewis Rumford persuasively argues that the first differentiated social organization in prehistory was probably the Church, so too the first health place probably had sacred connotations and priestlike proprietors. Remember that even the Hippocratic oath and the promises contained therein were offered and made *to the gods* and not to sick men and also that a strong body was the quintessence of Spartan values.

In even earlier times, villages of any size whatsoever probably possessed "inns" where the homeless, infirm, and penniless could count on to find solace, some rest and food, and some reassurance. Health care as we know it? Surely not. But these early sick places were certainly holy places, whether Greek, Jewish, or early Christian. It seems that very early in the history of civilization, being sick was often an essential qualifier for kindness; being poor neither then or now necessarily enhanced one's position in this regard. As Eliot Freidson has sagely observed:[5]

> In the most general sense, the hospital is a place in which ailing people sleep and receive care. Because ailing people live in it, the hospital will always have some attributes of the hotel or dormitory: some of its personnel will play domestic roles and others will supervise them. Because ailing people receive some sort of care while they are living there, the hospital will always have some of the attributes of the school or prison: some of its personnel will assume responsibility for the inmates. Provision of hospital care thus implies a profound division of people into those who assume responsibility, those for whom responsibility is assumed, and those who keep house. The nature of that division has varied with prevailing notions of what ails people and what must be done to help them. In all, the word "hospital" has been applied to institutions that have on one occasion or another resembled a Skid Row hostel, a religious retreat, a school, a prison, a hotel, an elephant's graveyard, and a hospital. Such variation is not entirely historical.

The relatively short-lived link between hospitals and the citadel has been traced to Roman times, and especially to the pre-Christian era, in which the traveling Roman legions carried with them members whose special task it was to care as best they could for their fallen comrades, a more concrete and secular expression of the service of the healers to the interests in the state than was probably true of the situation in earlier times.

It seems clear that, as medicine inched forward in its technological capabilities, the more valuable a resource it became the more did it become an object of competition for "interested parties" who might benefit from it—however illusory those benefits might in fact have been. Historically, therefore, it is not inaccurate to say that the sociopolitical implications of medicine were more and more elaborated as the technology acquired increased utility, and the early state surely became one of the earliest manifestations of structural differentiations in early civilization to articulate and utilize that resource. Health, therefore, historically was as an expression of *collective* rather than *individual interest* (that was to come much later in historical development). Health, as an expression of a higher order of service, was certainly given long-lasting impetus by early Christian teachings, in which the link between the care of the ill and benevolence becomes highly specific. This continued through the long years of the medieval period and up to the Renaissance. As Lewis Mumford has it:[6]

> Hospitals, for the general care of the sick and ailing, were not provided on a remarkable scale. The sanatorium was no longer a health resort set apart from the city and catering mainly to those who could afford to travel, but a place in the heart of the city, near at hand, open to all who needed it, under the care of men and women willing to undertake all the repulsive officers demanded by sickness, wounds, and surgical operations.

And the link to early Christianity is also clear enough:[7]

> Both the hospital and the isolation ward were direct contributions of the monastery; and with them came a more general kind of hospitality for the healthy, in need of overnight rest and food. Through all the centuries when inns and hotels were lacking, when private lodging was meager and wretched, the monastic hospice provided decent free accommodation.

And so to a condition of general welfare even in an era combining low technology with special privileges for the few who were rich, and alms for the hordes of the poor and the aged:[8]

> The provision of almshouses was likewise a medieval municipal institution, for the care of the poor and the destitute was an obligation of Christian charity, and not the least handsome buildings in the late medieval city were in fact almshouses—though their existence shows that poverty kept pace with increasing wealth. Finally, for the first time again, institutions for the care of the aged flourished in the late medieval city: sometimes, as in Bruges, Amsterdam, Augsburg, forming little neighborhood units, with their common gardens and their chapel; pools of civic comeliness to this very day.

So widespread was the growth of this type of institution that by the end of the 1400s England contained over 600 of these hospitals, some of the larger ones with the beginnings of differentiations into "departments" which catered to clients with differing needs—medical, indigency, the aged, and so forth.

But with these early beginnings in the spiritual realm, even it could not forestall the drift in the later medieval period toward guildism, in which work in the hospital came to be more in the nature of an occupation than of service in the name of God and in the interests of salvation. The growing rationalism of the hospital is evidenced also in the later Renaissance period with the increasing links of the hospitals to the national government in its civilian aspects and with the processes and structures of mercantilism and industrialization.

These changes from health spa to a differentiated urban institution were surely profound. Still, "As it emerged from the medieval period the hospital was essentially an instrument of society to ameliorate suffering, to diminish poverty, to eradicate medicity, and to help maintain public order."[9]

But although these changes foreshadowed a more contemporary view that the nurturing of good health was in the national interests of the societies involved, hospitals in the Western world at least remained essentially under local control, and this militated against the implementation of any really effective society-wide health plan or policy. This situation continued in most of the Northern European countries until the end of the last century and is still the case in the United States. In fact, one of the striking paradoxes in the present milieu is the enunciation of the importance of health as a civil right while promoting the continuation of the pattern of political and cultural pluralism that anchors the hospital to the local community rather than rendering it responsive to the articulated need for a working national health policy.

The Renaissance and the Age of Rationalism were undoubtedly important in effecting the importance of rational administration in hospitals as well as increasing the base of pluralistic control. And these in turn, can be readily traced to democratization and economic growth in the Western world.

In broad historic outline, we now possess a complex of hospitals in which in terms of operational policy and programs the physicians have emerged as supreme, surpassing all others in the scope and effectiveness of their influence, and of predominating importance in reacting to possible insults occurring from outside forces.

HOSPITALS AS INSTITUTIONAL EXTENSIONS

Our present hospital system has not taken root and arisen without retaining important elements of normative systems that at one time in history may have been preeminent in the structure and functioning of hospitals.

Hospitals still retain some shadow of their former *sacred* nature, conveying to patients as they do expectations of humanism, diffuseness of interest, and omnimpotence. Second, hospitals have become a center for the promotion of the *scientific* norms of empirical truth and validity, certain important self-correcting functions, the communistic sharing of ideas and information, a search for logical consistency, and, perhaps above all, a pervading organized skepticism. Third, the *professional* norms entered the hospital quite early in its history: guildism and its associated protectionism, the claims to autonomy, lack of accountability, expertise, elite entrepreneurism, and the enforcement of monopolistic dominance over those served. In addition, the observer may note the presence of the associated *technical* norms of universalism, predictability, the maintenance of affective neutrality in human relations, and objectivity sometimes bordering on disenchantment. Entering rather later are the *bureaucratic* rules of rationality, order, rational predictability and calculation, a tendency to expand domains, and the tendency toward insulated self-perpetuation. Finally, note must be taken of the hospitals' fundamental general *collectivity* orientation, involving external democratization, surrounding political and social pluralism, and a continual threat of boundary permeation by others.

Only the last serves as a threat to the practice of organizational autonomy and professional dominance; all of the others—sacredness, scientism, professionalism, technocracy, and bureaucracy—have at one point or other entered into hospital structure historically, remained there, and presently contribute the enormous asymmetry that now characterizes the relationships of hospitals to their internal milieus and their external environments. No two of these sets of overarching norms are entirely consistent with each other. No matter. Even though logical consistency may be absent and conflict to be expected as the proponents of each compete for ideological, technological, organization, and resource dominance, their very liveliness and ubiquitousness contributes to the dominance the hospital is able to exercise over those who fall into its orbit.

SPONSORSHIP, CHARTERS, AND CONTEMPORARY TYPES OF HOSPITALS

Given the above generalizations concerning the overall normative structure of hospitals, it is not difficult to find concurrence with the assertion that "all hospitals are different but very much alike." And as we come closer to the contemporary scene, we are impressed with the vast array of different types of hospitals that are in existence. How may we seek for order amid the seemingly infinite array of types of hospitals we can observe around us? For there are *large* hospitals and *small* ones.[10] There is the big division between *private* hospitals, which treat people in relation to their capacity to pay and are therefore answerable to the special market forces sketched in Chapter 3, and the numerous *public* institutions, which accept patients merely on the strength of their citizen status and are answerable to monies generated in the political arena of a community.[11] There are those hospitals that distinguish themselves by dealing primarily, or exclusively, with specially selected diseases and disabilities.[12] Such as hospitals for the tubercular and rehabilitation institutes for the permanently damaged and the intellectually deficient.[13] There are places, often called "hospitals," where people who are summarily defined as insane are squirreled away.[14] There are institutions catering mainly to surgical as against medical regimens of care;[15] community general hospitals and teaching hospitals;[16] hospitals standing on the forefront of research and change and dealing with some of the intransigent and difficult medical problems;[17] an especially elaborated set of medical institutions for those in military service.[18] If we are to include the teaching of medical students as a primary component,[19] there are places where patients are seen, and sometimes treated, on a nonresidential basis. We must also include neighborhood and community health centers, where there is considerably more equity and symmetry in the relative influence exercised by persons other than medical doctors.[20] There is the important distinction between private hospitals that are nonproprietary and those of a proprietary character. And there is the important difference between what Belknap and Steinle have referred to as the two major types of private community-oriented nonproprietary hospitals—the so-called "restricted" versus the "nonrestricted" hospitals. Moreover, there are hospitals set aside almost exclusively for mothers or for the very young, or for people of advanced years,[21] or for those who are approaching a natural death.

The list could undoubtedly be lengthened. Suffice it to say, however, that the differences between hospitals are at least as striking as are their commonalities, and it is to these differences that we now turn.

At the beginning, it is important to keep in mind the dictum that structural differentiation in a society is a function of the twin processes of population density on the one hand and technological development on the other. That is, without a population sufficiently large and varied to support highly differentiated hospitals, and without at least the presumption of the existence of a technology and a division of complexity within the medical establishment itself, the vast range of different kinds of hosiptals we observe around us simply would not exist. The hospital systems of Boston, New York City, or Atlanta bears little or no resemblance to the medical facilities existing in Scituate, Rhode Island; Peterborough, New Hampshire; or Medina, New York. Nevertheless, rapid transportation and communication do make it possible under certain organizational circumstances for the residents of the latter three hamlets to find themselves receiving care in one of the three aforementioned medical centers. However true it might be that a hospital in one community may cover the uncovered contingencies that may arise in another smaller community, for the most part it remains true that the fate of most people, for most of their illnesses including fatal ones, is in the hands of the medical organizations in the community in which they and their physicians have direct involvement. Over and above population size and the condition of local technocracy, what determines the shape and form a hospital is likely to take? The answer seems to lie in the existing state of *functional differentiation* in a community and the sponsorship a hospital is able to establish; the first involves the *justification* a hospital may be able to secure for itself; the second is the *charter* by which a hospital is contractually constrained.

CHARTERS AND JUSTIFICATIONS: FROM RESTRICTED COMMUNITY HOSPITALS TO COSMOPOLITAN SPECIALTY HOSPITALS

The kind of work a hospital undertakes and for whom, as well as the degree of autonomy it enjoys in setting its goals and its freedom in pursuing them, is a joint function of its *charter* and its *justification*. Let use consider the charter first.[22]

All formal organizations, hospitals included, operate under the conditions of a charter. This refers to a legal or quasi-legal set of contractual relationships with external agents or institutions that legitimize the institution, offer it political and economic support of various kinds, sanction and authorize its goals, and in various ways monitor its performance and as a consequence either continue to charter it, alter its chartering arrangements, or cancel the charter altogether. In its essentials, the organization's charter delineates, either directly or by interpretation, the extent of control the chartering agents relinquish to the control of direct organizational participants, both in terms of the *ends*, or *goals*, to be pursued as well as the *means*, or *procedures*, by which goals are to brought about. In some cases both organizational *means* and *ends* are left more or less to the discretion of the direct organizational members. In others control of means and ends is retained by the chartering agents and agencies. In still other cases the charter may retain control of ends while relinquishing exclusive domain over means to be employed. Or the reverse may be the case. By such a manner of reasoning, the reader can quickly grasp that the independent of *organizational means* and *organizational ends* yields four distinctively different organizational types, as shown in Table 6.6.[23]

As suggested in Table 6.6 the hospital enjoying an *autonomous charter* is in the favored position of determining what tasks it will undertake and how it will organize itself to pursue those tasks. In the field of health, the large-scale privately sponsored proprietary hospital

TABLE 6.6

Control of organizational means and ends, and organizational charters

Internal control of means	INTERNAL ORGANIZATIONAL CONTROL OF ENDS	
	Yes	*No*
Yes	Autonomous charter	Professional charter
No	Negotiated charter	Constricted charter

SOURCE: Adapted from William R. Rosengren and Michael S. Bassis, *The Social Organization of Nautical Education: American, Britain, and Spain.* Lexington, Mass.: Heath, 1976.

comes closest to fitting this type. (There are presently rather few of these, although the newly developed community health centers, originally generated out of the Office of Economic Opportunity and other more recently sponsored federal programs, also resemble this type.) At the opposite extreme, the hospital with a *constricted charter* functions under close constraint in terms of both the goals it pursues and the means at its disposal and discretion to operate. What comes to mind when the term "typical state hospital" is used exemplifies such a situation. Third, the relatively large-scale privately sponsored hospital, although this may also be true of the "specialty" nonproprietary psychiatric hospital, exemplifies the *negotiated* type, while the university-based teaching hospital probably comes closest to the hospital with a *professional* charter.

In terms of locating prior causes, the nature of a hospital's sponsorship seems most critical in determining the type of charter under which it must operate, particularly whether external sponsorship is by multiple or single agents and whether the "charge" sponsors give to a hospital is loose or close in nature.

In the case of the first type of charter, the autonomous, the typical sponsorship pattern involves reliance upon multiple but uncoordinated sponsors working in loose coordination with one another in relation to a loose charge. The result of such an arrangement is a weak system of monitoring and control of organizational autonomy with regard to the establishment of means and ends. The large-scale multipurpose private community hospital most nearly approximates such a model. Accordingly, the autonomous hospital draws its financial resources from several sources rather than one, is likely to contain numerous semiindependent "boundary-spanning" units to influence and where possible coopt elements in the external environment, and is otherwise endowed with program flexibility and environment control denied to hospitals operating under different kinds of charters. Moreover, inasmuch as its charter contains a loose charge, it may pursue a variety of different goals, which may change as contingencies in the internal and external environment change, and is subject in only the most general way to accountability and monitoring links to the external environment. As will be explained later, such a charter has important consequences for the kinds of health care activities—at a programmatic level—that are likely to arise in such institutions. In sum, the autonomous hospital is more or less "in command" of organizational means and ends, and leads among other things to the development of a flexible and debureaucratized form of internal structure.

The hospital operating with a constricted charter is more frequently to be found in state psychiatric hospitals and other "specialty" hospitals. Here sponsorship is by a single external agency imposing a close charter. In effect, such a hospital is little more than a component and subordinate unit in a larger bureaucratic-type organization, the effects of which are felt directly at the program level. The tendency of such a hospital is to sharply delimit program flexibility and to adhere as far as possible to externally imposed bureaucratic constraints. As such, the "constricted" hospital is subject to all of the pathologies commonly attributed to such organizations while seeking for rational efficiency as well as standardized methods for measuring bureaucratic performance criteria. Whereas the autonomous hospital enjoys a considerable degree of freedom from bureaucratic constraint, it cannot avoid the hazards involved in engaging in organizational risk-taking.

Both the negotiated and professionally chartered hospitals represent mixed types. In the case of the first, sponsorship takes the form of a coordinated coalition of external interested parties who together exercise relatively strict control over the internal procedures and strategies to be employed within the hospital setting while leaving open the entire question of long-term hospital goals as far as the outcome of cases is concerned, either in the individual case or in the aggregate. In such a situation, hospitals with a negotiated charter are closely monitored in terms of procedural activities but are allowed considerable latitude as far as long-range treatment goals and ideology are concerned. Such a situation is most typically the case with regard to special hospitals or units therein—practicing highly specialized technologies and especially those that involve monitoring and licensing procedures on the part of external agents. Thus, a hospital or unit specializing in organ transplantation may experience very tight supervision and close monitoring of its operational procedures, while be left entirely open as to the moral and ethical questions of the justification for the use of this technology. The same situation may occur in institutes offering only hemodialysis services—close external control over the technology employed, but virtually without control or even guidelines as to the social psychological circumstances under which the technology is to be employed. Hence the negotiated hospital tends to be bureaucratized at the operational level but debureaucratized at the social output or policy level, thereby given enormous freedom in this second and most vital process linking such a hospital to the surrounding social order.

Now just the opposite situation is found in the hospital operating under a "professional" charter, which allows for internal organizational control over means or procedures but is restricted at the goals-ends levels. In such an institution (a teaching hospital approximates this) there may be general consensus, implicit in the charter, as to the primary purpose of such an institution, whereas the means to fulfill that purpose is given over into the hands of the direct organizational participants—to wit, the great diversity found in modes of medical education as sketched in the previous chapter. Again, some specialty hospitals may exemplify such a charter, and obstetrical hospitals again stand as a prime example in which general purposes are literally without negotiation, while modes for conducting steps toward those purposes may vary dramatically, from the factorylike assembly line of some such places to the more homelike atmosphere of the midwife-administered nursing home.

In any event, it should be kept in mind that there is no *one* form of hospital sponsorship presently serving as the single such model. The range of external interested parties who may combine in various ways to create a hospital chartering arrangement is virtually without limit in terms of possible sponsorship systems. And in that sense, vast arrays of "external interested parties" may exercise enormous influence on the program growth, development, and policy expression in the contemporary hospital scene.

In addition to the not-so-subtle effects of ethnicity as a factor in sponsorship as outlined earlier in this chapter, Belknap and Steinle have provided a somewhat more detailed, and in some ways more informative, look at the importance of sponsorship to charters and hospital operations.[24]

THE COMMUNITY HOSPITAL AND LOCAL COMMUNITY 'LIVELINESS'

Belknap and Steinle were concerned with the vital issue of what might cause one community to possess a general hospital delivering good quality and broad scope medical care, while another similar community had a community general hospital system of considerably lower quality and offering medical services of a sharply delimited kind. It is to be remembered that the studies of hospitals considered thus far have addressed the matter of quality of care in only the most indirect fashion. This one deals with it as a prime consideration.

Proceeding under the assumption that local general hospitals were in fact creatures of their surrounding community in ways that go deeper than mere objective measures of superficial community characteristics, the researchers selected two cities in Texas that were matched for certain basic socioeconomic features. The researchers then compared the structure and quality of the general hospitals in these cities, and finally examined some hypotheses concerning the relationship between the communities' social structure and the quality of their hospital programs. In order to conceal their true identity, one community was called "Centralia," which was determined to have a far less adequate hospital system than did its matched mate, "Watertown."

The two communities were remarkably similar in a number of important respects, as summarized in Table 6.7. In addition to sharing a similar surrounding social economic and cultural environment, the two cities were remarkably alike internally in a number of important respects: The average and aggregate income of the two populations were almost identical, as was the percentage of doctors in each who had achieved board certification in a medical specialty. The available medical talent was virtually the same. Moreover, although there was some difference in the patient load carried by doctors in the two

TABLE 6.7

Characteristics of 'Centralia' and 'Watertown': the search for community origins of adequate hospitals

Characteristic	Centralia	Watertown
Median per capita income	$3219	$3312
Percent of physicians who were board-certified	32.8	34.2
Number of persons per physicians	1220	1021
Number of hospital beds	430	470
OCCUPATIONAL STRUCTURE:		
Percent of Persons Employed in:		
Agriculture	9.5	8.0
Mining	0.3	3.5
Construction	7.7	11.0
Transportation-communication	7.5	7.7
Wholesale and retail	26.1	24.5
Finance, insurance, etc.	3.7	3.5
Business and personal services	7.1	8.0
Professional and semiprofessional	11.4	7.0

SOURCE: Adapted from Ivan Belknap and J. Steinle, *The Community and Its Hospitals.* Syracuse: Syracuse University Press, 1963. By permission.

towns, the difference was not great. At the same time, the hospitals in each town had approximately the same number of hospital beds in which to treat ill persons. Perhaps of most importance is the fact that the shape of the occupational structure in the two towns was strikingly similar. Each had roughly the same proportion of persons employed in all of the key economic sectors, indicative of an underlying similarity in educational attainment, income distribution, and, by indirection, probably differential distribution into illness categories. But important as these fundamental similarities may be, the similarities stop here and differences between the two begin to manifest themselves. Some of these differences are summarized in Table 6.8.

In very nearly every respect on which agreement can be reasonably expected, the hospital serving Watertown rates superior to that in Centralia: A larger proportion of Watertown's physicians are board-certified. As is typically the case in effective hospital administration, strong authority was vested in the chiefs of service in Watertown. Moreover, Watertown'had an active social service department, and each admission was routed through that department and dealt with on an individual-case basis. This was not true in Centralia. At the same time, the hospital in Watertown had strong working links with the local Social Welfare Department, whereas patients in Centralia remained only within the scope and purview of their private physician. There was an effort in Watertown to coordinate the hours of the clinic service with the prevailing patterns of work shifts in the community. Staff meetings were held regularly, and admissions were usually made directly to a specialty ward rather than to a general ward, the latter being indicative of specialty consultation prior to hospitalization. The internship program at Watertown was more highly developed and effective. As a rough indicator of referral efficiency, death rates in the hospital were higher in Watertown than in Centralia. The implications of this may not be entirely self-evident to the student but deserve some discussion in class. Watertown's link to the community was also evidenced by its active outpatient clinic. And while the implications of cost differentials may not be immediately evident, it is worth noting that costs were *higher* in Watertown than in Centralia. Finally, staff morale was good in the Watertown hospital but low and openly hostile to the administration in Centralia.

Furthermore, with but one or two exceptions, clinical procedures used in Watertown were superior to those in Centralia, *in spite* of the general availability of identical technologies to the staff in each of the hospitals.

Lastly, and in connection with the earlier discussion on medical care costs, differences in the physical plant are worth nothing. In general, the physical plant in Watertown was more completely geared

TABLE 6.8

Contrasts between a 'good' hospital and a 'poor' hospital system

Characteristics	Centralia's poor hospital	Watertown's good hospital
ORGANIZATIONAL FACTORS		
Percent of staff physicians board-certified	29%	34%
Authority of chiefs of staff	Weak	Strong
Social service	No case work; admission by each M.D.	Admission through Social Service Department
Relation to City Social Welfare Department	None	Strong coordination
Relation to work tempos of community	Clinic hours uncoordinated with community	Clinic hours coordinated with community work tempos
Staff meetings	Timing irregular	Regularly scheduled
Admissions	To general ward	To specialty wards
Internships	8, AMA approved; filled by U.S. M.D.s	4, none approved; filled by foreign M.D.s
Efficiency of referrals	Low death rate in hospital	High death rate in hospital
Community service	No outpatient clinic	Active outpatient clinic
Staff morale	Staff generally hostile	Staff identified with hospital
Cost factors	Low costs per patient	High costs per patient
CLINICAL FACTORS[a]		
Surgical procedures	2.4	3.7
Progress notes	2.8	3.8
Histories and physicals	3.1	3.1
Nurses' notes	4.1	4.2
Lab reporting	3.0	4.0
PHYSICAL FACILITIES		
Percent of Total Space Devoted to:		
Bed space for patients	33%	44%
Diagnostic and treatment	18%	24%
Public space	31%	15%
Administrative work	6%	10%

[a] Clinical procedures were rated on a scale from 0 to 5; the higher the score, the better were the clinical procedures.
SOURCE: Adapted from Ivan Belknap and J. Steinle, *The Community and Its Hospitals.* Syracuse: Syracuse University Press, 1963. By permission.

to patient services than was true in Centralia. In the latter hospital, an excessive amount of highly expensive space was allocated to non-treatment type activities such as public uses (lobbies, lounges, gift shops, restaurants, etc.), and administrative uses (office, record storage, and so forth). Watertown was particularly advantaged in the proportion of available space devoted to bed space for patients, and special diagnostic and treatment facilities.

Thus by whatever standard one wishes to apply, and for which data are readily available, Watertown's hospital was clearly better than Centralia's. Given the numerous similarities between the two cities, why should this be so and how can such situations be averted? Belknap and Steinle offer some valuable clues—some internal to the hospitals themselves and some rooted in the social organization of the *constituencies* of these hospitals.

First, there were major differences in the internal structure of the two systems. Centralia had what has been referred to as a "restricted" type of organization, while Watertown's system was "unrestricted." Schematically, the two types are shown in Figures 6.1 and 6.2, respectively.

The restricted hospital in Centralia was similar to the kind of hospital structure typically found in private hospitals started some 40 years ago. Centralia's had not changed much since that time. It was a hospital organized in response to the needs expressed by a limited sector of the local population and organized in direct relation to the expressed and felt needs of that minority—namely, the clientele of the private physicians who staff it. Accordingly, the internal system was simple, with power invested in a diffuse way among the members of the medical staff dealing *directly* with *their* paying patients. External linkages were primarily *informal* through the local medical society, and administratively by the Board through the hospital administrator. This represents a hospital with a limited set of goals and a highly constricted type of charter that sharply limits the scope of services such a hospital is likely to provide and experiences limited program or goals inputs from other sectors of the surrounding community and its citizenry.

By way of contrast, the internal structure of Watertown's unrestricted hospital is far more complex and linked to external interested parties in a much more elaborate fashion. Sectors of the local governmental system has formal tie-ins with the hospital, particularly through the departments of Social Welfare and Public Health. The relation between medical staff and administrators are much closer, as are the direct working relationships between medical staff members and residents and interns. And quite aside from considerations of size, the unrestricted hospital offers a wider range of specialty services, especially to nonpaying patients. In general, the unrestricted hospital is

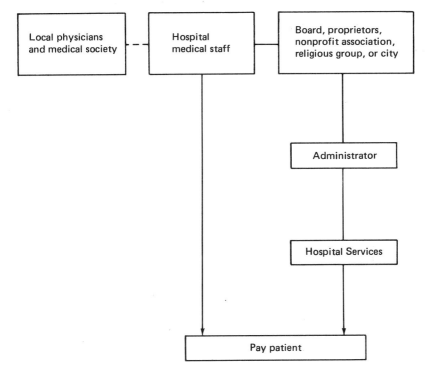

FIGURE 6.1 The restricted hospital.

Source: Adapted from Ivan Belknap and J. Steinle, The Community and Its Hospitals.
Syracuse: Syracuse University Press, 1963. By permission.

much more a part of the surrounding community than is the restricted hospital. It more nearly approximates a "community" institution as that term is normally applied. By present standards and ideology, the unrestricted hospital, offering a broad range of services to a wide spectrum of constituents, is currently to be preferred over the restricted model. How did these two types arise?

Although Belknap and Steinle offer an impressive amount of information of this important point, the answer seems to be that Watertown is a "lively" community, whereas Centralia is not. By "lively" is meant a community milieu in which people are aware of their community and its institutions and participate actively in their operation and elaboration. Some communities possess this elusive "liveliness," while others simply do not. It is not easy to generate artificially; it seems to depend on some processes of self-starting, which are not themselves altogether clear. In the case of Watertown and Centralia a number of factors seem to be involved in generating this liveliness, to which general responsiveness of the hospital system must be attributed.

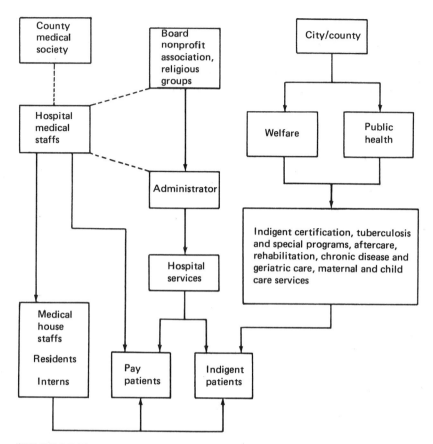

FIGURE 6.2 The unrestricted hospital.

Source: Adapted from Ivan Belknap and J. Steinle, <u>The Community and Its Hospitals</u>. Syracuse: Syracuse University Press, 1963. By permission.

First, Watertown had undergone rapid urbanization and population growth, increasing its population tenfold since 1920. Centralia, on the other, had experienced only sluggish growth and change during that period. But of most interest was the different composition of the governing boards of each hospital system, regarded here as the principal linkage to the community and serving as the charter-defining force in each community.

Watertown's Board was intimately linked to the local community power structure and tied in closely with the principal social institutions in the community. The Board was relatively young, and with low turn-over. The Board in Watertown had continuity over time, while Centralia's did not. In terms of power structure, however, the Board in Watertown was heavily loaded with members who were otherwise influential decision makers in the community. They were in addition continually in informal association with one another. Their relationship to the hospital was highly paternalistic, and they seemed to regard themselves as agents for the community at large and stewards of the townspeople. This pattern was very much less pronounced in Centralia, in which Board membership was essentially a sinecure for older members of community—a final accolade in a career of community membership—and not a charge of service yet to come, as was the case in Watertown. Moreover, the Centralia Board members were not informal associates as in the other town, nor did they represent a broad scope of community, population, and institutional interests in the community. In a sense the community, through the Board, was a participant in the structure and operation of the hospital in Watertown, while the absence of community "liveliness" in Centralia tended to yield a hospital insulated and isolated from the community and to encourage institutional atrophy. Centralia was operated on the basis of the prestige and influence that limited numbers of community groups are able to express in its constricted charter; Watertown was founded on the basis of multiple-interest groups, and its negotiated charter reflects that pluralism.

At one level, at least, a principal difference between Watertown and Centralia—currently an active debate in medicine generally—is the dispute between hospitals in which a strict "medical model" predominates, as against those leaning more in the direction of a "social model." This distinction, between a focused and specific versus a diffuse and multifaceted form of care, in one form or another constitutes a pervasive thread in this book. One way of considering types of hospitals from this broad perspective has been called the "client biography model," and we now turn to a discussion of that view of hospitals.

CLIENT BIOGRAPHIES AND HOSPITAL STRUCTURE AND DYNAMICS

People enter the medical establishment whether it be in a doctor's office or in a hospital as whole persons whose lives are a complex of experiences, commitments, engagements, and past and future directions. Although it may occasionally appear so, they do not enter as inanimate objects; however, they may sometimes be treated that way. Given the twin complexities of the human social personality and the multifaceted character of hospitals as organizations, the relations between hospitals and patients can be complex indeed. To what degree is it feasible, possible, or even desirable for hospitals to "take in" the whole person and still "get the job done"? The answer to this seemingly simple question is not at all simple. There is a very considerable literature indicating that the answer to this question of how hospitals elect to intervene in the biographical careers of their patients, sometimes influenced by some of the factors already mentioned in this chapter, can importantly affect the nature of life in the hospital for both patient and staff. Often this intervention goes far beyond the parameters of the mere technological efforts that are attempted.

In large measure, the variety of *types* of hospitals discernible is a close function of those client characteristics that a hospital *selectively* definies as being critical to its operation and that it attempts to incorporate into its spheres of activities.[25] Hospitals, that is, selectively intervene in the present and future lives of patients in varying scopes and in varying intensities. In fact, the delivery of any service such as health requires that hospitals intercede in the human careers of patients —to make an imprint upon the kind of person the patient will be, both in the here and now and later on in life. The fact that hospitals must be organized internally to bring about this desired change has important consequences for the kind of hospitals we experience around us.

From this point of view it must be obvious that a hospital may exhibit an interest in patients ranging from a truncated and abbreviated span of time—as in an emergency room—to a nearly infinite period— as in a long-term psychiatric facility, a chronic illness or rehabilitation hospital, or a tuberculosis sanatorium. Whatever the case, hospital resources, arrangement for work, and behavior toward patients are strongly influenced by the stake the hospital has in the patient's future, and the types of hospital that are revealed by such a view also range from those that are most compatible with a social model of illness as against a more strict medical model.

There is also a second type of career interruption, that is, hospitals may have an interest in a limited aspect of highly selected facets of their patients as products of an participants in society. Still others may elect for a broader scope of interest in patients, as in the case of some psychiatric services. In these, an effort is made to incorporate the entire person into the hospital system and to work on multiple facets of the human life simultaneously. In fact this perspective toward hospitals and patients yields four distinct types of hospitals, and hospitals within each category share certain important common organizational characteristics, however different their putative aims may appear to be. These are shown in Table 6.9. How do these general types of hospital affect the internal structure and dynamics of hospitals, and especially how patients are handled?

How are patients controlled?

The four types of hospitals outlined give rise to different kinds of patient control problems and to different arrangements for achieving compliancy.

TABLE 6.9
Hospital types and orientations toward patients

	PATIENT INTERVENTION	
Examples of hospitals	*Lateral (social space)*	*Longitudinal (social time)*
Acute general hospital emergency room	Specific (−)	Short-term (−)
TB hospital, rehabilitation hospital, medical school teaching hospital	Specific (−)	Long-term (+)
Short-term therapeutic psychiatric hospital	Broad (+)	Short-term (−)
Long-term therapeutic hospital; self-help community; neighborhood health center	Broad (+)	Long-term (+)

SOURCE: Adapted from William R. Rosengren and Mark Lefton, *Hospitals and Patients*. New York: Atherton, 1969, 125.

It is useful to make the distinction between *conformity* and *commitment* as modes of compliancy. In the case of compliancy through conformity, assuring patients' adherence to rules of conduct is the key problem. On the other hand, the investment of the patient in the ideology of the hospital is more at issue when commitment is desired. The broader the hospital's interest in the patient's life space, the larger will be the number of conduct alternatives on the part of the patient regarded as organizationally relevant. One important consequence is a large investment of staff time and effort in *determining* relevant rules for conduct and in devising strategies for enforcing them. In extreme cases this may lead to a reliance upon "control" expertise in the hospital, in which the distinction between clean work (service) and dirty work (control) becomes blurred, and the service ideology is informed by the need for control.[26] And these control contingencies may be increased when a "social model" is adopted.

Conversely, hospitals with a more focused interest in their patients are likely to be those in which the conformity of patients to *rules* is of lesser importance. In some cases, conformity may be regarded as given and therefore unproblematic. This may occur either because of the physical layout of the hospital (isolation wards and private rooms) or by the physical inacapacitation of the patient (e.g., quadraplegics in rehabilitation hospitals).

In the long-term hospital, however, the compliancy problem is different because the commitment to the patient's future biography may extend beyond the time when he or she will be physically present in the hospital. Here, rearrangement of the patient's life cannot be accomplished merely by manipulation or the exercise of coercion when the patient is "on the grounds." On the contrary, compliancy is best achieved by getting patients to believe in either the moral goodness or practical fitness of the future the hospital attempts to shape for them.

Here, the compliancy problem is attacked by transmitting an elaborate ideology to patients so that self-control may be exercised once he departs. Thus, although patients in a *medically* oriented psychiatric hospital are not expected to believe in or understand the theoretical grounds upon which the use of electroshock therapy rests, patients in a *socially* oriented hospital may experience a profound transformation because of the symbol systems to which they had been exposed.

A central difference between the long-term and short-term hospital is that in the former the patients are expected later to *control themselves*, whereas in the latter they are expected to conform in post-hospital life only insofar as enough was done *to* them in a mechanical sense while they were hospital patients. The broadly oriented hospital, however, is forced to impose a wide scope of conduct rules, which must then be accommodated in some way to its ethic of service.

Patterns of conformity and commitment take the shape as indicated in Table 6.10. Contrasting problems of patient compliancy—deriving from differential investments in the careers of patients—give rise to different types of problems for hospitals which are attended to by contrasting methods of resolution.

Problems of staff consensus

The nature of a hospital's concern with the patient also creates contrasting problems of consensus among the staff. A persisting dispute in hospitals has to do with whether agreement exists as to what work shall be done and how it should be accomplished. Hospitals confront this contingency in either of two ways. Conflict may be recognized and acted upon so that its resolution is given a formal place in the social structure of the hospital. On the other hand, conflict may be relegated

TABLE 6.10
How are patients controlled?

ORIENTATIONS TOWARD CLIENTS		COMPLIANCE PROBLEMS	
Specificity	*Time span*	*Conformity*	*Commitment*
—	—	No	No
+	+	Yes	Yes
—	+	No	Yes
+	—	Yes	No

TABLE 6.11
Problems of staff consensus

ORIENTATIONS TOWARD CLIENTS		CONSENSUS DIFFICULTIES ABOUT	
Specificity	*Time span*	*Means*	*Ends*
−	−	No	No
+	+	Yes	Yes
−	+	No	Yes
+	−	Yes	No

to an informal system of bargaining and negotiation. The patterns are indicated in Table 6.11.

In the short-term general hospital, for example, the specificity of orientation toward patients results in clear priorities as to the importance of different occupational skills in the quick repair job to be done. There is little basis upon which competitive processes can emerge to be incorporated in the officially sanctioned system of work. This finely graded system of status is reflected in nearly every sphere of activity in such a hospital, including the norms that guide interaction in the surgical team, permissible expression of humor among the staff, the adherence of staff members to official aseptic rules, and ceremonial standards governing the ways in which staff members of varying rank come together to constitute a working team.[27]

The specificity characterizing this kind of hospital, as well as the instant removal of the patient, implies little need to devise mechanisms for evaluating long-term outcome or to allocate hospital resources for this purpose. Nor is there a need to establish limits to long-term responsibility. In fact, the reverse is often the case: pressures exist to get the patient out quickly rather than to elongate his or her stay.

This does not mean that stress and strain do not occur in the highly focused "quick" hospital; rather, that it is seldom subject to formal procedures.[28] Conflict occurs at the informal, extrainstitutional level: claims for status are made by those whose place in the hierarchy of professional priorities is somewhere other than at the top. Power alignments develop among staff involving agreement of a *quid pro quo* type. But on the whole, structured competition for priority is blocked by the presumption of *rank inequality* that exists at both the operational and administrative levels.

This kind of socially oriented hospital is subject to pressures from the outside to take the "whole" person into account rather than some specific part of that person, and to intervene in the patient's life for a longer period of time. Considering the short-term general hospital as an archetype of the community institution, it is easy to see that its technical elegance and elaborate cadre of ancillary personnel lead to periodic interfaces with its "publics," which attempt to alter the hospital's existing priorities. Substantively, if the bane of the general hospital is the accusation that physicians are technically competent but often without human feeling, the cross borne by the more socially oriented hospital is that while general medicine may be well-meaning, its humane edifice rests upon a weak technological foundation.

Similar counterpressures are to be expected in terms of the hospital's intervention in the future life of the patient. Thus, the long-term tuberculosis hospital must somehow cope with patient's contention that they are retained as hospital property for too long. However, the short-term general hospital is often accused of discharging patients before they are fully recovered.

The reverse pattern is typical in the broadly oriented and long-term hospital. Here is to be found greater formal response to the presence of conflict. Such a hospital continually contrives official and new devices for dealing with conflict resolution. Although it may be true that the initial roots of conflict may arise out of the informal system of power alignment and personal negotiation, these issues are swiftly made subject to formal methods of solution. Here is to be found a proliferation of systems of communication, specialized staff and team meetings, and repeated attempts to develop a consistent and coordinate medical technology. The not infrequent outcome is a continual reorganization of systems of authority and decision making, continual addition of staff members with finely discriminated skills and techniques—all with an aim to resolving problems of technology coordination and staff conflict. In sum, the diffuse and long-term hospital involves a changing formal system of authority with a staff conflict culture.

The shape of hospital authority

The breadth of intervention in the patient's life space will have important consequences for the structure of authority within the operative or medical worker line, while the extent of intervention in the patient's future life course more loosely affects administrative authority.

In the general hospital, for example, the specific and short-term orientations will be accompanied by "pine-tree" forms of authority in both the operative and administrative lines. Conversely, broad and long-term interests in the patient's life will lead to dual "oak-tree" structures, as represented in Table 6.12.[29]

In contrast to the debureaucratized oak-tree pattern, one feature of pine-tree authority is a capacity for clarity and devisiveness in deicision making "at the top." Here the hierarchical pattern of authority renders decision making smooth, easy, and utterly understandable and acceptable to subordinates.

TABLE 6.12
The shape of hospital authority

ORIENTATIONS TOWARD CLIENTS		PATTERNS OF AUTHORITY	
Specificity	*Time span*	*Administrative*	*Operative*
−	−	△	△
+	+	▽	▽
−	+	△	▽
+	−	▽	△

Coser has pointed out some of the consequences of these differences as observed on both a surgical and a medical ward:[30]

> . . . the line of communication on the medical floor is clear-cut and follows a scalar system, decision-making there generally proceeds through consensus. On the surgical floor, however, where the line of communication is not strictly adhered to, authority is not, as might be expected, diffused and shared, but tends to be concentrated and *arbitrary,* with decision proceeding by fiat from the visiting doctor or the chief resident.

Jules Henry also has noted some of the problems connected with each kind of authority system, and especially how the oak-tree pattern arises out of a broad concern with the patient's life space.

In the typical general hospital the specificity of intervention in the patient's present and future life leads to a dominant technological core around which a priority of occupational skills can be devised. Moreover, task assignments are likely to be so highly differentiated that line workers—nurses, for example—have little difficulty in locating their place in the overall operation. Hence, this pattern of authority results in formalized rules for conduct that are more or less easy to follow.

Finally, a further important consequence of oak-tree structures for hospitals is staff dissatisfaction at the lower levels. As Henry says:[31]

> . . . the organizational structure was not considered satisfactory by the personnel; the data showed much agreement that it was difficult to work in the system, that there was a problem of definition of function, and that information did not "behave" as it should. Differences in orientations of hospitals not only result in these kinds of authority patterns in hospital, but also call for the presence of different kinds of professional and occupational representatives.

Hospital types and staffing shape

When hospital work is defined in different ways, it demands the presence of persons with different kinds of skills and of varying professional stature. Often when full professionals are not available, less talented and less trained people are elevated to professional status in a hospital and expected to do this work. More generally, however, variations in the hospital's efforts to alter the present and future life course of patients results in differing proportions of professional and administrative personnel, as shown in Table 6.13.[32]

A short-term commitment to the patient means that only a few highly specialized administrative tasks have to be accomplished. This is in distinction to a long-term hospital, where a larger administrative *cadre* is needed to maintain records and to seek out, codify, and nurture contact with *departed* patients.

By virtue of the short period of time for which patients are in general hospitals, administrative tasks are focused and routinized, requiring a small number of "officer" status personnel, and a correspondingly larger number of clerks, stenographers, medical secretaries, and so forth.

Administrative patterns in the long-term hospital are likely to be quite the reverse. Work here is not subject to routinization, but contains many of the elements of policymaking. It is, therefore, more frequently implemented by staff personnel rather than clerks.

Similar patterns will be the case among the *operational* contingents in hospitals. That is, specificity of orientation will lead to a comparatively small, though organizationally powerful, professional medical staff. Specificity of focus implies that the hospital's work rests upon an articulated technology, the implementation of which requires that work be organized around a single professional group whose "property" the technology is: physicians in general hospitals, psychiatrists in psychiatric hospitals, physiatrists in rehabilitation hospitals, and so forth. Moreover, the medical technology used in such a hospital is not the exclusive product, property, or domain of the specific hospital in which it is practiced. Rather, it stems from and belongs to a farflung professional and scientific community. This fact has implications for the *audience* to which different types of hospitals address themselves. This small conspicuous professional staff in the specifically

TABLE 6.13
Hospital types and staffing shape

ORIENTATIONS TOWARD CLIENTS		PROPORTIONS OF STAFF COMPONENTS	
Specificity	Time span	Professional	Administrative
−	−	Small	Small
+	+	Large	Large
−	+	Small	Large
+	−	Large	Small

focused hospital is supported by a correspondingly larger number of ancillary personnel whose skills are selected and differentially rewarded on the basis of their presumed contribution to the main professional focus.

A broad interest in the patient is likely to weaken the dominance of any particular medical group, through the employment of a large variety of semiprofessionals who are awarded at least the accolade of equal status and responsibility. This process may lead to the domination of the operative activities of the hospital by lower-level semiprofessionals or even nonprofessionals. Cooptation by lower-level workers can occur especially when the hospital is economically pinched, as in the case of many state psychiatric hospitals that attempt to treat the "whole person" without a corresponding increase in resources.

The pseudoprofessionalization characteristically occurring on the heels of a broad social orientation toward the client can have profound effects upon hospital policy in general and upon the degree to which novel and creative innovations in medical care emerge.

This is perhaps no better illustrated than by the following:[33]

> The desired end of such a meeting of minds is that it be on the common ground of investing energy in learning. On this basis, personnel can come to understand that Milieu Rehabilitation is not a matter of a professional person applying his knowledge and having orders carried out, but that it is a research enterprise every step of the way with every client. Viewed from this perspective *personnel are in no way providing purely ancillary services in the usual sense* . . . they are research workers whose powers of observation, thoughts, and communication are vitally important. (italics mine)

In contrast to the more specifically focused hospital, this kind is more likely to construct a special rationalization as well as a unique modus operandi. It is, in short, strong on ideology but weak on technique. This difference in the technological equipment of hospitals has important consequences for the introduction of innovations.

Innovations in hospitals

Hospitals may innovate in either of two ways. They may introduce *technological* changes such as new mechanical equipment, new ways to organizational efficiency, reduction of time-cost formulas, more accurate criteria for evaluating work production, and the like. Or hospitals may innovate at the *ideological* level. The development of new rationalizations, novel conceptions of the "meaning" of the work being done, alternate ideas to justify goals, and variations in cause-and-effect ideas are here involved.

It is proposed that innovation occurs as shown in Table 6.14. In

TABLE 6.14
Innovations in hospitals

ORIENTATIONS TOWARD CLIENTS		SUSCEPTIBILITY TO INNOVATION	
Specificity	*Time span*	*Technical*	*Ideological*
−	−	Yes	No
+	+	No.	Yes
−	+	Yes	Yes
+	−	No	No

the specifically focused hospital the presence of a selected and well-articulated technological core makes it possible for the institution to *add to this* repertory in an *additive* sense. The longer and more salient this additive process becomes, the less such a hospital is able to turn away from its highly focused orientation, reverse its course, and adopt a broad orientation toward its patients. The more elaborate and sophisticated the medical technology becomes, the less it will be seen as resting upon whatever ideological backdrop may have originally led to this establishment. The more specifically focused a hospital becomes, the greater is its propensity to accommodate technological innovations that can be rationally integrated with those it already contains. This may partially account for the oft-noted difficulties in attaching *functionally meaningful* social or psychiatric service departments in general hospitals.

But this kind of "quick-repair/quick-release" hospital is but minimally susceptible to ideological innovation. The lack of a long-term engagement with the patient means that such an organization has little contact with all those other organizations that may later be responsible for the patient's future. As a result, it has few occasions to take part in the dialogue of multiple organizations in contact, which can often be the source of reassessments of the aims and meanings of work. Because the patient's reorganized life is seen as satisfactorily accomplished through the application of a relatively specifit technology, such changes can quite easily be though of as separate form, and certainly not dependent upon, a coordinate ideological foundation. The specifically focused and short-term institution can be that which best embodies the process of cultural lag as found in organizations: dramatic advances in technological repertory combined with an ideological framework perhaps more relevant to an earlier era.

The more broadly focused and long-term hospital stands as a contrasting type, subject as it is to a great deal of ideological turmoil and a minimum of effective technological innovation. Such an institution contains a multiplicity of technologies, and as a result the central organizational problem is coordination rather than addition.

A third type of hospital—the specifically focused *and* long-term institution—is subject to *both* technological and ideological foment. The rehabilitation hospital exemplifies such a pattern. Here the operatives and administrators each sponsor a different form of innovation and change and must often face each other in conflict as to which shall have priority. The conflict centers on which shall take precedence, the changing conception of the "mission" of the hospital as it may influence the long-term social welfare of the patient or an increase in the hospital's machine technology. Such institutions may be suspended in a state of continual crisis and dilemma, with the patients as the most alienated of participants—confused about the hospital's claims for technological efficiency and its appeals for self-transformation.

This discussion relates to yet a further issue; decision making about patients and the pacing of the flow of work.

Work rhythms in hospitals

Imperative decisions are those regarded as inescapable, and compelled by forces and processes not reducible to persuasive strategies. These kinds of decisions about patients are ones in which the human being serves merely as the articulating agent or vehicle transmitting the decision to others so that its irreversible outcome may be implemented. *Judgmental* decisions are different; they are created out of interaction and communication and hence are tentative. In contrast to imperative decisions, these *are* reversible and permit numerous alternatives. In short, imperative decisions have a "thinglike" quality, whereas judgmental decisions are more nearly the product of social construction.

The distinction between rapid and slow is also one of degree. Work in some hospitals is done much faster than is work in others. In some hospitals one aspect of the treatment process follows more or less instantly upon the heels of earlier parts: a surgical sequence as compared with psychoanalysis is a case in point. The manner by which decision making and work tempos relate to the hospital's orientations toward the patient is shown in Table 6.15.

The specific orientation in the general hospital, combined as it is with a highly articulated division of labor, is often accompanied by the development of *sequential patterns* of work. Here, one activity must await the completion of a prior state. However subtly, the activation of stage B is contingent upon the empirical facts signaling the completion of stage A. Thus, the decision maker must be sensitive to the criteria that compel the work to move on to the next stage, rather than be

TABLE 6.15
Work rhythms in hospitals

ORIENTATIONS TOWARD CLIENTS		WORK RHYTHMS	
Specificity	Time span	Decision making	Work tempos
−	−	Imperative	Rapid
+	+	Judgmental	Slow
−	+	Imperative	Slow
+	−	Judgmental	Rapid

concerned with the readiness of other workers to express their agreement with the decision. Both patients and staff are carried along by forces that they can oversee but cannot reverse.

In the case of the obstetrical hospital, work has this sequential and imperative character:[34]

> The normal circuit: admitting room, to prep room, to labor room, to delivery room, to recovery room, and finally to the lying-in room is adhered to scrupulously. Timing may also be disturbed if key personnel happen to be absent from one of the places in the timing sequence. One evening, for example, a man rushed into the service claiming that his wife was about to have her child and that no one was in the admitting office. The doctor's advice—in all candor and sincerity—was that she was probably in false labor, and then encouraged the man to return to the admitting room.

The same generic pattern holds for administrative activities in the short-term hospital: admission, securing of insurance policy numbers, recording of expended hospital resources, totaling of fees, exacting payment, and discharge of the patient. The relatively rapid tempo is obvious—the quicker one stage is complete, the more rapidly will the next impress itself upon the transmitter. Whether the hospital's concern with the patient *really* extends for two days or two years, the significant point is the sense of urgency about the work.

Sometimes, indeed, the rapid pace of work in such specifically focused hospitals can produce what the objective observer can regard only as macabre practices. Mechanic, in referring to Sudnow's study of the handling of death in two different hospitals, writes:[35]

> He illustrates in various ways how the handling of the dying patient may reflect the needs of the staff to cope with their work, even at the cost of committing significant improprieties. Sudnow, for example, observed a nurse trying to force a woman's eyelids closed before she dies because it would be more difficult to do so after she had died. . . . On a busy ward, where death is a frequent occurrence, the wrapping for the morgue may be started while the patient is still alive.

Events such as this involving time moving in advance of itself are characteristic of the highly focused and short-term hospital in which the social structures of decision making and work rhythms seem to outstrip the more naturally expected series of physiological events. In the obstetrical hospital previously referred to, for example, it was observed that:[36]

> Lack of a natural tempo seemed to be handled in a number of ways in order to impose a "functional" tempo where a "physiological" tempo did not exist. . . . In the delivery room itself, there seemed to be an attempt to impose a tempo—to adhere to a pace of scrubbing, of administering anesthesia, and so forth. There was also emphasis upon keeping track of the length of time involved in each delivery. . . . The "correct" tempo becomes a matter of status competition and a measure of professional adeptness. The use of forceps is also a means by which the tempo is maintained in the delivery room, and they are so often used that the procedure is regarded as *normal*.

Perhaps the most dramatic view of the crisis atmosphere that prevails in this type of hospital can be observed in the postmortem investigations into why the elaborate machine technology failed. These often acquire the tone of a judicial investigation, with the implication that some failed to "read" the imperative clues or acted too slowly after having read them. But the weekly staff conferences in the elite socially oriented psychiatric hospital communicate little of this sense of urgency and technical breakdown.

In comparison with the mechanistic criteria for decision making in the general hospital, a particularistic stance toward patients is possible here. This stems from the fact that the hospital is faced with a technology coordination problem, in which the relative weights given to each social medical intervention can be tailored to each case. Sequential activities are seldom found. Simple cause-and-effect assertions are seldom the basis of action. In short, imperatives are absent.

As a result decisions are made more on the strength of plausible argument. In extreme cases the root of decisions is not the nature of observation of the patient but more the unfolding of interpersonal relationships among staff members (the outcome of the human relations approach to supervision), the latent roles of some members, or the charisma of one person.

In addition, there is not the sense of urgency so characteristic of the short-term hospital. Events need not occur overnight. There is time to reflect, to ruminate, and to come to considered judgments. The pace of work is slow, stages of progression for patients are elongated, and movement between each stage is hardly perceptible. The patient is gradually coaxed and induced through such a hospital, rather than marched in an orderly sequence through it.

196 SOCIOLOGY OF MEDICINE

Thus the term "hospital" calls forth a rich variety of types of institutions that cater to the ill. They are not drawn out of a single mold, as a casual reading of history might suggest. The complexity of this diversity is both a function of the diversity and pluralism of modern societies at large, a commentary of the rapid and recent proliferation of technologies that can now lay claim to having a right to control some sector of the hospital community, as well as to the democratization process, which has helped to place hospital systems in the realm of the "public good" and therefore a target over which multiple interest groups attempt to gain dominance and control. In a broad sense, the different types of hospitals we see reflect the variety of accommodations hospitals can make to their relatively new position as reservoirs of services to be rendered in the interests of the "community" at large; they represent compromises between merely "some things" for "some people" and "all things" for "all people." The specialty hospitals deriving from a "medical model" of illness, treatment, and professional organization lean toward the former. The more broadly based and community-oriented hospitals resting on a "social model" of illness, treatment, and professional power and influence are inclined toward the latter. Whichever the case, the situation of the participating ill person is different depending upon the social milieu he or she enters as a patient.

A more focused consideration of the patient is the topic of the chapter to follow.

SCENARIO II

A Guttman scale of patient improvement in the specifically oriented "medical model" hospital

In a tightly organized rehabilitation hospital for the severely physically impaired, the entire program of patient rehabilitation is under the close supervision of a physiatrist (a specialist in physical medicine), who monitors patient progress from beginning to end and directs a complex hierarchy of paraprofessional in the actions to be taken in the rehabilitation program. No step is undertaken unless the prior one has been satisfactorily completed.

These steps are arranged as in a Guttman Scale. Each is assigned a score of ascending magnitude, and it has been found empirically that patients who have completed step 3 can also satisfactorily perform the tasks in steps 1 and 2, but are as yet unable to proceed to step 4 and higher. Also, it can also be assumed that a patient who can perform at step 8 can also perform all steps from 1 through 7, but is as yet unable to act on steps 9 and above. This is useful for classifying patients, assessing their progress, billing funding sources, planning discharge, and numerous other ancillary activities that can then be rationalized. As for example, in the case of patients with high spinal cord breaks (quadraplegics):

Step 1.   Can breathe during waking hours without assistance.
Step 2.   Can breathe while asleep with assistance.
Step 3.   Can chew and swallow solid foods without monitoring.
Step 4.   Can "hunch" shoulders.
Step 5.   Can flex wrist tendons.
Step 6.   Can "hook" finger.
Step 7.   Can sit upright without support.
Step 8.   Can turn over in bed.
Step 9.   Can operate electric wheelchair.
Step 10. Can pull on sock and trousers with hooked fingers and "hunching."
Step 11. Can move from bed to wheelchair unassisted.
Step 12. Can live at home under supervised care.

All of this is programmed for each patient, and careful direction and monitoring can speed up progress toward maximum rehabilitation. The long-term nature of this process is indicated by the fact that the step can theoretically be increased as the bureaucratized rehabilitation period is extended.

Hence, we have a Guttman-type treatment program.

NOTES

1   Edward Hallet Carr, *The New Society*. New York: Macmillan, 1951, pp. 5–6.
2   David N. Solomon, "Ethnic and Class Differences among Hospitals as Contingencies in Medical Careers," *American Journal of Sociology*, 65 (March 1961), 463–471.
3   Stanley Lieberson, "Ethnic Groups and the Practice of Medicine," *American Sociological Review*, 23 (October 1958), 549.
4   George Rosen, "The Hospital: Historical Sociology of a Community Institution," in Eliot Freidson, Ed., *The Hospital in Modern Society*. New York: Free Press, 1963, pp. 1–36.

5 Freidson, Ed., *The Hospital in Modern Society*, pp. vii–vix.

6 Lewis Mumford, *The City in History*. New York: Harcourt, 1961, p. 267.

7 Ibid.

8 Ibid.

9 Ibid.

10 William R. Rosengren, "Structure, Policy, and Style: Strategies of Organizational Control," *Administrative Science Quarterly*, 12 (June 1967), 140–164.

11 William R. Rosengren, "The Rhetoric of Value Transfer in Organizations," *Sociological Inquiry*, 41 (Winter 1971), pp. 47–56.

12 Renee Fox and Judith P. Swazey, *The Courage to Fail: A Social View of Organ Transplants and Dialysis*. Chicago: University of Chicago Press, 1974.

13 Robert B. Edgerton, *The Cloak of Competence: Stigma in the Lives of the Mentally Retarded*. Berkeley: University of California Press, 1967.

14 H. Warren Dunham and S. Kirson Weinberg, *The Culture of the State Mental Hospital*. Detroit: Wayne State University Press, 1960.

15 Rose Laub Coser, *Life on the Ward*. East Lansing: Michigan State University Press, 1962.

16 Raymond S. Duff and August B. Hollingshead, *Sickness and Society*. New York: Harper & Row, 1968.

17 Renee Fox, *Experiment Perilous: Physicians and Patients Facing the Unknown*. New York: Free Press, 1959.

18 David D. Rutstein, *The Coming Revolution in Medicine*. Cambridge: Massachusetts Institute of Technology Press, 1967.

19 Robert K. Merton et al., *The Student Physician*. Cambridge: Harvard University Press, 1957.

20 Frank Riessman, Jerome Cohen, and Arthur Pearl, Eds., *Mental Health of the Poor*. New York: Free Press, 1964.

21 Ivan Belknap and J. Steinle, *The Community and Its Hospitals*. Syracuse: Syracuse University Press, 1963.

22 William R. Rosengren, "A 'Nutcracker' Theory of Modern Organizations," *Sociological Focus*, 8 (August 1975), 271–282.

23 William R. Rosengren and Michael S. Bassis, *The Social Organization of Nautical Education: America, Britain, and Spain*. Lexington, Mass.: Heath, 1976.

24 Belknap and Steinle, op. cit.

25 William R. Rosengren and Mark Lefton, *Hospitals and Patients*. New York: Atherton, 1969.

26 Rosengren, "Structure, Policy and Style," op. cit.

27 Robert N. Wilson, "Teamwork in the Operating Room," *Human Organization*, 12 (Winter 1954), 9–14.

28 Anselm Strauss, Ed., *Negotiations: Varieties, Contexts, Processes, and Social Order*. San Francisco: Jossey-Bass, 1978.

29 Jules Henry, "The Formal Structure of a Psychiatric Hospital," *Psychiatry*, 17 (1954), 139–151.

30 Coser, op. cit.

31 Henry, op. cit.

32 William R. Rosengren, "Organizational Age, Structure, and Orientations Toward Clients," *Social Forces*, 47 (September 1968), 1–11.

33 Robert Hyde et al., *Milieu Rehabilitation*. Providence: Butler Health Center, 1962, p. 27.

34 William R. Rosengren and Spencer DeVault, "The Sociology of Time and Space in an Obstetrical Hospital," in *The Hospital in Modern Society*. E.

Freidson, Ed. New York: Free Press, 1963, p. 283.
35 David Mechanic, *Medical Sociology: A Selective View*. New York: Free Press, 1968, p. 88.
36 Rosengren and DeVault, op. cit., p. 283.

SUGGESTED READINGS

Rose Laub Coser, *Life on the Ward*. East Lansing: Michigan State University Press, 1963.
A comparative study of the social organization and dynamics of a medical and surgical ward, integrating conflict and functional points of view.

Raymond S. Duff and August B. Hollinghead, *Sickness and Society*. New York: Harper & Row, 1968.
An account of the process of hospitalization as experienced by patients.

Renee Fox, *Experiment Perilous*. New York: Free Press, 1959.
The special organizational problems encountered in dealing with patients suffering from mysterious or unknown maladies.

Eliot Freidson, Ed., *The Hospital in Modern Society*. New York: Free Press, 1963.
Twelve original chapters on various aspects of the sociology of hospitals from several different points of view.

Wolf Heyerbrand. *Hospital Bureaucracy*. New York: Dunellen, 1973.
A nationwide comparative study of factors inducing and impeding the emergence of bureaucratic structures and processes in hospitals.

Charles Perrow, "Hospitals: Technology, Structure, and Goals," in *Handbook of Organizations*, James G. March, Ed. Chicago: Rand-McNally, 1965.
A review article on the social structure of the hospital from a technological imperative point of view.

William R. Rosengren and Mark Lefton, *Hospitals and Patients*. New York: Atherton, 1969.
A literature review and conceptual model for the analysis of types of hospitals and their relations with patients.

SCENARIO I

Medicine and urbanization: the mass media incorporate indigenous medicine

Diagnoses to letter writers by Dr. Chandrasekhar G. Thakkur, *Calcutta Press,* Sunday, December 12, 1965:

To C.D., Bombay: You are suffering from Gonorrhoea and you are advised by take Chandraprabha pills No. 1, 2 in the morning and 2 in the evening with water, and Sarivadhyarishta ½ oz with equal quantity of water after principal meals. Also take Rasavana Choorna with Triphala Choorna at bedtime and in the morning, with a cupful of milk or water. This treatment will help you a lot. You should continue it for a month. The burning will disappear. I would advise complete abstinence for a couple of months.

Editor's Note: Dr. Chandrasekhar Gopalji Thakkar, Ayurvedacharya, will prescribe remedies to ailments through these columns every week. Readers may send queries to the Editor, *The Bharat Jyoti,* under closed covers superscribed "Medical Advice." All queries will be treated in the strictest confidence. All questions must be brief stating the nature of the illness, treatment undergone, age of the questioner. Inquirers are requested to give their full name and address to enable the doctor to communicate directly in case he feels it is necessary. It will also help prompt attention.

CHAPTER 7

The great and marginal systems of medicine

The development of any social institution is not unilinear, nor does the present manifestation of any social institution necessarily represent its final elaboration. By the same token, it is neither reasonable nor true to fact to expect any major social institution, at whatever level, to be thoroughly orderly and systematic in its present functioning. So too with medicine as we know and experience it. In a historical sense, it is probably fair to say that so-called Western medicine has been *additive* in character, acquiring over centuries of growth and change, encorporating within its boundaries untold numbers of new technologies, new organizational forms, new belief systems, and perhaps most important, new rationales and justifications for its growth and change. In this sense "new" diseases are constantly being discovered; old ones are virtually eliminated but do reappear now and then; new machines for the clinical analysis of illness are always being invented, as are new ways of intervening in disease-producing conditions; and so on. So Western medicine is additive in the sense that it carries with it over the years much of the old as it acquires the new.

Even within the practice of medicine itself a situation of "antagonistic cooperation" prevails regarding notions as to the principal causes of illness and priorities as to the preferred treatment modalities. Moreover, when the supply of patients appears to be short, a competitive and protective arrangement between medical organizations and medical personnel emerges. In short, what we understand to be the medical system is hardly a system in the technical sense at all. Only by the broadest extension of the meaning of words is Western medicine an "assemblage of objects united by some form of regular interaction or interdependence; an organic or organized whole." Thus, as diverse and multifaceted as medicine is, it is not without some consternation that the layman is able to distinguish "regular" medicine from the other somewhat more integrated forms the practice of medicine may in fact take.

THE APPEARANCES OF WESTERN MEDICINE

We "know" and recognize Western medicine largely on the basis of the *appearance* its practitioners make and the *social settings* in which its practitioners usually work. We know little, however, of the ongoing processes of medicine as a way of manipulating the body so as to try to produce healthy outcomes. A hospital, like a funeral parlor or library, has a recognizable claim to being what it purports to be largely as a result of its reputation as well as by its appearance, its mood, and its odors and thereby commands our trust and our compliance. A doctor's office, as well as the deportment of the personnel employed therein may also lay similar claims by virtue of similar superficialities. In the world of medicine, therefore, and as in other worlds in which people congregate for special purposes, things are *often* (not seldom) what they seem. Beyond casual inspection of certificates decorating the walls of doctors' offices or the lobbies and business offices of hospitals, the authenticity of medical practitioners both individual and organizational are only periodically and infrequently questioned by the members of the medical community itself, let alone by members of the lay public, who presumably have the most to lose. With the exception of the run-of-the-mill maladies that drive us to the doctor every now and then, and the relatively small— though growing—number of persons whose entire lives revolve around an illness of one sort or another, our consequential encounters with the world of medicine are more unfamiliar and unusual than they are familiar and commonplace. Hospitalization is traumatic for most people as are the diagnostic and treatment procedures to which we submit ourselves there. Even the laying on of hands at the doctor's office for a "routine" checkup is strictly out of the ordinary for most people.

Thus, on the basis of unsubstantiated trust alone do we give our bodies and eventually our lives into the care of strangers in strange places to do with largely as they will. We do much the same, of course, in the case of schooling, although what goes on in schools is subject to somewhat more external monitoring than is the case in what transpires beyond the drawn hospital curtain or the closed door of the operating theatre.

Why this unqualified trust in a complex of institutional practices with so many faults and inadequacies? The answer seems to lie first of all in the monopolistic nature of medicine as practiced generally in the Western world, and second in the eclectic diversity of the "science" of medicine as it is actually practiced.

As in the case of doing business with the telephone company, the electric power company, and the water works, the vast number of consumers have no real choice when it comes to the selection of medical care. The choice is largely an illusory one, involving either no medical care at all (and there have been and are numerous elaborations of this choice into various dogmas of nonmanipulative self-help and self-care) or taking what is offered by the established practice of Western medicine. And where the latter option is picked up (and this is in the vast majority of cases) the nearly absolute asymmetry of the doctor-patient relationship ends the illusion of free choice once that step is taken. Medicine is in this sense a self-controlling monopoly that in the phraseology of the business world, is both *laterally* and *vertically* organized. That is, Western medicine possesses the very powerful tool of having defined health in the broadest terms possible, so much so that virtually every undesirable facet of the human condition can be called a "health problem" and therefore legitimately subsumed under the heading of "health"—and therefore under the purvue and control of the medical world.

The author, for example, had a conversation with a faculty member at a distinguished medical school, and during its course I asked him whether he thought alcoholism was a disease, and he said, "Of course it is." I then impudently asked him why he thought so and he said, "Because doctors treat it." The flaw in such reasoning is obvious but in fact constitutes the primary justification for the monopoly "standard" medicine now has: The *activities* of its practitioners are now used as a *justification for medicine's domain,* not the other way around. Hence, if the practitioners of medicine alone are empowered to define whatever phenomena they wish as health-related and if the health-illness definers are even loosely organized into a closed monopoly, then choices in medical care become increasingly superficial and "cosmetic" in character rather than representing real alternatives to the pursuit of health. Perhaps as a result of this, those taking part in the health market place who are not certified and authorized by "allopathic" medicine to do so run the risk of falling victim to the pariah status of all "unauthorized" practitioners whatever the worth their uncertified services might in fact possess. Thus, *other* "great" indigenous medical systems as well as other more limited and circumscribed "special" but unauthorized treatments must bear the designations of being either "marginal" or "fraudulent."

ALLOPATHIC MEDICINE: ECLECTIC AND PRAGMATIC

Allopathic medicine is what most of us understand to be "standard" or "regular" medicine, as practiced and distributed by the practitioners we recognize as being legitimate, true, and credible. Allopathic medicine, therefore, is to be distinguished from the several other "great" and marginal practices of medicine to be sketched here: the indigenous ayervedic medicine in the Asian subcontinent of India, indigenous medicine as developed and practiced in China, and others such as homeopathy, osteopathy, chiropractic, naturopathy, dianetics, orgonomy, iridiagnosis, zone therapy, virilium sticks, goat gland therapy, and metal dynamism, as well as others, which are far afield and range from being "complete and alternate" medical systems to the patently fraudulent, to those which presently occupy some indeterminant status of fad, fashion, cult, or social movement.

In broad definition, allopathic medicine is that practice which combats disease by the use of remedies producing effects *different* from those produced by the disease treated, including the use of all measures that have proved to be of some value in the treatment of disease. Thus, from such a view, the human body in its normal state is free of disease, and any disease found must be regarded as a foreign incursion into an otherwise healthy organism. Further, allopathic medicine is rooted in the rather general idea that inasmuch as disease is foreign, its cure can usually be brought by the application of some form of "opposites" to it: surgery to remove the affected part, the ingestion of chemically compounded substances to "reverse" the course of disease; the application of various physical manipulation and physical exercises to "retrain" misused, unused, or atrophied parts; and where deemed necessary the "temporary reversal" of the ill person's social behavior (the adoption of the role of sick, which will be discussed at length in a later chapter) so as to allow one's body to recover and regenerate itself.

In this sense, and one or two others to be enumerated, allopathic medicine is indeed a system resting on the generalized notion that "opposites cure," and we may observe this theme in the reputed therapeutic effects of the above four modes of intervention—correction through surgery, the taking of specially prepared compounds, the manipulation of the body mechanism, and the gradual restoration of one's capacity and inclination to reshoulder normal social responsibilities. The doctrinaire elements in allopathic medicine seem to end at this point, and lead to the preeminence of the "medical model" as outlined earlier, while the remainder of the substance of the rather special features in allopathic medicine are to be found more in the realms of technique and social organization rather than epistemological thought.

How shall cures be brought about? It is at this juncture that diversity begins to be manifest in the sense that allopathic medicine from this state forward exhibits its propensity for eclecticism and pragmatism, resulting not only in multiple technologies over which doctors themselves argue but also in a variety of organizational forms for the delivery of these technologies, over which the conflict and debate is even more heated. Further, the two important phrases in the lexicon of allopathic medicine—"differential diagnosis" and "treatment of choice"—are part and parcel of this pragmatic diversity.

Allopathic medicine, therefore, is a *conglomerate of technologies,* all of which are located within the same institutional differentiation in the division of labor. This exceedingly important point sharply distinguishes the "fit" that is customarily found between technologies and social organization in contemporary society.

This consolidation of multiple technologies under a single organizational umbrella is made possible, and even crystallized and legitimized, by the fact that allopathic medicine is empirical in its approach to its definitions of illness and both eclectic and pragmatic in the standards of authentication it applies. This is to say that allopathic medicine is continually involved in a "search" process, assisted by a commitment to the medical model previously outlined, and its practitioners are generally reluctant to place dogma in front of the evidence of signs, symptoms, and clinical observation. Hence, allopathic medicine is at least *partially* scientific in the sense that Max Weber used the term as a system of thought which is continually outdating itself and possessing the dynamics of self-correction.[1] There is therefore a kind of tentativeness in allopathic medicine that often frustrates patients and may sometimes make yesterday's practice of medicine seem far out of date or even bungling and incompetent. In short, the allopathic practitioner is trained to look for "results" that are empirically verifiable and has no comforting doctrine to which to turn in cases in which patients unexplainably experience "spontaneous remission."

Hence, because of its eclecticism, allopathic medicine is able to accommodate within its own organizational ranks ideas of cure that may appear as inconsistent and conflicting as are regimens of surgery, medication, physical therapy, or social-psychological counseling, even for the identical malady. If it appears to "work" in the practice and experience of the individual practitioner, it may then be expected to be regarded as authentic by other members of the profession itself. This slippage and apparent inconsistency between technology and professional organization is handled in more than one way and is functional for the perpetuation of the ongoing professional organization of allopathic medicine in a variety of ways. First, it is highly supportive of the enormous amount of autonomy granted to individual practitioners in judging and evaluating their own work, and allows for the side application of the ideology of "clinical experience," which makes possible the recollection and observation of a handful of cases to transcend the reported experience of a large number of cases. The phrase, "The experience in my practice has been that . . . ," is often heard. Doctrinaire medicine would not tolerate such slippage.

There is the additional factor that the experience and accounting of special cases favors the illusion that inasmuch as clinical experience is so important for the effective practice of medicine, patients really do have a choice, because "getting along" with your doctor on the basis of something that resembles a personal standard is often considered at least as important as the objectively assessed technical competence of a health practitioner or health organization. The right to "choose one's doctor" is one of the most prevalent shibboleths of allopathic medicine and remains as an institutionalized appendage in nearly every organizational form of allopathic medicine in the Western world of which we know.

Further, this lack of fit between technology and professional organization makes it possible for the astounding specialization that now typifies allopathic medicine and yet preserves a quite monolithic professional organization and basis for professional identity of its members. It seems true that the highly trained expert in neurosurgery can barely communicate with the specialist in proctology; yet, in spite of the differences that separate them, they are still members of the same profession. The same cannot be said of air-conditioning experts and interior decorators, both of whom contribute to the construction of a building. This slippage also makes possible for the sliding scale of clinical acceptability that the monitors of allopathic medicine find acceptable. That is, where the art is imperfect, as in heart transplantation, a rate of pragmatic success of fifty percent may be regarded by both practitioner and client as being "scientifically" acceptable, whereas the loss of one patient out of a hundred during a tonsillectomy may result in the revocation of staff privileges and the activation of a malpractice suit. In short, pragmatism and eclecticism combine with the "search" elements in the allopathic medical model to produce great diversity within the practice of medicine, an enormously vivid mosaic of tentatively acceptable technologies, and the growth of an overarching professional organization that itself consolidates the social power of medicine while preserving its flexibility and diversity and modulating sources of potential internal divisiveness and conflict. At the root of it, the lack of *dogma* must be laid down as the cornerstone of this technical-organizational edifice. Not much the same can be said for one of allopathic medicine's historic and prime competitors in the Western world: homeopathy.

HOMEOPATHIC MEDICINE: LIKE CURES LIKE

In some ways homeopathic medicine represents the antithesis to allopathic medicine in that its central organizing concept is not that illness is to be countered by a set of opposite forces or that the relationship between the practitioner and illness is essentially a *combative* one. It is, rather, that *similarities* promote good health and that diseases may be overcome by applying, in minute doses, substances making up natural compounds that themselves contain materials similar to those which perpetuate the disease. Organized as a system of thought in the early 1800s, the notion underlying the use of minute doses of the affecting disease can produce health *preceded* the development of and application of vaccination technologies by several decades. Like so many so-called "marginal" systems of medicine, homeopathy has been faulted for its lack of pragmatism, eclecticism, and diversity. It seems to rely on a *unitary* conception of the cause-cure link rather than on a more general philosophical edifice, such as the medical model of disease, which in large part has made possible the enormous explanatory power of allopathic medicine and has contributed so heavily to its adaptability and longevity.

However that might be, homeopathy in its original form constituted a complete medical system in that it contained a central organizing operating principle (the "law of Similia"), an elaborate pharmacopoeia, an elaborated system of education for homeopathic physicians, and a network of hospitals in which the technology was applied.

Homeopathy was the child of one Samuel Hahnemann, a doctor heretofore practicing the then "standard" medicine in Germany in the early years of the nineteenth century. According to Hahnemann, the body responded to and followed the "law of Similia," the central dictum of which is that "like cures like," that diseases can be cured through the ingestion of substances that contain materials identical to those producing the disease, and that *the more minute the dose the more potent was the effect, and therefore the more certain was the cure.* The extent to which the dosages were compounded is evidenced in prescriptions that were compounded to the "decillionth"— or 10^{-33} parts to one. Such a measurement has been likened to placing an eye-dropperful of the desired substance into the Pacific Ocean, stirring it well, and then taking a teaspoonful of the water.

It must be remembered that the law of Similia constituted a unitary explanation in that it applied to *all* disorders and complaints that the patient might bring to the homeopathic condition. Each disorder responded to a specific substance, rather than potentially to a range of therapeutic regimens, a guiding principle of allopathic medicine. The therapeutic substances were contained in the main text of homeopathy, the *Materia Medica*, which in its original form consisted of some 3000 different substances, one of the most recent addition to which is the use of metal cadmium to be taken for the cure of migraine headaches. Some of the more exotic substances contained in *Materia Medica* were as follows:

Materia Medica	Natural Derivation
Lachryma Filia	Tears from a weeping young girl
Asterias Rubens	Powdered starfish
Mephitis	Skunk excretion
Cimex Lactularioas	Crushed live bedbugs

Other sources of the substances prescribed in *Materia Medica* include powdered anthracite coal, powered oyster shells, and a new substance concocted from spider webs, which is discussed in a recent issue of the *Journal of the American Institute of Homeopathy*. The practice of homeopathy diffused throughout Europe during the 1820s and was introduced in the United States about 1840, where it reached its peak of popularity during the last quarter of the nineteenth century.

It is worth noting that such well-known and distinguished institutions as the Hahnemann Medical College of Philadelphia and New York Hospital were originally established as homeopathic institutions, and there are still some 1000 practicing doctors in the United States who refer to themselves as homeopaths, although they resemble their earlier counterparts only to the extent of having attended schools that were once under homeopathic sponsorship and are, by reputation, more inclined to prescribe medications of one sore or another as compared with their more allopathically oriented colleagues. In short, homeopathy was slowly assimilated into pragmatic and eclectic allopathic medicine, ridding itself of its notions of unitary causation as well as the mystique of the law of Similia and its associated dogmatic approach to health problems.

Bizarre and exotic as old-fashioned homeopathy may now appear to have been, it is worth noting that it drew to it numerous patient-adherents, some of them both wise and healthy: Oliver Wendell Holmes, the distinguished chief justice of the U.S. Supreme Court, was a devotee of homeopathy and died after a long, healthy, and productive life at age 85. Similarly, the renowned author, essayist, poet, and journalist William Cullen Bryant was also a long-time homeopathic devotee, dying in 1878 at the age of 84. Thus, in an era when allopathic medicine had not yet achieved the level of dominance of acceptance and authenticity it now enjoys, systems such as homeopathy could compete in the medical marketplace quite successfully. However, as in the case of most cults, even homeopathy was not successful in overcoming the dangers to organizational survival brought about by the crisis of the succession of charismatic leadership—although it is still true that it survived, if only in vestigial form. Osteopathy, by way of contrast, illustrates a marginal system of medicine exhibiting somewhat great survival abilities.

Osteopathy: physiatry in embryo

Osteopathy, borrowing crudely from the Greek derivation, means "sickness of the bones," and constitutes a medical theory and practice resting on the supposition that diseases are caused by a malfunctioning of the nerves and blood supply, which in turn is due to dislocations of the small bones in the spinal column and in the muscles surrounding the spine. Given this unitary concept of cause, therefore, proper therapy for all illnesses involved careful and specific manipulations of the spine and its associated muscular systems. Its creator, Andrew Still, in his original text claimed to have experienced a divine revelation that disclosed to him the proper manipulations needed to bring about cures in patients suffering from such maladies as yellow fever, malaria, diphtheria, rickets, piles, diabetes, dandruff, constipation, and obesity, among others.

After its inception in the rural Midwest in the last quarter of the last century, osteopathy thrived as a medical alternative until the threats posed by the Flexner report in 1910 became apparent to its principal practitioners.

Since that time, osteopathy, rather than falling victim to the growing rationalization and credibility of allopathic medicine as homeopathy had done, began to alter its theoretical and practical orientation so as to incorporate more and more of the regimens and points of view of general medicine. This process began gradually with such manipulative innovations as hydrotherapy, electroshock, and surgery, to the present stage, at which the technical training and practice of the osteopathic physician differs little if any from that of his allopathic counterpart. The D.O. designation, however, is still retained—and there seems little doubt that although osteopathy survived the threat of extinction brought about by the increased dominance of allopathic medicine, osteopathic physicians and institutions still suffer from their relatively deprived status in relation to prestige, to both formal and informal power and authority in the institutions of medicine, and to the occupational status of its practitioners. For many people, however, routing to an osteopathic physician still represents a deviant choice, and the choice of training in osteopathy is still regarded as a secondary choice by most medical school aspirants. In general, however, osteopathy competed tactically with allopathic medicine—relinquishing its claim to purist doctrinaire uniqueness in return for institutional survival, if not prosperity. The key to its survival appears to be diversity, pragmatism, and eclecticism. This is unlike homeopathy, which rejected all three and thereby failed.

In general, the recent history of marginal medical systems such as homeopathy and osteopathy has been to merge, in one form or another, with allopathic medicine in both the ideological and technical senses and thereby achieve some measure of durability, or retain dogmatic ideological purity and experience either elimination or the perpetuation of a kind of pariah status in nearly every respect. Chiropractic illustrates the latter situation of continued marginality, although the even more recent drift toward the seeking of alternatives to allopathic medicine in the form of deprofessionalization, demystification of medicine, and a search for less costly avenues to medical care through paraprofessionals and semiautonomous marginal practitioners has resulted in a resurgence of chiropractic on the contemporary scene. The latter half of this chapter will deal in more detail with this most recent phenomenon that is working at the edges of the monopolistic posture that allopathic medicine has enjoyed virtually unchallenged over the past half-century.

Naturopathy, in both its original and contemporary offshoot forms, probably represents the most enduring alternative to allopathic medicine by avoiding direct technical or organizational competition with the dominant medical form.

Naturopathy: nature cures

The reputed curative power of natural forces is probably as old as mankind, and there is little reason to doubt that nature itself must have been relied upon before the invention of even the primitive medicines or even the creation of the concept of mystical deities. It was almost certainly at the root of the early Greek conception of human perfection and follows us today in many guises. Strictly speaking, however, the loosely organized congeries of movements and beliefs subsumed under the heading of "naturopathy" rests upon the *rejection* of any and all forms of artificially manufactured intervention and manipulation of the human body as well as rejection of the idea that a special and esoteric body of health knowledge can be acquired only after a long period of formal training and that persons must rely on the ministrations of medical professionals in order to preserve one's health.

As an identifiable social movement, however, naturopathy has no individual who can be singled out as its founder, although in the specially institutionalized form of Christian Science, Mary Baker Eddy of course must be noted. But naturopathy was and is secular and does not possess any of the organizational or ideological components of theology. At the base of naturopathy rests the principle that "nature" itself can be relied upon to bring about cures and, perhaps most important, that *disease produces bacteria, not the other way around*. Once this assumption is accepted, it is an easy step to a generalized program of self-motivated behavior that would avoid any foreign tampering with the sites of diseases, lest the bacteria lying fallow there be activated, intensified, and dispersed. Cleanliness, therefore, is from the view-point of naturopathy not so near to godliness as it is to healthfulness.

One prominent disciple and widely heard spokesman for naturopathy was the long-lived health promoter, Bernarr Macfadden, who for many years operated a large chain of nature-oriented health spas throughout the country thereby making a fortune many times over by espousing the specific principles to be followed in a strict regimen of adherence to the laws of nature and the avoidance of the ministrations of professional medical personnel. So committed was he to the principles of "no professional medical care" that he once argued rather persuasively that cancer could be cured by restricting oneself to a diet composed strictly of grapes (many years in front of laetrille) and he offered $10,000 in prize money to anyone who could offer evidence to disprove it. No one can be certain how skilled Macfadden was in the art of logic or how familiar he might have been with the difficulties involved in disproving a negative, but he finally went to his own reward at an old age with his $10,000 still in his wallet.

Another prominent and remarkably healthy devotee of naturopathy was George Bernard Shaw, who took the position that drugs and other artificial medical palliatives merely suppress symptoms (a position with which many modern physicians would at least partially agree) but that diseases can usually be relied upon to break out again under such treatment unless nature is allowed to run its course. In fact, even in dramatic form, Shaw attacked conventional medical wisdom by arguing that most diseases were traceable to the commercial laundry where microbes from the soiled handkerchiefs and clothing of sick persons were randomly mixed up, infecting the clothes of others and hence redistributing diseases around the community on a weekly basis.

A classic case of naturopathy *in extremis* is no better illustrated than by the final days of Eugene Debs, the long-time leader of the American Socialist Party and several times the candidate for the American presidency who was also devoted for most of his adult life to the principles of "nature cures." In fact, Debs died in a naturopathic sanatorium in Elmhurst, Illinois, in 1932. After being in the sanatorium for two days, Debs lapsed into unconsciousness and was checked on by an M.D. at the request of his friend Carl Sandburg (also given to a belief in the powers of natural healing). In any event, it was then observed that the pupil of one eye was dilated and the other contracted, a sign which usually indicates the presence of a brain lesion probably brought about by either a brain tumor or a cerebral hemorrhage. Whatever the case might have been, Debs, being unconscious, had not asked the attending staff for a drink of fluid and of course the staff had not bothered to offer him one. So Debs was dehydrated. When his heart began to fail he was treated with extract of cactus— and he died.

MARKET ALTERNATIVES AND COUNTERCULTURES

It is to be noted that naturopathy, in the diffuse and unarticulated form here described (as well as so many other of the marginal systems which have appeared and disappeared in history) arrived on the scene *prior to* the watershed years of the 1930s when allopathic medicine began to crystallize its dominance in the medical field and before the two-generation drift toward the medical profession began to give way slowly to what we are now witnessing as the "demedicalization" of health phenonmena, with its accompanying reassessment of received dogma concerning medicine as presently practiced. Hence these were not so much medical countercultures in direct conflict with allopathic medicine but rather realistically perceived alternate choices in health care. This contrasts with the more recent rejections of "standard" medicine favoring deinstitutionalization, deprofessionalization, a denouncement of the mystique of the medical profession, and the movement toward democratization and self-help in matters of health. That is, earlier alternate and marginal modes of health care were not seeking sweeping institutional changes in the society of the time but were merely entering a market offering a different health product. They had not become social movements in the technical sense of that term.

The difference between medical market alternatives and countercultures in medicine is perhaps no better dramatized than by the ideology of this partially coalesced social movement. As Ivan Illich states:[2]

> The medical establishment has become a major threat to health. The disabling impact of professional control over medicine has reached the proportions of an epidemic. *Iatrogenesis,* the name for this new epidemic, comes from *iatros,* the Greek work of "physician," and *genesis,* meaning "origin." Discussion of the disease of medical progress has moved up on the agendas of medical conferences, researchers concentrate on the sick-making powers of diagnosis and therapy, and reports on the paradoxical damage caused by cures for sickness take up increasing space in medical dope-sheets. The health professions are on a brink of an unprecedented housecleaning campaign. . . . Limits to professional health care are a rapidly growing political issue. . . . A crisis of confidence in modern medicine is upon us. Merely to insist on it would be to contribute further to a self-fulfilling prophecy, and the possible panic.

In response to this sweeping rejection of the existing medical establishment and its documented accomplishment, Renee Fox somewhat less flamboyantly counters:[3]

> There are numerous grounds on which Illich's thesis can be criticized. He minimizes the advances in the prevention, diagnosis, and treatment of disease that have been made since the advent of the bacteriological era in medicine, and he attributes totally to non-medical agencies all progress in health that has ensued. He implies that modern Western, urban, industrialized, capitalist societies, of which the United States is the prototype, are more preoccupied with pain, sickness, and death, and less able to come to terms with these integral parts of a human life, than other types of society. . . . a disturbing discrepancy exists between the data presented in many of the works that Illich cites in his copious footnotes and the interpretive liberties that he takes with them. Perhaps most insidious of all is the sophistry that Illich uses in presenting a traditional orthodox, Christian-Catholic point of view in the guise of a vulgar Marxist argument. For he repeatedly claims that "when dependence on the professional management of pain, sickness and death grows beyond a certain point, the healing power in sickness, patience in suffering, and fortitude in the face of death must decline." In Illich's view, this state is not only morally dubious, but also spiritually dangerous. Because it entails the "hubris" of what he deems arrogant and excessive medical intervention, it invites "nemesis:" the retribution of the gods.

However eloquent Illich's attack on established allopathic medicine might be, there seems little likelihood that hospitals are about to close their doors in large numbers, that physicians are about to shut down their examination rooms and laboratories, that pharmacies are about to go out of business, that people are now prepared to carry their medicine cabinets to the town dump, or that the Department of Health, Education, and Welfare is about to return its portfolio to the White House. But while the medical castle seems to be in little danger of being breached by the gallant attack of Illich, a modern Man of La Mancha, it does seem clear the medicine—like education before it—has become politicized if not yet fully demystified. And in this sense at least, claims to a virtual technical monopoly are becoming less and less adequate to justify either organizational autonomy or hegemony over policy. As shall be detailed in a later chapter, these issues are more and more finding their way into the public arena of the courts where presumably the will of the people will find its expression before the bar in those cases in which it is not heard across the examination table.

In any event, the earlier partial and marginal systems of medicine we are discussing here were of an entirely different type than the ideologically based medical parallels now entering the scene. They were more in the nature of misconceived efforts to add to growing body of pragmatic and eclectic medicine or merely shady ways to corner a part of the health market and do as little physical harm to buyers as possible,[4] as we shall see in the next section.

FADS, FRAUDS, AND FIXATIONS ON THE MARGINS OF MEDICINE

The relatively short-lived fad of "iridiagnosis" involved an apparently complex method of diagnosing various diseases through careful visual examination of the eye. Accordingly, the eye was presumed to be divided—radiating from the center of the pupil—into 40 concentric zones. Thus, changes in the shape, size, and coloration, as well as the general configuration of the zones, would, through examination by the trained iridiagnostician, reveal not only the nature of the malady afflicting the patient but also its location in the body. After paying the iridiagnostician the appropriate fee, the patient would then be referred to a "standard" doctor already armed with this advance information so as to accelerate the treatment process. Incredible? Apparently not to a large number of people who availed themselves of this service.

Another fad, called zone therapy, was the brainchild of a graduate of the University of Vermont Medical School and a senior nose and throat surgeon in a hospital in Hartford, Connecticut. It rested on the premise that the body is divided vertically into exactly ten zones—five on each side of the body, and each one terminating at the individual finger and toe. According to this, every body disorder could be checked by putting pressure on the proper finger or toe, or some correct combination of them, relating to the zone or zones involved. According to zone therapy doctrine, headaches could be cured by pressing the thumb against the roof of the mouth. Nausea was to be treated by pressing a metal hair comb against the backs of both hands. Whooping cough was attacked by pressing a spot on the back of the throat. Other maladies were to be treated by similar digital manipulation or by applying stretched rubber bands on the appropriate combination of fingers and toes.

Then there was Dr. Elisha Perkins's idea of "metal dynamism," constituted of the notion that specific metals drew diseases from the body when applied to the surface of the flesh covering the offending part. This particular medical fad was blessedly short-lived, although it was apparently responsive to a market, however limited, during its brief life. The same can be said for the diagnostic contraption conceived by a Dr. Abrams called a "dynamizer," which supposedly directed special rays toward the body. Their registering on the machine would to the trained eye indicate the presence or absence of various diseases. The famous writer and iconoclast, Upton Sinclair, once wrote an article defending Abrams and his device in the *Journal of the American Medical Association,* but to little avail. Abrams, the "oscilloclast," as he was called by Sinclair, may well have been the inventor of the precursor to the *diathermy* machine, which was found in many physicians' offices in the 1930s. The diathermy machine was also supposed to direct special therapeutic rays into the body with generally healthful results. In point of fact, the diathermy machine directed rays of heat at such an angle that they intersected beneath the surface of the body, thus making possible a soothing warmth to be applied to aching parts without making the outer skin feel uncomfortable—much on the principles of the modern laser beam. Diathermy is, in fact, still to be found today as equipment in many physical education departments of schools, in sports team locker rooms, and in health spas as a device for the palliation of numerous aches and pains of halfbacks and tennis buffs.

The marketing of the "vrilium stick" also deserves brief mention. During most of the 1920s a Chicago businessman successfully sold an object called a "vrilium stick"—a small brass cylinder which was supposed to be worn around the neck as a talisman to fend off germs and bacteria. Thousands of them were sold at approximately $300 each and were worn by such individuals as Mayor Kelly of the City of Chicago. The federal government took action against the Vrilium Products Company in 1950 and its investigation found that the cylinders contained nothing more than a cheap grade of rat poison. On their side, the owners claimed that it was an *unrecognized* form of radioactivity in spite of the fact that it had no effect on a Geiger counter.

This laundry list of medical and quasi-medical inventions and discoveries could be lengthened, but at least one more is worth mentioning before we move on to the uncharted realm of psychiatric and psychological systems of a similar ilk. Another entrepreneur in Chicago made a handsome income some years ago by predicting the sex of unborn children, with a *money-back guarantee.* This service was presumably of considerable value to many purchasers because it made possible early planning for the purchase of the appropriate sex-related bassinet, toys, advance information to relatives and other potential gift-givers, especially where the uninformed baby shower invitee might otherwise offer forth a useless gift. Of course, given the rough probability that about half of all births could be expected to yield male children, the other half female offspring, the "predictor" was correct in approximately half of the cases—returned the $50 in the case of the wrong half and pocketed the other half so as to realize a substantial profit. Of course, these predictions are now on a far more scientific basis, and even to the point at which the would-be parents can exercise some degree of control over what sex child will be produced.

Perhaps one of the most bizarre examples of medical quackery and marginality demonstrating the persuasive power of the then-new mass medium of communication, the radio, it the meteoric rise to popularity of "goat gland" therapy, under the leadership of John Brinkley, one-time medical doctor with dubious qualifications and certification. In the small town of Milford, Kansas (following a brief period of service as an army doctor and the company surgeon with a large meat-packing firm in Kansas City), he developed the idea that people aged and became victims of disease merely because their glands wore out. By logic, then, it stood to reason that if he could supply people approaching old age with new glands, they could then resist the ravages of old age and deterioration of the body. Thus, a modern Fountain of Youth was discovered in the form of endocrine glands removed from goats and then "transplanted" into men. So successful was this notion locally that his "hospital" was constructed in the town of Milford in 1918, and before long the modest town of Milford and Brinkley's "hospital" became host to seekers from all over the world, anxious to be the receivers of goat glands.

At the time, goat donors were shipped into Milford at the paltry rate of 60 per month. But after Brinkley erected his own radio broadcasting station, more than 100 goats a month were required to answer the growing demands for the health-giving glands. Flushed with such success, Brinkley now easily expanded his market by claiming over the airways that goat glands were also potent to counteract the effects of rheumatism, heart trouble, failing eyesight, deafness, impotency, and a large variety of disease of the stomach, lungs, liver, spleen, kidneys, and bladder. And, like the ayervedic physician responding to the mass in Calcutta, Brinkley then began to make diagnoses over his radio station and to market his goat glands extracts through more than 500 druggists scattered over the Midwest.

After many years of this successful quackery, the Kansas State Medical Society succeeded in getting his medical license revoked, but the notoriety it brought him my means of the radio carried him to a very nearly successful bid for the governorship of Kansas. And much of his strong campaign involved inveighing against the medical establishment and other prosecutors from the status quo. And as his star was falling in Milford, Brinkley made energetic plans to move to Mexico, establish an even larger broadcast system, and there bring prosperity to the goat herbers in Chihuahua.

However that may be, just as the successful practice of allopathic medicine requires a diligent and cooperative client who tilts in the direction of gullibility and plausibility, even more does the successful execution of a medical fraud depend on the gullibility, ignorance, and often the greed and avarice of the waiting public.

MARGINAL SYSTEMS IN THE PSYCHIATRIC REALM— RELIANCE UPON MYSTICISM—MEDICAL ORGANIZATION WITHOUT TECHNOLOGY CRITERIA

An entirely different realm is entered into when departing the field of organic medicine and venturing forth into the effort to bring about alterations in persons' social conduct rather than in their organic condition. The range for plausibility is much enlarged, as is the invention of explanatory systems by which odd behavior can be described away in persons designated either by self or others as emotionally sick. The problem is dramatized by changes in the number of persons committed to psychiatric hospitals since 1900.

The pattern of institutionalization in the case of negative societal response to conduct deviations underwent a gradual increase in the first two decades of this century, followed by a sharp increase since 1920 up to the late 1950s, at which point a general decline was to be observed. In other words, institutionalization was the preferred mode of handling a large and growing number of persons designated as mentally ill for a considerable period of time. And as the definition of mental illness became more and more encompassing, the potential catchment population fitted in this category became larger and larger (recall the astoundingly high percentage of New Yorkers designated in the Midtown Manhattan study as being in need of psychiatric care!). And as hospitalization as a mode of deviance management gained popularity during these years, a dazzling variety of psychotherapies and other "communication technologies" competed for professional and organizational dominance in this lucrative and fascinating new medical arena. Some competitors for this specially ambiguous form of "illness," as shall be discussed in a later chapter, achieved far-reaching success in securing legitimization, authenticity, and organizational control. Others were less successful, although to some readers the theories of those who tried and failed may seem no more mystical than those whose ideas captured and caught the imagination of large numbers of the people and held it firmly, at least until the creation of the tranquilizer in the late 1950s—a period that corresponds almost exactly with the decline in psychiatric institutionalization rates. What are the stories of some of those psychiatric ideologies that were tried and failed? Like most of the unsuccessful systems touched upon the earlier part of this chapter and dealing with organically focused interventions, most forms of pseudopsychiatry represent some kind of exaggeration, extrapolation, expansion, or overgeneralization and indiscrimate application of some limited facet of the prevailing institutionalized and established practices in the realm of mental well-being. The comic-tragic story of Wilhelm Reich is highly illustrative of this process.

Reich's orgonomy: a neo-Freudian beyond the pale

Reich, an Austrian born physician and psychoanalyst, was one of Sigmund Freud's original students. He was one of the leaders of a small group of people who became known as "neo-Freudian" because of their later retention of much of Freudian doctrine concerning the dynamics of the psyche, but even more so because the revisionist position each of them developed. In his early years of writing and practice Reich concentrated his efforts on elaborating and polishing the psychodynamic view of human personality, especially in attempting to delineate basic personality factors attributable to forces of aggression and suppression on the one hand and the standard Freudian preoccupation with human sexuality on the other. None of this at the time was particularly radical even within the ranks of doctrinaire Freudians. His departure from it could be authenticated and authorized by any persuasive segment of the population began sometime in the mid-1930s when, while traveling in Norway, he claimed to have discovered the primary source of all life forces—not the internal power of libido as Freud insisted, but something Reich called *orgone energy*.[5] Orgone energy was postulated to be a till-then-undiscovered cosmic force invisible to the human eye but, when concentrated, having a light blue cast to it. Further, as a spin-off from doctrinaire Freudianism, Reich contended that the imperfections in the human condition were traceable to an inadequate supply of orgone taken into the body during the normal course of human existence in the modern world and made symptomatic by disturbed sexual impulses and activities, especially the inability to experience a satisfactory sexual orgasm. Now the chain of effect, cause, and cure is nearly complete.

To accomplish the desired result, Reich needed both a technology and an organization—the first to deliver orgone to patients, the second to deliver patients to Reich. In the early 1940s these final obstacles were overcome: technology in the form of the *orgone box*, and organization in the form of a summer encampment in the health-giving woods of Maine and an Orgonomy Society, which published the *Journal of Orgonomy*, a periodical distributed to friends and members. The orgone box was a small metal cubicle in which the nude patient was to sit in a position of relaxation, during which time the box would gather amounts of orgone from the environment and direct it toward the body of the patient. Given enough time and counseling, in exchange for the appropriate fee, the orgone would build up sufficiently that the person would be able to experience life-giving orgasm and hence a generalized cure. The therapeutic box could either be rented or purchased, thus allowing home treatments. Even better, patients could gather in groups during the summer months in Maine and experience collective orgasms after proper exposure to concentrated orgone. Until recently, thousands of people availed themselves of this new therapy—a precursor, in some ways, of modern outreach programs and sensitivity training.

The orgonomy movement prospered until the mid-1950s, at which time it experienced a precipitous decline, due largely to failure of Wilhelm Reich to perpetuate the movement's credibility as a result of the apparently felt need to continue innovating and improving the "therapy" involved—another distortion of standard Western scientific practice. The results were an organizational Waterloo for the movement and a personal tragedy for Reich.

It is instructive to take note of the fact that Reich's "theory and practice" of general sexual well-being finally was rejected, and Reich himself discredited, only a few brief years before Masters and Johnson sanctified sex as a legitimate area for health counseling and manipulation. Within a relatively short period of time this research led to the now widespread use of sexual therapy and counseling as an avenue out of one's life problems. In short, Reich's mystical view of sex was rejected, while the sexual scientism of Masters and Johnson rendered the subject somewhat sterile and therefore accorded it some measure of respectability. Reich's error was in promoting an idea before its time had come and in a way that did not fit with general public standards of acceptability and respectability.

In the course of the elaboration of his theory, Reich undertook some bizarre experiments in the creation of life from inert matter. In these quasi-experiments a combination of nonliving substances were boiled to a point of the appearance of a residue which he termed "bion" materials. "Bion" was hypothesized to be material at an intermediary stage between the living and the dead. And he further proposed that the presence of such material was a root cause of cancer. Further, Reich contended that orgone could assist in the enlivening of bion materials, and its growing presence could be evidenced by the heat that was generated in the orgone box. As a result of this "experimentation" Reich proceeded informally to announce a cure for cancer through the use of orgone treatments—supplemented now by exercises and body massaging—and to try to cure cancerous patients by attempting to work on their bion material. Since he was not licensed to practice medicine in New York State (although he had often been offered such a license), a court order placed an injunction upon any further activities in the health field. Reich ignored this order and was sent to jail, where he died during the appeal process.

A footnote to Reich's career lays in the fact that his philosophies and ideas experienced a rebirth among many European university student populations in the late 1960s, due mainly to his long-time rejection of all authority—political as well as parental—and his advocacy of sexual freedom at a time when a quite strict Victorianism still had considerable strength.

Dianetics: pseudoscience turned religion

L. Ron Hubbard, a former naval officer turned self-styled psychologist, seized upon yet another key element in the Freudian metaphor concerning human development, the importance of earlier childhood experiences (especially those long forgotten) in forming human personality, and the distortions and suffering that can be brought about when such experiences are buried in the unconscious. True to the Freudian arrow, dianetics was originally formed as a mode of psychotherapy involving recollection of very early childhood experiences, a long and costly process. A further innovation involved the contention that the most critical experiences were those which occurred when the patient was in utero. Hence the memory retrieval process was thereby made more difficult, time-consuming, and costly.

A final new discovery that led Ron Hubbard and his dianetic movement across the river and into the uncharted woods of mysticism was the contention that the even more critical experiences were those taking place before conception had occurred. Thus a believable bridge was constructed to the meditative and self-reflective philosophy of the religion of scientology, of which L. Ron Hubbard today remains the surviving high priest. Thus far, Hubbard continues to prosper, although he has outdone Reich in his leap from empirical therapy to untestable religion, partially by exploiting the modern opportunities for international legal immunities. For example, the following Associated Press report on Hubbard appeared in the February 15, 1978, edition of the *Providence* (R.I.) *Journal;* by-line Paris:[6]

> L. Ron Hubbard, American founder of the Church of Scientology, was sentenced yesterday in absentia to four years in prison and fined $7,300 for fraudulent business practices. The French criminal court issued a warrant for the arrest of Hubbard, a former U.S. Navy officer who founded the church in California in 1954. He reportedly lives on a yacht in the Atlantic off the French coast. In reading the court's decision, the presiding judge said the court was taking action against "the polished commercial activities" of the church and not its religious tenets. Scientology, as described by a church publication, is a "pan-denominational

applied religious philosophy which contains a remarkable system of effective techniques for increasing human ability and awareness."

In arguing the potency of his new discoveries, part of which involved the impact of what he called "engram" during pregnancy which have a lasting effect on the course of human life, Hubbard writes:[7]

Here is a list of chains—not all the possible chains by any means—found in one case which had passed for "normal" for thirty-six years of his life.

Coitus chain, father. 1st incident zygote. 56 succeeding incidents. Two branches, father drunk and father sober.

Coitus chain, lover. 1st incident embryo. 18 succeeding incidents. All painful because of enthusiasm of lover.

Constipation chain. 1st incident zygote. 51 succeeding incidents. Each incident building high pressure on child.

Douche chain. 1st incident embryo. 21 succeeding incidents. One each day to missed period, all into cervix.

Sickness chain. 1st incident embryo. 5 succeeding incidents. 3 colds. 1 case grippe. One vomiting spell-hangover.

Morning sickness chain. 1st incident embryo. 32 succeeding incidents.

Contraceptive chain. 1st incident zygote. 1 incident. Some past substance in cervix.

Fight chain. 1st incident embryo. 38 succeeding incidents. Three falls, loud voices, no beating.

Attempted abortion, surgical. 1st incident embryo. 21 succeeding incidents.

Attempted abortion, douche. 1st incident foetus. 2 incidents, 1 using paste, 1 using lysol, very strong.

Attempted abortion, pressure. 1st incident foetus. 3 incidents. 1 father sitting on mother. Two mother jumping off boxes.

Hiccough chain. 1st incident foetus. 5 incidents.

Accident chain. 1st incident embryo. 18 incidents. Various falls and collisions.

Masturbation chain. 1st incident embryo. 80 succeeding incidents. Mother masturbating with fingers, jolting child and injuring child with orgasm.

Doctor chain. 1st incident, 1st missed period. 18 visits. Doctor examining painful but doctor an ally, discovering mother attempting an abortion and scolding her thoroughly.

Premature labor pains. 3 days before actual birth.

Birth. Instrument. 29 hours labor.

In that mother was a sub-vocal talker this made a sizable quantity of to be erased for the remainder of the patient's life was in addition to this. This was a 500-hour case, nonsonic, imaginary recalls which had to be cancelled out by discovering lie factories before the above data could be obtained.

LSD: CULT OR POLITICS?

Finally, and most recently, the rise and decline of the LSD movement is further illustrative of the shift that can occur through the cycle from incipient medical innovation, to deviant cult, to quasi-religious zealotry, and finally to court declaration of illegality. The composition of the drug, LSD, had been known for a number of years before, but in the early to mid-1950s established psychiatrists began to explore the possibility of its potential therapeutic value when applied to some patients. It is to be remembered that this was in the era of the first great breakthroughs in psychomedication (particularly the tranquilizers, which, while highly effective in large number of cases of anxiety neuroses, seemed to be of little value in severely depressed and schizophrenic patients). So there was no reason not to believe that LSD might be helpful. Coincidentally, Timothy Leary, then a lecturer in psychology at Harvard University, was experimenting with its use with his classroom students at the university without any prior approval of the university officialdom and without any existing clinical evidence of the drug's safety or effectiveness. Shortly thereafter, Dr. Leary was fired from his academic job and began to head a loosely organized drug-oriented, and largely youth-dominated, cult whose byword was "Drop Out and Turn On." This group soon acquired many of the cosmetic qualities of a standard expressive social movement, with Leary as the charismatic leader, dressed in distinctive Eastern-styled garb, and migrated to southern California, where creative and exotic religious-oriented cults have always flourished.

Meantime, a handful of psychiatrists continued with their not very carefully controlled experiences, first with individual patients, then later with groups of patients. In the latter circumstances the effects were particularly noticeable and striking. This was, it is to be recalled, in the very early days of the deprofessionalized group encounter tactics in sociopsychological therapy that by now are so ubiquitous as to be "old hat." But this approach was very new in the mid-1950s and had none of the taint of suspected charlatanism or fraud that clouded the fading years of Reich's orgonomy or the out-and-out entrepreneurism of the successful Ron Hubbard. In any event, the final step was taken by a handful of psychiatrists who discovered that the results, both in verbal behavior and apparent deep psychological representation and symbolism, could be achieved if the psychiatrists subjected themselves to the LSD *along with groups of patients.* In more than one instance the sponsoring and authorizing agents of this exercise then drew the line, and LSD was barred from further clinical practice. Leary has since been arrested on drug possession charges, placed in jail, escaped from jail, fled to Europe, and remains now a fugitive from the law, apparently "dropping out" further than even he had hoped for.

A last, and in some ways even more ominious, footnote to the LSD story dramatizes the pitfalls that lie in wait for unwary sociomedical researchers and their unwary client-patients, who may pursue with too much zeal that continuing will-o'-the-wisp, the health panacea. The case to be described involved a highly regarded and "elite" psychiatric hospital that in its past had enjoyed high repute as one of the few "moral treatment centers" and had enjoyed a resounding success over a hundred years ago.

In the late 1950s and continuing into the early 1960s, the administrative staff of a small but respected psychiatric hospital in New England received a grant of money from a New York City–based foundation, which presumably was using nontraditional and innovative means to study factors involved in influencing human behavior. The grant the hospital received was for the purpose of studying the effects of alcohol consumption on communication content and capabilities. In order to get at this problem carefully, the following procedures were established: The hospital built, at grant expense, a mock-up cocktail lounge in its basement, with all the proper accoutrements of a quiet drinking establishment. Volunteers from the community (no drunks *or* teetotalers, please) were assembled who agreed to come to the lounge periodically by taxi at grant expense, and help themselves to as much liquor as was handed them. During the drinking sessions, grant workers taped the voices of the imbibing research subjects on recorders so as to capture the deterioration of the subjects' speech patterns as the alcohol content of their blood increased. But this was a "blind" experiment. Some of the drinkers got the genuine alcohol material, while others drank, unknown to themselves, a placebo containing little or no alcohol. A triumph for social science was announced at the close of the experiment when the tape recorders revealed that the people drinking sugar water seemed to get just as "drunk" as did those with the straight Chivas Regal.

Thus were the predispositions of the granting agency substantiated, as was the explanatory bias of the researchers who were eagerly searching for "hard data" that would support a "social causation" theory. Now for the shocking conclusion! More than a *decade later* it was discovered that the Fund for Human Ecology was actually a front organization for the CIA. What had actually taken place a decade earlier was not a double-blind experiment on the effects of alcohol, but rather a one-sided blind experiment on the effects of LSD. This fact was heretofore known only to the fund personnel, presumably the CIA, and a small handful of hospital administrators who were "in" on the original game, but kept the line research workers and the community volunteers ignorant of the facts of the scandal. The enormously important area of mounting ethical and moral issues in medical care and medical research, as suggested by this case, will be taken up in Chapter 12. It seems accurate, however, that much medical research ventures into the sphere of the noninstitutionalized. But only some, through later public reaction, cross the line between actual medical intervention, medical fraud, and charlatanism.

SCIENCE, FRAUD, AND AUTHENTICATION IN MARGINAL MEDICINE

It is customary to draw a simple distinction between standard, regular, allopathic medical practices that are justified and legitimated because they are "scientific" in character and marginal and irregular medical practices such as the ones here described as being deviant and fraudulent because they are "unscientific." But if science is used in its specifically technical meaning, namely "systematic and formulated knowledge," then regular medicine is only crudely differentiated, and only at a nonsociological level, from irregular or marginal medicine. If science is regarded as a set of procedures as well as a body of substantive knowledge, incorporating valid and reliability accountability and prediction of outcomes, then certain branches of regular medicine *may or may not* in fact be more scientific than some irregular medicines. In this sense, it is not difficult to dispute the fact that traditional psychotherapy, which seems so unscientific to most, enjoys very widespread acceptance in American society and *appears* to be of help to a large number of people. This may be compared, for example, with heart transplantation, which is based on a very reliable scientific foundation but is a rarity in Western medicine and avoided by most surgeons and patients. The reverse can also be true with hordes of ill people turning to physicians who have no scientific cure or ready explanation for many disorders of the mind and body, while only a small portion of the population turn to chiropractors who can claim to have a sound scientific basis for much of what they do. How may we explain this paradox by going beyond the mere scientific-unscientific distinction? An answer seems to be in the fact that "regular" physicians are the agents of choice for most people not because of what they do but rather who they are.

This is to say that it is faulty logic to equate "science" always with helpful and worthwhile, and nonscience or "mystical" with the fraudulent and useless. As far as the activity of patients are concerned, at least, it is the *social organization* and cultural accreditation accorded allopathic medicine that draws them to it, not its scientific content or its quasi-scientific procedures. However that might be, the routing of persons outside the orbit of allopathic medicine must be understood not as gullible innocent acceptance of "quackery"; nor must one's continued embrace of allopathic medicine be regarded as evidence of wisdom and rationality. The former represents a vast range of social, economic, and political situational factors that result in at least the temporary rejection of the now dominant form of medical practice—allopathic medicine.

Some irregular medicines (such as osteopathy and chiropractic) seemed to flourish best in rural areas that had little if any allopathic medicine. Others, particulary the organic types, seemed to prosper at a time prior to the 1930s when allopathic medicine had not yet achieved dominance. Thus it was possible for irregular medicines to compete at the organizational level, as well as "empirically," with the poorly articulated technology available to allopathic medicine at the time. Still others, especially the limited and entrepreneurial forms, seemed to do best in the confusion and anonymity of the urban centers—always fertile ground for razzle-dazzle and the flimflam artist. Still others, such as Christian Science, naturopathy, orgonomy, and the numerous "self-help" movements that can be observed in the contemporary medical scene, seem to represent quite widespread disenchantment of fairly large segments of the population with the prevalent social order and its indigenous medical establishment. They also may represent something of an effort to seek to retain an element of "folk" medicine in the affairs of health and to reestablish effectively potent and viable *gemeinschaft* relationships outside of the cool bureaucratic rationality that had developed within and along with allopathic medicine. Many of these irregular forms represent as much a rejection of the *organization* of allopathic medicine as they are a rejection of its *technological claims.*

Figure 7.1 is a way of depicting the extent to which the long-standing and ongoing authenticity of a medical practice rests upon the authorization given to it by those to whom its appeal is made. This authorization stems from "credibility" on the one hand and the presentation of the technology by those making claims to technical expertise on the other, in terms of its apparent "truthfulness."

The vertical axis, running from "credibility" to "incredibility" relates most directly to the content of the "theory" involved in the public expression of the medical practice at issue, whether it is believable or unbelievable. Believability, remember, is not related in a strictly unilinear way with scientific *procedures* or *content,* but rather the *apparent* empiricism in which the practice is rooted as well as the degree of its mystification in the public mind. Where both *empiricism* and *mysticism* are invoked, the chance of a practice achieving public authentication through credility is increased. The former refers to the extent to which the practice appears to be founded on scientific procedures, whereas the latter relates most directly to the practice's "miraculous" nature. We are, for the most part, enchanted by the impossible, and the impossible is enchanted when it appears to have been arrived at by what appear to be scientific means. Thus heart transplantation as a technique of allopathic medicine seems *plausible* partly because of the cautious scientific steps involved, and even more so because of the miracle it appears to be. And this is *quite aside* from its outcome—death in at least 50 percent of the cases.

Much the same can be said for the authenticity accorded other modern "radical" medical interventions. It is not that they do much to

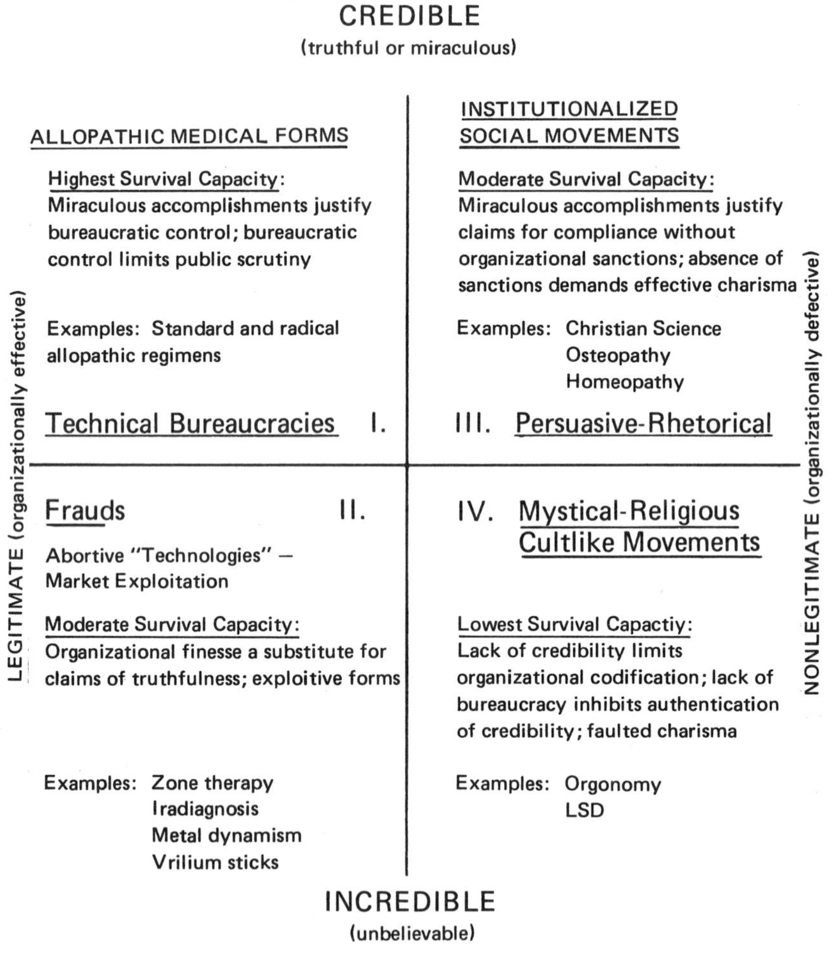

CREDIBLE
(truthful or miraculous)

ALLOPATHIC MEDICAL FORMS	**INSTITUTIONALIZED SOCIAL MOVEMENTS**
Highest Survival Capacity: Miraculous accomplishments justify bureaucratic control; bureaucratic control limits public scrutiny	Moderate Survival Capacity: Miraculous accomplishments justify claims for compliance without organizational sanctions; absence of sanctions demands effective charisma
Examples: Standard and radical allopathic regimens	Examples: Christian Science Osteopathy Homeopathy
Technical Bureaucracies I.	III. Persuasive-Rhetorical
Frauds II.	IV. Mystical-Religious Cultlike Movements
Abortive "Technologies" — Market Exploitation	
Moderate Survival Capacity: Organizational finesse a substitute for claims of truthfulness; exploitive forms	Lowest Survival Capacity: Lack of credibility limits organizational codification; lack of bureaucracy inhibits authentication of credibility; faulted charisma
Examples: Zone therapy Iradiagnosis Metal dynamism Vrilium sticks	Examples: Orgonomy LSD

LEGITIMATE (organizationally effective)

NONLEGITIMATE (organizationally defective)

INCREDIBLE
(unbelievable)

FIGURE 7.1 The authentication of medical practices.

bring about good health, but merely that they can be done at all. I would include here the rehabilitation of the spinal cord patient, limb and organ transplants, the use of life-sustaining machines, and the prediction of the sex and mental conditions of unborn infants and other miraculous medical exercises.

Along the other axis, that of *legitimation*, medical practices can be arrayed along a continuum ranging from those on the left of the horizontal axis, which are assisted in their claims for authenticity not by the content of their rhetorical persuasion, but rather by their organizational characteristics, both structural and cosmetic. The possibilities for legitimation, therefore, rest upon such factors as licensing and accreditation procedures (which may be as much political as they are technical), a source of funding (which gives at least the appearance of a rejection of the "profit" motive), and the ability to rest quietly at the receiving end of an effective referral network (which makes it appear that clients are neither wooed nor recruited but come for treatment on a strictly volitional basis instead, and which rests its case on its public respectability rather than on its zealotry).

In short, the life chances of mystical, fantastic, and extraordinary medical practices are increased when rooted in the rhetoric of science and are further augmented when buttressed by bureaucratic organizational forms. As was sketched in a previous chapter, the success of Western (allopathic) medicine is closely related to that of science and bureaucracy as dominating organizational forms. Other new medical practices, however, may fail in their mystical appeal, perhaps because they were introduced to the public before their time. These seldom evolve beyond the cult or social movement stage. But chances for successful innovation are enhanced when a novel medical innovation is associated in some meaningful way with indigenous 'folk' conceptions of health practices. This now appears to be the case with the recent health-food fad, small-group lay counseling, and other self-help movements.

AYERVEDIC MEDICINE—TIES TO TRADITIONAL COLONIALISM

It is probably a truism to say that no medical system can long survive if it transcends the prevailing cultural milieu in which it functions and the standards of public plausibility on whose survival it depends. This is perhaps no better illustrated than to mention only briefly the two other "Great" medical indigenous medical systems on this globe: ayervedic medicine, which predominates throughout the Indian subcontinent; and Chinese medicine, presently limited almost exclusively to the mainland of China and operating under the sponsorship of the present government of China. Each represents major departures from what we understand to be "regular" medicine, and each is regarded in its homelands as being both credible and legitimate.

Ayervedic medicine, and its present-day "Unani" physicians, can trace their roots as far back in history as can its Western counterpart, allopathic medicine. As a complete medical system it contains an institutional complex involving an overarching theory of disease, with much the same eclectic elements as allopathic medicine. There is a network of ayervedic hospitals in which much of the practice, including surgery, takes place, a large and highly diversified pharmaceutical industry, a set of medical schools in which new physicians are trained and apprenticed, and a set of prescriptions concerning the ideal doctor-patient relationships—parallel to but substantively different from, what is found in allopathic medicine. Moreover, there are historically founded medical "texts"—the books of the Veda—which are a combination of ancient Muslim, Greek, Arabian, and Persian tracts delineating the causes of disease and modes of diagnosing medical problems. The latter rely heavily on the interpretation of verbalized symptoms as well as certain signs as in allopathic medicine, although the modern forms of ayerveda represent a complex evolution from the folk-based originals, and contain elements of homeopathy, naturopathy, and extensions of modern pharmacology as introduced by the British during the last century. In terms of body theory, ayervedic medicine holds that one's state of health is determined by the interrelations between the body forces of "equilibrium." These consist of five elements: (*panchbhuta*), seven basic body substances (*dhatus*), and three humors (*tridoses*).

As the anthropologist Charles Leslie writes:[8]

> Ayervedic theories as they are taught by learned practitioners in relation to the classic tests are based on Nyaya, Vaisesika, and Sankhya philosophies. They conceive of man as a conglomerate (samudaya) of the panchabhutas, or five elements: earth, water, fire, air, and ether. There are subtle and material forms of the elements, each element possessing five subtle and five material forms. The physiological expression of these elements are the dhatus: chyle, blood, flesh, fat, bone, marrow, and semen. Semen (ojas) stored in the heart and diffused through the body sustains its vital tone. In addition, the tridosas, or three humors, in their role as supporters of the body are called dhatus. The aggregation of elements in the human body is a microcosmic version of the universe in which an equilibrium of the humors, wind (vayu), bile (pitta) and mucus (kapha or slesman) is necessary to health. The nature and severity of illnesses are diagnosed according to the dominant humor and the number of humors involved.

Evolutionary and assimilative as ayervedic medicine has been, particularly since the period of British colonialism, the indigenous medical system has in many ways *aped* allopathic medicine—and at the present time, especially in the urban areas, it occupies a status parallel to the paraprofessionals in allopathic medicine.

However that might be, the conceptual foundation of ayurvedic medicine is the idea that illness represents a disequilibrium between the panchbhuta, the dhatue, and the tridoses. These can be corrected by some combination of the three following therapeutic regimens— surgery, changes in dietary intake, and the ingestion of one or more of the vast number of pharmaceuticals contained in ayervedic medicine. Training for ayervedic practice retains much of its original character, although the formal structure of medical schools—presently training groups of students rather than individuals—is similar to allopathic schools, including a heavy emphasis on gross anatomy. In terms of the doctor-patient relationship, the clinical detachment and functional specificity so characteristic of the tenets of allopathic medicine are absent, and this is replaced by a functionally diffuse orientation emphasizing the particularistic manifestations that diseases can take in the individual case. Hence, the effective ayervedic physician is one who is broadly versed in the entire life space of each individual client—not merely with clinical signs. In a way, the social versus the medical model distinction drawn in this text is not applicable to the ayervedic scene, and indigenous medical institutions in India are, to use Riggs' terms, diffuse and *defracted* rather than specific and *differentiated* as in allopathic medicine.[9] However, as the Scenario selection introducing this chapter indicates, the coming of modern mass society, literacy, and the mass media have altered even this foundation so much that ayervedic physicians now feel they can deal with individual illnesses in the daily press.

Seemingly paradoxical is the fact that the coming of Western medicine to India in the guise of British colonialism did not result in the total replacement of ayervedic medicine with the allopathic medicine of the colonial rulers, but rather in a revisionist posture of indigenous medicine as a way by which the ruled might reassert their cultural and political identity and autonomy. If, for example, as has been argued, Western allopathic medicine appears most closely linked to scientism, bureaucratization, and professionalism, ayervedic medicine seems to have a stronger institutional link to cultural traditionalism. But as a medical system, the important point to keep in mind is that ayervedic medicine in India, like allopathic medicine in the West, is sustained and perpetuated not so much by the empirical "evidence" it may muster to demonstrate whether or not it "works," but more on the strength of its being there with certain historic and structural supports that are lost when one moves from one sociocultural tradition to another. In our terms, ayervedic medicine may seem in our organizational terms to be legitimate, while its operational principles and philosophy lean more in the direction of the incredible.

Much the same might be said for indigenous Chinese medicine, with the possible important distinction that Chinese medicine has been *politicized* to a degree that is true neither of allopathic nor ayervedic medicine. That is, the link between cultural purism, political orthodoxy, and the perpetuation of indigenous Chinese medicine may have been strengthened by the isolation of the Communist forces during the long Chiang-Kai-Shek reign when the civil revolution survived Western assimilation, as well as the battle with the Chiang and Japanese forces. Thus, adherence to traditional Chinese forms of medicine signifies not only one's cultural purity but one's loyalty to political dogma as well. This adherence has nothing to do with the concepts of legitimation and credibility, which when applied to allopathic medicine and Western alternatives may seem of some classificatory use but seem less useful when applied to the indigenous and dominant medical systems in other historical and cultural settings.

Thus eclectic and pragmatic allopathic medicine remains the dominant form in the Western world, accommodating itself in a gradual evolutionary sense with the marginal and partial medical systems that periodically arise as alternatives to it. In general, however, it is safe to say that the social organization of allopathic medicine encorporates partial and incomplete medical alternatives into its division of power and authority only when it can exercise explanatory and organizational power over it. Much the same can be said for the wide range of paraprofessionals now counted as legitimate and credible "medical personnel," again because of their subordination to the control of the agents of allopathic medicine and not strictly because of the degree of professional autonomy they may have achieved.

THE SELF-HELP MOVEMENT: INCIPIENT MARGINAL SYSTEMS OF MEDICAL COUNTERCULTURES

The link between demonstrated technical expertise, professional designation, and received authority is an exceedingly strong one in Western social organization. Yet it is not complete; there are strong countercurrents favoring common sense, self-reliance, and the democratization and diffusion of authority that do not necessarily always retreat when confronted with affairs medical. In an intellectual sense, the former linkage may well be traced to the mind-body dualism that runs through much of contemporary psychology as well as throughout medicine. The argument proceeds something as follows: If the behavior of the body, as a system, can be both analytically and empirically distinguished from minded behavior, then it is possible to construct a science of the body, resulting in the "medical model of illness" contained in shorthand in this book. Once such a distinction, based on the premises of physical science, has been made, it is then possible to justify an additive and accumulated tradition of training basic to the creation of the medical professions and their organizational justification, with which we are all familiar.

If the mind-body dualism is rejected, as Sigmund Freud was so instrumental in bringing about, then the foundation underlying the contemporary and prevailing medical institutions are, if not shattered, at least very significantly weakened. If minded behavior and the behavior of the body are indeed manifestations of the same systematic processes, then it is possible to demystify science and its accompanying professional dominance—along with its subsidiary infrastructures such as medical education, its elaborate mechanisms producing high medical care costs, and most of all the ascribed authority with which standard medical practice has been endowed.

Now in a manner of speaking the marginal medical system here accounted—when they are not out-and-out market frauds—do represent a demystification of the medical establishment, involving a rejection of its legitimation and the foundations of its credibility. None, with the possible exception of chiropractic, has been successful for very long in sustaining its challenge. This may be due at least *partially* to the fact that whichever one we choose to look at, they constitute an attempt to "ape" allopathic medicine, and none can do as well what allopathic medicine can do; hence in the long run they are doomed to downright failure and rejection.

Out of such premises, often not well articulated, have grown such movements as the elaboration of a fairly widespread *natural foods* movement; physical exercise, weight reducing, and body-caring enterprises and activities of one sort or another; various community-based counseling enclaves for marital problems; sexual behavior and performance groups; introspective meditation groups; numerous patient and ex-patient congeries offering help by those who "have been there" —parents of battered children, alcoholics, drug users, those who are high risks for venereal disease; pregnancy and abortion counseling centers; referral agents routing callers to other deprofessionalized self-help groups and agencies; parent associations for the promotion of the well-being of the mentally retarded; various information centers to promote the avoidance of health risks for cancer; hypertension control; health care payment advice; medical legal counseling; counseling centers for health matters peculiar to women; deprofessionalized centers for the help of the aging; genetic counseling; rape and suicide "hot-line" centers; and college and university wart clinics; as well as a host of others.

The self-help movement represents, perhaps oddly enough, *functional specialization* without *technical specialization* and *professionalization,* and the return to a "folk-based" health practice without the antiquity that these roots imply and without partial disintegration and assimilation by the dominant allopathic medical forms.

Let us consider some of the current spate of "self-help" activities that are on the fringe of the domain of health and examine whether they in fact constitute incipient marginal systems of health promotion, which will soon be either assimilated into the orbit of allopathic medicine, fade and die at the precult stage, or develop into authentic and long-lasting alternatives to the existing allopathic megasystem.

The term "self-help" refers to a conglomerate of groups, associations, and ideas concerning the promotion of health that, different though their focus may be, seem to share certain common characteristics:

1. Group efforts at health maintenance are to be preferred over individual-patient-practitioner relationships.

2. The concept and status of "patient" implies a childlike dependency and ignorance that only exacerbates the asymmetry between those giving help and those receiving help.

3. "Official" sanctioning of medical practitioners through license procedures, the control of admission to "professional" status, and governmental authorization impede rather than promote good health and well-being.

4. The residential isolation of those receiving help causes more health problems than it cures.

5. Persons who are afflicted with a health problem, or have recovered from one, are better able to help their fellow sufferers than are certified professional "specialists" who have not actually had those experiences.

6. The promotion of good health and well-being is enhanced when social distance between helper and helped is minimized.

7. Rigid and "standardized" regimens of health represent a bureaucratization and distortion of the health promotion processes.

8. Any person of reasonable intelligence and good intention is capable of helping others. It does not require the status differentials and mysticism that surround the practitioners of allopathic medicine.

9. Standard medicine now includes in its domain far too many possible forms of social deviance, and its efforts to incorporate other and additional avenues to well-being should be intercepted and forestalled by the further mobilization of self-help strategies.

Perhaps at the apex of this loosely organized self-help movement is the recent resurgence of fundamentalism in religion and the rebirth of the mass.

The range and variation in this protosocial movement is immense: An Episcopal Church in New York City holds "healing services" at noon every Thursday employing the work of "psychic healers," who claim to abolish pain through prayer;[10] "sensitivity training sessions" are used aboard a U.S. Navy aircraft carrier to resolve a ship's company racial tension problems;[11] interest is becoming aroused in Philippine and Tibetan "mind surgery," in which the skin is presumably parted and internal parts restored without the use of anesthesia or scalpel; prayer sessions are claimed to make cancer tumors regress;[12] apricot pits as a cure for cancer cause a legal and professional brouhaha throughout the country; "psychorelaxation exercises" are reported in a distinguished British medical journal to reduce hypertension in a longitudinal study of patients (statistical controls are employed);[13] parents (especially those of ill young children) turn away from doctors and the hospitals and to the church in the search for solace if not cures; a spiritualist church in Chicago has been raising money for nearly 20 years in order to build a cancer hospital that will be faith-oriented;[14] a well-known Evangelist raises nearly $26 million to build a faith-oriented medical center, which will not be permitted by the regional health facilities planning council; the proprietor of an occult bookstore in Chicago claims to have cured his slow blindness by rubbing urine into his eyes each morning;[15] an estimated 40 million American citizens were served by some 5000 astrologers for various health and health-related matters—a $200 million per year business; and the National Council of Churches reports over 400 "spiritualist" and "healing" churches in the United States, with at least 150,000 members;[16] a witch's coven in Brentwood, New York, claims to have cured a blocked tear duct and bleeding ulcers.[17]

The health of women has become politicized in the past decade with strong repercussions on the prevailing handling of obstetrical and gynecological programs: feminist protagonists travel from group to group demonstrating self-help methods of breast examination and cervical cancer tests, as well as a controversial method of menstrual period termination used also as an early method of self-abortion;[18] a female promoter of "home remedies" brought about by a diet made up strictly of yogurt is found guilty of fitting a diaphragm without a medical license. A phonograph record is marketed for $3.95 promising a self-hypnosis for the purpose of easy weight loss; a self-administered urinalysis test is offered in conjunction with a specified purchase of vitamins;[19] in spite of the lack of demonstrated success, 16 acupuncture clinics operate in Washington, D.C., alone, offering acupuncture treatments for cure of nerve deafness;[20] and in an article entitled "A Surgeon's Magic Touch That's Too Good to Be True," William Rice is reported to describe a psychic surgeon whose operations take between

15 and 30 minutes.[21] A soothing potion is rubbed over the area to be operated and cotton is placed over it. What looks like blood is said to appear and the surgeon produces what is said to be a tumor. No tools or implements seem to be used during this procedure. This particular psychic surgeon has been forced to migrate to the Philippines where so-called psychic surgery has been practiced, and where it is said to have prospered for two decades. These practitioners do not claim to possess special powers; that is attributed to God. It must be said, however, that none of the tissues reportedly removed from patients in this fashion have ever been authenticated as having come from human beings.

One thing of great interest with regard to the many manifestations of the self-help movement is not so much their validity but rather the very fact that they exist and continue to proliferate—representing, as it were, a growing disillusionment with the bureaucratization and elaboration of "standard medicine" occurring alongside an increasing health awareness and growing health expectations.

A similar proliferation is occurring within the medical division of labor itself, and that is the subject of the next chapter.

SCENARIO II

Allopathic medicine and mass society: clinical diagnosis by mail

Diagnosis by George C. Thosteson, M.D., *Providence Journal,* Friday February 3, 1978:

Question from Miss L.:
   Q. What does it mean when the eye twitches? I have heard superstitions that if your right eye twitches you have trouble and if your left eye does, it is a good sign.—Miss L.
   A. Superstition and medicine don't mix. It is a habit or a tic. They are common in children from age 5 to 12 and usually begin as purposeful movements, but can develop to automatic ones. It's rare for this kind of tic to be a sign of a disease. Some may occur with excessive fatigue.
   I knew a doctor whose eyelid twitched only when he did not

take his thyroid medication. Most childhood tics are more disturbing to parents than harmful to the child. In children, watch for other signs. Could be signs of the Tourette syndrome, a special problem.

Dr. Thosteson's Note:
Your thyroid plays a critical health role for you—in everything from eyesight to fertility. Dr. Thosteson explains this important, and misunderstood, gland in his booklet, "Your Thyroid: How It Works for You." To get a copy, enclose 50 cents and a long, stamped and self-addressed envelope to him care of this newspaper.

NOTES

1 Max Weber, "Science as a Vocation," in *From Max Weber,* H. H. Gerth and C. W. Mills, Eds. New York: Oxford, 1946.
2 Ivan Illich, *Medical Nemesis.* New York: Random House, 1976, p. xi.
3 Renee Fox, "The Medicalization and Demedicalization of American Society," in *Doing Better and Feeling Worse,* J. H. Knowles, Ed. New York: American Academy of Arts and Sciences, 1977, pp. 9–10.
4 James Cornell, *Fakes, Frauds, and Phonies.* New York: School Book Service, 1974.
5 David Elkind, "Wilhelm Reich—The Psychoanalyst as Revolutionary," *New York Times Magazine* (April 18, 1971).
6 Associated Press Bulletin, "Scientology Founder Sentenced," February 15, 1978.
7 Ron Hubbard, *Dianetics.* New York: Grosset & Dunlap, 1978, pp. 363–364.
8 Charles Leslie, "The Modernization of Asian Medical Systems," in *Rethinking Modernization,* J. Poggie and R. Lynch, Eds. Westport, Conn.: Greenwood Press, 1974, pp. 43–44.
9 Fred W. Riggs, *Administration in Developing Countries.* Boston: Houghton Mifflin, 1964.
10 "Healing: Mind Over Matter?" *Newsweek,* 83 (April 29, 1974), 67–68.
11 Personal field experience, *U.S.S. Wasp,* U.S. Naval Air Station, Quonset Point, Rhode Island, July 1972.
12 William Rice, "A 'Surgeon's' Magic Touch That's Too Good to Be True," *Today's Health,* 52 (June 1974), 54–59. By permission.
13 Chandra Patel, "12 Month Follow-up of Yoga and Biofeedback in the Management of Hypertension," *Lancet,* 1 (January 1975), 62–64.
14 F. Glen Loyd and Theodore Irwin, "How Quackery Thrives on the Occult," *Today's Health,* 48 (November 1970), 20–23.
15 Ibid.
16 Ibid.
17 "The Yogurt Cure," *Newsweek,* 80 (Dec. 18, 1972), 44.
18 Ibid.
19 E. J. Kahn, Jr., "A Stamp of Disapproval for These 'Medical' Malpractitioners" *Today's Health,* 52 (March 1974), 20–23.
20 Samuel Rosen, "Beware of the 'Quackpuncturist' Who Operates for Profit," *Today's Health,* 52 (August 1974), 6–7.
21 Rice, op. cit.

SUGGESTED READINGS

L. Ron Hubbard, *Dianetics: The Modern Science of Mental Health.* New
York: Grosset & Dunlap, 1978.
*Originally published in 1950, this is the doctrinaire and standard text for the
Church of Scientology. Worth scanning as an exercise in science fiction,
futurology, religion, and mass persuasion.*

Sigmund Freud, *The Psychopathology of Everyday Life.* New York: New
American Library, n.d.
*The original tour de force on "slips of the tongue" and other evidence of the
sickness all around us.*

Earl L. Koos, *The Health of Regionville.* New York: Columbia University
Press, 1954.
*An interesting section on folk medicine in a modern community; common
health practices before the doctor is consulted.*

Wilhelm Reich, *Character Analysis.* New York: Orgone Institute, 1945.
*Reichian analytic thinking before some of his more exotic ideas were formu-
lated.*

Henry E. Sigerist, *A History of Medicine: I. Primitive and Archaic Medicine.* New York: Oxford, 1951.
An historical account of a variety of "prescientific" medical systems.

The "granny" midwife: cooptation of a folk practitioner

Midwifery, considerably reduced in scope, is still practiced among Negroes in a Southeastern rural region. Seen as a social institution in partial disintegration, marginal to modern medical practices, and subject to powerful official opposition, it permits the study of institutional adaptation to stress. The old midwife practiced with the sponsorship and personal support of the white physician. She was "called" to her occupation and trained through a familial apprenticeship. The new midwife is trained and officially appointed by a Health Center. The old midwife has continued to retain by far the largest share of practice by reliance upon her power and prestige in the Negro community, but urban influences are affecting her clientele, and she is faced with competitors rather than successors.

From B. Mongeau, H. Smith, and A. Maney, "The 'Granny' Midwife, Changing Roles and Functions of a Folk Practitioner." *American Journal of Sociology,* March 1961.

CHAPTER 8

Paraprofessionals in medicine: the decline or crystallization of medical dominance

Although it is true that the most prevalent current drift in demedicalization is in the direction of "self-help" models on the one hand and the deprofessionalization of relatively small sectors of the growing medical domain on the other, it remains true that the umbrellalike network of established allopathic medicine does not now have, nor did it have in the past, any serious competitor. Indeed, even those counterthrusts sketched in the preceding chapter never posed any real or long-standing threat to the viability of "regular" medicine. That is evidenced by the fact that with the exception of a relatively small number of dedicated antimedicine zealots—some Christian Scientists and naturopathic enthusiasts of varying degrees of religious or secular commitment—nonlegitimate and nonallopathic health patterns have tended to be "add-ons" to the ongoing allopathic medical practices of most members of American society. That is, few persons actually *reject* the regular medicine system (although they may occasionally denounce it), despite the fact that the lay referral system and the persuasive powers of the mass media may somewhat influence them to "try other things as well."

At the moment, therefore, the dominance of allopathic medicine continues unabashed in the face of the kind of attack that someone of Illich's powers of elocution may be able to launch. But it must also be said that the present codification of allopathic medicine is both enhanced and potentially threatened *internally* by the growing complexity of the division of labor in medicine over which the physician attempts to exercise dominance and control. The astounding proliferation in the complexity of the medical division of labor over the past quarter-century stands as evidence of the army of occupational forms and organizational potentials over which the central figure in allopathic medicine—the doctor—might increase his dominance. Its sheer size and complexity, however, may lead to significant alterations in some of the key elements in the medical enterprise—access to patients, the initiation of services, the determination of treatment priorities, and the general establishment of medical priorities. That is, medicine may be unable to avoid some of the inescapable consequences of its own magnitude.

MEDICAL OCCUPATIONAL STRUCTURE

As seen in Table 8.1, there are now no less than 297 distinct occupations in the health industry. This does not include the fully 50 different M.D. specialties, ranging in alphabetical order from aerospace medicine specialist, to laryngologist, to nuclear medicine specialist, to urologist. Nor does this list include the large categories whose members *may or may not* work directly in collaboration with or *under the control of a physician* (this includes health administrative services—14 different jobs; medical data processing—3 different positions; dentistry and allied services—18 occupations; funeral directors and embalmers—2 occupations; library services—3 positions; pediatric medicine—12 occupations; psychology—15 different occupations; medical secretarial and office services—3 occupations; speech pathology and audiology—3 occupations; vocational rehabilitation counseling—2 occupational headings; medical sociology, anthropology, and economics—3 occupations).

TABLE 8.1

Medical occupational categories and job specializations

Occupational category	Number of specific occupations
Basic sciences in the health field	24
Biomedical engineering	8
Clinical laboratory services	29
Dietetic and nutritional services	25
Environmental sanitation	12
Food and drug protective services	11
Health and vital statistics	8
Health education	5
Health information and communication	6
Medical records	10
Medicine and osteopathy (allopathic physicians)	50
Midwifery	2
Nursing and related services	38
Occupational therapy	3
Opticianry	10
Optometry	8
Orthotic and prosthetic technology	15
Pharmacy	16
Physical therapy	5
Radiologic technology	6
Respiratory therapy	4
Specialized rehabilitation services	15
"Miscellaneous" health services	37
Total number of doctor-related health occupations	297

By this method of calculation, the division of labor in the health industry—broadly refined—contains no less than 375 different occupations. Further exempted from this list are the quite large number of lower-level housekeeping and maintenance personnel whose work, though undertaken in medical settings of one kind or another, is not medically involved, nor is their character shaped in any significant way by medical surroundings in which the work is accomplished. The same exemption also holds for personnel who are only incompletely or temporarily involved in medically related work—construction workers of varying types and even architects and engineers, some who actually spend their entire careers designing medical establishments along the lines suggested by medical personnel.

So when all of these ancillary and periodic personnel are added to the total list, there are well over 400 different occupations directly or indirectly related to the health enterprise, *most of whom* work only or primarily at the behest of physicians, but with varying degrees of autonomy that they may exercise in the initiation, interpretation, and judgment of the course of medical treatment. There are a number of useful ways to classify such occupations, with the degree of "professionalization" being perhaps the *least* enlightening as to the operation of the internal dynamics of the complex division of labor in this growing field of human endeavor.

The following reordering of these occupational forms in medicine represents one way of organizing the array of occupations involved in some classificatory scheme that captures some of the important dynamics of health care, particularly in relation to how and by whom medical decisions are made and how and by whom they are carried out.

The term "profession" carries with it the notion that people who are so designated are in the possession of knowledge superior to that held by nonprofessionals. The concept presupposes therefore that "professional" knowledge is more difficult and costly to acquire than is "nonprofessional" knowledge and is capable of being assimilated by only a few people. This is in contrast to "nonprofessional" knowledge, which is commonly understood to be a good deal easier to come by, is less time-consuming and costly to acquire, and can be acquired and applied by pretty nearly anyone.

A further shibboleth of the term "professional" is that since such knowledge is imbued with a certain acquired sanctity, people who possess it have a right to apply it quite aside from the willingness of consumers to have it applied to them. This is in contrast to nonprofessional knowledge and services, which operate more fully in the open market and are far more subject to the "will" of the people. It is further commonly accepted that professionals, because of their superior specialized knowledge, also are *generally* more wise and knowledgeable and therefore ought to be in authoritative positions superior to those occupied by less knowledgeable (and therefore less professional) workers. Hence we have a neat and reasonable scheme to explain the superior authority and power surrounding the role of physicians and those who are inferior to them in the realm of knowledge—and therefore necessarily in general wisdom, power, and authority.

It goes without question that the physician occupies the key role in this enormous division of employment. In virtually every case the physician is *nominally* in control, whether practicing in solo fee-for-service practice or as chief of service in a large hospital employing dozens of ancillary and subprofessionals in medicine. On what does this authority rest?

PHYSICIAN DOMINANCE

The criterion of "superior" knowledge, while obviously true in some or even many instances, is neither always true nor is it even at the root of the physician's authority in those cases where he or she is more knowledgeable. And while it may also be the case that the formal period of training for physicians is probably considerably longer than it is for the occupants of most other health occupations, this generalized authority is not traceable to that fact, nor is it justified on that basis. By the same token, the seeming *imperative* of medical technology—that its application can be seldom be easily turned down—does not stem from any observable *demonstration* of its laudatory effects. In fact, the aftermath of medical applications may in many cases seem to be worse than merely living with the affliction: Parts may be individually improved, but one's whole quality of life may in fact be diminished. If, then, the physician's authority cannot be easily traced to the possession of superior knowledge, nor to an extended period of training, nor to prior claims about "results," what does it rest upon? In a general sense, the authority of the physician is traceable to his *organizational* or *bureaucratic location* and the *moral authority* that falls upon his or her shoulders as a result of the fact that it is the physician who is both *organizationally accountable*—and even personally *liable* in cases in which patients may seek redress for presumed wrongdoings. Let us explicate that point, because it relates directly to the solidarity and compliancy sought in the complex division of occupations in which the physician is presently involved. It is the combination of *organizational location* and *moral responsibility* that forms the basis for the consolidation of the exercise of broad-scope authority in the person of the physician and in the capacity of the physician to influence others in the medical scene.

A central feature of this authority is the physician's *generalized* capacity to influence others in the medical scene. While "hard" data are not adequately reflective of this fact, physicians exceed all other members of the medical division of labor in the aura and mystique that surround them and their utterances. This capacity is not unrelated to the fact that it is the physician group that has been authorized the right to declare what is properly in the domain of medicine and therefore properly under its direction and control. In this regard (as we shall discuss in somewhat more detail in the next chapter) the scope of normative and behavioral deviations that have come to be included under the "medical" rubric has broadened nearly beyond definition in the past few decades, to the point where nearly anything that seems to interfere with a person's capacity for the "fullest realization of the human potentiality" has to be regarded as a medical matter to be dealt with in medical terms and under the purview of the principal medical overseer—the physician.

This generalized influence and the right granted to make "medical" definitions lie at the root of the physician's power—not necessarily superior knowledge.

Second, an important fact is the physician's professionally established and organizationally supported right to *initiative* medical action and to direct others in carrying out such action. It is literally true, as Freidson has pointed out, that the patient's decision to enter into a medical relationship has its roots in some locatable "lay" referral system. But however true that might be, the impetus given to such apparent patient initiative is based on medically established precepts and not strictly on lay knowledge as such. At the same time, it is the physician who sets forth a plan of action to be followed by ancillary personnel, is a prime mover in coordinating their efforts, assesses outcomes, and terminates medical involvement with the patient. This means of course, that the physician is both a *manager,* a *programmer,* and *coordinator* for the division of labor involved in all cases, however simple they might be.

Stated in schematic form, the exercise of physician dominance is made possible through the authorization of the physician to determine means and ends in the medical enterprise, to set their content, and to direct others in task assignments to see to their fulfillment. In general terms, the medical decision-making process can be schematically presented as in Figure 8.1. The composition of the medical team and its members' relationship to cases take the broad distribution as shown. Where the division of labor and the societal authorization processes endow a medical occupation with control both over the ends (cell I) to be pursued and determination of the means by which these ends are to be attacked, a "professional" decision may be said to exist, and the physician in charge of a case possesses that decision-making power.

This is quite aside from the *content* of the physician's technical knowledge; it has to do with the allocation of decision making as a process and not its substance. In the opposite cell, number IV, personnel who hold positions regards as strictly supportive in nature (typically housekeeping, clinical volunteers, maintenance personnel, personnel services, and others) are denied access to the determination of both means and ends and are excluded from the decision-making power altogether, although in unanticipated crisis situations their presence and experience might be taken into account. It is to be emphasized that the mere *occupational title* carried by a worker is not necessarily an accurate predictor of his or her decision-making position. The two—title and power —can be both analytically and empirically quite separate.

Program and policy decisions by way of contrast tend to predominate in the general area of goals rather than a combination of goals and means, and are reserved for sponsoring functionaries who are nominally outside the organization altogether. This may include "close" sponsors such as members of boards of sponsoring agencies—trustees, hospital councils, federal funding agencies, or local funding agencies such as the United Way and Blue Cross–Blue Shield. Other external parties, such as local medical societies are protective of the professional cadres' right to determine *means* and at the same time preserving that group's right to act in a strong advisory capacity vis-à-vis making pro-

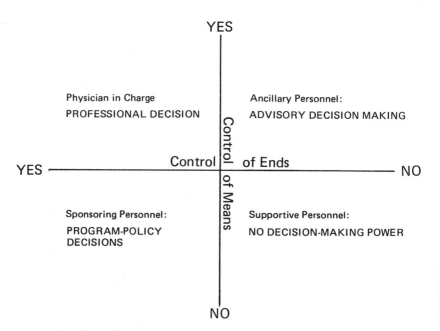

FIGURE 8.1 Authorization for control of medical "means" and "ends."

gram and policy decisions. Finally, ancillary personnel–nurses as the prototypical case but including many of the occupational groups specified in Table 8.1—hold strictly advisory decision-making power, although at the same time they exercise considerable authority over the activities of the "supportive" personnel. The drift, of course, is for specific occupational groups to seek greater influence in all three sectors; for supportive personnel, largely through unionization, to achieve "ancillary" status, thereby securing some measure of advisory decision making; for ancillary personnel, including nurses, some medical specialist such as anesthesiologists, pathologists, and physiatrists, to claim "physician" status and hence some degree of professional decision-making power; and for those presently making professional decisions to gain some measure of program-policy decision-making authority, largely by means of securing external support and authorization that goes beyond the extant sponsoring structure of the institution.

Thus the differential allocation of professional status results in these three broad categories of health workers, each with distinctive decision-making prerogatives. Each has a tendency to seek greater degrees of control over medical means and ends, thereby achieving increased autonomy from others and hence codifying its claims to professional status. Out of this status, claims may be made and imputations secured from others concerning these groups' superior knowledge, their relative importance, and their right to *initiate* action, to *direct* others in the conduct of their work, and to declare *closure* in a case. In general, however, means *and* ends control is reserved for those who are granted the privilege of making professional decisions, and this is why nearly every occupation in the health division of labor seeks to become authenticated as professional. The consequences of this trend —both in terms of skyrocketing medical care costs as well as complexities and ambiguities for organizational structure and dynamics in the field of health—are so obvious as to require no further comment. In short, the physician's heretofore exclusive claim to exercising such control is no longer unchallenged by those who presently enjoy only ancillary and supportive stature.

There is a second derivative of varying control over means and ends that importantly affects the *salience* and *cogency* of the decision-making authority assigned to different functionaries in the medical world. It has to do with the occupational group's "professional" stature and the *form* taken by decision-making influence. This is shown diagrammatically in Figure 8.2.

Again, the quadrant occupied by "professionals" represents the most highly elaborated and convincing decision-making style. Their control over the discourse of both means and ends bestows upon decisions an imperative character that acquires much of the facade of computation. Links between cause and effect are accorded a logic that they may not in fact have when subject to empiric test, but nonetheless they are regarded as inevitable by the uninformed observer. The "reasoning" behind any specific professionally authorized health pursuit and the strategies for bringing it about carries with it the weight both of reason and of science, and hence are "computational" in character. Thus it serves effectively as a buffer between the carrying out of such decisions and those who would impose alternatives from one of the other three decision-making occupational sectors. The hoary phrase "follow the doctor's orders" is a standard dictum applicable to both co-workers and patient alike.

Again, the supportive personnel in the opposite quadrant represent the most contrasting type, possessing little or no decision-making power except insofar as they may exercise some degree of information control and either its "leaking" or "suppression." They may, in some circumstances, "ape" the language and style of authenticated ancillary personnel and occasionally attempt to coopt some degree of decision making on those rather shaky grounds.

Coming closest to the "computational" form of decision imposition available to the professional cadre are ancillary personnel (nurses, etc.) who have access to advisory decision making. And this is based upon skills of "judgment" rather than the seemingly irrefutable "computation" of the professional. It is the ancillary personnel's increased

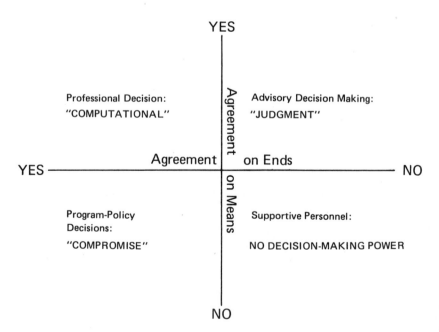

FIGURE 8.2 Means-and-ends agreement and form of decision making.

access to the patient and his records, in addition to their increased pool of specialized technical knowledge, which strengthens their judgmental role in influencing the final decisions of the professionals.

Finally, in cell IV are to be found the program-policy decision makers whose sphere of influence is circumscribed by alternatives in broad compromise with respect to general goals, interfering with the work of the professionals in the broadest sense of the term, delineating the contours of the economic restraints and limitations within which professionals must work and the medical goals toward which the resources of the enterprise will be addressed.

Summarizing the implications of Figures 8.1 and 8.2: Where there is agreement as to means and ends, "professional" decisions are called for, those of a "computational" character predominate, and in the ranges of cases from a simple one-on-one doctor-patient relationship to the integration of a "team" effort in a large medical complex, the physician cadres hold sway in this quadrant. Where no agreement as to means and ends occurs, then "supportive" personnel who are involved exercise no control and are generally regarded as inferior to all others in the enterprise. Closest to the professionals are the ancillary personnel on the one hand and the policymakers on the other. In the first instance, there is agreement as to the means to be employed but not the ends. In this case ancillary personnel exercise control over the means to be employed and exercise their influence by means of persuasive judgment. In the case of policymakers (boundary-spanning personnel such as top-level administrators and boards of trustees come to mind immediately as examples), control over the determination of ends is possessed and decisions come to take the form of a series of compromises.

So within the framework here set forth, physicians occupy a key and pivotal position in the sense that they have a complex array of specialized subprofessionals working *more or less* under their control, but only partially so due to the fact that at certain points in the flow of work, physicians relinquish some degree of autonomy over "means" to these ancillary and subprofessionals. On the other side, physicians are themselves partially subordinate (are themselves in a sense ancillary) to more general-level policymakers represented by sponsoring agencies, funding sources, and other external quasi-members. This paradigm does not include the *patients* as a force to be reckoned with. This factor will be treated in the chapter to follow.

STRAIN IN THE DIVISION OF RESPONSIBILITY

Given this rough distribution of rights, obligations, and authority within the medical occupation, complex internal stress and conflict may be noted to be as enduring and lasting as is equanimity and quietude.

The members of each of these four sectors are continually, if not always openly, involved in maneuvering and negotiation concerning their domains.

This may be an opportune point to say a few words about the doctor-patient relationship insofar as the patient may in fact be regarded as a "sponsor" of medicine, who is at the same time its consumer and its source of resources. With the possible exception of extreme crisis or seemingly hopeless situations, doctors are not free to do "anything they want" with patients. First there are certain restraints against this, found in legal statutes, professional ethics, and the general normative system surrounding medicine. Patients may not be openly exploited either financially or with regard to the gross abuse of their bodies; patients have a right to be informed of their diagnosis and at least some of their family members informed of the prognosis, especially if it is a poor one; the doctor is behaving under considerable risk if he engages in surgical procedures not agreed upon in advance, no matter how imperative they might appear on the face of it. In general, the patient has a right to honest and informed treatment, and should not be subject to bizarre treatments unless informed of their uniqueness.

Should any of these general prescriptions be violated, doctors (either on "means" grounds or on "ends" grounds) face the possibility of severe retribution brought either by their patients in the form of malpractice suits or by their peers through rebuke, loss of hospital staff privileges, or (in extreme cases) in the loss of license. It should be pointed out that professional *self-control* and the fear of malpractice suits are probably more effective as deterrents to this kind of behavior than are the varieties of possible peer rebukes. However true that might be, the doctor must provide his or her consumers, within admittedly quite broad limits, what they will accept—if not always what they openly desire. In a sense, the structure of medical practice (particularly its economic arrangements) in this society makes the physician something of an "employee" of his or her patients. Should the "customers" not like the services rendered to them and for which they pay, they can always take their trade elsewhere. Although such "doctor swapping" may often be based on trivial causes and grievances, it is the fact that it occurs that is consequential. The ambiguities that enter into the seemingly simple one-on-one doctor patient relationship will be elaborated in the chapter to follow.

The imposition of restraints on the physician from formal sponsoring agents is probably somewhat more subtle in its effects. No medical treatment team—solo fee-for-service practice or full-time hospital complex employment—is capable of satisfying all interested third parties to the activity. In the most general sense, medical facilities are *public resources,* which are answerable to the citizenry either in the marketplace or in the courts. Although they may appear to operate in vacuo, they actually do not. They are subject to a variety of thinly camouflaged "voter" and owner sovereignties, which very importantly affect the degree of self-control implied in the diagrammatic schemes in Figures 8.1 and 8.2.

In the case of practice forms which go beyond the relatively simple organization of solo fee for service, medical practitioners are subject to a rich array of program policymakers that may limit very strictly their autonomy relative to the ideal of open choice of professional means and ends. Let us consider just a few of the limiting circumstances that stem from above and make practicing physicians somewhat subprofessionals themselves.

There is first the general sponsorship of the medical practice in which the allopathic physician engages—public versus private sponsorship perhaps being the most dramatic in their differences. As has already been discussed in Chapter 6, the charter of a medical practice is pivotal in the constraints set upon the practitioner, quite aside from the limitations imposed by bureaucratic settings generally. The public institution sets restraints of a unique kind upon the presumed omnipotence of the physician. The public hospital or other facility is usually merely one component unit in a network of publicly supported agencies, each one of which seeks maximum autonomy and financial independence in a situation of intense competition for public attention and support. Because of the depressed socioeconomic status of most of the clients of services such as these, they are engaged in negotiation and exchanges with their environments of a highly asymmetrical kind. They are caught in a spiraling decrease of available resources *along with* an increase of lines of external accountability. The "Catch-22" treadmill situation of the typical public institution is related to its initial low esteem in the public eye, which in turn leads to inadequate political and economic support; this leads inevitably to all the intraagency problems of short resources, low morale of both patients and staff, a scruffy and defeatist physical appearance, and so on, and inexorably to an unimpressive performance of service delivery. This last outcome helps them to affirm the earlier low esteem, which appears to bolster the cycle, and the whole series of events begin once again in a more intensified form.

Not infrequently such an institution represents something of a deviant career for medical personnel at all levels, producing on the one hand enormous problems in attracting and retaining highly qualified workers and on the other an insidious demoralization that extends down from the medical staff and throughout the patient populations. It is common in such institutions for many of the medical officers to have been foreign-trained, and their facility in the English language is often not impressive. Many have foresaken the relatively high rewards and risky entrepreneurism of private practice and have settled for the relatively secure institutional life, which often provides free housing, very cheap or free household and gardening labor, the use of an automobile, and other amenities that are found on "reservations" of all such fiefdoms. Hence, an ever-present danger in institutional medicine is its isolation from the very public it is chartered to serve and thinly veiled antagonism both toward the keepers of the public purse and toward the vagaries of the state legislature or city council that has the power to will reduce appropriations and favor some other equally dependent and underfunded public facility. There is often resentment of the down-and-out patient population it must serve, who may lack even the veneer of affability and sociability that often makes doctor-going and patient-seeing tolerable or even pleasant over the long haul of a life and a medical career.

In short, the contingencies brought about by the public institution being merely one, often small unit in a large *public* bureaucracy account for many of the sponsoring constraints on the ideal practice of medicine in such settings. Though isolated from the community, they are still a part of it; though charged with serving the public at large, their meager budgets, thin staffing charts, and patient overcrowding make such a charge more theory than reality. Life for patients in such circumstances will be touched upon in a later chapter. Suffice it to say that medical doctors in such an institution may appear to enjoy a certain special freedom and autonomy; in reality they are caught up in a bondage no less constricting than that of the patients. Whereas the physician practicing in the private sphere is a victim of the tyranny of the market on the one hand and the patient on the other, the doctor in the public sphere is a victim of the tyranny of the public bureaucracy and the partially self-imposed isolation that only serves to deepen community neglect and avoidance. The "constricted" charter of such a medical practice is at the root of these problems. Much the same has to be said for the military practitioner.

The continual mission of the military to be prepared to mobilize combat-ready troops places special opportunities as well as limitations on military doctors. On the one hand, they are caught between the sometimes conflicting possibility of awarding "sick status" (more than merely the sick role as conceptualized by Parsons in that it is a formal readjustment—sometimes of a permanent nature) in cases where it is not objectively justified, or holding up strict medical military criteria and hence be responsible for fielding debilitated troops. The peculiar opportunity such practice offers the medical professional, however, is the chance to practice in a dazzling array of different practice settings

—from the elaborate and sophisticated Walter Reed Hospital in Washington, to the most isolated backpack field medical station of the M*A*S*H variety on the other—all without endangering the long-term development of a career. There are other distinct advantages of military medicine, advantages both to the practicing professional and to the patient: the movement of patient from one facility to another as needed constitutes no great problem, as it often does in private medicine, in that organizational boundaries are easily permeated and no bridges are "cut." Since price is not an issue, it need not enter into the mind of the potential patient as he or she crosses the line between feeling well and feeling ill and doing something about it. On the doctor's side, since profit as a possibility has been contracted out of the situation, that motive need not hover as a specter as it surely does in the private practice of medicine. As the patient is moved from one level of service to another, the physicians involved are not "taking someone else's patients," and as the patient moves around the system, so too does a complete and long-term medical record to facilitate continuity and assure uniformity of the medical history. In a very real sense, military medicine stands as one of the prototypes of so-called "comprehensive care," and civilian medicine has much to learn from it. The nagging question always remains, however: What is the military doctor, the servant or the server?

In a different vein, both the teaching hospital and the specialty hospital pose certain other kinds of constraints on the ideal means-ends control exercised by medical professionals.

In an analytical sense, the teaching hospital occupies a position analogous to the public hospital in that its "prime beneficiaries" are *not necessarily nor always* those who are its proximate patients. Since the teaching hospital is also almost always a research hospital as well, it must not only treat patients, conduct research for the future well-being of those not present, and provide students with useful learning experiences, it must also be organized in such a manner that all three of these masters are served to an "acceptable" level. But the university teaching hospital is also an economy and as such relies upon patients' fees over and above revenue from gifts, research grants, and interest from endowments.

The admissions officer is a key figure in balancing this set of often competing interests, and it is this person's conception of his or her role that is critical in shaping the broad contours of the opportunities and contrasts imposed upon the practice of medicine in this type of setting.

As Hollingshead and Duff describe, the teaching hospital relies heavily upon "walk-ins" not only as a source of revenue but also to supply useful teaching materials. "Walk-ins" are patients who enter the hospital without sponsorship of a staff physician and therefore can be more easily assigned to the teaching wards where the teaching and treatment functions occur simultaneously. The admissions officers, according to the authors, can be classed broadly as being either "sieves" or "rocks," respectively, depending upon their propensity to admit only good teaching walk-ins to the hospital regardless of their capacity to pay, or their inclination to admit nearly all walk-ins regardless of the usefulness of their clinical picture but more strictly on the basis of their capacity to pay. In the ideal situation, of course, the teaching hospital is blessed with an abundance of walk-ins, a large number of whom are not only stricken with curous illnesses and diseases but also display a capacity to contribute to the monetary economy of the hospital. Thus the admissions officer becomes something of an "instant diagnostician" as well as a sociological assessor—in the first capacity by selecting the most interesting cases and in the second by judging the walk-ins' social status by a quick assessment of their dress, their demeanor, and whatever can be determined about the candidates' occupation. Hence the sponsorship of such institutions and the mission set forth in their charter pose special limiting parameters on the kind of practice likely to occur in them and, in the long haul, upon the kinds of clinical experiences that will form the central core of clinical experiences their trainees are likely to have. The "rock" contributes to a sound institutional economy at the possible cost of clinical depth and variety; the "seive" fills the wards with interesting and baffling cases, although the till may be simultaneously emptied.

The practice of medicine taking place in a corporate setting is somewhat analogous to the case of the military doctor and is to be distinguished from the "proprietary" type of hospital discussed earlier, in which the owners of the enterprise are also its practicing professionals. (See Chapter 3.) But perhaps more so than in the army or navy, the special privileges stemming from being ill are placed in possibly more serious jeopardy when the doctor is in the employ of the owners rather than by the patients. The reason is that although it may appear that the doctor serves merely a series of isolated cases, he or she is actually serving the interests of a more generalized collectivity. For as Carl Gersuny has indicated in connection with a study of the social history of industrial accidents, illness is sometimes used by workers as a strategy to avoid coercion by owners and managers. To call such behavior 'malingering' implies a value judgment favoring the attitudes and judgment of administrators over those of workers. And it is clear that other kinds of subordinates in organizational settings, including school children and members of the military forces, often resort to the sick role as a way of confronting authority figures.[1]

In addition, "specialty" hospitals (notably those limiting care to patients suffering from particular kinds of illness) create special circumstances that limit and shape the professional's attitude toward work. Renee Fox, for example, in a study of a hospital dealing exclusively with patients suffering from incurable—though not necessarily fatal—diseases found special limitations on the establishment of a traditional doctor-patient relationship and even more so on the applicability of the classical "sick role" otherwise found to be so widespread in the handling of most acute short-term and curable illnesses.[2] She found similar special limiting circumstances in a hospital dealing with kidney dialysis patients and others on whom radical technologies were employed.[3] And the uncertainties produced by maladies such as tuberculosis and recovery from the effects of polio in children brought about special contingencies not found in other practice settings, as reported by Fred Davis[4] in the former case and by Julius Roth in the latter.[5] The present author found parallel kinds of limiting circumstances in studies of a children's psychiatric hospital[6] and an obstetrical-gynecological hospital.[7]

Thus the practice of medicine under special conditions of work reduce physicians' autonomy and in the colloquial sense their "professionalism" as well. And in some sense the history of collective bargaining is to guard against the corruption of the role of the physician by third-party conditions, as well as its corollary, the illegitimate use of the sick role by goldbrickers and featherbedders. And it is surely often the case that the company doctor, the prison doctor, and others emerge as instruments of groups whose interests conflict with those of the patient. In the absense of a recognized union the company doctor was often a dreaded figure who was viewed as threatening the livelihood of employees. Today many collective bargaining agreements provide for adjudication of conflicting medical opinions, thus implicitly recognizing the role of the physician as an agent of conflicting interest groups.[8]

The same kind of ambiguity and conflict can often be observed in the case of student health services in colleges and universities and in school nursing activities in which there are enormous pressures due to the double functions brought about through sponsorship structures. In the extreme cases, the professional role can become vulgarized to perform mere review and certifying functions rather than treatment.

In these ways at least, the professional authority of the physician is seldom of a pure type. Modifications of a somewhat different order are brought about by the growing presence of a virtual army of sub- and paraprofessionals on whom the physician is becoming increasingly dependent. Let us consider the situation of nurses.

THE NURSE: SUBORDINATE OR CO-WORKER?

The original assignment of women to a subordinate and even subservient role in health care seems to be as old as antiquity. However, the mystique that surrounds the female nursing role includes not only the notion that women possess special talents in the realm of nurturance and affective capabilities but also that such primordial capabilities require careful supervision and scrutiny by male overseers. Some have interpreted this link between mothering and magic as exploring the exploitation and torture of extraordinary women as witches during the Middle Ages. For as Ehrenreich and English have argued:[9]

> Witches lived and were burned long before the development of modern medical technology. The great majority of them were lay healers serving the peasant population, and their suppression marks one of the opening struggles in the history of man's suppression of women as healers. The other side of the suppression of witches as healers was the creation of a new male medical profession, under the protection and patronage of the ruling classes. This new European medical profession played an important role in the witch-hunts, supporting the witches' persecutors with "medical" reasoning: "Because the Medieval Church, with the support of kings, princes and secular authorities, controlled medical education and practice, the Inquisition (witch-hunts) constitutes, among other things, an early instance of the 'professional' repudiating the skills and interfering with the rights of the 'nonprofessional' to minister to the poor." The witch-hunts left a lasting effect: An aspect of the female has ever since been associated with the witch, and an aura of contamination has remained—especially around the midwife and other women healers. This early and devastating exclusion of women from independent healing roles was a violent precedent and a warning; it was to become a theme of our history. The women's health movement of today has ancient roots in the medieval covens, and its opponents have as ancestors those who ruthlessly forced the elimination of witches.

Whatever the historic facts might be concerning the link between witchery and nursing and the present asymmetry between doctors and nurses, it is true that the occupation of nursing is predominantly female, including nursing services provided to largely male populations—the military forces, for example. And it is indisputable that the nurse—as influential as she might be—is still greatly inferior to the doctor. This persisting difference seems to be due not so much to the imperative effects of differences in technical knowledge (the nurse is privy to a great deal of esoteric information as well as trained and skilled in activities not within the ken of the physician), nor can it be attributed to outstanding inferiority in the formal professional organization of the occupation. Nursing shares along with medicine an enormous amount of control over its own educational processes, its standards of licensure, and numerous other elements thought to distinguish a true profession from a mere occupation. To what may this asymmetry be attributable, and how vulnerable is it to erosion and a drift toward equality?

First, there are important differentiations of rank within the occupation itself, which may be as divisive as is the domain disputes between doctors and nurses generally. These differentiations have primarily to do with the different social organization of training to which nurses are subjected and their consequences for career commitment on the one hand and efforts at domain expansion on the other. They also have to do with the *level and scope* of training received and the fact that membership in the occupation of nursing is, to a considerable extent, a self-declared membership, a fact that does not help nursing in its efforts to distinguish itself sharply from the workaday population.[10]

There are presently four identifiable streams of training for nursing work, each of which involves a different level and scope of certification, and it is the level and scope of certification that authorizes the nurse's location in the medical authority system and confers generalized social status. And it is the combination of these two that forms the basis for workable claims to heightened professionalization. At the lowest level is to be found training as a licensed practical nurse. Here, the level of training has its equivalent in a relatively short-term vocational training program, which falls somewhere between the completion of high school and the beginning of junior college, and bestowing upon the recipient an equivalent generally low social status. The practical nurse's training is both narrow and relatively shallow, qualifying that person to work at medical tasks only under the close supervision of others—mainly nurses with higher levels of training. This kind of certification encourages membership by persons of relatively minimal ambitions for autonomy and increased social status, and does not reward the kind of deep and lifelong commitment typically found in the more highly professionalized occupations. As a result, work as a licensed practical nurse is undertaken as a kind of stopgap occupation, which persons move into and out of as other life circumstances demand and warrant. Sacrifices, that is, which may need to be made in other spheres of life may require a L.P.N. to work for varying periods of time, and not the other way around.

Somewhat higher in level and broader in scope is the "diploma" program, which also offers training strictly within a medical setting and is geared almost exclusively to supervised work under the direction of other nurses. Again, the generalized social status conferred by such training is not high, career commitment can be expected to be somewhat qualified, and movement in and out of the occupation easily facilitated. Somewhat higher is the associate degree program, offering a level of training roughly equal to that of junior college graduation, with some strictly academic studies, but still mainly subprofessional in nature. Next is the baccalaureate training, which is typically housed in a university setting, with students held responsible for a general course of study as well as technical nursing training. Such program certification is considerably higher than the previous two. It evokes greater career commitment on the part of its members, producing fewer nurses than the previous lower certification programs, but at the same time facilitating mobility out of the occupation because of the generalized transferability of certification made possible by the general education degree candidacy through which the candidates have passed. An even smaller number go on to the master's degree level, with its increased specialization and greater transferability. Finally, an even smaller number progress to the Ph.D. level, which often involves commitment to administration and/or research rather than on-line nursing work.

Thus, the lines of differentiation within the nursing profession tend to create schisms in the occupation itself along lines of level and scope of training which are likely to produce differences in career commitment, preparation for the autonomous exercise of skills, and the facilitation of movement out of the occupation as a result of the nature of the generalized social status conferred. All of this produces problems of uncertain solidarity within the occupation itself that impede the movement toward nursing autonomy.

Variations in the level and scope of training open to members of the nursing profession weaken its base for internal solidarity and do not contribute to its ability to identify itself in the public mind as a distinct profession worthy of increased autonomy and self-direction. There is a strong public feeling that, like elementary school teaching, "anyone" can become a nurse, that even a planned temporary commitment to the work (until marriage, or until the first child is born) is a thoroughly acceptable motivation, and that the income derived from it is strictly supplemental to that of the "real" breadwinner. So the ranks of the nursing occupations are filled with workers who come and go, who take a marginal role, if any, in the affairs of the professional association and with countless others who work strictly part-time.

In a very real sense, the present social organization of nursing is an adaptation to and accommodation to the secondary status it holds relative to those certified as "medically" rather than "nursing" trained. And with the possible exception of the situation in some nursing homes and homes for the aged, the nurse cannot properly speak of "her" patients; they are almost invariably those of doctors. Nor can she speak of her "turf," for the hospital is *always* the place and property, putatively if not nominally, of the physician.

It seems unlikely that merely adding layer upon layer of levels of training, and revising and rerevising curricula around changing concepts of the scope of the nursing role will in the foreseeable future bring about a substantial difference in the asymmetry between doctors and nurses. Although the functional roles of nurses might change in various ways, the *legal* responsibility almost always is held by the doctor, and it is out of this legal responsibility that functional power and authority are fundamentally rooted. Nurses may be perfectly willing to take on the status of "responsible agents," but physicians are unlikely to be willing to relinquish that burden because to do so involves relinquishing the fundamental sources of their power. As shall be indicated later, the transfer of medical functions to nonphysican personnel, while at the same time retaining legal responsibility, has been a central strategy by which the division of labor in medicine has been astoundingly expanded without fundamental alterations in the structure of authority and dominance.

Whatever diminution in the autonomy of the physician that has occurred from the nursing quarter must be laid to the growing reliance of the physician on the nurse as a source of information upon which medical judgments must be made.

As Rene Dubos has pointed out, one of the important consequences of this expanded division of labor in medicine is the limited amount of time each doctor actually spends in the presence of and in interaction with patients:[11] Charts are inspected, laboratory reports are reviewed, and nurses' notes are assimilated, while more and more of the patient's time is spent either alone or in the company of nurse and other para- and subprofessionals. As a result, doctors, largely by means of the burgeoning character of medical technology and its associated expansion of the division of labor, have relinquished and given over to others their traditional role of tending the sick. Thus, although doctors have greatly increased their authority options in terms of possible technical alternatives, they have lost out in a more subtle and yet profound way: by having to rely more and more upon information to which they are not directly privy and by the dispersion of the foundation for patient-doctor trust among a host of paraprofessionals. In this regard, Rose Coser's comparative analysis of a medical versus a surgical ward is instructive.[12]

According to Coser, the medical and surgical wards differ profoundly in the *functional* power and authority possessed by nurses as a consequence of their structure of authority and the manner by which work is conducted. In sum, nurses in the medical ward possess a much stronger component of "judgmental" authority than do their counterparts on the surgical ward, so much so that it "tilts" in the direction of moving to the left and across the perpendicular in Figure 8.1 into the "professional" cell customarily thought of as the exclusive domain of the physician. On the surgical side, in the most typical cases the outcome of surgery is known relatively soon, and the convalescent period can normally proceed without a great deal of medical monitoring once the immediate outcome is known. In such a circumstance the surgeon is quite literally in operational charge of the case. He or she conducts the procedures and follows the course of the outcome personally with little dependency upon the independent skills and knowledge of the nurse. In a sense, in the surgical ward the doctor is the nurse for the surgical patient, and the nurse's authority is strictly minimized.

On the medical ward, on the other hand, the clinical situation can be far more complex, with changes in the patient's condition occurring as the result of body alterations in response to changes in medication, physical therapy, or any number of manipulations in the patient's life environment. Unlike on the surgical ward, the attending physician may actually see and observe the patient for only very brief periods of time —perhaps a few minutes each day or even less. Accordingly, nurses and other paramedical specialists are likely to spend far more time with the patient than is the doctor and are often required to make decisions that are denied the surgical nurse. Perhaps more important is that the nurses and other ancillary personnel are in a key position to determine what information will be made available to the physician in charge—and with what degree of imperativeness and urgency. Thus they constitute a strong factor in determining the progress and development of a case. Much the same situation can be found in the case of the relative positions of the psychiatrist and ancillary personnel in a broad-based milieu-oriented psychiatric hospital and their counterparts in specifically focused single-therapy psychiatric institutions.[13] In these former cases, the division of labor involved in the care of patients is "flooded" with information stemming from paraprofessionals in the system. So in this *functional* sense the sharp distinction between "professionals" and "paraprofessionals" is most apparent than real.

Nevertheless, it remains true that at least at the initial stages, new occupational additions to the medical division of labor enter as strictly subservient to the authority of the doctor. The extreme case is dramatized by the virtual irradication of the "granny" midwife and her replacement with the "nurse-midwife."

THE SURVIVAL OF THE MIDWIFE ON POLITICAL
RATHER THAN MEDICAL GROUNDS

As has correctly been pointed out, the supervision of childbirth for pregnant women, regardless of their station in life, was undertaken almost exclusively by female midwives, who were not doctors.[14] And although men had begun to take up midwifery as a lucrative line of work by the middle of the eighteenth century (at least two had been knighted for their work with members of the royal family in Britain), it was not a recognized part of the medical establishment until nearly a century later when the practice of midwifery came under medical supervision and control. Some time later it was almost entirely subsumed as a medical specialty in its own right and became, almost de facto, strictly a man's occupation. What remained in the United States following this transformation was the so-called "granny" midwife—a folk practitioner primarily in the rural South who assisted women during pregnancy and birth without official medical authorization or supervision. Thus, by the beginning of this century, pregnant women were attended almost exclusively by male doctors, sometimes in the home, but more and more in a hospital context in conditions designed to facilitate the work of the physician rather than enhance the experience for mother and child.[15]

It is not unwarranted, therefore, to view the recent history of the transformation of care during pregnancy from midwivery to medical specialty as something of a prototype of the course of medical bureaucratization and until very recently, an inexorable explanation of the physician–hospital-dominated medical division of labor.

The virtual eradication of the "granny," or "lay," midwife over the past 30 years is shown dramatically in Table 8.2. The granny midwife, rare as she is today, is a true folk practitioner, plying her trade without formal medical or nursing training, operating without official authorization or sanctions, and gaining stature, respect, and a growing clientele as she herself grows older. But as the data in Table 8.2 clearly reveal this vestigial medical institution—itself the child of slavery and the world of rural preprofessionalism of the antebellum South had, by

TABLE 8.2
Lay midwives in relation to population: selected years, 1948 through 1973

| Year | LAY MIDWIVES | |
	Number	Number per 100,000 population
1973	2,503	1.1
1972	2,880	1.4
1971	3,736	1.8
1970	4,089	2.0
1969	4,425	2.2
1968	4,760	2.4
1967	5,201	2.7
1964	6,690	3.5
1956	11,500	6.9
1948	20,700	14.3

SOURCE: National Center for Health Statistics.

1973, been almost completely eliminated from the American scene. That the South survives as the dwindling last bastion of the granny midwife is evidenced in Table 8.3, which shows the geographical distribution of the 2500 who were still known to be in practice in 1973.

How was the granny trained and what did she do? Younger women became apprenticed, over a period of many years, to an established midwife, and they tended to work together until the older women began to relinquish her practice. At this stage an apprenticed woman then acquired the status of the "granny," and then she herself took on a younger person as her own apprentice. Practice was limited almost exclusively to the rural areas, and although the vast majority of southern grannies were black, their practice was not limited to black mothers or necessarily to those of low social economic position. Sometimes the granny would work as an adjunct to a physician, but the relationship was not of the ancillary type discussed in this book but more as a master-apprentice relationship in its own right. There were no established "rules" under which the granny functioned; she was in no way involved in an associational network of the type presently characterizing units in the medical division of labor. Her roots were to her local community, and her identity appeared to be more with the patients she served than with her calling as a rationalized occupation.

The origins of her art being lost in the antiquity of all folk heritages, however, even the granny midwife could not withstand forever the inexorable drift toward professionalization and bureaucratization in the forms of the establishment of formal rules and regulations, bureaucratization of all medical practice, and the growing dominance of the authorized physician and the emergence of the doctor as the

TABLE 8.3
Location of lay midwives, 1973[a]

Location	Number	Percent of total
All locations	2503	100
Alabama	369	14.7
Georgia	104	4.0
Louisiana	75	3.0
Mississippi	304	12.1
North Carolina	20	0.8
South Carolina	169	6.7
Texas	1000[a]	39.9
Virginia	115	4.6
Total in "Old South"	2156	86.1

[a] 1972 estimate.

model to emulate in the process of the transformation out of the rural South. As Mongeau, Smith, and Maney put it:[16]

> The midwife looked to the physician for her sanction to practice; he stood almost, but not quite, on the par with the Lord as her authority figure. . . . It was mainly through him that she added to her knowledge and skills and retained or abandoned her old beliefs and folk practices. She observed him as she assisted him with his white practice, and she became acquainted with the ways of the white people and his advice to them as they stayed on with the family after the baby was born. She kept her patients immobilized in bed with darkened rooms for days on end, with tightly bound abdomens, in a state of semi-starvation, just as he did. She prided herself that she no longer used a great ball of freshly made pig lard for a cording dressing but now used a piece of linen baked brown to which she added a powder made of flour baked even browner. And, when her doctor abandoned this for boric acid and made it possible for her to carry boric acid as part of her equipment, she quickly followed his procedure.

And further aping the physician:[17]

> The doctor had his own methods for reducing pain, and she had hers. She gave up her ways more readily when he made it possible for her to take on his. If he gave her ergot to prevent hemorrhage, she abandoned her pepper tea; if she learned from him an effective method for expressing the placenta, she no longer set her patient on a pot of burning feathers. . . . She continued to slip the ax under the bed to cut the pain, and she tied thin copper wires or cords high on the thighs to keep the pains in the abdomen from slipping down into the legs. Sometimes, *to make double sure of success, she used the doctor's technique and threw in her own for good measure!* (Italics mine.)

Thus, the practice of midwifery became an undifferentiated blend of traditional folk medicine and contemporary authorized medicine, and the process of assimilation into the prevailing medical model continued until in most states the supervising of childbirth is accomplished only by licensed M.D.s or by licensed nurse-midwives who have received formal training in a medical center prior to the administrative, instructional, and licensing procedures set down by the representatives of allopathic medicine.

In fact, the return to midwife practice is still relatively new, having taken place on the heels of rising medical care costs, the movement of women to take control of their own destinies, and the generalized drift away from the "overmedicalization" and "overprofessionalization" of human services of all kinds, including pregnancy and childbirth. At present, the nurse-midwife *never* practices alone outside of a medical setting and strictly as a member of the "obstetrical team," the head of which is invariably either a general practitioner or an obstetrician.

The widwife has been transformed from a folk practitioner to a technical specialist in the expanding division of labor in medicine. And in becoming strictly *ancillary* to the physician in spirit and outlook as well as in authority, so too do her patients, and the experience of bearing children has taken on a reflection of this rationalization and bureaucratization.

As far as the impact upon patients is concerned, the key to this lies in how the experience of pregnancy is defined as an "illness" which must be attended by the kind of technical bureaucracy which is implicit in the "medical model" of illness set forth earlier in this book, or as normal life experience which is better viewed in its holistic implications for the life experience of the pregnant mother and the child, as is more nearly implicit in the "social model" of illness.

In a sense, as the midwife becomes ancillary to the physician, so too pregnancy falls under the purview of both the medical and bureaucratic models.

THE SICK ROLE IN PREGNANCY: DOCTOR-PATIENT RELATIONSHIPS AND BUREAUCRATIC CARE[18]

> All women ought to know that invalidism, speaking generally, is a carefully cultivated condition. . . . Pain is ordained by God. . . . How can a mother love her child without suffering for it? . . . Be careful and guarded as to your society demands, lest they steal your time and strength and you be unfitted for the real duties of your home. . . . The sedentary life of many men renders them a prey to the gratification of their lower natures. . . . Look at beautiful pictures, study perfect pieces of statuary, forbid as far as possible, the contemplation of unsightly and imperfect models. . . . Above all, keep croaking companions away.

Such was the character of advice offered to pregnant women in a handbook for "young wives" that sold over a million copies in English alone at the end of the last century. The daughters and granddaughters of the "young wives" to which this early document was addressed are given the following advice in an equally popular book published in 1956 and in reference to an obstetrical case taking place less than 20 years after the publication of the older book:[19]

> One of my earliest private patients was a dancer in a night club. She first consulted me when she had successfully completed three months of pregnancy. In taking the history and discovering her occupation, I was curious to see just how much dancing she did. Not only did she twirl, pirouette, and leap in the air, but two strong-muscled gentlemen tossed her back and forth between them like football ends warming up before the game. . . . Difficult labor is uncommon today, and the likelihood of being so penalized is small. . . . Don't become a stay-at-home

introvert. . . . Sexual intercourse is permissible, desirable, and safe. . . .
We now realize that pregnancy is a normal, simple, physiologic state.

Although these contrasting images of pregnant women may well correspond to more basic changes in the definition of proper ladylike conduct during the past half-century, from the fragile Victorian lady-in-waiting to the blasé sophisticate of the present day, still the "role of the sick" remains a legitimate conduct alternative for persons who are incapacitated or who otherwise regard themselves as faced with a crisis situation that not only prevents them from following their usual round of life but also obliges them to retire into the exempt, dependent, and self-transforming status of the "sick." In American society, at least, illness has this joint physiological and social character about it. Illness has physiological imperatives about it, as well as socially motivated roots and personally satisfying consequences.

The study summarized here is intended to shed some light on the social conditions under which pregnancy comes to be regarded as a personal crisis obligating the expectant mother to enact the "role of the sick" with special emphasis on the part that social-class position seems to play in motivating one to play the "ill" role.

Three indicators of physiological problems were used: Length of labor time was drawn from the hospital records, as were indicators of gross difficulties during labor and delivery. Finally, the number of psychosomatic complaints that each patient had brought to the attention of her doctor was drawn from the records kept routinely in the examination room. It was anticipated that women who regarded themselves as "ill" during pregnancy would make many more psychosomatic complaints, have longer periods of active labor, and experience more gross problems and difficulties during the course of childbearing.

Finally, the extent of each woman's belief in a series of common folk superstitions about nonnaturalistic and magical forces influencing pregnancy and childbirth was assessed. This included such ideas as "if a husband and wife quarrel, their baby will be ugly," "the absence of morning sickness is a sign the baby will be a boy," "the baby might die if you rock its cradle before it is born," "if a mother craves sweets, it is a sign the baby will be a girl," "shocking experiences to the mother tend to leave birthmarks," and "morning sickness is a sign of a strong and health baby." We expected to find that lower-class women would be more committed to such forms of magical thought and would, at the same time, be more likely to regard themselves as "ill."

Women of blue-collar status tended to regard themselves as more "sick" during pregnancy than did women of middle- or upper-middle-class status. Moreover, women who viewed the future and the present in negativistic and escapist terms were more drawn to the role of the "sick" than were women whose value commitments were not of the alienated variety. Also, women with low self-images regarded themselves as more "ill" than did women and more positive self-esteem. And those women who were socially mobile—either upward or downward—were more likely to act the role of the sick than were those whose class position had remained more stable. In addition, women who were most likely to stand in a role conflict situation with their doctor were those who regarded themselves as most "sick," which means, in turn, that the typical orientation of the physicians was one that viewed pregnancy as a normal, rather routine, and nonexempting event. Furthermore, women whose prenatal care took place in the hospital clinic were not only more likely to stand in a role conflict with their physicians than were those under private care but also were more likely to regard themselves as "ill" during the course of their lying-in. Finally, there was some evidence that women who regarded themselves as most sick were in fact those who subsequently experienced more gross difficulties and complications during labor and delivery—a near-classic example of the old dictum, "If a situation is defined as real, it is real in its consequences."

More important, however, was the consistent pattern with which blue-collar women were not only more prone to enact the role of the "ill" but also more likely to be characterized by other factors that were associated with high regard for self as sick. In comparison with the middle-class women, the blue-collar women were more likely to view the future in negativistic and grim terms, more likely to show a pattern of alienation in terms of attachment to values not normally in keeping with their social status, more likely to have a negative or otherwise inadequate self-image, more likely to have experienced recent upward or downward social mobility, more likely to have been confronted in the treatment setting by a physician who viewed pregnancy in different terms than they did, and more likely to have been treated in the hospital clinic with all the "illness"-invoking symbolism inherent in such establishments. It is not surprising, then, that it was the lower-class women who had the longer labor time and more other difficulties during childbearing.

THE MIDDLE CLASS AND PSYCHOSOMATICS: THE BLUE-COLLAR CLASS AND MAGICAL THOUGHT

Just as there were many blue-collar women who regarded themselves as ill, so too were there a number of middle-class women who so thought of themselves. However, the ways in which each group expressed the fact of their having become "ill" were quite different. These middle-class women who saw themselves as sick tended to express such an attitude *in the context of the medical treatment setting* by complaining to their doctor about a wide variety of body ailments and problems from which they said they had been suffering—each complaining about earaches, headaches, nausea, dizziness, and the like. In short, they expressed their perception of self as sick in ways with which the medical professional could deal on his or her own medical terms. The blue-collar women who regarded themselves as sick, however, expressed remarkably few psychosomatic complaints. Rather, they resorted to a belief in the folklore of pregnancy and childbirth, which involved nonnaturalistic explanations of cause and effect and which lay beyond the pale of modern medical science.

Thus, in general, four contrasting patterns existed among the middle-class women, on the one hand, and the blue-collar women on the other. The middle-class women were less likely than the blue-collars to regard themselves as sick. They were less often involved in those social situations in which becoming "ill" was a likely alternative. They were less often plagued by lengthy labor and complications in giving birth to their offspring. Finally, in those cases in which they did regard themselves as sick, they expressed such an attitude in the context of the medical treatment setting and in terms that had both meaning and sense for the professional healer. The blue-collar women, however, were more likely to conceive of themselves as "ill." They were more' often involved in patterns of life and situations likely to lead to the acceptance of the role of the sick. They were more often beset with actual physiological problems during labor and delivery. And, insofar as they did regard themselves as "ill," they eschewed the enactment of sick role in medical terms and turned instead to folklore and magical thought.

'ILLNESS' AS A PERSONAL CRISIS

If relatively high educational attainment and greater exposure to the inroads that the "great tradition" of modern science makes upon the "lay traditions" of a people are considered, it might be expected that middle-class women would be sensitized to the more currently popular professional images of sickness and health and would be somewhat knowledgeable concerning the objective medical contingencies of childbirth in terms of physiology and morphology. Combine this with the middle-class woman's very real better chances for the survival of herself and her baby, and the pattern of low sick-role expectations among middle-class women is not at all surprising. As one physician put it, "When a middle-class woman wants to try natural childbirth, it is usually because she wants to experience the whole affair of having a baby; when a lower-class woman wants to try, it is usually because she doesn't want to go under anesthesia because she is afraid she won't wake up."

Consider the blue-collar woman, the relative personal and social isolation in which she lives—isolated, at least, from the personal contacts and formal experiences by which one assimilates the meaning and significance of professional ministrations. Consider also the relatively minimal education she has achieved and the life milieu in which she lives, where illness, incapacitation, and the like abound; and also the very real, heightened chances that either she or her baby may encounter either insult or accident during pregnancy. All of these factors and others combine to make the pattern of high sick-role expectations among this group particularly understandable. Moreover, the blue-collar woman is likely to be cared for in a clinic setting rather than by a private doctor, and thus it is easy to see why she might regard herself as "ill." The middle-class woman chooses her own physician— usually on the basis of word-of-mouth advice from friends and relatives. She appears for her prenatal care in a treatment setting that has little of the symbolism of sickness—a quiet "living-room-like" waiting room, perhaps occupied by a nurse without a uniform. This is in dramatic contrast to the clinic-attending woman who experiences her treatment within the confines of a hospital—with ambulances going to and fro, uniformed nurses and interns scurrying about (sometimes in apparent anxiety), with stainless steel, tile walls, and medicinal odors intermixed with medical machinery and equipment. Not only, then, does the life milieu and its attendant contingencies conspire to move the blue-collar woman toward the enactment of the role of the sick, but so, too, does the peculiar character of her obstetric treatment episode.

The pattern of high psychosomatic complaints among the comparatively few high-sick-role middle-class women might be understood in something like the following fashion: For whatever reason the middle-class woman regards herself as "ill," it seems understandable that this should be expressed in psychosomatic terms in the context of the doctor-patient relationship. Given over as she is to the ultimately "normal" nature of pregnancy, and in view of what is sometimes regarded as the middle-class pattern of internalization of anxieties and conflicts, one might expect that the manifestation of concern about perceived illness should be expressed in covert psychosomatic terms. Considering also her greater knowledgeability about modern medical terms and practices, it seems natural that she should bring her complaints and worries to the attention of her doctor rather than to nonmedical persons to whom she might otherwise turn.

The enactment of the role of the sick by the lower-class woman, however, must be understood in somewhat different terms. Alienated as she is from the mainstream of medical knowledge, more prone to externalizing her difficulties rather than internalizing them, and standing in a position of great social distance from her educated and urbane physician, it seems unlikely that she will seek solace in psychosomatic or quasi-medical terms. And in further consideration of her local social-class position—with a lack of formal education and with extended kinship ties with grandmothers and great-aunts as lifelong agents of socialization—it seems likely that she should act out the anxiety she has over her "illness," not in the context of the doctor-patient relationship but rather within the framework of her own lower-class subculture. Part of that subculture consists of a body of lore and superstition to which persons turn in the face of personal crises—not unlike the ways in which groups sometimes turn to bizarre and incredible ideologies that also deny the "real world" when faced with a perceived collective calamity.

Returning once again to the two contrasting images of the expectant mother, both of which are still current and available in American society: the trend appears to favor the "pirouetting dance" above that which would "keep croaking companions away." If, indeed, there has been a very real change in the more appropriate model of conduct for expecting ladies, the material from this study would indicate that the blue-collar woman more often aspires to a form of conduct that has largely disappeared from the repertoire of conduct alternatives of the middle class. The blue-collar woman, in short, reflects a pattern of cultural lag in this respect. Students of collective behavior have taught us for many years that the circuit of fads and fashions is from the upper reaches of the system of social stratification to the lower. And if we include as fad and fashion all those patterns of behavior that are learned, that have symbolic meaning for persons, and that have sources within an identifiable social structure, then it seems particularly fitting to find that the blue-collar women in this study patterned their illness conduct upon a model that was "fashionable" among the middle class perhaps a generation or two ago.

Briefly, social-class position seems to be basic in defining the conditions—social, psychological, and medical—under which women come to regard themselves as "ill" and in molding the processes by which persons attempt to confront those situations which they regard as critical.

In this regard, Bockoven has said:[20]

> One lesson which can be derived from the history of institutional care . . . is that human beings are molded by whatever authority they respect and that ideas about human beings of authoritative origin eventually influence human behavior in the direction which confirms the authoritative idea.

The recent history of the sociology of pregnancy is in fact a history of skirmishes between those who would impose a medical model of disease on the condition and thus treat pregnancy women "as if" they were ill and those who would view pregnancy as basically a social and personal experience that falls beyond the pale of bureaucratic medicine. The reintroduction of the midwife in the guise of the nurse-practitioner signals a major relinquishment of the physician's dominance. Thus, while there has been a drastic decline in the folk or "granny" midwife, the resurgence of the concept of pregnancy as a holistic experience is signified by the fact that as of this mid-decade there were an estimated 1800 licensed nurse-midwives who in 1974 were in attendance at nearly 8000 births. And although the nurse-midwife is still putatively subordinate to the physician, the attitudes that she welcomes on the part of the women she attends—the demystification of childbirth, predelivery counseling, and the general debureaucratization of the childbirth experience—reflects in large measure the return of the lay midwife in modern costume. And as shall be pointed to in the next chapter, just as the nurse-midwife represents an altogether new force to be reckoned with in the medical division of labor, so too she may also be largely responsible for a growing trend toward the demechanization and deinstitutionalization of the birth experience as well. The case of the "physician's assistant" constitutes a somewhat different aspect of this growth in the medical division of labor on the one hand and the potential erosion of the autonomy of the physician on the other.

THE PHYSICIAN'S ASSISTANT—A PARAPROFESSIONAL IN UTERO

At the present time, the job of the "physician's assistant" or "assistant physician" is an occupation without a job description. This ambiguity in the *de jure* and *de facto* status of many "new health workers," including the so-called physician's assistant, is attributable not so much to the rationality and rightness or superiority of the status quo in the medical division of labor as to the inherent difficulties involved in institutionalizing new "enacted" social forms of *any* kind. Whatever the terminology used, however, the "physician's assistant" functions as an extension of the physician—not as an adjunct, as is more typically the case with nurses. In this sense, a variety of activities normally undertaken by doctors themselves, many involving direct patient contact, are allocated to the assistant. He or she serves almost directly under the control of the physician, who in many cases is quite literally the assistant physician's employer. Being generally not organized to define his or her own sphere of work, the assistant is paid by the doctor and is allowed to do only whatever his employer wishes. The range and variation in the kind of work undertaken by the military physician's assistant is exemplified by May's description:[21]

> It is commonly said that increasing the productivity of the physician will require the delegation of selected tasks together with briefer, less expensive training. A notable current example of this, often cited, is provided by military medicine. The range of tasks performed by corpsmen, nurses, and technicians in that setting is indeed remarkable to one unused to such flexibility. At one extreme is the medical corpsman trained to work with special forces teams. He is expected to cope with medical situations ranging up through an emergency appendectomy on the assumption that no physician will be available. In non-combat zones and peacetime situations, the corpsman performs a screening role at sick call and is the practitioner of a wide range of routine procedures. With no adverse affects many a soldier has had his superficial laceration stitched by a corpsman. Military medicine has its shortcomings and civilians might not be satisfied with it on a regular basis, but it does have valuable lessons to offer us.

As far as the range of acceptance of the civilian physician's assistant by practicing doctors, Roemer reports the following range of attitudes toward what kinds of work they felt a physician's assistant could reasonably be expected to perform, in rather sharp contrast to the expandable role of the military corpsman:[22]

> In responses to questions concerning the likelihood of delegating clinical chores to qualified aides, again 25 percent of all the physicians queried were *dead set against the idea* (italics mine). Younger men were likely to be more willing to consider it than were older men, physicians involved in a partnership type of practice were more willing than those in solo practice, and physicians practicing in rural settings were more willing than those in urban or suburban settings.
>
> When they were asked what specific clinical tasks they felt could be safely delegated in the future, nearly three-fourths listed procedures running the gamut from ear irrigations to application of casts. Heading the list with about one-fourth of the procedures named are those involved in *routine* physical examinations—blood pressure, temperature, height and weight, pulse and so forth. More than a fourth of the doctors who listed procedures mentioned history taking.
>
> Injections, lab tests, eye test, dressing applications and work with casts and sutures were also commonly mentioned. When asked to single out the one approach that seemed most workable to them in the interest of increasing productivity, the surveyed physicians gave us the popular answer, "more aides." . . . The reason apparently is that this option is clearly open to nearly every doctor regardless of his specialty or his type of practice.

As far as the possible impact of the physician's assistant upon the efficiency and economy of medical care costs are concerned, there are yet only skimpy data on which to work, although the writings of both

May and Roemer seem to agree with the survey done at the McFarland Clinic:[23]

> . . . he (the author) found that, by and large, the higher the ratio of employees per physician the higher the average number of annual visits, the higher the average gross income for the clinic, the *lower the average overhead expenses and higher the income.*

And in further support of this general finding:[24]

> Without exception, as the number of aides per physician increases and as the number of hours of work on the part of the physician increases, the number of patient visits and the annual patient billing per year also increases.

In general, it can be concluded that:[25]

> Task realignment and the development of new types of paraprofessionals may well provide a good start of the solution to the manpower problems facing the health field.

The equivocal words "may provide" are central to any discussion of the possible impact of the physician's assistant upon the basic contours of the social organization of medicine on the one hand and medical care costs on the other.

How widespread the use of physician's assistants will eventually become and their subsequent final place in the medical decision-making process is not now entirely clear. Although there are a number of serious impediments to their total acceptance and to their securing a firm domain of service with its attendant professional decision-making authority, it does seem likely that the heretofore unquestioned and overall dominance of the physician is threatened by them, although his economic well-being might in fact be enhanced through the use of the P.A.

What are some of these impediments to granting P.A.s a clear sphere of activity and reducing their present equivocal status as merely employees of the doctor to be told what and what not to do? Below are some of these obstacles:

The licensing laws of most states are written in such a way that very little scope of medical care remains to be assigned to a new medical category. Most, for example, provide that only a physician can "prescribe" and "furnish," and the most that nursing laws are allowed is the right to "dispense" and "administer." Given this global definition of the rights of doctors and nurses, what is left for the physician's assistant to "call his or her own"? Largely what the physician is willing to delegate. Moreover, the delegation of medical tasks always entails some measure of risk, particularly in terms of what has already been mentioned about the special problems entailed in relinquishing a medical function while retaining legal responsibility.

Although the delegation of traditional "doctor's" tasks occurs with unremarkable frequency, the specter of legal action is always present. As one observer puts it: Malpractice suits involving task delegation from doctor to a paraprofessional almost always involved charges of negligence rather than of strict violation of the licensing laws:[26]

> In the leading case of *Barber v. Reinking*, a physician and a licensed practical nurse were held liable for damages to a child patient from an injection given by a practical nurse in a physician's office. During the injection, the child moved and the needle broke off, remaining in the child's body. The court instructed the jury that it could take into account the restriction of the licensure law that authorized only registered nurses to give injections, and thus could presume negligence from the practical nurse's acting beyond her legal scope of functions.

And similarly:[27]

> When a justice of the Pace Court in Shasta County, California, held a neurosurgeon and a former army medical corpsman guilty of violation of the medical practice act on facts in which the neurosurgeon placed the Geigle saw on the patient's head and the corpsman drilled the holes in the presence of and under the supervision of the neurosurgeon, fear of liability mounted. The growing numbers of malpractice actions contributed to this concern, even though *compliance with the licensing laws would not relieve practitioners of liability for negligent conduct.* (Italics mine.)

There are usually certain exemption clauses in the malpractice insurance carried by most physicians that do not cover suits involving illegal acts performed by the insured physician. And in many cases patient financial coverage through various health insurance plans differ considerably in the kind of coverage included, depending upon the extent of use of ancillary and paramedical personnel.

There are other impediments to realizing the full potential of paraprofessionals such as the assistant physician. First, the economics of solo practice work against the hiring of more and more personnel, thus adding to his administrative and overhead burdens, even though at some point the addition of ancillary personnel is economically advantageous. The attitudes of patients must also be taken into account in the sense that patients are often treated in depth by others, and many complain bitterly already that "they never see their doctor."

But at the root of the underutilization of the physician's assistant lies the fact that "medical efficiency" has always been measured either in terms that are convenient to the rationality of hospital organization or to the practice of the physician. Seldom has the impact of paraprofessionals on patients been seriously taken into account. And the same might well be said for the future of the Parsonian norm of the "role of the sick"—a posture of convenience for the social and economic behavior of the physician and the hospital, with only passing attention to the functions of the patient as a person.

A further impediment to the fuller utilization of the physician's assistant that is worth mentioning has to do with the presence of inter-occupational protectionism characteristic of all occupational networks. In this regard, by the year 1972 twenty-four states had enacted legislation pertaining to the rights and privileges of physician's assistants. In two to ten of these states the legislation has been shaped by the special interests of optometrists, dentists, dental hygienists, pharmacists, and chiropractics so as to prevent the new occupation from preempting the prerogatives of those professionals and semiprofessionals.[28] In every case, however, it is unclear whether the physician delegating the responsibility of the physician's assistant makes the physician liable for possible malpractice on the part of the P.A. In those many states without such authorizing legislation, both the doctor and the assistant may be open to conviction of illegal practice of medicine or aiding and abetting illegal practice.

In general, however, it seems safe to say that as of now physician's assistants do not possess a mandate or a "charter" that transcends their immediate work situation in the sense that doctors and nurses have such an extrasituational charter. Rather, the rights and obligations of the P.A. for the moment are strictly *situationally derived and negotiated,* as a function of the degree of risk a given hospital, clinic, and practice might be willing to undergo in exchange for the probable cost benefits to be derived therefrom. The point is made clear by the study of the P.A. by Morris and Richard in a Dallas hospital. That conducted study showed that a significant number of P.A.s were utilized in surgery, and as a result of that particular work situation specific rules were adopted related to duties in the operating room. The rules set up provided a format for dealing with the situation existing in that one hospital and were neither generalizable to nor functional for all hospitals.[29]

The problem of legal versus functional responsibility seems to be at the root of the problem encountered in developing a generalized set of prescriptions for the physician's assistant, and so long as the work delegated to the P.A. can be *routinized* and *programmed* so as to produce empirical outcomes virtually identical to those which physicians themselves can bring about, such physician extensions are likely to be enlarged. Where this is thought to be impossible to bring about, the position of the P.A. is likely to be ambiguous, with the physician reliance upon the P.A. remaining substantially at the *organic* rather than the *mechanical* level.

If the P.A.'s role were institutionalized, it is likely that cost-efficiency considerations would lead to the more widespread adoption of this new medical function whether or not the P.A. was "trusted." So long as such routinization and institutionalization are lacking, the acceptance of the physician's assistant is likely to be contingent strictly upon situationally derived trust. Counterpoint to this, however, is Barish's contention that the restriction of the activities of medical auxiliaries to the "professional judgment" of the physician unnecessarily impedes the utilization of such personnel. Barish argues that such judgments are influenced in far too many instances by ideosyncratic factors and points out that "configurational" judgments are not necessarily enhanced or improved by the mere fact of having longer periods of formal "professional" training.

The preoccupation with establishing work tasks that the P.A. can be relied upon to perform without "close" supervision by a physician is evidenced in the study of the diagnostic ability of paraprofessionals by Dellaportas, Swords, and Ball.[30] They were specifically concerned with the ability of such ancillary personnel to derive accurate "clinical impressions" of venereal disease patients, both from patient histories and direct physical examinations. Accuracy was determined by the verification of the laboratory test specimens collected from the patients, and by comparing the results with the judgments made independently by physicians. They found that sensitivity of diagnosis for patients with V.D. was somewhat higher for physicians (96 percent in male patients, and 87 percent in female patients) than it was for the paraprofessionals (90 percent in males and 70 percent in females). For both groups, the proportion of false positive diagnoses was higher than the false negative diagnoses. Both groups, that is, were skewed in a conservative direction.

The role of the P.A. is not institutionalized and therefore is ambiguous. In an effort to overcome this lack of clarity, it is tempting to develop into finer discrimination in this ambiguous role—to make the medical division of labor even more complex than it already is. And so, Ford proposes that the physician's assistant is in fact three separate occupations:[31] (1) The *physician's associate*, the most highly trained of the subtypes, assists in diagnostic and therapeutic procedures, usually under the supervision of a physician; he or she may be expected to exercise a degree of medical judgment. (2) The *specialist assistant* possesses specialized skills in one clinical area only and in this area has knowledge generally exceeded only by a physican specialist in the same clinical area, but is less capable of independent action than the *physician associate*. (3) The *Nonspecialized Assistant* performs a wide variety of tasks all under the supervision of a physician but cannot and may not *integrate* or *interpret* findings from testing a patient.

However the occupational pie is cut, the question still remains as to whether we are faced with a proliferation of discrete jobs, each chasing a technology, or a burgeoning medical technology, each part of which is chasing an occupational designation worthy of stature and authority.

The future status of the physician's assistant remains uncertain. What is certain is that the division of labor is going to continue to expand, bifurcate, and become even more awesome in its complexity,

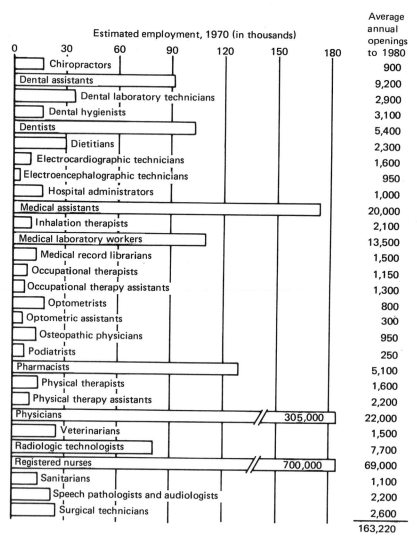

FIGURE 8.3 Employment in health service occupations in the United States, 1970 to 1980.

Source: U.S. Bureau of Labor Statistics.

especially with regard to the expanded managerial role of the physician *and* continued "technocratization" of the patient. Indeed, as shown in Figure 8.3, the U.S. Bureau of Labor Statistics has made an assessment of the extent of employment in merely *selected* paraprofessional occupations. Also shown are forecasts of increases in each that are likely to be realized during this decade.

With these impending changes in the work force of medicine, the client as a patient faces a complex technical, professional, and organizational edifice when incorporated as a lower-level "worker" in the medical "industry." It is to this issue that we turn next: the place of the patient in the world of the ill.

SCENARIO II

Cathleen Moran: hospital aide

Q. What is your work?

A. Makin' beds and bed pans and rotten stuff like that.

Q. What are you called?

A. Nurse's aide, dumb aide. I really don't know if I mind the work as much as you always have to work with people, and that drives me nuts. I don't mind emptying the bed pan, what's in it, blood, none of that bothers me at all. Dealing with people is what I don't like. It just makes everything else blah.

Q. How often do you work?

A. As least as possible. Two days on a weekend, just to get me through school, like money for books and stuff. We start to work at seven, but I get up as late as possible, get everything on and run out the door. I ride my bike to work. I usually have someone punch me in, 'cause I'm never on time. You're gonna think I'm nuts, but I do my work well. If I come a quarter after seven, they're surprised. They don't mind, because I get my work done before the allotted time. I won't have anybody saying I did something lousy. I don't know why.

We get on the floor and you have to take thermometers and temperatures or you have to weigh people or pass water, and go in the rooms, and they yell when you get 'em up so early in the morning. Then they don't want to get out of bed when you weigh 'em. They complain, "How come the water wasn't passed earlier?" "We couldn't sleep all night with the noise." Or else you'll walk in the room and you'll say, "Hello" and they'll say, "Good morning, how are you?" So I'll say "Fine," and some of 'em will say, "Well, gee, you're the one that's s'posed to be asking me that." They don't even give you a chance.

I really wonder why I do have such a rotten attitude towards people. I could care less about 'em. I'll do my work, like, you know, good, I'll give 'em the best care, but I couldn't care less about 'em. As far as meeting their emotional needs, forget it. That's why (a little laugh) I don't think I should go into nursing.

I used to work in a hospital, it was more of a cancer ward. Young women, men. I got along great with the men, they could care less. But I always hated working with the women. They drive you nuts. I really can't sympathize with 'em unless sometimes, rarely, I think, What if I was in their place? Like the younger girls, they want you to feel sorry for them. I just can't feel that. Some of 'em are okay, but they're always crying. That doesn't depress me. I have no feelings at all.

From Studs Terkel, *Working: People Talk about What They Do All Day and How They Feel about What They Do.* New York, Random House, 1972, p. 121 passim.

NOTES

1 Carl Gersuny, "Coercion Theory and Medical Sociology," *Case Western Reserve Journal of Sociology*, 2 (1969), 14–19.
2 Renee Fox, *Experiment Perilous.* New York: Free Press, 1959.
3 Renee Fox and J. P. Swazey, *The Courage to Fail.* Chicago: University of Chicago Press, 1974.
4 Fred Davis, *Passage through Crisis.* Indianapolis: Bobbs-Merrill, 1963.
5 Julius Roth, *Timetables.* Indianapolis: Bobbs-Merrill, 1963.
6 William R. Rosengren, "Status Stress and Role Contradictions," *Mental Hygiene*, no. 45 (January 1961), 28–39.
7 William R. Rosengren and Spencer De Vault, "The Sociology of Time and Space in an Obstetrical Hospital," in *The Hospital in Modern Society*, Eliot Freidson, Ed. New York: Free Press, 1963, pp. 266–292.
8 William B. Werthes and Carol A. Lockhart, *Labor Relations in the Health Professions.* Boston: Little, Brown, 1976.
9 Barbara Ehrenreich and Deirdre English, *Witches, Midwives, and Nurses.* Old Westbury, N.Y.: Feminist Press, 1973, p. 6.
10 William R. Rosengren and Michael Bassis, "Ship Contingencies and Nautical Education," *Maritime Studies and Management*, 2 (January 1975), 154–164.
11 Rene Dubos, *The Mirage of Health.* New York: Harper & Row, 1959.

12 Rose L. Coser, *Life in the Ward*. East Lansing: Michigan State University Press, 1962.
13 William R. Rosengren, "Structure, Policy, and Style: Strategies of Organizational Control," *Administrative Science Quarterly*, 12 (June 1967), 140–164.
14 Jean Donnison, *Midwives and Medical Men*. New York: Schocken Books, 1977.
15 Beatrice Mongeau, Harry L. Smith, and Ann C. Maney, "The 'Granny' Midwife," *American Journal of Sociology*, 66 (March 1961), 497.
16 Ibid., 502.
17 Ibid., 502–503.
18 William R. Rosengren, "Social Class and Becoming Ill," in *Blue Collar Worker*, A. Shostak and G. Gomberg, Eds. Englewood Cliffs, N.J.: Prentice-Hall, 1964.
19 Ibid.
20 J. Sanbourne Bockoven, "Moral Treatment in American Psychiatry," *Journal of Nervous and Mental Disease*, 124 (August 1956), 112.
21 Joel May, "Increasing Productivity of Existing Health Care Teams," *National Congress on Health Manpower* (Chicago), 1970, 2. By permission.
22 Ruth Roemer, "Legal and Other Institutional Impediments to Realignment of Health Service Functions," Ibid., 5. By permission.
23 May, op. cit., 5 et passim.
24 Ibid.
25 Ibid.
26 Ruth Roemer, op. cit., 7.
27 Ibid., 8.
28 Ibid.
29 Anselm Strauss et al., in "The Hospital and its Negotiated Order," *The Hospital in Modern Society*. Eliot Friedson, Ed. New York: Free Press, 1963, pp. 147–168.
30 G. Dellaportas, William Swords, R. Ball, "Diagnostic Efficiency of Paraprofessionals," *American Journal of Public Health*, 64 (October 1964), 991–993.
31 A. S. Ford, *The Physician's Assistant: A National and Local Analysis*. New York: Praeger, 1975.

SUGGESTED READINGS

Fred Davis, Ed., *The Nursing Profession*. New York: Wiley, 1966.
A group of five original essays on sociological aspects of nursing as a profession.

Barbara Ehrenreich, and Deirdre English, *Witches, Midwives, and Nurses*. Old Westbury, N.Y.: Feminist Press, 1973.
An avowedly feminist activist view of the subordinate position forced upon female health helpers by males over the centuries.

Norman Metzger and Dennis Pointer, *Labor-Management Relations in the Health Services Industry*. Washington, D.C.: Science and Health Publications, 1972.
Some special problems of labor relations in the health industry.

National Center for Health Statistics, "Health Resources Statistics." Washington, D.C.: U.S. Department of Health, Education, and Welfare, various years.

Valuable statistics on health division of labor. Useful for discussion and class reports.

Ruth F. Odgers and Bruness C. Wenberg, *Introduction to Health Professions.* St. Louis: Mosby, 1972.

A series of brief articles dealing with numerous paramedical occupations.

William R. Werther, and Carol Ann Lockhart, *Labor Relations in the Health Professions.* Boston: Little, Brown, 1976.

Some particular issues arising from the fact that nonprofit hospitals must now abide by the conditions of the recently amended National Labor Relations Act as well as maintain patient welfare as the preeminent concern.

Chronic illness—status without passage

Last September my kidneys failed. As a consequence I am on a rigidly restricted diet and must limit my fluid intake. In addition, I am attached to an artificial kidney machine three days a week, five hours each day, undergoing a blood-cleansing process called hemodialysis. It is a regimen I will have to endure as long as I live or until I get a successful kidney transplant. When people ask me how it feels, I say, "Great—considering the alternative." The alternative is death.

My life-style has been radically altered. I love to cook and to eat. I have written about gastronomy and edited a cookbook, but now I am forbidden many of my favorite foods and denied all but small portions of others. I have always been a big drinker—I don't mean liquor—and now I have to think twice before I take a single sip of water, soup, coffee, wine, anything liquid. I am the assistant travel editor of the *New York Times,* but I have had to say goodbye to carefree trips. I can travel no farther than two days from a kidney machine, and to use one away from home I have to make arrangements weeks in advance. Such is my life with failed kidneys. I also have osteoarthritis of both hips, cannot put on my own shoes without a long, specially made shoe-horn, and walk with a cane.

Connected to the main tubes are four subsidiary tubes. One runs to a gauge that indicates the pressure being built up by the machine. A second leads to a device that automatically turns off the blood pump if the pressure gets too high. A third is attached to a saline bag for the administration of saline solution should my blood pressure drop sharply as the result of excessive loss of fluid, causing dizziness and muscle cramps. A fourth permits Leslie to raise or lower the blood level in the chamber that traps air bubbles. On the face of the machine are switches and dials that I operate or monitor as dialysis proceeds. When I first began dialyzing, I felt like a flight engineer at the control panel of a Boeing 747.

Lee Foster, "Man and Machine: Life Without Kidneys," *Hasting Center Report* (June 1976), pp. 5–8. Reprinted with permission.

Things can go wrong during dialysis, so even when I'm fully relaxed I can never be completely oblivious of the machine. Needles often need adjusting, connections can loosen, and on rare occasions the tubing can split. Although it has not happened so far, the membrane can even rupture despite all precautions, which would cost me a pint of blood I can ill afford. I have to watch the pressure gauge and adjust the pressure, be certain the heating element is keeping the dialysate bath at the right temperature, and observe the color of the bath by means of a mirror attached to the machine to make sure the membrane hasn't sprung a slow leak. I have to watch the air chamber for bubbles, which would indicate that a loose connection is allowing air to mix with the blood. I have to watch a small plastic chamber called the pillow; if it collapses, the pressure drops sharply and a needle has to be repositioned or a line unkinked. I also have to take my blood pressure and pulse every hour, sooner if I don't feel well, and give myself saline, lower the pressure and slow down the blood pump if I get faint, dizzy, or start getting muscle spasms.

What does the future hold? I could stay on dialysis for the rest of my life, however long that may be. The record for longevity on a kidney machine, the last time I checked, was 14 years, and if I stay on dialysis I aim to break the record. Or I could opt for a transplant. However, no one in my family is capable of donating a kidney to me, and the statistics on cadaver transplants are not too encouraging. Half reject within two years, about two-thirds within five. Some patients have had two or three transplants.

CHAPTER 9

The patient: partner or adversary in medical care?

It is patently obvious that people have an enormous stake in remaining well. Although, as we shall show, there may well be a number of "secondary gains" associated with embracing—even inappropriately and for short periods of time—the contingent "role of the sick," the disadvantages in becoming dependent upon the ministration, manipulations, and solicitude of the agents of health far outweigh what may appear to be the advantages. Certainly it is to be set down that to remain "ill" for too long without at the same time adopting the posture and attitude of one who is "sick" may lead to even worse consequences. To ignore a lesion or to pretend that it does not exist and to hope that it will merely "go away" may seem to work in some instances. In the vast majority of cases, however, illnesses do not go away of their own accord; they hang on or get worse.

Entering into the medical system, either voluntarily as in the private sector or involuntarily as in the public sector of medicine, signifies in a sense that one has given up and surrendered over to others the care of one's self, including one's sense of personal integrity and viability. It lays one's body open to some of the more dramatic outrages modern technology has yet devised, and in many cases it is tantamount to giving a small group of total strangers a blank check. Even the possession of health insurance does not fully allay that feeling of sharp economic loss. And in the case of serious and/or long-term illness one's family also joins the ranks of the suffering and is led, along with the patient, into the tunnel at the end of which some light may or may not be visible.

Now, obviously this feeling of having been defeated and overcome is obviously sharper and more poignant with some illnesses than with others. This differential horror at having been discovered to be ill is largely attributable not to the sheer mechanics of the affliction involved, but more to the social symbolism surrounding specific ailments and incapacities as conveyed in the collective unconscious of a people, portrayed in the mass media, as well as in high and popular culture. Young people in the skiing season wear a limb cast like a badge, weekend sailors and spring skiers proudly display their badly burned epidermis, equestrians have been known not to conceal too effectively a slight limp, and young children often seem to regard their surgical scar as a prized new possession. And Susan Sontag has written recently of illness as a metaphor in which specific diseases are embodied with a set of meanings and connotations that transcend any simple and objective measurement of the body lesion itself.

With the exception of the very minor and pesky health problem for which going to a doctor is a strictly casual affair and a mere diversion from one's usual round of activities, other health encounters (and many of us experience at least one of these sooner or later in our lifetime) are highly consequential. For both of these reasons—the casual and seemingly inconsequential nature of the periodic checkup and the possible profound impact of the "big one"—the surprising fact is not that so many people seemingly in need of medical care do not get it; rather, given the impediments to health care it is surprising that so many do!

Consider the following: Even with the now widespread availability of some form of health insurance, medical care is only one of an infinite variety of services that compete with one another for a portion of our discretionary income (those funds left over for spending after the "essentials" of life have been provided). This of course is just as true for publicly provided health services as for private expenditures. The former competes for our tax dollar in the voting booth, whereas the latter competes for a larger slice of the same discretionary pie in the crucible of the marketplace. As such, health care is one of the most expensive and unpleasant ways of letting go of a family's discretionary money; measured against any number of other ways of spending one's surplus money, paying a $15,000 hospital bill doesn't seem like much of a bargain to most people unless their situation is desperate.

And, appealing as the official "role of the sick" has been touted to have been, it is an unpleasant encumbrance: The "right to be exempt from normal social responsibilities" can just as easily be read as "being prevented from taking part in normal social intercourse." The prescription to be "excused from work, at home or outside of it" also means that one is deprived of useful activity that one has relied upon in the past to fill the hours. To organize oneself around the central motive of "getting well" is to say that illness is to become one's central interest— perhaps, in the case of some maladies, for the remainder of one's life.

The imposed obligation to stick with one doctor and not "shop around" also means that you must remain with a regimen of care even though you dislike it, do not think it is doing much good, and believe is too expensive. The only facet of the "role of the sick" that few would dispute is the notion that when sick one should be expected to want to get well. But beyond that, becoming an appreciated patient in the modern health institutions can be a complex and cumbersome burden and for that reason alone (not to speak of the large number of people who actually do it), it should be a matter of some curiosity. What makes the patient role possible and feasible? It is expensive, often painful, too frequently ineffective, often humiliating and degrading, sometimes disfiguring, and nearly always an awkward intrusion upon our life.

SOCIALIZATION TO THE PATIENT ROLE

Patienthood is learned behavior, probably as complex in its origins as the other key learned role repertoires which most of us possess, including studenthood, workerhood, spousehood, and parenthood, among others. Certainly for most middle- and upper-middle-class persons, going to the doctor is among our earliest of memories—and not always an unpleasant memory. As babes we are carried to the doctor cradled in our mother's arms and are cuddled by her in the pediatrician's office while we learn to be examined. The mother nearly invariably sides with the doctor and we learn to obey the doctor just as at the same time we learn to obey our mother. Being sick as a child stays with us not always as a "bad" memory; being sick means being allowed to stay out of school, being presented with small gifts at times of the year that are not otherwise distinguished or memorable, having special foods prepared and being "waited on." And so we enter into the health industry in a kind of logical transition from family to bureaucracy without ever really realizing when we pass from one to the other.

THE SICK ROLE—THERAPEUTIC INSTRUMENT OR TACTIC OF SOCIAL CONTROL?

If indeed the assumption of the role of the sick is fraught with the kinds of tensions and ambiguities suggested here, why has a concern become so widespread in the sociology of medicine with measuring the circumstances under which people who are ill adopt it? First, there has always been a strong tradition in contemporary sociology to try to put theoretical "ideal types" to empiric test, and the sick role formulation lent itself admirably to this task. The second is that given the widespread popularity of Parsonian system theory of equilibrium during the late 1950s and early 1960s, the sick role idea as a way of formulating deviancy in the conceptual framework of social stability and continuity seemed to be especially suited to empirical application amid the astounding level of abstraction at which most of social system theory was written. Thus, tradition coincided with convenience along with the early beginnings of medical sociology. As a result we now have hundreds of journal articles recording the variable conditions under which ill people do or do not adopt the accorded role of the sick. The following attempts to summarize the main points of agreement in this literature: the conditions under which medical system and patient come together in the nexus of the role of the sick and the implications of this consensus in the light of the more contemporary understanding of total compliance with classical medical regimens as merely one of several real options now regarded as open both to patient and to practitioner.

According to its originator, Talcott Parsons, illness must be regarded as a special form of deviancy, and therefore the members of the medical system are agents of social control whose function is to bring sanctions to bear so as to restore health deviants to "normal" social functioning.[2] So far so good. Moreover, inasmuch as such deviancy is special in that ill persons are not personally responsible for their deviancy (not necessarily so far so good), the handling of the ill person ought not to contain the element of coercion and punition found with respect to some other forms of deviancy (good so far as it goes but not necessarily true). Further, given that medical personnel, as agents of social control, relate to ill persons on behalf of some larger social good (social stability and normal, nondeviant social functioning) they can be expected to act without regard to their own special interests (also not necessarily true). Finally, it is recognized that the role of the sick can in fact carry with it so-called "secondary gains" (the secondary gains of medical personnel are not really mentioned, although they exist), but these are to be regarded as minor deviations from conformity to the sick role professional model (also not necessarily true). But given this somewhat shaky conceptual and empirical underpinning, the "sick role" stands along side "professionalism" and "bureaucratization" as one of the central dominating themes in American medical sociology over the past quarter-century. What do we know about it?

First, the role of the sick is both *contingent* and *temporary*. This means that the sick actor must really have an authentic illness that is judged *professionally* to be incapacitating, and that the occupancy of the sick role is not to be regarded as permanent. Thus, both the right to bestow as well as to withdraw the role of the sick is in the hands of the medical officialdom—which, as we have already seen, may in fact be the legal personality of an organization—or indirectly in the hands of a paraprofessional.

Once the hurdle of authentication has been successfully overcome, the person elevated to the role of the sick is subject to the following special rights and obligations:

1. *Exemption from usual "instrumental" responsibilities.* Obviously depending on the severity of the incapacitation and the particular

social needs of their normal round of life, sick people are not expected
to carry on with their work routines and with other customary com-
ings and goings. They generally are allowed to "let things go" without
being accused of laziness, neglect, or goldbricking. Often this takes
the forms of self-exemption rather than an official nod from a doctor
that one should stay home from work for a while.

2. *Exemption from usual "affective" responsibilities.* Persons who
are sick are allowed a degree of latitude in attitude and mood swings
that are denied well people. This may range from tolerating the can-
cellation of social engagements, the "cutting down" on outside activities
and "sticking close to home," and signs of crankiness, irritability, or
testiness. Thus we speak of people who are "off their feed" and not
acting their "old selves." This kind of mood variation is tolerated and
even expected of sick people.

3. *The sick person is not to be blamed.* If the illness is of the
normal variety, a special condition of adopting the first-mentioned two
rights is that people should not be regarded as having "caused" their
own illness. They are blameless and therefore should not be treated
harshly or with any tone of moral reproof. This is an expectation that
seems to attach with special affinity to sick children, who seem to elicit
great outpourings of sympathy; those of advanced age, who seem
especially incapable of coping; and others afflicted with "mystery"
diseases where blame or cause cannot be at all fixed. In any event, and
in Western society especially, being legitimately authorized as sick is
a special qualifier for benign treatment. It is the special contingency
that has thus far excused, although not completely, such deviancies as
substance abuse (including alcoholism), hyperkinesis, and certain
other behavioral deviancies.

4. *Being ill is to be regarded as undesirable.* The persons allowed
to act as if they were sick must also regard their condition as strictly
temporary and undesirable and must wish to "get well" again. While
probably the least problematic of the four thus far enumerated, this
expectation seems to hold up least well among some children, among
childlike adults who may find enormous secondary gains, much like
the "Hawthorne effect" in being pampered as an ill person, and among
some longtime institutionalized patients who have become colonized
to life behind the walls. In the former case it is more a distortion of
the age-grading process and in the latter a pathology of organizational
life that is at issue rather than the role of the sick itself.

5. *The obligation to secure "competent" help.* A special condition
of being allowed to skip work, slack off on social obligations, and to
be regarded as blameless is that the sick person must seek out competent assistance in getting well. In the typical case this means going
to see an allopathic physician and doing what he or she tells you to do

without an argument. As reasonable as all of this sounds, we all know of people, including ourselves, who delay going to the doctor, engage in home dosing, or ignore following the doctor's orders when we know them to be in our own best interest. And everyone is familiar with the story of the ill person who went to the doctor, received an unpleasant diagnosis, and therefore changed to another doctor. Now both the new health professionals and the highly fragmented self-help movement have been added to the list of reasonable alternatives to standard help competencies.

6. *To follow the doctor's orders and not to shop around.* Finally, another condition of the role of the sick is that the doctor is justified in withdrawing his services if the patient either refuses to follow orders or goes from doctor to doctor for the same illness, and especially if the patient leaves a residency in a hospital "without doctor's orders." Any one of these ways of short-circuiting the system relieves the doctor of moral as well as legal responsibility, even though the increasing popularization of medical knowledge and easy direct access to specialist services has made such blinded obsequiousness to the authority of the doctor seem somewhat quaint and obsolete.

Research over the past several years has centered mainly around the problem of delineating those social categories and groups of illnesses that seem to conform most closely to the classical "sick role" model. It must be said that this effort has not been entirely successful, although there does appear to be some consensus on some points:

First, the concept does not seem to hold very well for chronic conditions—whether so defined by the sufferer or by the objective observer. More important, it is unclear as to whether the lack of fit between chronicity and the sick is attributable directly to the nature of the condition involved or to whether the condition happens to be *treated* on a long-term basis, as diagrammed in Chapter 10; there seems to be some evidence to suggest that it is the medical agents' *definition* of the condition rather than its objective characteristics. And as shall be pointed out later, the problem of condition definition is *especially* acute in the case of intellectual impairment and is strongly related to the role into which such persons enlist the aid of "normals" in helping them to appear to be normal themselves. There is the additional problem of whether the classical sick role conforms most closely to role behavior expected of ill people on the part of main stream medical practice, whereas it may in fact represent a distortion of the expectations held by the public at large and therefore be a prescription for patient behavior only when under the purview of the medical officialdom; it may, in short, be *role taking* rather than *role playing.*

Thus, although there are variations in the degree of generalization of which the sick role concept is applicable, there is little doubt that illness, as a lesion, is often accompanied by role behavior of a special sort, the enactment of which is dependent upon subjective as well as objective factors that are *primarily* sociological and psychological in nature. And the mere presence or absence of "symptoms" is not sufficient to explain differentiation adoption of this special set of roles. Of crucial importance in this regard is how symptoms are perceived by the person experiencing them, and how such perceptions may or may not lead the suffering into a "lay" referral system that will ulti- mately lead him or her into the network of professional medicine. In short, it seems to be the interactional networks in which persons are involved that either accelerate or impede the adoption of some con- figuration of the role of the sick.[3] How may we usefully conceive of the effects of one's interactional network upon symptom definition and the world of human correction?

DEVIANCE AND THE DIVISION OF SERVICES

Let us concede that the sick role represents one way of defining illness and therefore but one way of handling it, and it is the medical division of labor, and its organizational configurations, which are the substance of this text. But the other major divisions of service must also be mentioned briefly at this point. They include education, welfare, the law, and recreation. All other organizational sectors involve either industrial production and distribution and their ancillary administra- tive, political, and supportive industries. Recreation, as a division of service, need concern us only tangentially to the extent that is repre- sents yet another manner by which human potentialities may be tapped, expressed, and made manifest. But health, education, the law, and welfare (in addition to recreation) are the four major systems that attempt to designate forms of deviance, define them as properly within their domain, and are organized to process people into the appropriate conditions or attitudes that, from the point of view of the processing agents, represent an "improvement" of the human condition. The *clienthood* expected of lower-level members in each is strikingly differ- ent, with "sick role" behavior of one form or another being exclusive to the health and medicine division of service. Let us conceive, dia- grammatically, as in Figure 9.1, of these four "serious" divisions of service as taking the form of *overlapping* umbrellas. Each of these umbrellas has its domain elites at the "top," and at the bottom each has the appropriate gatekeepers who "patrol" the populace in search of deviants and defects who may be swept into one or the other of these divisions of service.[4]

Each major division is composed first of "elites," who diffuse

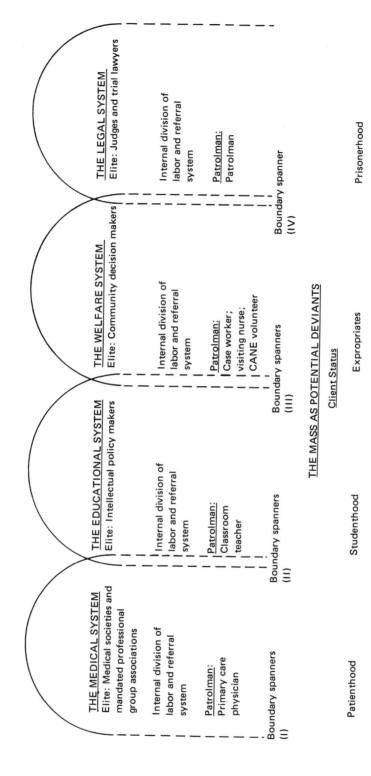

FIGURE 9.1 Elites and gatekeepers in the division of human services.

THE MEDICAL SYSTEM
Elite: Medical societies and mandated professional group associations

Internal division of labor and referral system

Patrolman: Primary care physician

Boundary spanners (I)

THE EDUCATIONAL SYSTEM
Elite: Intellectual policy makers

Internal division of labor and referral system

Patrolman: Classroom teacher

Boundary spanners (II)

THE WELFARE SYSTEM
Elite: Community decision makers

Internal division of labor and referral system

Patrolman: Case worker; visiting nurse; CANE volunteer

Boundary spanners (III)

THE LEGAL SYSTEM
Elite: Judges and trial lawyers

Internal division of labor and referral system

Patrolman: Patrolman

Boundary spanner (IV)

THE MASS AS POTENTIAL DEVIANTS

Client Status

Patienthood

Studenthood

Expropriates

Prisonerhood

throughout a major prevailing *philosophy* concerning what is at the source of the deviants who fall into its orbit and prescribe, in a *general sense*, the procedures to be used in bringing about a correction in the perceived defect. They establish, as it were, the *means* and *ends* format of their division. In the case of the medical division, and the one that is primarily at issue here, a model of detection that usually resembles what has here been called the "medical model of illness" is the prevailing and dominating mode, although in the case of some of the functional illnesses and in some long-term disabilities involving major personal adjustments, something patterned after the "social model of illness" might be found. It should be noted that the elites in each of the four divisions—medicine education, welfare, and law, tend to overlap with one another at the elite level, the internal division and referral system level, and the patroller level.

At the elite level, one typically finds overlapping sponsorship group membership with the same names appearing on the boards of directors or trustees of specific organizations within each sphere. This usually bears some relationship to the local community power structure of the host community and is functional to the extent that it is helpful in the formal and informal allocation of available funds as well as in seeing to it that undue interdivision competition does not take place and that domains of influence are more or less protected.[5] Perhaps more important, each elite structure assists in defining the "catchment area" and probable client pools for each division as well as the *means* by which clients are attracted. Hence overlapping elites protect operational domains as well as insulate against *visible* competition for clients.

Each division also contains internal subdivisions of labor of varying complexity, each with an array of paraprofessionals and subprofessionals analogous to the one for medicine described in the previous chapter. But in medicine the internal subdivision process is far more elaborate and differentiated than in the other three divisions. At the internal level, however, the somewhat more interesting functionaries are the "boundary spanning" personnel who help to link each major division together at the operational level. It is to be noted, that once into the orbit of one or the other of the major divisions of service, regardless of whether it is medicine, education, or one of the other two, clients are seldom referred *outside* that division; that is, each attempts to extend its dominance to encompass the broad client intervention schematically depicted in Chapter 5. Hence, hospitals have their own welfare department and social workers; many provide instructional services, especially for long-term patients and for children; all include some range of recreational facilities; and many even act as the legal agent for clients when people become official clients of the division. The same internal dominance tends to be true of the other divisions as well. The boundary spanning personnel are useful in securing such ancillary services, sometimes from quasi-members such as volunteer groups who enter the system strictly at the behest of the elites, in referring into another major division if that cannot be avoided, and in screening clients who approach the division after a history of clienthood in another division.

Finally, the "patrollers" are the line workers who apply the elites' definitions upon the pool of individuals who are in the appropriate clienthood pool. They seek for persons who are appropriately faulted so that they may be incorporated into the clienthood status of their division, and they compete however subtly with one another for the on-the-line preeminence of the deviancy definition that constitutes the core of their respective divisions. The patrollers in fact constitute boundary spanning personnel of a very special kind in the sense that their extensive day-to-day interaction with "persons in contact" make them especially vulnerable to lay influences and lay definitions. Hence they are a primary source for the infusion of deprofessionalized conceptions and definitions into the formal structure of the divisions of service.

But since each defines deviation in its own way ("health" problems for the medical division, insufficient knowledge for the educational system, social incapacitation for the welfare system, and criminal culpability for the legal system), each division quite understandably imposes a different kind of "clienthood" upon the persons who enter as patients, students, recipients, or prisoners, respectively. *Clienthood* refers to the *status* dimensions of the expected behavior of service recipients, whereas *client role* refers exclusively to the interactional dimensions of such situated behavior. Thus, the sick role refers to a fairly circumscribed set of expectations having to do with the behavior patients are expected to exhibit strictly in the context of treatment *per se;* it does not include the full range of changed status dimensions being ill may in fact bring about, especially the kinds of personal transformations that might be required as a result of such treatment taking place within an institutional *context.* Thus, clienthood in a *total institution,* such as that described by Goffman or for child polio patients such as those depicted by Davis, in hardly any way resembles the clienthood of a pregnant woman in a lying-in hospital, even though the patients in all three are subject to most of the constraints of the sick role. It is, therefore, differential clienthood that offers the distinctive patient experiences, not the sick role itself.

Now it is to be remembered that for many behavioral manifestations the proper routing of clients is quite well institutionalized and not at all problematic: simple inability to find employment clearly qualifies one as a welfare recipient, age qualifies one for studenthood, and so on. But in a growing number of instances, definitions are less clearly institutionalized, and with the burgeoning of the service sector of the American economy, persons exhibiting such "new" deviations come to be the objects of competition by both the elites and the patrolmen for each division of service: What shall we do with child-beaters? Shall we jail them, counsel them, rely upon the schools to teach such tendencies away, subject them to psychiatric treatment, or what? Who holds domain over those who inject mind-altering substances into their veins: doctors, lawyers, teachers, or social workers? How shall we handle alcoholics? Put them in the lockup time after time, get them to join AA, put them on the public dole, or dry them out in a hospital? These questions are *not* academic, they represent "where the action is" in the service scene and illustrate the powerful competitors the medical division of labor really has.

Clienthood in the legal division of service dramatizes the *adversary* nature of client status, whereas studenthood more strongly illustrates the partnership character of client status. Both the medical and social welfare divisions contain enormous ambiguities in this regard, and therefore a close examination of specific types is required before it is possible to go far beyond delineating the nature of the sick role as it can be distorted by having to be enacted in special kinds of treatment contexts.

Eliot Freidson has given us a useful scheme by which to appreciate how rich the variation may be in this regard.[6]

RESPONSIBILITY AND PROGNOSIS IN THE DEFINITION OF CLIENTHOOD

The definition of and reaction to perceived deviance is not at all self-evident in the cognitive aspects of the behavior. They are, rather, a function of a complex interplay of factors with both historical and contemporary ramifications and extensions. What is regarded as appropriate patient behavior at one historic moment or in one inter-actional context may not be so regarded at another time and in other circumstances. The social perceptions of and organizational reactions to deviance, and therefore the patienthoods into which persons are cast, are not inherent. This point will be elaborated in more detail in Chapter 10, which deals with the so-called "functional" illnesses. By Freidson's scheme (see Table 9.1), organizational reactions to deviance may vary independently along two intersecting axes—an *imputed* prognosis ranking from conditions regarded as "curable," such as a fractured limb, to those that are "incurable," such as certain forms of cancer. A second axis involves the degree to which the victims of ill-ness are regarded as being personally "responsible" for the condition in

TABLE 9.1

Managing deviance by imputation of responsibility and prognosis

Imputed prognosis	Responsible	Not responsible
Curable	Limited punishment I	Treatment, education, or correction
Incurable	Execution; life imprisonment III	II Protective custody IV

SOURCE: Adapted from E. Freidson, "Disability as Social Deviance," in *Sociology and Rehabilitation,* Marvin B. Sussman, Ed. Washington, D.C.: American Sociological Association, 1965. By permission.

which they find themselves. This may range from "responsible," such as the growing attitude toward lung cancer, to "not responsible," such as usually the case with pneumonia. It is to be emphasized that under different historic and situational conditions, any condition can theoretically fall *anywhere* along either of these two continua.

In cell I (conditions perceived as curable but involving patient responsibility) a limited form of punishment is the preferred mode of management. The organization dealing with patients in this fashion exhibits some of the characteristics of a prison, and the typical model of *patienthood* therein is some form of *inmate* status analogous to that of a prisoner in a penal institution. Some psychiatric institutions take this form, as do some restorative institutions involving substance abuse. In cell II (incurable conditions perceived as involving personal responsibility) a harsher form of punitiveness is typically involved, one generally no longer found in the medical division of labor. However, in an earlier era lepers and those with syphilis and certain forms of mental aberrations were perceived and managed in this way. In a marginal sense, persons found guilty of especially heinous crimes—sex murderers, for example—still find themselves subject to this mode of management and occupy the status of one who has been officially condemned. In cell II (curable but without personal responsibility), in which a vast array of marginal medical conditions presently fall, the management tilts in the direction of a *social model of illness.* The preferred type of management is that prevailing in the educational division of service—that is, some form of reeducation. Clients enter as students or quasi-students, and the organization incorporating this conception takes on some of the characteristics of schools rather than medical treatment centers. Various chronic illness treatments and programs of preventive care are model types in this regard. Finally, conditions judged to be *incurable* but without the culpability implied in the victim's being personally responsible fit into cell IV. Here, patient management is a benign protective custody, clienthood takes on the tone of a kind of permanent childlike status, and the posture of the "treatment" agents is that of protective custody. Many of the mentally retarded, the aged and infirm, and some with gross morphological damages—the blind, the deaf, kidney patients, and some persons with severe spinal column damage—are treated in this way. It is to be pointed out that strong themes of the "sick role" run through all of these variants of clienthood.

Friedson goes on to make a finer distinction between those conditions that are "not curable but are improvable," and along the other axis between those conditions that carry some form of stigma and those that do not. But such a means, the four major types discussed above become bifurcated into 12 different types of management and clienthood, each with distinctive features of the patient role on the one hand and medical management strategies on the other. It is easy to speculate that the current drift—even more so since the beginning momentum given during the watershed years of the 1930s is the increasing numbers of "medical" deviations which have come to be classified in the "not responsible, improvable but not curable, no stigma" cell, with its associated extension of the dominance of the medical division of service, its high cost and long-term management implications, and the increasing reliance of the voluntary participation and general goodwill of clients to suffer even lifelong subservience to extensive medical regimens.

By whatever patterns the sick role may manifest itself with regard to the social and psychological characteristics of patients on the one hand and the perferred style of clienthood on the other, it is axiomatic that patient acquiescence to medical regimens is critical; but it should not necessarily be taken for granted, for some of the reasons specified in this chapter. If the *assumption* of ready patient willingness is accepted, then a persuasive and semicollegial relationship is likely to emerge between client and practitioner. At the other extreme, if patients are assumed to be reluctant or downright unwilling to render cooperative conduct, then less subtle means of securing cooperation are likely to be employed. Consider, for example, the case of the flow of patient conduct in a large lying-in hospital, the officialdom of which made the judgment that patient cooperation cannot be expected to be automatically forthcoming.[7]

PATIENT SUBSERVIENCE IN THE PLACE OF TREATMENT

The two places of greatest spatial segregation are the clinic examination rooms and the delivery service itself. The clinic is located in a wing completely separate from the delivery service. Thus, the patient has no contact with the delivery service until the day of delivery arrives, except in the case of some private patients who are given a "tour" of the service during their prenatal care. For most patients, however, the transition from the prenatal area to that of the delivery service represents—both spatially and symbolically—their retirement from one world and their entrance into a totally new and different world, produces a corresponding spatially enforced change in self-image.

More than that, each region in the service is itself set apart from the others in several ways. This segregation is accomplished not only by space but also by rules of dress, of expected behavior, and of decorum—all of which present an image of the place that will ease both patients and staff into desired roles with respect to one another.

First, the residents' quarters are separated from the other parts of the service by a long corridor and heavy doors. The atmosphere here is not unlike that of a modern motel—comfortable but austere and suggestive of the fact that people never settle down here, as indeed the residents do not. In large part, the residents' quarters serve, in Goffman's terms,[8] as their backstage area, to the extent that it is here that the interns and residents may enact among their own kind the informal roles that attach to their formal status as hospital staff members. As a backstage area it is not complete because there is a rather massive "scoreboard" on which is noted essential information about deliveries taking place in the service during the past 24 hours. Thus the tempo, timing, and rhythm that invade the backstage area reassert the raison d'etre for the residents' presence at the hospital and modulate the effect of the spatial segregation of their quarters.

The admitting office is just beyond the residents' quarters. Here there are no barriers of any kind, almost as a symbol of welcome to the incoming patient. A mood of friendly casualness characterizes the behavior of the admitting room staff, which is most casual in regard to decorum in both attitudes and dress. This is consistent with the function of the admitting office as the intermediary stage in the hospitalization of the patient. The physical setting, the spatial location, and the behavior of personnel in it serve to gradually introduce the patient to the new world of the service.

Directly opposite the admitting room is the preparation or "prep" room where the incoming patient is stripped of her self-image as "person," and promptly cast most effectively into her new status of "medical phenomenon." Segregation of the prep room was accomplished not only by physical and symbolic barriers but also by an atmosphere of anonymity exceeded nowhere else in the service.

This aura of *mystique* surrounding the prep room does not seem to conform to the popular image of childbirth. Ordinarily, modern hospital childbirth produces an image of immaculate lying-in rooms, attentive doctors and nurses, the drama of birth, and subsequent visits by a proud father, friends, and relatives. The total reality is, of course, considerably more mundane. The organizational stages of delivery involve the performance of tasks that do not conform to the popular image. And it may not be unique to this one obsterical hospital that the distribution of "deviant" functions occurs in the context not only of the status system of the organization, but within the ecological system as well. Nevertheless, it is true that it is in keeping with the professional image of the modern obstetrical hospital, as well as the folklore of childbirth, that the "climax" of the human career in the hospital should take place in the delivery room, in which the miraculous and often dramatic birth takes place. But it is equally obvious that much more takes place—both before and after this single climax time and place—that is essential to the operation of the organization. In a larger sense, these other activities—prepping, labor, and recovery in particular—are the deviant but necessary functions of this particular place. It is fitting that these deviant activities should be accomplished in regions segregated both physically and symbolically from the rest of the service and that the overseers of these activities should be the lower-status personnel—nurses and student nurses in particular.

In the area of the labor rooms, one is isolated from the nurses and the patients by a shoulder-high and seemingly nonfunctional barricade. This not only segregates the patients from those who pass by but also symbolically segregates the attending nurses from others in the hospital. Perhaps implicit in this mode of segregation is the notion that the nurses are definitely "in charge" and that others in service have no authority beyond that point. Moreover, the area of the labor rooms in some sense corresponds to the residents' quarters insofar as it serves as the nurses' backstage area. Also, the physical barrier—serving to maintain status differences—seemed to be reinforced symbolically by the dim lighting and drab decor of the interior of the labor rooms. The staff was in agreement that the patients seemed to "behave better" while in labor under the quieting effect of the gray decor of the rooms. At the same time, here the nurse was most likely to behave with most confidence in the role of the nurse in the presence of other personnel and least like a nurse when interacting only with other nurses. From a slightly different perspective, both the physical and the symbolic segregation of the labor rooms may be understood to be a function of labor as a kind of "deviant" activity in the service. That is, there is none of the "highlighting" of the place or of the patients here to suggest that what takes place in the region is actually germane to the entire process.

Thus far it may read as though some of the regions of the service had distinct boundaries. Of course, this is not true; if it were, it would suggest that moods, attitudes, and behaviors had discrete boundaries as well. It is more proper to speak of the overlapping of regional boundaries—a frame of reference that may account for the periodic times and occasional places where the behavior patterns among the staff are less distinct than they are when observed well within a bounded area. This overlapping of boundaries could be seen most clearly in the hallways, where the regions of the labor rooms, the doctors' lounge, and the delivery rooms converge. This area was ambiguous not only as to its spatial relationship to the several other regions but also with regard to the relationships between the functionaries in the service who interacted there. Doctors and nurses appeared to know quite clearly what the appropriate modes of interaction were between them when they were within one of the distinct regions, but this was less true in overlapping areas. The formalized aspects of doctor-nurse interaction seemed to break down here, and those persons tended to interact in a more spontaneous and less formalized fashion.

On one occasion, for example, an attending nurse rushed into this "interstitial" area, announced to a private obstetrician that a patient who had recently been ordered to the delivery room by the doctor should not have been so ordered, and insisted that the doctor return the patient to the labor room. A heated discussion ensued between the nurse and the doctor and the outcome was that the patient was returned to the labor room. The tenor of the encounter was not that of a subordinate-superordinate relation, but rather that of a dispute between professional equals with a disregard for the possible impact the exchange might have upon the surrounding audience. The stresses and conflicts among and between the doctors and nurses that were less manifest within a specific region became considerably more apparent in such interstitial areas. Whereas each particular functionary group in the service had, to a greater or lesser extent, its own backstage region, areas of overlap between distinct regions served more as the backstage place for interaction between functionaries.

The administrative nurses hold forth in the area of the delivery rooms. At this point, which is really the "community center" and the point of both physiological and social climax, the projected image of the hospital and consequently the expected roles and attitudes of both staff and patient are cast most effectively by symbols—uniforms, stainless steel, medicines with their odors, brilliant lighting, and so forth.

The operating arena is just beyond the delivery room; it is segregated from the rest of the service by a wide red line painted wall to wall and ceiling to floor. No one without surgical cap, face mask, and insulated shoes is allowed beyond that point.

Farther along this corridor, and perhaps significantly farthest from the community center, is the recovery room. This is a large, dimly lit room attended by one nurse. The functions here are also of the "deviant" variety. The mother is relegated here after delivery of the child, while the newborn is retained in the community center where much attention is paid to it by high-status personnel—obstetricians and pediatricians. This spatial indication of the importance of the child may, in fact, account for the emphasis that is placed upon administering anesthesia. Without anesthesia the patient may become troublesome to the obstetrical team, and their reassuring and comforting gestures toward the patient often give way to irritability.

A further mode of segregation indicative of status differences seemed to relate to having delivery room doors open or closed. A delivery room door was never closed when a clinic patient was there, but this frequently happened with private patients, thus limiting access to the place of climax.

The fact that the "fathers' room," adjacent to the recovery room, is unattended is suggestive that the father is regarded as the least important person in the process. By its sparseness of furnishing, its physical isolation, and its small size, this room seemed to communicate symbolically the idea that the fathers are unnecessary and functionally peripheral.

Behavior in each of the several regions in the service is at least partially a function of the kinds of spatial, symbolic, and physical segregation that set each region apart from others.

RHYTHM: THE CONTINGENT NATURE OF THE ROLE OF THE PATIENT

An important factor in establishing rhythmic patterns of behavior in the hospital is the fact that the patient is potentially both "ill" and "not ill." Pregnancy does not necessarily entail abnormal complications, but that possibility always exists. Because of this the demeanor of the doctors and nurses takes on a studied casualness about childbirth, but always with a watchful eye toward unforeseen difficulties. This was most pronounced when the team included student externs. The students were always more oriented toward complications and pathology in labor and delivery than were the resident doctors. As a consequence a modulated crisis seemed always to exist on the service. In cases where no complications were medically indicated, an atmosphere of general apprehension pervaded the team. In cases with possible imminent complications, the members of the team seemed to be considerably more at ease, tension lessened, and they appeared able to set about their tasks in a more relaxed fashion. To the students, the latter situations were those in which they were actually "learning something."

As in most hospitals, the nurses and doctors refer to the complaining and excitable patients as "crocks." This most frequently meant that the patient was demanding too much sedation while in labor. The term "crock" was often applied by the residents to the patients of private obstetricians, but it was also used to refer to clinic patients under their care as well. The clinic-patient "crock," on the other hand, was usually regarded as having been "pampered." In terms of rhythm, however, the clinic crock is simply disturbing the usual periodicity with which medication is ordinarily offered; she is upsetting the rhythmic expectations to which the term members have become accustomed. The disturbance of rhythm by the private-patient crock, however, relates to other rhythms in the social morphology of the service. In such cases, the residents are usually reluctant to administer medication over and beyond what the private doctor might have ordered—a case not only of status differences but of the sacredness of private clientele as well. Thus, the "crock" label was most frequently applied to private patients during the late evening and nighttime hours when the private obstetrician was least likely to be on the service to minister to his or her complaining patient. The former, then, related to the rhythm of medication, while the latter was associated with the work rhythms of the establishment.

CONCEPTIONS OF THE 'NORMAL' IN THE HOSPITAL

The number of deliveries taking place in a given period of time particularly relates to the tempo of the service. In the clinic service, the number of births in a 24-hour period may range from as few as one or two to as many as fifteen or twenty. This lack of a natural tempo was handled in a number of ways in order to impose a "functional" tempo where a "physiological" tempo did not exist. For example, when deliveries were occurring at a naturally slow pace, the residents showed much anxiety and concern over the one or two women who might have been holding up the tempo of events in labor—constantly checking and rechecking for signs of change. Similarly, in the delivery room itself, there seemed to be an attempt to impose a tempo—to adhere to a pace of scrubbing, of administering anesthesia, and so forth. There was also an emphasis upon keeping of the length of time involved in each delivery. In terms of tempo, the unusually prolonged delivery was as upsetting to the team as was an unusually rapid delivery—even though both might be equally normal or abnormal from a medical point of view. As one resident put it, "Our (the residents') average length of delivery is about 50 minutes, and the pros' (the private doctors') is about 40 minutes." Thus, the "correct" tempo becomes a matter of status competition and a measure of professional adeptness. The use of forceps is also a means by which the tempo is maintained in the delivery room, and they are so often used that the procedure is regarded as normal.

The student externs showed particular reluctance about admitting patients to the service because of the possibility that the patient might be in "false labor." This would upset both the rhythm and the tempo. It may not be unrelated to the fact that such a "mistake" on the part of low-status personnel is much more crucial than a similar mistake on the part of higher-status personnel. In addition, the potential high tempo for the obstetrician is necessarily limited; he or she can be in attendance for just one case at a time. When the physiological tempo begins to outrun the functional tempo, the margin of safety can be partially maintained by the anesthetist, who can hurry cases along or delay them, depending upon the kind and amount of anesthesia administered. As one anesthetist joyously announced one night when the physiological tempo was very high, "I've got five going (ready for delivery but delayed) at once now."

EXPECTATIONS OF THE NORMAL COURSE OF EVENTS

In the naturally expected sequences of events, it is of interest to note how the coming together of the team members for delivery differs from the situation in the regular surgical setting. Ordinarily the high-status personnel—the surgeons—arrive last.[9] In the obstetrical service, however, it is difficult to know whether the patient can actually wait for the doctor. Frequently, therefore, the doctors arrive on the scene before the subordinates do, and not infrequently before the patient herself. This disturbance in timing usually leaves the doctors either making "busywork" with the administrative nurses or leaving the region to check another patient in labor whom minutes before they may have referred to as a "crock."

The normal circuit: admitting office to prep room to labor room to delivery room to recovery room and finally to the lying-in room is adhered to scrupulously. The physiological tempo would often indicate that at least one or more rooms might better be forgotten, but the patient must adhere to this timing of movements from region to region, even if it means at a fast trot.

Timing may also be disturbed if key personnel happen to be absent from one of the places in the timing sequence. One evening, for example, a man rushed into the service claiming that his wife was about to have her child and that no one was in the admitting office. The doctors' advice—in all candor and sincerity—was that she was probably in false labor, and they encouraged the man to return to the admitting room. In a second instance, a woman who had previously given birth to seven children appeared in the last stages of labor. There was not enough time to administer the usual anesthesia, even though it seemed obvious that she could bear her child easily without it. The obstetrical team, however, was in a state of much agitation until the baby suddenly appeared. These inroads upon the timing of events are highly disturbing to the service personnel. And, in general, it may be said that there appeared to be a kind of gradient of the temporal organization of the hospital, with the greater emphasis upon rhythm, tempo, and timing, the closer one got to the community center.

THE ECOLOGY OF PAIN

To express more fully the interrelationships between time, space, and social behavior, the discussion turns now to the ways in which the hospital is organized to define, legitimatize, sanction, and handle the expression of pain by patients.

As Parsons[10] has pointed out in his theoretical analysis of the doctor-patient relationship, a requisite for the maintenance of the professional self-image, and therefore professional behavior toward patients, is the maintenance of an affectively neutral orientation toward the patient. The patient must be regarded as a clinical phenomenon rather than as a person in order for the doctor to behave as doctor. It may well be that an important function of the "prepping" process in the flow of work is to reassert both the clinical nature of the patient and the professional self-images of the personnel. Certainly the expression of pain by a patient as well as the recognition of painfulness, as such, by the doctor is a salient means by which the affectively neutral orientation may be changed to that of an emotionally involved or affective orientation. Such a contingency is handled in a variety of ways.

There are, first of all, certain places in the service where pain is legitimated and defined as such, and others in which it is not. By and large, pain is not sanctioned in any place other than the delivery room, for it is only here that the hospital provides the means to handle pain in an affectively neutral fashion—namely, anesthesia. The acceptance of pain in any other regions—the admitting room, the prep room, and even the labor rooms—would necessitate a more personalized orientation toward the patient by the staff rather than the technical, mechanical, and personally neutral means that are so characteristic of the delivery room. This is not to say that women are in pain only in the delivery room, but merely that it is neither accepted nor dealt with as such by the staff, particularly high-status staff. And not only does the staff segregate pain in this spatial sense, but this meaning appears to be shared by the patients as well; many patients seem a bit apologetic about having pain when in these other regions. In places not sanctioning pain, when the patient's discomfort intrudes itself upon the staff, various means are employed to cope with it in an affectively neutral fashion. In the prep room it is handled by the use of humor and comparatively low-status personnel, and by defining the phenomenon as something other than pain—complaining, pampering, nervousness, or what have you. In the recovery room it is handled by spatial and symbolic segregation as well as by defining it as unconscious behavior of one who is still under the effects of anesthesia.

The symbolism of lighting, individual segregation of patients, and perhaps even the mood and attitudes of the nurses on duty serve to minimize the patient's attempts to legitimatize her discomfort as genuine pain. Spatially there appeared to be a kind of gradient as to the legitimation of pain, with the greater sanctioning of pain found the closer the "place" is to the delivery rooms, and a corresponding decrease as one moves away from the community center.

Significantly, it is in this "climax" region of the delivery room, where pain is most fully sanctioned and accepted by the staff, that the affectively neutral orientation is most likely to break down. For here, perhaps for the first time, the entire obstetrical team is confronted, and at close quarters, with the patient and her discomfort. She is highlighted not only in a physical and interactional sense but in an organizational sense as well. An important relation between status and "place" is clearly evident here because the anesthetist has no part to play in the labor room, even though the manifestation of pain there may actually be as great as, or even greater than, that shown in the delivery room. Once pain is accepted as such—in the delivery room— there is then a special functionary to handle it in an affectively neutral fashion: the anesthetist. Pain is not only sanctioned in the delivery room; it is expected. If there is no pain, this would mean that the anesthetist, who occupies a position of considerable prestige, would be superfluous. Moreover, the legitimation of pain is also organized temporally. There are patterns according to which pain is sanctioned and expected—only so often and for only so long. To show pain either too frequently or too infrequently (or, indeed, not at all) is disrupting to the obstetrical team.

On one occasion, for example, the team was preparing for the delivery of a patient, a mother of several children. The chief resident was heading the team and he was assisted by an intern, a staff nurse, and a student nurse. The anesthetist, of course, was on the service should he be needed. All phases of the preparatory stage were going according to schedule until the staff nurse attempted to administer anesthesia by means of a nose mask. Apparently for technical reasons, the apparatus failed to operate. There are three masks in each delivery room—each containing a different form of anesthesia—and the nurse tried the other two; neither one worked. Although the patient did not appear to be suffering undue pain, with each failure of the apparatus the team members, particularly the chief resident, became increasingly agitated, excited, and alarmed. This pattern of deprofessionalization of the doctor continued until he excitedly hurried from the room in search of the anesthetist who, he hoped, could somehow handle the situation.

What was apparently happening in this instance, and according to our frame of reference, was first that pain was sanctioned and expected by the physician in the delivery room. Second, the delivery room was the place where the hospital was organized to maintain affective neutrality in the face of pain by means of the anesthesia apparatus. When this apparatus did not function properly, an important mechanism by which affective neutrality is maintained broke down. With it the affective neutrality of the obstetrical team also broke down.

In sum, both the spatial and the temporal organization of the service seemed to be geared to cast the incoming patient into a role and mood that would allow the personnel of the service to behave in the ways which they had learned to expect that they should. The staff members themselves—residents, interns, and so on—seemed to be subject to the same proscriptions that stemmed from the morphology of the hospital. In the case of both staff and patients this process was accomplished apparently less by verbal instruction, or even by informal socialization processes, than by the erection of both physical and symbolic barriers to the undesired behaviors and attitudes.

DYING

There is a strong tendency for patients *not* to be accorded a full participatory role in the contexts of medical care, *nor* is a strictly *adversary* relationship expected and tolerated, however much a variety of rationalities may seem to be predisposed one way or the other. The reason for these denials is that in the vast majority of treatment regimens medical technology and technique is thought to be *maximized* where it is possible to assign patients a *nonrole*, as in the obstetrical hospital—that is, a *nonstatus*, in which the medical defect or anomaly is *efficiently* attended to in spite of the fact that it is encumbered by being attached to a living person. And even though there may be broadly oriented attempts to implement a "social model of illness," in the treatment setting the whole person who is presumably the object of attention is something of a cartoon of a real person, not unlike Jeremy Bentham's "auto-ikon," who had the appearance of full life but without the liveliness and range of reactivity of his living counterpart. Thus, in spite of the apparent symmetry of benefits accruing both to patient and doctor in the treatment center, genuine treatment experiences tend to be skewed in the direction of convenience to the doctor, in the worst distortions of which one may find its pathological manifestation in the kind of "pseudodemocracy" described by Lefton, Pasamanick, and their associates.[11]

An especially difficult problem faced in all medical treatment contexts involves managing the dying patient—those unfortunate individuals for whom whatever modification of the standard sick role one wishes to consider has become patently irrelevant. The medical treatment setting and its overseers become especially vulnerable in that a workable *clienthood status* has not yet been institutionalized for patients in general, let alone for dying patients. It seems fair to say that doctors and nurses are probably the only two professional-occupational groups whose members sometimes weep when their services and technologies have failed. The "concerned detachment" of which Fox writes concerning the medical training career does not always work. What sort of a clienthood should one strive for in the case of the terminal placement? Shall, as Glaser and Strauss write, the revelation and acceptance of death be left patients to work out on their own?[12] Shall "outsiders"—family members, friends of the soon-to-be-deceased, clergymen, and others—be recruited to pass on the news and deal with the arrangements? Shall, as Sudnow suggests, the medical term harden itself to death and merely assume the role of expediting bodies[13] from room to morgue? Or shall, as the newly organized "Hospice" institutions are currently attempting to do, we redefine death as an experience of life to be guided, organized, cognated, and cathected just like any other significant life status passage? As of yet, we have no clienthoods for dying people. Still as the changing age-sex pyramid and the changing disease-illness patterns of American society continue to change, death will come less and less frequently as a quick, unanticipated event that therefore can be excused from medical rationality. More and more it will come slowly, forecast with frightening accuracy, and will continue to force itself to the consciousness of those who control it, witness it, and are in a position to give it at least temporal meaning through the establishment of workable death clienthoods.

Basking in the power of a dominant profession also carries with it onerous burdens, and the dual uniform of patrol officer for health as well as for death are not adornments easily worn.

Much the same kind of burden has come to be assumed as a result of medicine's claiming domain over those illusive disorders called mental illness, emotional disturbance, or mental imbalance. It is this "other side" of medicine and patienthood that is the subject of the next chapter.

SCENARIO II

Death: a passage without status*

Camera, action, fade in toward a huge bed surrounded by a multitude of somber figures. Grandpa is slowly dying, comforted by his adult offspring, his wife, his friends, his neighbors . . . fade out as grandpa, smiling, passes on.

Is this what death is all about? Certainly not in our day and age. . . .

The picture goes more like this: camera, action, fade in toward a silent hospital ward in which a white-coated figure looks at a flat reading from an EEG machine. Grandpa lies in a small white bed, breathing normally, with a normal pulse and a normal body temperature. Suddenly the white-clad arm reaches over and disconnects the life-sustaining apparatus hooked up to grandpa. The verdict from the doctor is death.

In the next scene we see the life-sustaining equipment back on, and so is grandpa. Or so it seems. But the oxygen is pumped only to support his heart and kidneys which are being snatched away. Grandpa is dead. . . .

The problems of death and dying in an age in which the ethical and moral problems have surpassed the technical problems is of concern. What constitutes death, prolonged dying, refusing treatment to the terminally ill, telling the patient, are all topics in Veatch's journey inside the moral meaning of death. The morally explosive suggestion of organ banks for breathing cadavers is also presented in this book.

Veatch goes beyond the examination of death as a

*From A. Fontana, "Book Review: *Death, Dying, and the Biological Revolution: Our Last Quest for Responsibility,* by Robert M. Veatch," *Contemporary Sociology,* 7:1 (January 1978), 108–109. By permission.

controversial topic of an era besieged by a cultural lag between technological advances and moral concerns about death and dying. The book offers social policy solutions for the various problems, while never losing sight of the patient's freedom of choice and dignity in the face of death.

This volume is a must for all individuals interested in death: from public administrators to academicians, from college students to lay people.

Andrea Fontana, University of Nevada, Las Vegas

NOTES

1 Susan Sontag, *Illness as Metaphor*. New York: Farrar, Straus & Giroux, 1978. By permission.
2 Talcott Parsons, *The Social System*. New York: The Free Press, 1953.
3 Eliot Freidson, "Client Control and Medical Practice," *American Journal of Sociology*, 65 (January 1960), 374–382.
4 Elaine Cumming, *Systems of Social Regulation*. New York: Atherton Press, 1968.
5 Sol Levine and Paul White, "Exchange and Interorganizational Relationships," *Administrative Science Quarterly*, 5 (March 1961), 583–601.
6 Eliot Freidson, "Disability as Social Deviance," in *Sociology and Rehabilitation*, Marvin B. Sussman, Ed. Washington, D.C.: American Sociological Association, 1965.
7 William R. Rosengren and Spencer DeVault, "The Sociology of Time and Space in an Obstetrical Hospital," in *The Hospital in Modern Society*, Eliot Freidson, Ed. New York: Free Press, 1963, pp. 266–292.
8 Erving Goffman, *Presentation of Self on Everyday Life*. New York: Doubleday, 1959.
9 Robert N. Wilson, "Teamwork in the Operating Room," *Human Organization*, 12 (Winter 1954), pp. 9–14.
10 Parsons, op. cit.
11 Mark Lefton et al., "Decision-Making in a Mental Hospital," *American Sociological Review*, 24 (1959), 822–829.
12 Barney Glaser and A. Strauss, *Awareness of Dying*. Chicago: Aldine, 1965.
13 D. Sudnow, *Passing On: The Social Organization of Dying*. Englewood Cliffs, N.J.: Prentice-Hall, 1967.

SUGGESTED READINGS

Michael Balint, *The Doctor, His Patient and the Illness*. New York: International Universities Press, 1957.
A standard text on the doctor-patient relationship.

Fred Davis, *Passage through Crisis*. Indianapolis: Bobbs-Merrill, 1963.
The experience and treatment of polio victims and their families.

Fred Davis, *Illness, Interaction and the Self*. Belmont, Calif.: Wadsworth, 1972.
Ten papers by the author-editor on the social psychology of illness.

Robert Edgerton, *Cloak of Competence*. Berkeley: University of California Press, 1967.

Deinstitutionalized mentally retarded and "normals" assist one another in pretending that nothing is amiss.

Shizuko Y. Fagerhaugh and Anselm Strauss, *Politics of Pain Management*. Reading, Mass.: Addison-Wesley, 1977.

A symbolic interactionist approach to the social psychological and organizational constraints and opportunities for the expression and management of pain.

Erving Goffman, *Stigma*. Englewood Cliffs, N.J.: Prentice-Hall, 1963.

How persons who carry visible damages on their bodies attempt to sustain the social self intact.

Charles Dickens tours a "moral treatment" center in 1842

Charles Dickens' account of his visit to the Boston State Hospital in 1842 brings to light still more facets of hospital life in the moral treatment era. He commented on the wide variety of activities available to patients including carriage rides in the open air, fishing, and gardening, and several kinds of indoor and outdoor games. Patients worked with sharp-edged tools and ate their meals with knives and forks. The patients organized themselves in a sewing circle, which held weekly meetings and passed resolutions. They also attended weekly dances. Dickens was particularly surprised with the self-respect that was inculcated and encouraged in the patients by the superintendent's attitude toward them. He made special note that the superintendent and his family dined with the patients and mixed among them as a matter of course.

In support of such impressions, Dr. Pliny Earle wrote on moral treatment in 1845:

In the moral regimen at this institution, every practicable effort is made to pursue that system, at once gentle, philosophical, and practical, which has resulted from the active and strenuous endeavors of many philanthropists, in the course of the last half century, to meliorate the condition of the insane. The primary object is to treat the patients, so far as their condition will possibly admit, as if they were still in the enjoyment of the healthy exercise of their mental faculties. An important desideratum for the attainment of this object is to make their condition as boarders, as comfortable as possible; that they may be the less sensible of the deprivations to which they are subjected by a removal from home. Nor is it less essential to extend them the privilege, or the right, of as much liberty, as much freedom from personal restraint as is compatible with their safety, the safety of others, and the judicious administration of other branches of curative treatment. The courtesies of civilized and social life are not to be forgotten, tending, as they do, to the promotion of the first great object already mentioned, and operating, to no inconsiderable extent, as a means of effecting restoration to mental health.

CHAPTER 10

The functional disorders

An official sociological posture toward the various behavior disorders and aberrations lumped under the heading of "mental illness" cannot be said to have been taken until 1939, when Robert Faris and Warren Dunham published their landmark book *Mental Disorders in Urban Areas*.[1] Yet another mark was passed when the sociology profession adopted its still viable "policy" position toward professional mental health workers with the publication, by Kingsley Davis of his now often forgotten "Social Values, the Mental Hygiene and the Class Structure," in the early 1950s.[2] Finally, the heretofore insularity of psychiatric institutions from external academic examination was broken, probably forever, with the publication in 1955 of their now modestly regarded study, *The Mental Hospital*, by the psychiatrist-sociologist team of Alfred Stanton and Morris Schwartz.[3]

At any time prior to those years, we did not have even the beginnings of a sociology of "mental disorder." Such matters were left to be worked out through the pens of journalists or historians of medicine and by pronouncements of "case results" by former patients or isolated practitioners who were usually doctors of a Freudian persuasion. Therefore, what passed as knowledge and perspective toward such behavioral anomalies and deviancies has either been thickened by sensational scoops by newspaper reports, forced through the strainer of psychoanalytic theory, or left to sometimes esoteric record keeping by medical historians. As shall be shown, the intellectual and public insulation of affairs mental had been made fairly complete by the closing years of the last century and was not to be fully broken until the rush of social-psychiatric research and practice that marked the 1960s. But more of that later. If the sociology of medicine now has a distinctively "critical" wing, however, it owes at least half of its parenthood to the four sociologists and one psychiatrist just named. What did they do, and what new understandings and perspectives toward the mentally ill were they responsible for triggering?

THE SOCIAL ECOLOGY OF MENTAL ILLNESS

Let us consider the work and implications of Faris and Dunham first: They studied the ecological distribution of schizophrenic and manic-depressive psychoses in the city of Chicago by examining the record of residents in psychiatric hospitals in the Chicago area. These were plotted on a map of the city of Chicago, along with the home addresses of institutionalized mental patients. It should be parenthetically stated that their interest was more in the social morphology of city life than in emotional disturbance as such. They were at the time members of a small army of sociologists from the University of Chicago interested in the city as a laboratory and social organ and stood in the mainstream of a whole generation of Chicago-trained sociologists who were devoting their entire professional lives in filling out the agenda on needs in urban research laid out by the founder of the "Chicago School of Sociology," Robert Park, in 1925.[4] To date this agenda remains only partially complete.

Faris and Dunham limited their study to various forms of schizophrenia (regarded as the most serious and intransigent of mental disorders, characterized as it is by a generalized withdrawal from meaningful social intercourse and the display of behaviors and symbolism that carry with them meanings and motives different from those apparently intended by the initiator) and to manic-depressive disorders. The latter involve deep and relatively long-lasting mood swings, from great and exhuberant elation inappropriate to the situation in which they are expressed, to deep periods of depression and withdrawal (often to the point of suicide attempts), also in response to stimuli and circumstances others would regard as minor if not downright inconsequential. In addition, psychotic diagnoses, along with addiction to alcohol, were also considered as major mental disorders. The ecological distribution of the home residence of institutionalized "schizophrenics" conformed closely to the pattern for alcoholic psychotics as depicted in Figure 10.1. The overall pattern was striking for its time: namely, that the incidence of schizophrenia increased markedly as one approached the center of the city—passing from the generally middle- and upper-middle-class suburbs into decaying slum and lower-class residential areas surrounding the nonresidential city center. And while the pattern for manic-depressives was not quite so striking, there was some indication that, opposite to the case of schizophrenia, manic-depression seemed to be more prevalent in the middle-class regions of the city than in the deteriorating regions toward the center of the city. All of this, of course, was taking place before the rush to the suburbs in the post–World War II years, the great expansion of the black ghetto of Chicago taking place during those same years, and the only partially successful efforts of the 1960s to regenerate the blight spreading out from the center of so many large American metropolitan cores.

Nevertheless, from a sociological perspective, mental illness had been as firmly established empirically as a correlate of social forces as the city itself and was therefore traceable directly to social causation

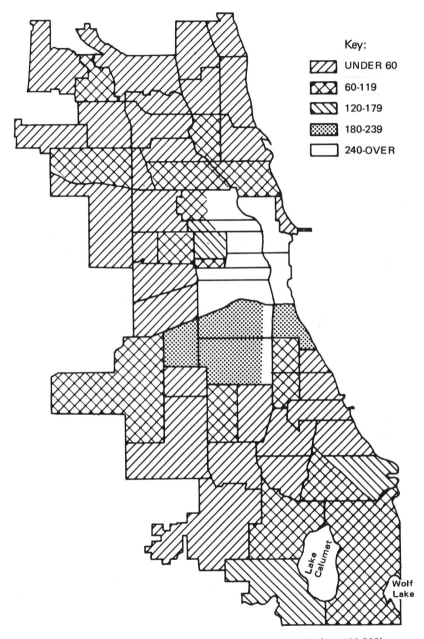

FIGURE 10.1 Alcoholic psychosis rates in Chicago, 1922-1931 (per 100,000).

Source: Adapted from Robert Faris and Warren Dunham, <u>Mental Disorders in the</u> <u>Urban Areas.</u> Chicago: University of Chicago Press, 1939. By permission. (Prepared by H. W. Dunham, Jr., from the records at Chicago, Elgin, and Kankakee State Hospitals.)

rather than to the capriciousness of early childhood experiences, a theory fostered by the then-prevalent social pathology view of mental disturbance. Never mind the fact that by contemporary standards the research methodology employed by Faris and Dunham was rather unsophisticated and that there may have been special attributes of the city of Chicago as a geographic and political entity that lent itself to widespread application of the so-called "concentric-zone hypothesis." Never mind also that the diagnoses as *assigned* were accepted at face value and not challenged either on validity or metaphysical grounds or—perhaps most telling of all—that the cases dealt with were drawn from the three major *state* psychiatric hospitals in the region. Patients in private practice or in residence at private hospitals were not included in the study. All of these today stand as devastating shortcomings of the original study. But that is not the point. The point is that the Faris and Dunham study clearly established the study of mental disorder as legitimately within the purview of the discipline of sociology and not the exclusive property of its then-temporary gatekeepers and custodians.

In fact it is arguable that Faris and Dunham were the cork-pullers who allowed the issue of mental disorder to spill into the public forum, thereby making both the psychiatrist's couch and the hospital corridor objects of public scrutiny and judgment—a process that 30 years later is not yet completely finished. Let it be said, however, that this single study established mental disorder as a social phenomenon, subject both to social causation and, by implication, to social amelioration, a fact that is still slowly emerging in the realm of more strictly organic illness. Its recent history is therefore something of a model of social change to which general medicine may or may not slavishly conform.

But even with these sharp limitations, the "urbanism–mental illness" link lent itself to numerous implications that would extend and expand the social view of behavioral deviations. First, the Faris and Dunham findings were thoroughly consistent with the general theme of antiurbanism that the Chicago ecological studies embodied: the idea that the nature of urban life was somehow antithetical to good mental health, not to speak of good morals. We were then still sufficiently close to our rural heritage and ideology as to welcome an explanation for mental illness that would authorize such a bias.

Second, the study is responsible in many ways for the enunciation of the hypothesis that one's *general* sociocultural milieu (in this case the alienating nature of modern urban life) itself fostered serious psychological breaks with a reality that was not worth embracing anyway. And this perspective was soon to be accompanied by a rapidly produced literature of social anthropological and social psychological studies of "national character." These were efforts to delineate the common types of social character produced in different national cultural-political contexts,[5] as well as home-based studies of the kinds of small social enclaves (mostly rural or semirural in nature) that seemed to be conducive to the preservation of "good" mental health. Here, the now-famous Eaton and Weil study of "mental health among the Hutterites" is a prime example.[6] More than that, however, the Faris and Dunham study was the spark that later developed into a major effort in the social sciences to delineate factors producing differential diagnosis and management of "mental illness." Ultimately it led to the recent widespread "labeling" theory, which holds that mental illness and its several offshoots are in fact a product of linguistic manipulation and differential status assignment. They have little or nothing to do with "illness" as an analog to the kinds of cellular anomaly foundation on which general allopathic conceptions of illness rests.

The impact of these later developments on social action and sociopolitical attitudes in the entire field of mental illness will be sketched later in this chapter. Suffice it for the moment to say that the early Faris and Dunham study clearly established the capacity of the discipline of sociology to say something worthwhile, even revolutionary, about mental illness. So much for the early beginnings of a social causation theory of mental illness—from symptom manifestation to differential diagnosis to differential institutionalization.

SOCIAL STRUCTURE AND HEALTH IDEOLOGY

What about the content of *mental health as a social organization?* A review of Kingsley Davis's study of the relation between the social values running through the early mental health movement and the class structure of society is instructive here. As Davis writes:[7]

> Our interest lies in our own mobile class system and its accompanying world philosophy. The latter, which may conveniently be called the Protestant ethic, and which receives its severest expression in Puritanism, is: (1) *Democratic* in the sense of favoring equal opportunity to rise socially by merit rather than by birth. (2) *Worldly* in emphasizing earthly values such as the pursuit of a calling, accumulation of wealth, and achievement of status. (3) But at the same time *ascetic* in stressing physical abstinence and stern sobriety, thrift, industry, and prudence. (4) *Individualistic* in placing responsibility upon the individual himself for his economic, political, and religious destiny, and in stressing personal ambition, self-reliance, private enterprise, and entrepreneurial ability. (5) *Rationalistic* and *empirical* in assuming a world order discoverable through sensory observation of nature. (6) *Utilitarian* in pursuing practical ends with the best available means, and conceiving human welfare in secularized terms as attainable by human knowledge and action.

Davis's argument is a cogent one and it is that the mental health complex is an active extension of these core middle-class values in American society. It serves therefore, a watchdog function against possible disruptive behavior of those whose actions indicate that they do not subscribe to these core values, and then as either a resocialization center to "rehabilitate" deviants to basic middle-class morality or as holding stations for those incapable or unwilling to accommodate themselves to the central values of the middle-class world. Thus, the mental health movement from Davis's point of view is not so much an organization for the diffusion of a new and modern "science" of man as an agent of strict social control at best and an instrument of punitive retaliation at worst. For as Davis says, "Mental hygiene turns out to be not so much a science for the prevention of mental disorder, as science for the prevention of moral delinquency. Thus, an author may state that every individual has a need for some kind of useful work, then draw the conclusion that every individual *must* have useful work to be mentally adjusted, and finally declare that any social customs which do not permit this are irrational and unworthy."[8] To make his point, Davis quotes extensively from the statements of policy—both written and spoken—made by the then-leading advocates of the mental health movement:[9]

> The ultimate in mental *hygiene means mental poise,* calm judgment, and an understanding of leadership and fellowship—in other words, *cooperation,* with an attitude that tempers justice with mercy and humility.

> Mental hygiene . . . presents many wider aspects. *Industrial unrest* to a large degree means bad mental hygiene, and is to be corrected by good mental hygiene. The various antisocial attitudes that lead to crime are problems for the mental hygienist . . . but mental hygiene has a message also for those who consider themselves quite normal, for, by its aims, the man who is fifty percent efficient can make himself seventy percent *efficient.*

> . . . the ideal democratic group today is one where each member of the group has the opportunity *to become superior* in something according to his special ability.

> Wells assumes that the *aim of life is to get ahead,* and that ambition is a prerequisite to a well-functioning mind.

> The free imagination of wished-for things results well for the mind through pointing in more glowing colors the excellence of what is wished for, and *firing the ambition to strive for it* the more intensely.

> Your birth means that you have been selected as a player in the greatest game ever devised.

. . . the worth of existence depends on success in a game infinitely more complicated than that of chess, in which *no mistake is ever overlooked* and no move ever taken back . . .

. . . one symptom of bad adjustment found in the inferiority complex is a *poor reaction to competition.*

Facing life squarely is the first principle of mental health.

The devotion of some leisure time to recreational pursuits is of positive value outside of the enjoyment which it affords, for it enables the individual to return reinvigorated to *the more serious routine of study or work.*

In life, *the lubricating function of money* to the social machinery is well known. It plays an equally essential part in the smooth operation of one's mental trends.

Life is ever-changing and demands continuous readjustment. It is a game with a continual challenge which you must meet if you are to keep alive. Stagnation and death come when you cease to *rise to the challenge.*

For a person to satisfy all his motives with regard for their functioning as an interrelated system, is good adjustment. To achieve this *requires unified and integrated* behavior.

By this means, Davis presents a persuasive argument that the claims of mental health promoters are faulty in arguing that the capacity to identify and classify behavior and motives that depart from standard and mainstream middle-class morality is sufficient evidence to say that an "illness" exists that must be treated in a manner which constitutes a "shadow" system of that mode of management prevailing for the treatment of acute infectious and morphological lesions. Further, it is an early identification of the politicalization of an expanding wing of medicine and triggered more recent and more avowedly radical attacks on the psychiatric bastions. In this regard, the work of Thomas Scheff on "labeling" theory and that of the psychiatrist Thomas Szasz on the historical accidents that have produced the psychiatric establishment as it is presently constituted and now exists under considerable criticism are the key cases in point.

Whereas Faris and Dunham opened hte door to the possible and widespread social causation and management ideas of mental illness, Davis's tour de force dramatized the class bias involved in its identification, control, and coercion. But it took the detailed social ethnography of a small psychiatric hospital by Alfred Stanton and Morris Schwartz to seed the suspicion that even *institutionalized* patients exhibited a wider range of "normal" behavior than their official designation as "mentally ill" might lead one to believe, thus opening up the home territory of institutional psychiatry to sociological analysis and critique.[10]

SOCIAL CONTEXT OF TREATMENT

The Stanton and Schwartz study, a three-year on-the-grounds analysis of life in a small elite private psychiatric hospital, stems from the assumption that ill behavior is a function of identifiable elements in the social milieu to which institutionalized patients are subjected and not merely the unfolding of the natural history of mental illness or the effects of specific psychiatric intervention modalities (much like the medical model of illness heretofore described) as such. In general, the underlying theme in this work is the contention that the organizational context of psychiatric treatment is more conducive to *maladaptive responses* on the part of patients than it is to the promotion of *adaptive forms* of patient behavior. In short, and as Perrow has argued:[11]

> It was assumed that the problem of the hospital was to correct the *hospital's* failure of communication which accounted for her disturbance. While expressly noting that not all of the disturbed behavior of patients was due to the hospital, the impression remains that most of it was. It is clear from several descriptions of discrete behavior of patients that they were very ill indeed, but their illness was not treated as a dynamic factor in the hospital by the authors (though it is by some hospital psychiatrists); only the interpersonal relations were so treated, and here the underlying theme is that the doctors were responsible for the manifestation of illness, almost as if they were the ones that were ill.
>
> This interpretation crops up repeatedly in Stanton and Schwartz. Staff tensions led patients to go on pass singly, instead of in groups, and to get into trouble and create disturbances the next day. Their needs (realistic, legitimate) were frustrated by staff tension, but the staff blamed the patients.

By focusing on the occasional recurrence of the appearance of symptomatic behavior on the part of a limited number of patients, the authors' general conclusion is that poor hospital organization and communication create maladaptive patient behavior through administrative bungling and staff disputes and disagreements more frequently than did "normal" behavior seem to follow the "professional" ministrations of the treatment personnel in the hospital. The *factual* basis for such a conclusion is, however, open to serious question. For as Perrow continues to say:[12]

> This curious emphasis upon the rationality and sanity of mental patients and the irrationality and sometimes repressive behavior of doctors, attendants, and nurses is a key theme in much of the current literature.

It receives its most forceful and repetitive statement in Goffman's *Asylums* (1961). However, the theme generally exists side by side with another, contradictory one, and again, Goffman's work provides many illustrations. When the patient does exhibit behavior characteristic of mental illness and which thus demands understanding and tolerance, it is claimed that the staff tends to regard such behavior as conscious, sane, and manipulative. Either way, the patient appears as misunderstood, the victim of irrational or predatory staff behavior. That patient behavior may be sane at some times and insane at others is, of course, true. But is striking that the staff is always seen as selecting the wrong interpretation.

The analysis of collective disturbances, attributing them to cover disagreements among the staff, is the most famous of the contributions of Stanton and Schwartz, and it is a brilliant *tour de force*. It is no doubt true that some disturbances occurred for the reasons they stated, and since this is a pioneering insight, some exaggerated claims for it are to be expected.

This theme of the rationality of the insane and the irrationality of the sane is picked up at about the same time in popular literature, reaching its fullest expression in Ken Kesey's now well-known *One Flew Over the Cuckoo's Nest*.[13]

What is important in these two works is not that the latter is a work of fiction and the Stanton and Schwartz conclusions are in fact based largely upon observations of *one* patient, but rather that both reflect a rejection of the heretofore received truth that inasmuch as the psychiatric profession had, through a series of historical accidents, come to possess management and control over the mentally disturbed, it *necessarily* had a clear understanding of what its responsibilities entail on the grounds on which they rested. In the absence of a convincing technology, its claims to organizational and policy preeminence were seriously called into question, especially in that the treatment ethic and philosophy stemmed from some special adaptations of the medical model illness without fully embracing, up to that time at least, anything closely resembling a social model of illness.

Before examining some of the historical events and circumstances producing the crisis in mental health care which can be dated as occurring in the decade of the mid-1950s to the mid-1960s, one final sociological step that should to recounted is the work of Thomas Scheff, who went far in rejecting the psychiatric ideology altogether—philosophically, ideologically, technologically, and organizationally.[14]

MENTAL ILLNESS AS SYMBOLIC CONSTRUCT

Having its origins in modern American pragmatism in general and in symbolic interactionism in particular, there is a special wing of social behaviorism of which the works of George Herbert Mead and Charles

Horton Cooley remain as the substantiating texts, along with W. I. Thomas's now famous dictum, "if a situation is defined as real it is real in its consequences." The proponents of this principle claim it to be one around which all understanding might be organized. According to Scheff, the special set of definitions, interactional networks, and organizational complexes called "psychiatry" and "mental illness" are little more than symbolic constructs about which sufficient consensus has been achieved that coordinated action "as if it were real" can be brought about.

By focusing more upon social reaction to persons referred to as mentally ill rather than upon the search for internal causes, these conceptual tools (according to Scheff) are utilized to construct a theory of mental disorder in which psychiatric symptoms are considered to be violations of social norms, and stable "mental illness" to be a social role,[15] and in fact a metaphorical usage in which the etiology of organic illness is regarded as having an analog in behaviors classified as mental illness. Such a view has major implications both for an understanding of mental illness (we use the term for the lack of a better one) and for collective action with regard to the mentally ill. The use of the medical metaphor is followed by a number of auxiliary conceptions concerning the mentally ill that Scheff and others regard as serious pathologies which deface the recent psychiatric scene. And it is to be kept in mind that these corollaries are *rejected* when one assumes a labeling theory perspective:

1. Persons with illnesses are best isolated from well people and handled in a clinical setting so that their illness will not pose a threat to others.

2. Illnesses represent the presence of internal "foreign" entities that must be combated and exorcised.

3. Illness is the domain of certified specialists (doctors), and therefore doctors should treat the mentally ill.

4. Ill people are unable to fulfill their normal social responsibilities and therefore should be relieved, by court action if necessary, of the *right* to perform their usual social responsibilities.

5. Institutions modeled on the "hospital" are the best places to handle people with mental illness.

6. Lay explanations of mental illness are superficial and inadequate; a professional lexicon that captures the "real" nature of mental illness is required.

7. Since people do not willfully become ill, it therefore follows that "mental illness" is not motivated and is in no way functional for the individual.

8. Since the history of modern medicine is the history of the accumulation of "specific" causes and "specific" cures, mental illness

research and treatment should follow that model wherever possible. A social model of mental illness, while it may be temporarily necessary as a stopgap measure, will eventually give way to the kind of medical specificity characterizing historical experience with regard to virtually every other illness.

By way of contrast, a social, "normalizing," or comprehensive view of the management of the ill differs in the following respects:

1. Whenever possible, ill persons are best managed outside of traditional medical contexts and interaction, and contact with persons who are not ill should be maximized.

2. Illness is an integral part of the social and cultural milieu, and an emphasis upon health is to be preferred over a preoccupation with illness.

3. Certified medical expertise is only one of several ways—many of them nonprofessionalized—in which ill persons can be helped; wherever possible, "illness" as an institutionalized status degradation should be avoided.

4. The continued performance of customary social roles should be facilitated, not impeded, wherever possible. Many patients can be counseled to "cope" in areas in spheres heretofore thought to be beyond their capabilities.

5. The acute-crisis-oriented hospital is only one of several ways of organizing medical care and is not always the preferred mode.

6. Professional labels for illness tend to be stigmatizing, and therefore the use of folk-based labels can often foreshorten the illness career.

7. Illness carries with it a number of "secondary gains"; therefore ill persons should be exposed to as many incentives as possible to see to it that they remain well.

8. The "organic illness" model is counterproductive in the case of most functional disorders.

The macrodifferences and their confrontation with the "over-medicalization" issue may be exemplified in the current debate over childhood hyperkinesis.

The medicalization issue derives from the conviction that far too many incursions into heretofore poorly defined areas of deviant behavior on the part of the medical profession constitute malevolent, unwarranted, and technically unfounded preemption of patients' human rights and are, in fact, exploitation of a gullible public in order to extend the scope of medical power rather than render new services to clients. Although each such case must be examined in its own right, the recent dispute over the use of drugs for the treatment of hyperkinesis illustrates some of the dynamics underlying this charge. It also highlights the caution that should be exercised in totally accepting one critic's conclusions, that "In the last analysis medical social control may be the central issue as in this role medicine becomes a de facto agent of the status quo."[16]

THE MEDICAL-SOCIAL MODEL DISPUTE— THE CASE OF HYPERKINESIS

The situation with regard to hyperkinesis dramatizes the ongoing dispute between the proponents of a medical versus a social model of a functional disorder and its differential treatment. It poses also something of a natural experiment of the social and medical models.

Hyperkinesis—or hyperkinetic impulse disorder, as it is sometimes called—is typically displayed by preadolescent boys in explosive and unexplained overt aggressive outbursts; an inability to concentrate, difficulty in formulating, engaging in, and sustaining stable human relationships; generalized anxiety; and poor development of language and other verbal skills. At the formal psychological testing and psychiatric examination levels, boys displaying this syndrome are not otherwise extraordinary and in most cases come to the attention of psychiatric authorities through an avenue of referrals and treatment and counseling efforts that are almost always unsuccessful. These efforts include school counseling and special instruction, social service agency contacts, direct one-to-one psychoanalytic treatment, as well as contacts with the police and delinquency authorities.[17] Thus formal institutional psychiatric referrals are typically regarded as last-ditch efforts because as boys such as these approach adolescence their generalized deviancy seems quite firmly fixed: repeated failure at school to the extent that most of them at age 11 or 12 read at levels typical of normal 5- or 6-year-old children; a history of court contacts and brushes with the law; extremely unhappy and unrewarding peer relationships, including long histories of fighting; as well as an accumulation of family tensions that make it impossible for the mothers and fathers to contain the children in a normal home atmosphere.

In several special treatment institutions for problem children such as these, a 20-year history of testing with a variety of early psychomedications[18] uncovered data suggesting that children who had received this diagnosis (which heretofore had been thought to have an etiology consistent with extensions of Freudian hypotheses concerning early child rearing and had been treated psychodynamically in those terms) reacted in a surprising manner to properly monitored dosages of the central nervous system stimulants subsumed under the heading of the amphetamines. Typically, the amphetamines ("uppers" in street language) had been used clinically to manage conditions of depression, debilitating lassitude, narcolepsy, and to help weight reduction by the artificial generation of high energy levels. In other words, amphetamines are *stimulants* that generally produce abnormally high levels of activity when administered in proper dosages. For hyperkinetic boys, however, the effect was *usually the opposite;* the amphetamines served as depressants rather than stimulants. Their use, in at least one clinical setting "under double-blind conditions,"[19] showed that these patients slept more soundly and for longer periods of time, were able to concentrate for longer periods of time in the school situation, seemed to get along much better both with their peers and the adults with whom they interacted in the hospital, got along better with their parents on visiting days, and generally tended to act more like "normal" pre-adolescent boys. The results were, for those of us who were watching during these years, little short of miraculous. Of course a great deal of adaptive damage had already been done, and their verbal IQ scores still lagged far behind their performance scores; interactions with others still tended to be somewhat testy as the memories of the past were always elements in behavior in the here and now. In any event, they were no longer the uncontrollable, unpredictable, aggression-prone time bombs that they had been.

Now the medical model, as we have seen, requires evidence of a "lesion" on which to rest its case, and here the real research work began. Over the years hundreds of electroencephalograms were run and analyzed revealing no particularly outstanding profiles. Patient after patient was referred to a large general hospital for the running of photometrazol tests, and no extraordinary patterns were seen. At the same time, continual psychiatric and psychological examinations, both standardized and clinical, were conducted in order to find some clues as to the organic roots of this problem and to search for some explanation as to why the amphetamines had this striking effect. It should be also said that the work involved periods of time during which double-blind placebo studies were undertaken to determine whether or not a "Hawthorne effect" may have been operating, and no positive results were obtained. Then in the very early 1960s some quite astounding results were found in the use of the so-called Archimedes spiral, which in fact pointed to an organic root to hyperkinesis. The figure is a black spiral painted on a white background card about 8 inches in diameter. This is attached to a small rotating electric motor that can turn the spiral either clockwise or counterclockwise. The spiral is depicted in Figure 10.2.

In the classical spiral test, the subject stares at the spiral as it rotates to the right. The spiral *appears* to be fading into the distance and *getting smaller;* then as it is actually stopped, the spiral *appears* only to slow down, then to *reverse* itself and *get larger* and move toward the observer. Further, as the spiral is mechanically rotated to the *left* it *appears* to be coming toward the observer and getting larger. As it stops, it appears to slow down, then to reverse itself and "go away" while getting *smaller*. This is the classic "Archimedes spiral effect," and in the "normal" case the perception lasts anywhere from two to five seconds. *Hyperkinetic children, however, do not observe this effect* or do so only for very short periods of time. When the machine stops, so too does their perception of it.

And it is primarily this finding on which the organic argument for hyperkinesis rests: that the differential perception of the Archimedes spiral is indicative of malfunctioning in the thalamus of the brain to such an extent that *perceptual stimuli* are imperfectly selected and differentiated. Thus the sufferer's capacity for concentration, attention span, and perceptual acuity are severely impaired. These, in turn, are *behaviorally altered* under proper levels of medication with amphetamines.

It must be said that the *exact mechanical* link between amphetamines and functional change in the brain thalamus is somewhat unclear, but it remains an empirically convincing and *plausible* explanation for the changes being brought about in these children. Although the "early childhood experiences" hypothesis as a way of explaining

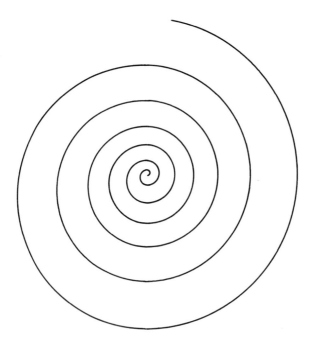

FIGURE 10.2 The Archimedes spiral.

the cause of hyperkinesis may also seem plausible, working with that presumed cause has not produced results. On the other hand, from a medical model point of view, the "malfunctioning thalamus" hypothesis is *equally* plausible, and working in terms of it *has* produced results. Hence the experience with hyperkinesis and amphetamines stands in the mainstream of allopathic medicine in that it is squarely in the "credible and true" quadrant.

In view of the quite spectacular results obtained, why the present dispute, raised sometimes to fever pitch, over the treatment of hyperkinesis through amphetamines? The main answer seems to be that we now live in a time during which the "medicalization" of social problems has become an epithet that one can apply with some confidence that it will elicit negative attitudes toward the medical profession and enterprise. That is, the arguments against the medicalization of hyperkinesis rests upon a *de facto* rejection of the medical model and its proponents and elevation of the social model to a sometimes unjustified stature of preeminence. As one such critic wrote in 1975:[20]

> Defining deviant behavior as a medical problem allows certain things to be done that could not otherwise be considered; for example, the body may be cut open or psychoactive medications may be given. This treatment (the use of amphetamines for hyperkinesis) can be a form of social control.

Furthermore:[21]

> The medicalization of deviant behavior is part of a larger phenomenon that is prevalent in our society, the individualization of social problems. We tend to look for causes and solutions to complex social problems in the individual rather than in the social system. This view resembles Ryan's notion of "blaming the victim"; seeing the causes of the problem in individuals rather than in the society where they live.

And finally:[22]

> By defining the overactive, restless and disruptive child as hyperkinetic we ignore the meaning of behavior in the context of the social system. . . . Depoliticalization of deviant behavior is a result both of the process of medicalization and individualization in social problems.

Suffice it to say that counterpoint to this political critique is the *fact* that the parents of such children who have been treated with amphetamines experience an enormous relief from feelings of diffuse guilt because the social model presumed that the problem was somehow "their fault." Boys, themselves, seem to acquire a far more positive self-image, and are able to make friends, tend to avoid trouble with the police, and have more rewarding experiences (some for the very first time) in school. So much for "victim blaming."

Assuming that to "cut the body" is necessarily a bad thing it is in this context nonetheless an *ad hominen* argument. No "body cutting" is involved in the medical treatment of hyperkinesis. A few small pills are swallowed each day, usually with few or no side effects. In return for this the boy avoids the probability of getting his body cut in a street fight, possible abuse by his parents in retaliation for his excessive aggressiveness. Small price for a mere acknowledgment that the "social model of illness" is not always and everywhere all-powerful.

Perhaps most important, the treatment, taken early enough, avoids in nearly every case the need for institutionalization with all the pitfalls that is known to involve. Families remain intact and functioning. Young children do not have to face sometimes long periods of time as "inmates" of the very kind of institutions that the critics of the medical model have been castigating since the days of the classic Stanton and Schwartz study.

In fact, one might easily argue that hyperkinesis has not been politicized by the small group of doctors who over years cautiously tested the uses of psychomedication. Indeed, it has been brought about by the spurious nature of the critics, such as the one quoted here, whose political persuasions blind them to the dramatic and basically benign effects that empirical and eclectic medical science can bring about.

The complex interplay of medical versus social factors in the institutional behavior of boys such as this is indicated in a study of 20 such children—10 of them from solid middle-class backgrounds, and 10 of them from working- or lower-class backgrounds. Attention also centers around the highly qualified causal statements that are justifiable with regard either to exclusive medical or social causes:[23]

> The family settings of the middle-class patients were usually characterized as "overmoralistic," with strict ethical and achievement standards imposed upon the children. The fathers were generally described as weak and ineffective and the mothers as hostile and domineering. The descriptions of the family included such remarks as "father disinterested in children because of career demands," "mother too busy in community activities," "competitive rivalry between siblings," and the like.
>
> The family settings of the lower-class patients, on the other hand, were more often characterized as "undermoralistic," with weak and unloving mothers and hostile and irrationally brutal fathers, the implications often being that the patient had grown up without available role models or meaningful behavior norms. The descriptions included such comments as "alcoholic father," "common-law marriage," "transient residence and sporadic unemployment," and so forth.

It is of interest to note that the factors in family relationships indicated for each class also appear to be somewhat typical of families in each class that apparently do not have emotionally disturbed children. Whether or not these reports reflect actual objective differences between family settings, in the records they tend to result in the implicit judgment that the lower-class child had been handled in much too lax a fashion, while the middle-class boy had been handled far too rigidly. In substance, these case materials suggested a perspective toward the lower-class child which might be summed up as *blame-control*, and a frame of reference for the middle-class child which might be summed up as *explain-treat*. From this starting point in the patients' hospital careers, it becomes increasingly difficult to determine what differences are a function of social class and what differences are a function of differential expectations that staff members have of patients.

Career sequences and staff responses

There were marked differences between the two classes in the processes of adjustment to the hospital setting. The phases of the hospital career may be referred to, in sequence, as (1) *intake*, extending up to the first six-month staff conference on the patient; (2) *treatment*, extending to the last six-month staff conference preceding the boy's discharge; and (3) *predischarge*, extending to the actual discharge date.

During the first period, the ward reports—as well as the first six-month conference transcripts—reflected an initially poor adjustment by the middle-class boys and an initially good adjustment by the lower-class boys. The lower-class patients fell rather quickly into hospital routines and adjusted to discipline expectations quietly and without turmoil. The middle-class boys, on the other hand, had quite a difficult time during the intake phase, adjusting poorly to both peers and adults. In short, during this period the middle-class boys appeared to be classic examples of their diagnostic category, whereas the lower-class patients did not.

During the second, or treatment, phase, the early good adjustment of the lower-class boys gave way to increased "acting out," while the middle-class patients adapted more satisfactorily to the routines and behavior standards of the institution.

During the predischarge phase, the lower-class patients shifted from poor to good adjustment, and the middle-class boys from good to poor.

Regarding the staff responses to these sequences, the initially poor adjustment of the middle-class patient suggested to many of the staff that the diagnosis was correct and the treatment plans were appropriate. The long period of adequate adjustment during the treatment phase, moreover, gave the staff the feeling that the treatment was effective and that the patient was making remarkable progress, usually formalized in an optimistic prognosis. The poor adjustment during the predischarge phase, however, was then associated with some dis-illusionment and pessimism among the staff regarding the middle-class patient.

The staff's shift from optimism to pessimism was reversed with the lower-class patients. The initially good adjustment resulted in some misgivings among the staff as to whether a proper diagnosis had been made and whether the patient might be more neurotic than a case of behavior disorder. Those who held out for the original diagnosis, how-ever, tended to be vindicated by the middle phase of acting out, and at this low ebb in the patient's career a rather pessimistic and negative prognosis was made—not infrequently with some staff members recom-mending discharge on the grounds that the case might be hopeless, since the patient appeared to have gotten "worse" rather than "better." But the generally good adjustment during the predischarge phase tended to justify those who had held out for continued treatment and resulted in a general spirit of optimism concerning the outcome.

Relations with the system, with peers, and with adults

The peer group among the patients was lower-class dominated. Throughout the ten-year period covered by the cases studied, the lower-class boys were always numerically dominant, and the mantle of indigenous group leadership was passed from one lower-class boy to another. As a result, the middle-class patients found it difficult to gain entree to the informal structure of the group and found themselves either tacitly excluded or only provisionally accepted. Insofar as one might speak of a patient subculture, the middle-class patients were only marginal participants in it. The differences between the two classes may actually be a function of the middle-class patients' time lag in acculturating to a lower-class-dominated subculture. Perhaps as a result of this, the middle-class patient did not learn the tricks of the institutional trade. The lower-class boys had a rather sophisticated awareness of the hospital as a system, a keen sense of the deviancies that would be tolerated, and considerable ability to manipulate or "con" the system. The middle-class boys appeared, on the other hand, to be somewhat overwhelmed by the experience of institutionalization, were typically in awe of the system, had little awareness of its toler-ance limits, and made few successful efforts to manipulate it.

But although the lower-class boys found it relatively easy to gain rapport with the system, they found it difficult to do so with individual adults within the organization. The middle-class patients, however, found the institutional system difficult to manage, but were better able to gain rapport with, and acceptance by, adults within the hospital, and frequently attached themselves to some one adult. This difference may have arisen from the greater sociocultural similarity of middle-class patients to higher-status members of the staff as well as from the inability of middle-class boys to manipulate the organizational system, which made them less threatening to the staff than were the lower-class patients.

Yet there appeared to be a certain superficiality in the middle-class patients' reciprocity with adults, paralleled by a superficiality in the lower-class boys' reciprocity with each other. While the lower-class patients received the tacit acceptance of their peers, there was little indication that they strongly sought it or valued it; instead they seemed to seek the acceptance of the adults, which they did not generally receive. The middle-class boys did not seek or value the acceptance they received in many instances from the adults, but they did actively seek the acceptance of the peer group, which was usually withheld. Thus a general lack of interpersonal reciprocity characterized relations within the patient group and between the patient and staff groups.

Behavior in hospital activities and routines

Competitive sports, which provide an important focus of the preadolescent round of life, seemed to offer more of a problem for middle-class boys than for lower-class boys. A great many of the lower-class boys liked sports and were proficient at them. Those who did not care for them seemed usually to have other interests that occupied their time in a manner acceptable to the staff. But many more of the middle-class boys not only did not like such activities, but were poor at them, and, in fact, abhorred physical contact. In addition, these middle-class boys often seemed unable to substitute other acceptable activities.

This self-exclusion from competitive sports and failure to substitute other acceptable interests may have been, in part, a function of the lack of acceptance of the middle-class boys by the peer group. Many of the staff, however, tended to view it as an indication of lack of therapeutic progress, and made attempts to cajole or coerce the middle-class patients into accepting the appropriateness of competitive sports. When the middle-class patients, during their absence from sports activities, were involved in deviancies such as fire setting, window breaking, stealing, and the like, the staff usually viewed these as clinical evidence of continued illness. Similar deviant forays by lower-class boys, however, were more likely to be reacted to with the attitude that such deviancies were psychologically unnecessary; the staff assumed that the lower-class patient was proficient at and liked group activities, and there was no reason why the deviancies should have taken place. Thus, while much of the acting out of the middle-class boys was regarded as a manifestation of inner turmoil, that of the lower-class boys were regarded as deliberate delinquency.

The lower-class patients who had difficulty in retiring and arising tended to manifest this by a variety of somatic complaints, such as headaches, backaches, nightmares, and so on. The middle-class patients, instead, manifested such difficulty by oversocializing—resisting going to bed by running from room to room, attempting to carry on conversations with reluctant lower-class boys or adults, and getting out of bed early in the morning to socialize. It appeared that the ward situation at night and in the morning provided the middle-class patients with a captive audience and an opportunity of making inroads upon the solid leadership core of the lower-class-dominated peer group.

According to the hospital records, there was a significant difference in the behavior of the patients in the hospital dining room; that of the lower-class boys was reported as acceptable, while that of the middle-class boys was unacceptable. Although this may reflect a genuine difference in symptom manifestation, it may also reflect the difference in expectations that the staff held of the two groups. It may, too, reflect the greater awareness of the lower-class patients of the tolerance limits of various areas of hospital routines.

Inadequate personal hygiene and sexual manifestations on the part of lower-class patients were noted very early in the case records, whereas such notations appeared for middle-class patients much later, usually in the predischarge phase. When sexual behavior was noted for middle-class patients, it was usually masturbation or other covert practices, but the sexual practices of the lower-class boys were more often of an overt nature. This later appearance of such data may have contributed to the disillusionment of some of the staff with the middle-class patients during the predischarge phase.

The middle-class patients showed a significant lack of enuresis, whereas the lower-class patients tended to have long-standing records of bed-wetting in the hospital. But there also appeared to be some discrepancy in the recording of enuresis; it seemed likely to be noted less consistently for the patients who were highly regarded by the staff.

The psychological differential

Although there were many common characteristics in the psychological profiles for both groups, the chief reason for their common diagnosis, a few major differences could be identified in the psychological reports. The typical lower-class profile was that of undercontrolled ego functioning, with volatile emotional responsiveness and accompanied by considerable guilt feelings that were interpreted as being quite close to the surface of consciousness. The profile of the typical middle-class patient showed a pattern of overcontrolled and inhibited emotional responsiveness, with a flattened form of ego functioning. Also there was much less indication of guilt, and what little could be identified was apparently far less close to the surface of consciousness than was the case with the lower-class patients.

These differences might suggest that in a psychodynamically oriented setting the lower-class acting-out patient is more likely to receive a hopeful prognosis than is the middle-class patient. But as a consequence of different case data, differences in symptom manifestations, and differences in staff expectations, the situation appeared to be somewhat the reverse. The greater interpersonal sophistication of the middle-class boys seemed to suggest to the staff a depth of emotional potential that in fact was not proved to be present. And the spontaneous and hostile impulsivity of the socially naive lower-class boys appeared to suggest the absence of emotional depth. The shell of sociability of the middle-class boys was of such a nature that they were likely to be viewed in much more accepting terms by the staff than were the rather unsophisticated lower-class patients. This combination of patient attributes and staff attitudes made the middle-class patients rather proficient on a one-to-one basis during the treatment phase of their careers, but quite inept in regard to the total hospital system. Conversely, the absence of social skills on the part of the lower-class patients appeared to make them inadequate in face-to-face relationships, despite their expertise within the total organizational system.

Differential responses to amphetamines[24]

There was a striking difference between the two groups in their reaction to psychomedication. Most of the patients in the study group had, at one time or another, and for varying periods of time, received dosages of amphetamines—usually benzadrines and dexadrines. The lower-class patients frequently did not react as clinically expected, but showed either little behavioral change or a slight increase in symptomatic behavior. In addition, they showed a variety of somatic side effects such as loss of appetite, loss of weight, nervousness, or sleeplessness. The middle-class patients, on the other hand, responded as expected, with decreases in hyperactivity, increased ability to concentrate, and few or no side effects.

There were some independent data which suggested that the middle-class patients regarded medical manipulation in the hospital, including psychomedication, as benign, potentially helpful, and indicative of the staff's concern for them, while the lower-class boys tended to view it as a punitive measure, as reflected in the statement by one patient, "If you don't behave you have to get needles."

More recently with respect to the hyperkinesis issue, however, there has been a contention that the condition can be markedly improved through the application of a suitable *diet*, hence eliminating the need for either medical intrusion or the calamity of institutionalization. On this issue the results are not yet in, but it illustrates the continuing dispute between the medical and social models of disease causation and strategies of cure.

Having said all this about the major sociological perspectives toward mental illness, it remains to ask how the present situation has evolved and what the present scene now has in view.

MENTAL ILLNESS AND PSYCHIATRY—WHITHER AND WHENCE?

We shall briefly sketch the major turning points in the history of the conceptualization and social organization for the handling of the "mentally ill," including the Freudian breakthrough that swept a rich variety of behavioral deviancies into the domain of medicine, following a brief 35- to 40-year period of apparent astounding success of an episode of care referred to as the age of "moral treatment." This age saw the rise of the state hospital and individual psychotherapy as the prime ideological and organizational forms, then the period of the "therapeutic milieu" or "total treatment center" following the groundbreaking work of Maxwell Jones in Great Britain, and a handful of others in this country—notably Stanton and Schwartz, William Caudill, and Bruno Bettelheim for children, followed by the current phase of the demedicalization and deinstitutionalization of the "mentally ill," of which Thomas Scheff's "labeling theory" was an early bellwether.

Although the development of organic medicine—at least throughout the past century—has a very strong *linear* characteristic, but technically and organizationally, no such single thread is discernible in the growth and expansion of psychiatry. It is filled, rather, with competing ideologies and technologies, false starts and countless unsatisfactory endings, and is to the present day a scene of considerable conflict and ambiguity. Part of this ambiguity has to do with the difficulties that have been repeatedly encountered in disentangling the *medical* aspects of mental illness from the *social* circumstances surrounding its etiology and management and from the obvious ideological and sociopolitical implications of empowering specialty groups to declare people incompetent to act on their own behalf. That is essentially what psychiatry has attempted to do ever since the great Freudian breakthrough of the last century: the right to impose a sick role status on people in the absence of workable technologies capable of extricating them from that deprived role. Stated yet another way, social and political circumstances have, since Freud, made it possible to declare persons who behave in a deviant fashion to qualify for, in Freidson's terms, "nonresponsible and improvable" benign management without an available technology to restore persons so categorized to a suitable level of social functioning.

How did the management of the functional disorders fall under the purview of the medical system and what are some of the implications of the fact that they did? For the lack of a less clumsy and more easily understood term, the phrase "mentally ill" will be used, without necessarily embracing its management and control implications.

Mental illness was not always the rationalized congeries of behavior that it now is. As an example, consider the famous event in France during the latter years of the French Revolution when Dr. Pinel unchained the mentally ill in that country and released them from their dungeons. This was not an act done in the name of medicine, but rather one of humane mercy and an expression of the revolutionary spirit. Pinel's act did much to set in motion a series of historical events that made it possible to approach the mentally ill in ways sharply differentiated from the pool of lore, mysticism, and religious zealotry that had been its lot in the Western world for so long. So far as we knew, prior to this time the mentally ill were either ignored and allowed to act out in the open community until found guilty of criminal acts, were subjected to various forms of religious exorcism or, in the case of Pinel's unfortunates, were merely locked up and forgotten. So much for the tender mercies of the eighteenth century's moral and medical community and the chances of effective *noblesse oblige* under the ethics of the *ancien régime*. Of this time, in 1785, the inspector-general of French hospitals put the then-existing situation quite clearly:[25]

> Thousands of lunatics are locked up in prisons without anyone even thinking of administering the slightest remedy. The half-mad are mingled with those who are totally deranged, those who rage with those who are quiet; some are in chains, while others are free in their prison. Finally, unless nature comes to their aid by curing them, the duration of their misery is lifelong, for unfortunately the illness does not improve but only grows worse.

Still others, as Rosen has described, lived quite contentedly and at peace in the open community but as identifiable "social personages," known locally as "imbeciles," "addlepated," or "crackbrains," who did little harm to themselves or to others and were often a source of amusement for the surrounding citizens. Illness, as we understand it to be both an obligation and a social role as well as a complex of professional networks, simply did not exist. And just as Pinel's emancipation stemmed from political and philosophical, rather than medical, roots so too the next major step, taken mainly in the United States during the first quarter of the nineteenth century, stemmed also from political and philosophical considerations, not from medical imperatives. This relatively brief episode in the premedical care of the mentally ill came to be known as "moral treatment" and constituted something of an early prototype of the kinds of demystification of mental illness that we are witnessing today.[26]

The first moral treatment center was established in 1817, and numerous others followed during the next two decades. Moral treatment rested upon the twin assumptions that persons who were mentally ill were not morally responsible for their condition, which was traceable only to their inability to function effectively in the community at large. Moral treatment, therefore, stemmed from the idea that the entire milieu of the "retreat" was to be carefully controlled so as to make possible "guests'" restoration of their living skills. Most of the early moral treatment centers were the creations of private philanthropy, although in later years a large number were taken over by the several states and by the turn of the twentieth century resembled the kind of overcrowded nontreatment institutions that we presently associate with the term "state hospital." In a social and political sense, the rise of moral treatment seemed to owe a powerful debt to the rationalism traceable to the idealism of Plato, the democratization and equalitarianism of the writings of thinkings of such as John Locke, and the general drift toward humanitarianism and democratization that characterized the sweep of history in the eighteenth and nineteenth centuries, culminating as far as moral treatment was concerned in the Jacksonian era of the rationalism of the common man.

The founders of moral treatment, for example, though putative "doctors," were in fact classically educated men whose ideas were formed not so much by a presumed psychiatric technology, but by the prevailing ideas that governed the institutions of their time. Hence, they were aware that Hippocrates had contended that psychosis was due to a brain lesion, while being equally aware that Plato wrote that "he who is depraved becomes so through an ill governed education. . . . The vicious are vicious through two involuntary causes, which we shall always ascribe to the planters than to the things planted, and the trainers rather than to those trained." Thus the wisdom of the ages freed the victim of blame and guilt, as well as rejected the Renaissance notion that human behavior is totally idiosyncratic and governed by inscrutable forces outside of human control. It was, recall, the time of the development of natural law, which held also that human behavior was also subject to discoverable patterns and uniformities. Hence, the humanitarian drift of the times coincided with the burgeoning scientific revelation that the world (including the rational understanding of humanity) culminated in the idea that "lunatics" had undergone stresses in life that had robbed them of their *reason*, which they would otherwise still possess as creatures of the loving God of a William Channing. Thus there was a surge in the belief in the fundamental good virtue of people and the conviction that the marks of insanity were merely overexaggerated personality traits that in mild form were only partially disagreeable. The task, therefore, to be borne by those who shouldered the burden of the mentally ill was to provide a benign setting for communal living in which the best traits of human nature —kindness, love, reason, and responsibility—would be fostered, encouraged, and rewarded.

To bring this about, centers were established for the care of small groups of "guests," who would live together with the "superintendents" and their families, along with the kindly motivated but untrained local people who served as helpers in a living environment designed to promote a return to reason and love. Included were "healthful" activities, congenial and convivial activity groups, strick discipline coordinate with the times, serious work responsibilities, "moral and philosophical" instruction, an attention to the amenities of life such as proper dress, good table manners, politeness to one another, a respect for other peoples' rights, and a growing sense of personal worth and social responsibility. The stress was on Kingsley Davis's "middle-class morality," if you will, and the reestablishment of gracious images of self and others so as to foster "right reason." "Guests" (the words "patients" and "inmates" were never used) in the retreats retained their street clothes; professional experts from the outside delivered edifying lectures; programs of activities included dances, concerts, games, and picnicking on the grounds; visitors came and went quite freely; all "guests" were expected to work; punishments for poor behavior were meted out; men and women mingled together in normal social intercourse; guests were even allowed to use knives and forks and took their meals with the superintendent's family. How did all of this credo work and why didn't it thrive?

As to the first, Horace Mann reports that on his first visit to the Worcester State Hospital in the early 1830s (before it became a moral treatment center) there were 100 patients there who would attack any human being who came near them. A year later there were fewer than a dozen assaultive patients. Charles Dickens upon visiting Boston State Hospital in 1842 was astounded to find guests going to Saturday night dances, enjoying outings in horsedrawn carriages, and fishing in the stream passing through the grounds. All the while Ralph Waldo Emerson was encouraging educated men to adopt the view that the key to democracy was self-reliance and arguing that "the world is nothing, the man is all."

The available information of an objective nature is equally encouraging about the effectiveness of moral treatment as a premedical and pre-Freudian "Camelot" in the care of the mentally ill. As far as recovery rates are concerned, the case records of the Worcester State Hospital between 1831 and 1848 are reproduced in Table 10.1.

In both the early and late years—though somewhat less in 1848

TABLE 10.1

Worcester State Hospital admission and recovery rates, 1831–1848

Year	Number admitted	Recovered	Percent improved
1831	300	70.0	8.3
1833	434	74.6	3.2
1843	742	63.9	4.6
1848	791	61.3	4.7

than in 1831—this moral treatment center recorded an astonishing rate of recovery, ranging from 61 to 70 percent of the patients admitted. We of course do not know what criteria were used or much about the reliability of their data; this information is lost to history. But even allowing generously for changes in circumstances, methods, or even severity of disablement, the reports of the honest, pious, intelligent, and educated persons who ran these places cannot be dismissed altogether. In fact, there is much in historical methodological research that would suggest that these reports have a high level of credibility,[27] and in any event are impressive if only for the levels of accomplishment thought to be within the realm of believability. They are unapproachable in the modern scene even by the most tolerant of standards.

But more impressive, and perhaps even less biased, supportive data are given in Table 10.2, which summarizes a follow-up study of patients discharged from the Worcester State Hospital during the years

TABLE 10.2

Results of 1882–1893 follow-up of recoveries of 1833–1846, Worcester State Hospital

Remained well, still alive	317	
Remained well through life	251	(568, or 48%)
Relapsed and again discharged	67	
Total well or had died mentally well at 36 to 60 years, follow-up point (subtotal)	635	(54.13%)
Relapsed, still living	100	
Relapsed, died in relapse	239	
Relapsed, nothing more known	10	
Total mentally ill, or had died mentally ill at 36 to 60 years, follow-up point (subtotal)	349	(29.75%)
No information	189	(16.12%)
Grand total	1173	(100%)

SOURCE: Data for this table were adapted from the Annual Report of the Worcester State Hospital, 1893.

1833 to 1846 whose life circumstances were traced many years later between 1882 and 1893.

The follow-up figures are striking, particularly in view of the fact that such a long period of time elapsed between the years of treatment and the actual time of the follow-up. Again, the methodological and performance criteria remain problematic, but it is inescapable to draw the conclusion that some quite remarkably normal and adequate lives were led after the moral treatment experience. As promising as the moral treatment episode seemed to be, it was short-lived and soon replaced with a national system of "state hospitals" of the type with which most of us have some passing knowledge, as well as by the professionalization of the care of the mentally ill with its substitution of a medical for a social model of mental illness. What in fact caused the decline of moral treatment?

Certainly of some importance was the growing urbanization of the society and the dramatic increase in the heterogeneity of the population, the first contributing to the kinds of macroproblems pointed to 100 years later by Faris and Dunham, and the second making it exceedingly difficult to create a "community" within the walls. As to the first, the problem of size alone contributed to the loss of community, as indicated by the growth of the institutionalized mental ill population since 1833 as shown in Table 10.3.

Most of the original moral treatment centers numbered no more than 200 residents, with a large number of staff members who could spend with each person an enormous amount of time devoted to the task of resocialization; this was no longer the case by the end of the

TABLE 10.3
Worcester State Hospital residents per physician, 1833–1943

Year	Residents per physician
1833	88
1843	127
1853	128
1863	156
1913	205
1943	230

	Residents per attendant
1833	8
1883	13
1903	15
1923	20
1943	24

Civil War. For as the data in Table 10.3 clearly show for Worcester State, the number of patients per doctor increased nearly threefold by the middle of World War II, and the number of patients each attendant was held responsible for increased by an equal magnitude during that time. The situation worsened further in the years following World War II.

Of equal importance was the erosion of financial support. At Worcester State, for example, in 1833 the weekly per capital expenditure per resident was approximately $2.00 per week, which at the time was fully two-thirds of the average American per capita *weekly income.* Moral treatment was costly by Jacksonian standards. By the late 1940s, however, the weekly expenditures per patient had risen only to about $8.00 per week, while the average per weekly national income had risen to nearly $50.00 per week. The care of the mentally ill had lost a great deal of ground in its competition for dollars over the years, and that competition has become no less intense during the past quarter-century.

An even more biting cause is pointed to by Bockoven in his data on the percentage of foreign-born residents in these treatment centers, as shown in Table 10.4. Prior to the 1850s, the real start of the decline, the moral treatment centers were culturally homogeneous. Residents and staff came from the same communities; they shared a common language, common customs, and a common religion, and in general identified with one another. The influx of European immigrants—especially Irish Catholics—just after the Civil War presented the receiving communities with a problem they had never heretofore encountered: What should be done with poor people who were "different" from themselves? Ethnic prejudice was not an uncommon reaction, as evidenced by a Worcester State Hospital Annual Report during this period, in which the Irish were castigated as follows:[28] "[The immigrants] receive high wages in prosperous times, gratifying vicious in-

TABLE 10.4
Worcester State Hospital foreign-born guests, 1844–1933

Year	Number of admissions	Percent foreign born
1844	236	10
1854	288	38
1863	215	47
1873	470	38
1893	534	67
1903	553	67
1913	515	46
1923	402	53
1933	484	45

dulgences, seeking labor in the most menial capacity, huddling together in the objectionable places, neglecting all rules of health, and preferring the solace of rum and tobacco to the quiet, intelligent influences of well ordered homes." As we see in Table 10.4, by the turn of the twentieth century the new asylums for the insane were almost completely filled by the foreign born—Irish, Italian, Scandinavian, Germans, and others, many of whom had failed to find in the promised land anything that resembled what they had hoped for. They found, instead, life in a back ward in institutions that had largely given up hope. And as Bockoven clearly contends:[29]

> Passages from the Annual Reports of the Worcester State Hospital leave little doubt that racial prejudice played a role in the breakdown not only of moral treatment but of ordinary decent hospital living standards. Mention of foreigners as a problem was first made in the Annual Report of 1854, in which the lament was made that the State Hospital was fast becoming a hospital for Irish immigrants rather than for the intelligent Yeomanry of Massachusetts who could pay their board and would not ask for charity. A special plea was made for the "classification" of patients by which was meant the segregation of foreigners from native New Englanders. The basis for the plea was that the sensibilities of patients reared in the proverbially neat and orderly households of New England were offended by close contact with those who were accustomed to and satisfied with filthy habitations and filthier habits.
>
> "Foreign insane pauperism" was the name given to the problem of mental illness in the immigrant population. Its disrupting effects were due not only to racial and religious incompatibilities, but also to economic factors. Patients without settlement in Massachusetts were paid for by the Commonwealth. All other patients' bills were paid either by their families or by the towns in which they resided. The Commonwealth paid so little for its pauper patients that the hospital was forced to charge the towns and families more. . . . Rapid population growth, immigration, and pauperism forced the metamorphoses of mental hospitals from homelike havens of moral treatment to huge custodial asylums.

Thus, the creation of new "diagnostic" categories produced different societal reactions and totally different organizational responses to mental illness. Other things were happening as well: the twin processes of medical professionalization and an ill-fated form of democratization under the banners of Dorothea Dix.

First, at about this time in history the French neurologist Charcot (Freud's prime intellectual father) discovered that hysteria in fact was "genuine" even in the absence of a physical lesion, and that it could be effectively eliminated by talking with the sufferer who was under hypnosis. This "discovery" by a physician was a turning point in history in that since the discovery was made by a physician, it therefore represented a form of "illness" that qualified one for the adoption of the role of the sick, and thus it subjected the person to the requirements and rights of that role. Hence, by such logic, mental illness began a long process of medicalization and professionalization, which led ultimately to the many kinds of abuses and misuses that Thomas Szasz popularized and lay at the root of the critique leveled by Scheff.

Freud, of course, created an enormous intellectual edifice that firmly established mental illness as the domain of specially trained doctors who, given enough time with a patient, could ferret out the psychodynamic causes of mental illnesses, and through deep probing could "cure" the patient's affliction. Individual psychoanalysis was born, and the growth of an enormous division of labor in the realm of medical psychiatry was set into motion. The fact, however, that only the rich could afford it and only the educated could understand it naturally limited its usefulness and has to this day effectively prohibited the diffusion of this "linguistic technology" to the population at large. The distinction between individual psychiatry and institutional psychiatry was an early one that continues to this day under the guise of private individual treatment on the one hand and mass institutional management in large state hospitals on the other.

The flood into the state hospitals was made complete by the energies of Dorothea Dix, who argued with great success that the receipt of care for mental illness was a right of citizenship that should be denied no one on economic grounds and should be made available in spite of the fact that the new "field" lacked a viable technology. "Moral treatment" had been forgotten in the rush toward medicalization and professionalization, and psychiatry became an offshoot of neurology and was given lasting legitimation with Kraepelin's "discovery" of *dementia praecox* (schizophrenia), which was then officially designated a "deteriorating" condition. Along with Dix's misguided equalitarianism, this discovery resulted in a nationwide movement of great numbers of the afflicted, the untolerated, and the manifestly deviant from their private places in almhouses, work houses, homes for the aged, jails, and even the back bedrooms of family homes into the state hospitals for the insane. Here the level of technology and sheer numbers made possible only a custodial environment (benign at best and abusive at worst) rather than a therapeutic surrounding.

At this point we begin to see the dramatic increase in institutionalized psychiatric "patients" reported earlier that was not to experience a decline until the coincidence of three major forces took hold beginning at about the time that Stanton and Schwartz did their work and the experimentation with amphetamines began. These forces were the emergence of the "therapeutic milieu" philosophy; the dramatic breakthroughs in psychomedication, starting with Miltown about 1958; and the sudden drift *against* institutionalization and *favoring* normalization, which has marked the past decade.

THE RISE OF THE THERAPEUTIC MILIEU

The dilemma brought about by the failure of the state hospital type of facility and the lack of accessibility of individual psychotherapeutic methodology seemed to find an avenue of resolution through the later work of neo-Freudians—Harry Stack Sullivan, particularly—who argued that mental illness reflected a disturbance of interpersonal relations and that these lent themselves to the treatment of *groups* of patients rather than strictly on a one-to-one basis.[30] There was also a sense of desperation over the failure of the state hospital type of facility in providing even benign custody, as evidenced by the devastating critique leveled at it by Erving Goffman in his discussion of "total institutions."[31]

> The inmates, as well as the staff, actively seek out these curtailments of the self, so that mortification is complemented by self-mortification, restriction by renunciations, beatings by self-flagellations, inquisition by confession. Because religious establishments are explicitly concerned with the processes of mortification, they have a special value for the student.
>
> In concentration camps and, to a lesser extent, prisons, some mortifications seem to be arranged solely or mainly for their mortifying power, as when a prisoner is urinated on, but here the inmate does not embrace and facilitate his own destruction of self.
>
> In many of the remaining total institutions, mortifications are officially rationalized on other grounds, such as sanitation (in connection with latrine duty), responsibility for life (in connection with forced feeding), combat capacity (in connection with Army rules for personal appearance), "security" (in connection with restrictive prison regulations).
>
> In total institutions of all three varieties, however, the various rationales for mortifying the self are very often merely rationalizations, generated by efforts to manage the daily activity of a large number of persons in a restricted space with a small expenditure of resources.

And so the time was ripe for a dramatic break with the past and the new idea (remarkably similar to the now defunct "moral treatment") of the "therapeutic community" came on the heels of World War II with the work of Maxwell Jones in England.[32] Jones dealt with what were occupational rehabilitation centers for ex-servicemen who were having difficulty adjusting to civilian life after long periods of war trauma and deprivation. The theme in the therapeutic community was that a properly organized "minor society" within an institution could bring about a palliative effect on defective role performance through the prime forces of a hospital milieu organized around (1) *rehabilitation* through a guided series of confrontations with reality, (2) the *democratization* of hospital life, (3) a spirit of *permissiveness* in patient conduct, and (4) the fostering of a sense of *communalism*. Various forms of the "medical model" were rejected with a specially conceived "social model" set in its place that would be an effort to mimic, within the confines of an institution, the satisfying and self-fulfilling elements of social life.

Rehabilitation through reality confrontation involved making the hospital as similar to the outside world as possible. Theoretically, adjustment to this environment prepared the patient for adjustment to the real world. The aim was to reduce the passivity and dependency fostered in the context of the repressive state hospital. "Milieu" therapy involved the use of "nonprofessional" personnel to encourage the establishment of supportive but nonmedically related human relationships, in contrast to the patient-staff schisms existing in the old bureaucratic state hospitals. Permissiveness was encouraged to bring about more effective and self-rewarding relationships with authority figures, while democratization of patient life was encouraged as a way of helping patients down the road to feelings of self-control and self-worth. Finally, communalism (the creation of familylike relationships) was encouraged in order to minimize the kind of isolation and depersonalization often found in the kind of institution criticized by Goffman and others.

In short, the *social setting itself* was an object of therapeutic manipulation and creation, not the *technical* events taking place within that setting. The reports on the results of this cultlike activity in the late 1950s and early 1960s were almost always enthusiastic and positive. But even the "therapeutic milieu" was not without its shortcomings, not the least of which was the fact of institutionalization itself.

This debureaucratization of mental hospitals took place over a decade or more. The trend is, however, related to even more fundamental changes that have occurred in the place occupied by mental institutions in American society—changes that began long before the ideology of therapeutic milieu was conceived.

Two fundamental changes crucial in accounting for the recent rise of the therapeutic community have taken place. First has been the shift in ideology, including both acceptable procedures for handling patients and ultimate goals, from a tradition of "custody" to an ethic of "treatment." Second has been the movement of psychiatric hospitals from the rural hinterlands into the mainstream of urban life in both an ecological and social psychological sense.[33]

A consequence of the first change has been a decline in the confidence such establishments have in the efficacy of the techniques employed in achieving the altered goals of the hospital. This has meant that a rigid defined and enforced division of labor is either superfluous or impossible to construct, or both. Where custody is the main purpose of hospitals for the mentally ill, knowledge concerning physical restraint and even benign care is adequate to lend a kind of uniformity and predictability to the tasks to which the old-style bureaucratic hospital addresses itself. Such an institution is able to devise and enforce a rigid and systematic division of labor. With the emergence of the ideology of total treatment and cure, however, such uniformity in task assignment fails in two ways. First, the goals of treatment become different for each member of the clientele population; thus the organization's stance toward patients becomes particularized and individualized. Second, the institution embarks upon the task of disavowing its commitment to custody-type knowledge with its associated rigid division of labor and reorganizing itself around the frontier-type knowledge of psychodynamic interpretation in which it is admitted that the casual and friendly "hello" by a janitor to a patient may be as significant as long hours of psychotherapy with a psychiatrist. This, in turn, implies not only that rigid division of labor may well be ludicrous, but that both traditional professional prestige and power are endangered. Thus, the shift from an ideology of custodial care to one of individualized psychiatric treatment has resulted in a decline in the efficiency and workability of the body of professional and occupational techniques the members have at their disposal, in the means by which they may empirically affirm its effectiveness, and in the plausibility of maintaining a rigidly defined bureaucratic structure.

The second major trend—that of the movement of psychiatric hospitals away from a condition of rural enclave into the urban milieu— has resulted in a lessening autonomy on the part of such institutions. They are less able than they were before to organize and run themselves without regard either to the wishes of the patients themselves or to those of interested parties on the outside. The larger community has come to have a greater stake in the activities of mental hospitals and in the fate of their patients. Part of this scrutiny may have arisen because of the publicity in recent years concerning the probability that something like "one out of three" persons will be hospitalized for a mental illness at some time during their lives. A more symbiotic relationship has come to characterize the relations between the hospitals and other agencies, professions, and establishments in the community. This has meant that the patients are no longer so fully given over to the institutions as they once were. Patients are followed into the hospital by a wide variety of identities and reciprocal commitments. Unlike the situation of the late-nineteenth-century custody hospital, patients are identified by friends, family, and professionally organized power groups —schools, physicians, welfare agencies, and the like—as being still part of the larger community to which they will return and which they have never completely left, at least in a social psychological sense. Indeed, the *sense* of the phrases "community as doctor," "community mental health," and "therapeutic community" suggests that the mental hospital is no longer an appendage of the real community but rather an essential part of its basic institutions.

Most important, perhaps, is that patients in the modern therapeutic community are not only regarded by their significant others as still a part of the larger community, but they so regard themselves as well. It is partially this ethic of potential cure, buttressed as much by spatial and symbolic closeness to the outside community as it is by statistical reports of rates of cures, that influences the posture that the patient assumes in the hospital—not quite the complete inmate but never fully the powerless captive. All of this means that the patient in the modern urban hospital retains a quality of autonomy from the institution that was much less characteristic of the inmate population of the old-style enclave type of facility. This in turn conspires to make the inmate population of the modern treatment-oriented psychiatric hospital much more volatile and less tractable to total bureaucratic control and manipulation than it once was. Parenthetically, therefore, one may well ask whether the "techniques of making out" in the psychiatric hospital so convincingly described by Goffman are not only a reflection of the patient's attempts to maintain an intact self-image, but are also evidence of the organizational gaps that exist in such institutions.

Thus, the changes from custody-type to treatment-oriented hospitals and from enclaves to community-involved hospitals have led to two major organizational factors that have made the rise of the therapeutic milieu feasible and in many ways imperative. First, there is a decline in the uniformity and predictability of the kinds of tasks such establishments set about to accomplish; this has made it difficult to devise a systematic division of labor. Second, the increased autonomy of the clientele served by psychiatric hospitals has meant that authority is no longer the basic means for manipulating patients and staff; it has been replaced by interpersonal relations. Further, in the more bureaucratized hospital the line of command is down the administrative hierarchy with little need for a clear distinction between policy and administration. Where the officials have to reckon with inmates under such circumstances, it is mainly in terms of clear-cut administrative face-offs involving a comparatively brief but overt confrontation, with the solution taking the form of directives. Where a schism exists in the bureaucratic hospital, it is commonly between the inmates and the administrative staff.

In the treatment-oriented institution, on the other hand, authority typically is divided into administrative and professional lines; the continuous difficulties associated with separate lines of authority in hospitals as well as in other organizations has been well documented. But further, while the importance of repeated bargaining between members of the administrative and professional lines is well known, it is also important to recognize that under a situation of divided and sometimes conflicting authority the inmate population may often be able to exert the leverage necessary to codify administrative decisions and clinical policy. Indeed, many of the well-known "conning" techniques so frequently attributed to a presumed viable patient culture or informal organization may be little more than evidence of the processes by which members of the patient clientele become activated to resolve standoffs and conflicts between the administrative and clinical perspectives in the establishment.

Many psychiatric establishments have met these trends by persisting in an application of a form of administrative structure that approximates a bureaucracy. Others, however, have disavowed the bureaucratic model and attempted to reorganize along nonbureaucratized lines with attendant changes in the form, content, and lines of communication. It is these establishments that resemble a therapeutic milieu.

Communication and decision making

The careers of psychiatric patients appear to move imperceptibly from beginning to end without clearly articulated points of shift and change. On closer scrutiny, however, it is clear that the apparently courseless histories of institutionalized persons are interrupted at key points when decisions are made about them by staff. In the bureaucratized institution, such decisions tend to be of a highly formalized nature, based upon well-understood and established criteria: they may elevate the inmate involved to a higher status with its attendant open-ward privileges, or reduce him or her to the status and the deprivations of a closed ward.

Decisions in the therapeutic milieu, however, are less rigidly prescribed in terms of impelling factors and subsequent meaning for the patient. They stem less from periodic formal staff review of cases than they do from the grass roots in the organization, that is, from informal disputes and discussions among persons involved with a case. These decisions affect not only staff behavior toward patients but the patients' own conceptions of themselves. Frequently these kinds of decisions—and the basis for them—are not clearly reported in case records because the criteria as to what constitutes relevant and reportable staff action in the diffusely organized nonbureaucratized hospital are unclear. The contingencies and alternatives in the career of inmates in the bureaucratized system are relatively simple: They either improve according to some reasonably clear criteria and move "up and out," or they get worse and move "down and back." This means that such patients can be ranked and judged by staff members in relation to all others in the patient population along some dimension of comparability, and the patients can themselves grasp the meaning of what has happened and may conceivably understand the basis for the decisions made.

In the therapeutic community, however, the situation of both patients and staff is markedly different. In the first place, not only are the social contexts of professional decision making unclear and changeable, but the bases for decisions are similarly diffuse. There are no clear-cut contingencies for the patient's understanding of his or her own career. The patient does not simply get better or worse but *periodically* improves *and* deteriorates depending upon the nature of the communication–decision-making process itself. Thus, since the staff has difficulty in achieving consensus, the patients themselves have little basis for understanding where *they* stand along some dimension of "health" and "illness" and have considerable difficulty in understanding how, when, and why decisions are made about them.

Moreover, in the nonbureaucratized institutions there comes to be an increased relation between the sheer amount of communication flow and the frequency of change and decision making; that is, the greater the quantity of staff interaction and communication about a patient, the more often is the patient the object of administrative and policy decisions. The changing and dynamic ideology of the total treatment hospital is such that communication is regarded as meaningful and valuable only if it is, first, spontaneous and informal; and, second, only if it results in the initiation of change, the alteration of staff attitudes and staff relationships, the reevaluation of patient progress, and ultimately the inception of a new course of action. In short, policy comes to be formed by the nature of the communication processes rather than by the formal system of offices.

Thus pressures in the therapeutic milieu enhance and magnify communication among staff about patients. This in turn leads to the felt need to come repeatedly to crucial decisions regarding the fate and situation of the patients, and this results in continual reassessment of the efficacy of the therapeutic interventions being employed and their subsequent frequent alteration. This sequence of communication and decision making is related to the absence of unequivocal standards of patient assessment and the associated diffuse division of labor in that the psychiatric hospital of the type characterized here seldom has at its disposal the means by which to judge adequately the consequences of many policy decisions.

A neglected question, however, seems to be whether there is any verifiable relation between the amount of communication flow and the number of policy decisions made and subsequent patient change. It is not likely that positive evidence could easily be obtained, inasmuch as the lack of a hierarchical structure renders coordination of problem-solving efforts difficult if not impossible to achieve. In this context, an essential feature of the total treatment institution is its attempt to coordinate a wide range and variety of professional perspectives and skills and bring them together into some integrated form with respect to a particular patient whose problem is defined differently from each perspective. Nonetheless, although the enterprise may often founder on problems of coordination, the ethic of maximum communication persists, for it is decidedly functional insofar as it maintains staff esprit de corps, even if it may be of a peculiar type: consensus at the broad ideological level and frequent discord at the operational level.

Communication, the self-fulfilling prophecy, and disenchantment

In spite of all of these pressures to minimize status distinctions among staff and between staff and patients, the inmates are still psychiatric patients. As such they retain a remarkable sensitivity to the expectations they perceive in others of greater power, prestige, and esteem. Albeit in a disturbed and often inaccurate fashion, they are similar to persons in all other interactional settings in that they make some attempt to meet what they regard to be other persons' expectations of them. A central characteristic of mental patients, which makes them no different from persons everywhere, is that they conduct themselves less on the basis of their own definitions of themselves and of situations than on the basis of perceived definitions of significant others in their immediate environment.

In relation to this, therefore, the pseudocrisis and the personalization of communication are *real* in their consequences: The pseudocrisis as an organizational strategy communicates to the patient what he or she should be like, and more often than not the patient acts upon that staff definition. In this sense, the staff calls forth from the patient those forms of behavior and attitudes that they fear on the one hand and need on the other. The staff fears the realization of their crisis-invoked patient misconduct primarily because such behavior reaffirms the suspicion that in spite of all that has been done, the patient is still sick. More important, however, the staff members need the realization of crisis-provoked prophecies to validate consensually the saliency of the complex communication processes in which they have engaged and to justify the emotional expenses they have suffered.

What is suggested, of course, is that patients make inferences about what is expected of them, and the nature of the inferences made is determined largely by how the staff members behave toward the patients. Thus, the pseudocrisis and personalization of communication elicit from the patients those attitudes and behaviors that in the first instance continually reaffirm the staff's judgment that the patients are still sick and in the second give the staff self-created evidence that the patients are only "using" them and the system.

The course of the total treatment ideology in the nonbureaucratized hospitals runs, therefore, the full cycle from initial optimism to subsequent disenchantment: disenchantment from the staff's point of view in the fashion just described; disenchantment from the patient's point of view in that the course of a patient's career always leads to a stage of discharge or the ever-present threat of the use of force, at which point the personalized relations the patient may have had with the staff are revealed as unreal after all.

Policy, organization, and communication

At the outset it was argued that the distinctive organizational features of the therapeutic milieu had to do with the character of the division of labor on the one hand and the nature of the communication system on the other. If we may equate for the moment the custody-type institution with a bureaucracy and the therapeutic milieu with a debureaucratized system, it may then be possible to suggest the conditions under which a complex organization may retreat from the bureaucratic mold and begin to approximate what has here been described as the therapeutic milieu.

Bureaucracy, with its rigid division of labor and clearly articulated communication system, seems to rest first upon the availability of a body of knowledge in terms of which tasks are uniform, predictable, and tractable to rational calculation in terms of cause and effects, and second upon the presence of a compliant clientele. The first allows a systematic division of labor with the assignment of specific tasks to different persons; the second allows the organization to persist in stable form over time without a great deal of sensitivity to the actions and reactions of its clients. As has been pointed out, however, not only a shift in therapeutic ideology but a long-recognized need for change has placed many psychiatric hospitals in the situation of having to work with a less than complete body of rational knowledge and a less than compliant clientele. This leads to a flattening of the authority system in the manner that has been described in the context of the therapeutic milieu. And this, in turn, leads to all those processes by which client compliancy is lost and by which the organization is faced not only with a diffuse and changing organizational structure but also with an increasingly autonomous clientele with which it must then contend.

Indeed, there is an implicit suggestion in Hyde's description of one "therapeutic milieu" that points out these problems:[33]

> The experience gained . . . in this project has resulted in the conviction that the majority of rehabilitation *failures* [italics in the original] were due to failure to acquire knowledge . . . or failure to apply knowledge already acquired by using already known methods . . . Failures which result from oversights and compounding of oversights are . . . a cause of great concern and are demoralizing to the rehabilitating team. For this reason there is a strong tendency for oversights to go undiscovered and . . . failure to be explained in terms either of *the client's intractable disability or intractable personality* [italics mine].

PSYCHOMEDICATIONS AND DEINSTITUTIONALIZATION

However loudly the "therapeutic milieu" was heralded, hard and convincing evidence that "proved" its efficacy was difficult to secure. It was also very costly and in any event the spector of Goffman's "total institution" still hovered over this modern hybrid of institutional life. Inmate democracy, as Pasamanick and his associates were to demonstrate, turned out in most cases to be "pseudodemocracy," and life in an institution still left much to be desired. Inmates were still not free, and there was the persisting suspicion that human rights were still being violated in the name of humanism.

In a major historical accident, the public-wide movement toward the deinstitutionalization and demystification of mental illness (along with Scheff's theoretical critique) occurred with the coincidence of John F. Kennedy's new program on mental illness and mental retardation in 1963 and the emergence of the "wonder" drugs in the early 1960s. The present mental health scene remains under the twin influences of these forces. Kennedy said:[34]

> I propose a national mental health program to assist in the inauguration of a wholly new emphasis and approach to care for the mentally ill. This approach relies primarily upon the new knowledge and new drugs acquired and developed in recent years which make it possible for most of the mentally ill to be successfully and quickly treated in their own communities and returned to a useful place in society.
>
> These breakthroughs have rendered obsolete the traditional methods of treatment which imposed upon the mentally ill a social quarantine, a prolonged or permanent confinement in huge, unhappy mental hospitals where they were out of sight and forgotten.

Thus the past decade has seen a flight of patients from the hospitals and into the community to remain as family members, to pursue employment and continue in their normal round of life wherever possible, to live in halfway houses and sheltered homes of one sort or another to receive the support and assistance of their fellow community members, to rely upon occasional supportive visits by home nurses, social workers, or college student volunteers. In short, there has been a mobilization of the entire community on behalf of those with difficulty in adjusting to and working within the normal constraints of the social order. In other words, we have what appears to be a "social model of illness" that in fact is almost isomorphic to the social order itself. Does this set aside the medical model once and for all? Hardly, because much of what has been possible must be attributed to the "wonder" drugs. What are they and how do they work?

An untold number of persons designated as "mentally ill" bear the brunt of that label—and its social consequences—because of the inappropriate behavior they exhibit in public places. Vast numbers of them suffer from some strange mix of *anxiety* and *depression* that effectively inhibits them from conducting themselves in ways that appear to others to be "normal." Now anxiety as a clinical entity does have identifiable *symptoms* on the one hand and *signs* on the other. Symptomwise, persons suffering from anxiety experience a generalized feeling of panic and a sense of impending doom; they are nervous and agitated and have great trouble sitting still, paying attention to what is taking place around them, organizing their actions in goal-directed ways. They have difficulty in concentrating, are subject to insomnia, and are in a general state of panic. The condition is often accompanied by a rapid pulse rate, shallow but rapid breathing sometimes to the point of hyperventilation, tremor in the hands, the dilation of the pupils of the eye, and a measurable alteration in the galvanic skin responses. All of these symptoms and signs can be artificially created in the laboratory through the alteration of the chemical compound in the blood called epinephrine-nor-epinephrine. When these are out of balance in one direction, what is known as *anxiety* is exhibited; when they are out of balance in the other direction, the signs and symptoms of *depression* are displayed. The first "causes" *neurotic* behavior; in the second, *schizophrenic* and *psychotic* types of behavior are brought about. In their earlier forms, the tranquilizer drugs did much to alleviate the debilitating anxiety symptoms but not their associated depressionlike symptoms, and thus their use had to be monitored very carefully. The new version attacks the anxiety symptoms and depressive symptoms *at the same time,* hence making possible a degree of self-control and self-regulation that never in the past been achieved in large populations of patients. In sum, with the use of these new psychomedications, thousands of persons who had been designated as mentally ill, and who had accepted that definition, no longer *acted* as if they were mentally ill and others did not react to them in that way. Hence, an enormous breach had been made in the vicious cycle of irrepressible signs and symptoms, manifest deviant behavior, and subsequent social reaction, and institutionalization no longer arose as the chief way to handle people who were experiencing these kinds of difficulties. An early bell-wether of the changes that were possible was heard in the double-blind study in the late 1960s of medicated and nonmedicated schizophrenic patients placed in the community by Pasamanick and his associates, who reported the following striking findings:[35]

> Despite the tremendous difficulties encountered in its implementation, this carefully designed experimental study confirmed our original hypothesis that home care for schizophrenic patients is *feasible*, that home care is at least as good a method of treatment as hospitalization by any or all criteria, and probably superior by most.
>
> Even apart from these striking results, which we believe to be both reliable and valid, are the implications which can be drawn from this work. These implications extend beyond the confines of the study itself and its immediate consequences. This study, for example, permits certain interpretations about the nature and management of schizophrenia and other neuropsychiatric and related impairments and their treatment. Just as the treatment model in tuberculosis became the basis for this home care investigation, so the latter has relevance as a model for the problems of aging and of mental retardation, to mention but two, and on a somewhat different level, for chronic alcoholism and other addictions. In theory, the home care model should have utility for various chonic conditions which impair social and psychological functioning to the point that the afflicted become burdensome members to society and require institutionalization. An extension of this home care model to other such chronic conditions now seems warranted, at least at the demonstration program level.

There has been a tremendous ripple effect of the psychomedication revolution and its subsequent reinterpretation into a new social model of the treatment of mental illness leading to a discarding of hallowed doctrine beliefs about the causes of mental illness, a total reassessment of the kinds of personnel central to these new tasks, and a rather thoroughgoing rejection of the hospitalization model. The treatment of mental illness has, to this point, at least partially begun to ape allopathic medicine in its emphasis on eclecticism and pragmatism. Mental illness is no longer regarded as a generalized debilitation incapacitating people in all of their behavioral respects. In its place has come a *situational* focus, an attempt to intervene in helpful ways in the pre-illness stage and by the use of on-the-spot teams to help people through immediate stress situations. Above all, the focus is on the developing of individual "coping" mechanisms and strategies so that the potentially mentally ill patient becomes, as it were, his or her own psychiatrist before the fact.

This development of "coping strategies" to substitute for traditional modes of professionalized-institutionalized management of the mentally ill has been put as follows by Powell:[36]

> Coping systems are social networks which deal with stress-producing long-term problems; they deal with these problems by means of available resources. Supportive coping systems are social networks in which primary responsibility for dealing with problems is assumed by the problem bearers themselves. Resocializing coping systems assign primary responsibility for dealing with long-term problems to assisting specialists.
>
> Supportive coping systems are, for example, family and staff networks of probation departments, open prisons, halfway houses, therapeutic communities, drug institutes, community health centers and after-care programs which cope with long-term stress through social support.
>
> Resocializing coping systems include maximum security prisons, custodial mental institutions, tuberculosis hospitals, detention camps, reform schools and military academies. Insofar as such programs minimize the use of the resources of those immediately confronting the problems they are deficient as coping systems.

This "return to the community" is not inconsistent with the recent and numerous efforts to develop an adequate philosophy of "comprehensive medical care" and to devise efforts and programs to bring such conceptions into realization. It is this overarching task that is the subject of the next chapter.

SCENARIO II

The collapse into hopelessness

Following the decline of moral treatment, William James writes in 1907 of the state of the State Hospital:[37]

> Nowhere is there massed together as much suffering as in the asylums. Nowhere is there so much sodden routine and fatalistic insensibility as in those who have to treat it. Nowhere is an ideal treatment more costly. The officials in charge have resigned to the conditions under which they have to labor. They cannot plead their cause as an auxiliary organization can plead it for them. Public opinion is too glad to remain ignorant. As mediator between officials, patients, and the public conscience, a society such as you

sketch is absolutely required and the sooner it gets under way the better.

Sincerely yours, William James

The "sodden routine and fatalistic insensibility" to which James refers is the damaging product of the incurability myth within the walls of mental hospitals. The stigma that it, in conjunction with exaggeration of the role of heredity, places on the mentally ill is as effective as the medieval belief in demon possession in denying them their rights not only to the means of recovery but to decent living standards.

And of another hospital over a half-century later, Dunham and Weinberg say:[38]

> Another tradition of the hospital which is particularly pertinent to the doctor's role is the attitude that many patients are incurable and eventually become chronic hospitalized types. ... in practice they tacitly accept the idea that all one can do for many patients is to furnish them with good custodial care. This tradition, which pervades all mental hospitals and which the staff doctors eventually if not immediately come to accept, has been strengthened by the Kraepelinian viewpoint concerning the poor prognosis for schizophrenia. About two thirds of the doctors on the staff operate conceptually within this tradition. The remainder have adopted a psychological dynamic viewpoint toward the development of functional disorders.
>
> But more specifically, the acceptance of the idea that many cases are incurable is reflected in the type of medical concern with chronic wards. Only the most routine rounds are made on these wards. Patients on these wards often report that they haven't spoken to a doctor for years other than to say "Good morning." The chief *medical* concern is with *physical aliments*. (Italics mine.)

NOTES

1   Robert Faris and Warren Dunham, *Mental Disorders in the Urban Areas.* Chicago: University of Chicago Press, 1939.
2   Kingsley Davis, "Mental Hygiene and the Class Structure," in *Mental Health and Mental Disorder*, Arnold M. Rose, Ed. New York: 1955, Norton, pp. 578–612. By permission.
3   Alfred Stanton and Morris Schwartz, *The Mental Hospital.* New York: Basic Books, 1954.
4   Robert Park, "Suggestions for the Investigation of Human Behavior in the Urban Environment," in *The City*, Robert Park, Ed. Chicago: University of Chicago Press, 1925.
5   Alex Inkeles and Daniel J. Levinson, "National Character," in *Handbook of Social Psychology, Vol. II*, Gardner Lindzey, Ed. Reading, Mass.: Addison-Wesley, 1954.

6 Joseph Eaton and R. J. Weil, *Culture and Mental Disorders*. New York: Free Press, 1955.
7 Davis, op. cit., p. 580.
8 Ibid., p. 589.
9 Ibid., p. 578 et passim.
10 Stanton and Schwartz, op. cit.
11 Charles Perrow, "Hospitals: Technology, Structure, and Goals," in *Handbook of Organizations*, James G. March, Ed. Chicago: Rand McNally, 1965, p. 936. By permission.
12 Ibid., p. 936.
13 Ken Kesey, *One Flew over the Cuckoo's Nest*. New York: Viking Press, 1962.
14 Thomas Scheff, "The Role of the Mentally Ill and the Dynamics of Mental Disorders," *Sociometry*, 26 (1963), 436–453.
15 Ibid.
16 Peter Conrad, "The Discovery of Hyperkinesis," in *Dominant Issues in Medical Sociology*, Howard D. Schwartz and Cary S. Kart, Eds. Reading, Mass.: Addison-Wesley, 1978, pp. 72–79.
17 William R. Rosengren, *Special Group Program for Acting-Out Children*. Report of National Institute of Mental Health, 1965 (mimeograph).
18 M. W. Laufer, E. Denhoff, and G. Solomons. "Hyperkinetic Impulse Disorder in Children's Behavior Problems," *Psychosomatic Medicine*, 19 (January 1975), 38–49.
19 Ibid.
20 Conrad, op. cit., p. 77.
21 Ibid.
22 Ibid.
23 William R. Rosengren, "The Hospital Careers of Lower and Middle Class Psychiatric Patients," *Psychiatry* (February 1962), 16–22.
24 Ibid.
25 George Rosen, *Madness in Society*. New York: Harper & Row, 1968, p. 151.
26 J. Sanbourne Bockoven, "Moral Treatment in American Psychiatry," *Journal of Nervous and Mental Disease*, 124 (August 1956), entire issue.
27 Louis Gottschalk, *Social Science Research Council—Committee on Historical Analysis*. Chicago: University of Chicago Press, 1963.
28 Bockoven, op. cit., p. 24.
29 Ibid. By permission.
30 Ibid.
31 Erving Goffman, *Asylums*. New York: Doubleday, 1961, 46.
32 Maxwell Jones, *The Therapeutic Community*. New York: Basic Books, 1953.
33 William R. Rosengren, "Communication, Organization, and Conduct in the Therapeutic Milieu," *Administrative Science Quarterly*, (June 1964), 70–90.
34 Robert Hyde et al., *Milieu Rehabilitation*. New York: Basic Books, 1953.
35 John F. Kennedy, "Message to Congress: Mental Illness and Mental Retardation," February 5, 1963.
36 Benjamin Pasamanick et al., *Schizophrenics in the Community*. New York: Appleton, 1967, p. ix.
37 Francis D. Powell, *Theory of Coping Systems*. Boston: Schenkman Publishing Company, pp. 1–2, 1975.
38 Bockoven, op. cit., p. 22.
39 Warren Dunham and S. K. Weinberg, *The Culture of the State Mental Hospital*. Detroit: Wayne State University Press, 1960.

SUGGESTED READINGS

J. Sanbourne Bockoven, "Moral Treatment in American Psychiatry," *Journal of Nervous and Mental Disease*, 124 (August 1956), entire issue.

A fascinating account of a short-lived "premodern" miracle in the handling of the emotionally disturbed; a landmark in history and in historical psychiatry.

A. Deutsch, *The Mentally Ill in America*. New York: Columbia University Press, 1949.

A levelheaded indictment of the care of the mentally ill at midcentury; modern psychiatry depicted at its worst.

Erving Goffman, *Asylums*. New York: Doubleday, 1961.

Contains the now-famous tour de force on "total institutions," comparing mental hospitals to prison camps, religious orders, military institutions, concentration camps, and others involving systematic self-degradation.

R. N. Rapoport and R. Rapoport, *Community as Doctor*. London: Tavistock, 1960.

An examination of the virtues of milieu therapy written when the idea was reaching its peak of popularity.

Stephen P. Segal, *The Mentally Ill in Community-Based Sheltered Care*. New York: Wiley-Interscience, 1978.

A study of former patients treated in various nonhospital environments; implications for social planning and social policy.

Thomas S. Szasz, *Law, Liberty, and Psychiatry*. New York: Macmillan, 1963.

An academic psychiatrist continues his scathing critique of contemporary psychiatry: civil rights and their violation in the name of psychiatric care.

SCENARIO I

The search for the total patient

Jeremy Bentham, political economist, logician, and encyclopaedist, had among his other eccentric characteristics an addiction to the coining of new words. Very often these neologisms were combinations of entirely unrelated languages, but they expressed his ideas precisely. Some of the more peculiar of these ideas were apt to look even more incongruous when presented in this way.

His frequent meditations on death, for example, led him to suggest that everybody should be embalmed, coated with varnish to preserve the face and with india rubber to maintain the garments. The whole ensemble would constitute an "auto-ikon," which could then be erected on an appropriate site or against a woodland background.

Nevertheless, not all Bentham's verbal creations had such a dubious survival value, for it is to him that we owe such words as "international," "codify," and "minimize." He also invented "mesology"—the science of the means of attaining happiness, which in turn was a part of "eudaemonics"—the art of applying to life the maximum of well-being.

More than 50 years later, in 1873, Louis-Adolphe Bertillon rescued "mesology" from oblivion, enlarged its empire to include all animals and plants, and indicated in detail his concept of the "social mesology" of man. He suggested that as a discipline it would be concerned with the effect upon human beings as individuals and in society, of temperature, light, humidity, gravity, atmospheric pressure, meteorological and electrical influences, food and drink, urbanization, sanitary conditions, occupation, domesticity, religion, institutions, laws and psychological factors.... According to Bertillon, "there are only two possible ways of modifying man, either individually or in the mass:—

(1) by modifying his ancestry, which is possible so far as future generations are concerned, but extremely difficult to apply.

Sir John Charles, *The Social Context of Medicine.* Oxford: The Nuffield Provincial Hospitals Trust, 1962, pp. 1–2.

(2) by modifying the natural or social environment.

This description of the content of "mesology" with certain modifications is the epitome of "social medicine" as we know it today.

CHAPTER 11

The search for comprehensive medical care

The expression "comprehensive care" is usually taken to have desirable and wholesome connotations as compared with its presumed opposite, "limited care," by which is usually meant health care that is inadequate in scope, too specialized, and episodic rather than programmatic. In point of fact, however, when specifics are called in the debate over comprehensive care, the term "comprehensive" carries with it a wide range of meanings and definitions that may or may not coincide with the simple and commonplace assumption that *any* health care program that asserts itself to be "comprehensive" is *ipso facto* necessarily good and desirable from all points of view and in terms of all possible criteria of evaluation. In sum, the myriad of health programs—both real and ideal—represent some reaction to a defect in the present medical complex and as ways of correcting a specific and limited number of these perceived definitions. They are not necessarily a panacea for improvement of the entire system as it presently operates. Few if any of such critiques and proposals would suggest complete scrapping of the present multifaceted system and its replacement with an altogether new or overhauled machinery for the delivery of health care.

The aim of this chapter is to examine some of the specific comprehensive health programs that have already been created as well as those still in the proposal stage, to examine some of the considerations that have led to them, and to discuss the social forces that impede their fulfillment. This chapter will also introduce the last major theme of this book, the sociopolitical implications of the fact that the idea of health care as a right of citizenship is now closer to a reality than it ever was. This topic is examined in detail in Chapter 12.

THE IDEA OF COMPREHENSIVE CARE

In an official sense, the idea of comprehensive medical care became an effective force in the politics and economics of health at about the time of the passage of Public Law 89-749, 1966 which is quite clear in its language and in its implications:[1]

> The Congress declares that fulfillment of our national purpose depends on promoting and assuring the highest level of health attainable for

every person (and) that attainment of this goal depends on an *effective* partnership, involving close inter-governmental collaboration, official and voluntary efforts, and participation of individuals and organizations . . .

Of more importance is the stipulation that the agencies charged with developing these overarching medical plans are expected to:[2]

. . . provide for encouraging cooperative efforts among governmental or non-governmental agencies, organizations and groups concerned with health services, facilities, or manpower, and for cooperative efforts between such agencies, organizations, and groups and similar agencies, organizations, and groups in the fields of education, welfare, and rehabilitation.

Finally, this legislation provides that these goals shall be attained:[3]

. . . without interference with existing patterns of private professional practice of medicine, dentistry, and related healing arts.

Thus was set into motion a gargantuan, nationwide machinery whose aim was to mobilize existing health care facilities in such a way as to bring better health care to more people than had heretofore received it. Every level—state, local, and national, and public as well as private—has seen more than a decade of experimentation with forms of health care delivery, both organizationally and technically, that depart (sometimes radically) with the long-standing tradition of individual fee-for-service treatment arrangements and the most simple economic arrangements for the payment of health care. For the financing of "alternative" systems of health care cannot be realistically discussed without some attempt to assess their economic impact on the industry as a whole as well as on the private economics of individuals. Now in a sense the search for a workable and acceptable program of comprehensive medical care requires a considerably complex operational system that would allow the "medical" and "social" models of illness to work *simultaneously* on both a broad-based and long-term basis. As we shall observe, there are certain intractable points of conflict between the medical and social models at the ideological, technical, and organizational levels that make integration and cooperation extremely difficult if not impossible to achieve on any long-lasting basis.

Diagrammatically, the interface between the kinds of program linkages that stem from a medical model on the one hand and a social model on the other are depicted in Figure 11.1. It can be seen that movement of patients up the "left," or "medical," side of the health care pyramid involves: (1) an *increasing detachment* of patients from their community roots and further disengagement from the world of the nonsick; (2) increased reliance upon the *imperatives of medical technology* and submission into an asymmetrical status relationship with its practitioners; (3) an *increased* probability that patients will be subject to health care modalities in which the line between *treatment* and *research* is but thinly drawn, and that require extraordinary strategies of "coping" by patients and their significant others; (4) an increased probability that patients will be called upon to adopt on a long-term basis roles somewhat analogous to a *lifetime sick role;* (5) a heightened probability that the impact of "medicalization" will reverberate throughout the entire life space of the subjects of comprehensive care; and (6) an ever-increasing expansion of the scope and influence of the medical "division of service." This seems to be the main by-product of the preeminence of those levels of care implied toward the top of the health care hierarchy.

In the opposite sense, retention of patients toward the lower end of the "right" side of the pyramid: (1) aims to minimize patients' disengagement from the world of the healthy; (2) relies upon non-technical and normal social supports for patients' coping strategies; (3) expands upon the scope and salience of patients' rights so as to minimize their exploitation for possible nontreatment goals; (4) seeks,

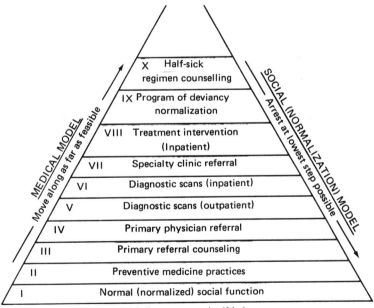

I-III: Lay and folk support and self-help
IV: Gatekeeping stage
V-X: Sick role establishment and medicalization stages

FIGURE 11.1 Stages in the health care pyramid: medical versus social dimensions.

wherever possible, alternatives to the "role of the sick" and seeks a partnership role for patients vis-à-vis practitioners; (5) aims to roll back the effects of life medicalization and to minimize its deleterious impact upon the patients' significant others; and (6) mobilizes community and lay resources to inhibit the expansion of the medical division of service and to permit access to its domain by "nonmedical" interests and influences. In short, the coincidence of these two models of illness would lead to a democratization of the medical establishment in which Rouseau's General Will would achieve a status of influence at least on a par with the technical imperatives of medicine as a dominant profession.

Before examining some of the recent efforts to bring about the kind of "comprehensive care" implied by such a model, let us spell out in somewhat more detail what such a comprehensive care program might involve. Its complexities are far greater than what one might infer from a quick glance at the health care pyramid, aside from the considerable problems in coordinating the medical and social perspectives.

It seems clear that comprehensive health care in American society is not likely to be achieved through the establishment of the kinds of monolithic health care systems that have proved to be possible in smaller and more homogeneous nations in the western hemisphere, although there are also some current critical economic considerations and impediments that did not exist, say, when the National Health Service was established in 1948 in Great Britain. Plainly put, society-wide comprehensive health services paid for directly from general tax revenues did not encounter the kind of monumental escalation of costs and consumer expectations that we now face. Nevertheless, it seems that in the foreseeable future comprehensive health care, where it is achieved at all, it is likely to be brought about through the manipulation and realignment of existing semiautonomous units at all levels in the existing health care system.

PROBLEMS OF PROGRAMMATIC CARE—
THE CARE OF THE MENTALLY RETARDED[4]

As has been pointed out, illness is a special case of deviancy in that it is typically regarded not only as undesirable but also temporary. Because it is temporary it carries with it no stigma, nor does it become the defining characteristic of the ill person for his or her total life course. Neither does it form the relation of other people toward the patient, except for the limited number of medical practitioners who temporarily intervene in the illness so as to cure it. This is made possible as a consequence of a viable medical technology by which the etiological roots of disease can be identified, the appropriate therapies applied, and reasonable predictions as to outcomes made. Hence, it is *technology* that makes most cases of somatic illness both temporary and non-stigmatizing.

At the organizational level, the availability of a vast set of viable medical technologies makes possible the type of delivery system that predominates in the United States, typically referred to as "hospital based." A distinguishing feature of such a system is that each separate delivery unit—typically the hospital—can independently administer these technologies, with only the occasional need for extensive inter-organizational coordination and collaboration. The focus of the units of such a delivery organization may be easily limited to individual ill persons as they pass through the hospital on a near-casual basis. The hospital as an organization, moreover, can be effectively sealed off from the organizational network in which other patients with similar illnesses may be undergoing similar treatment. Hence with respect to acute illnesses the acceptable goal is restoration of patients to a *normal* state of bodily health so that they may resume their normal social activities and responsibilities—familial, occupational, ideational, re-creational, and the like. This goal is reached through the application of technologies best administered and applied within the context of delivery units that maintain relative independence, autonomy, and self-direction.

The medical system here described is the prevailing and dominant one. Suitable as it may be for acute illness, it also tends to be the prevailing model for illnesses of all kinds. But in these cases it is un-suitable both in its treatment mode and its interorganizational char-acteristics. Furthermore, not only is the composition of the traditional medical system model in cases of chronicity unsuitable, it becomes pathologically distorted in that it tends to lead to long-term, stig-matizing, institutionalization of clients. That is, just as the acute patient in a general hospital remains a patient only so long as is tech-nically necessary for a cure to be effected, so too in the case of chronicity, long-term custodial residential "care" appears to be the logical extension of the medical model. It is the great power of medical technology that makes possible the perpetual and widespread diffusion of the "restoration" idea. Where that *technology* is absent, the *idea* of restoration becomes meaningless and its application pathological.

Herein lies the dilemma for the care of the modern ill, the re-tarded especially: Inasmuch as cures are difficult if not impossible to achieve, what shall the goals of comprehensive care be? If defining the intellectually incompetent leads to the ideological unacceptable outcome of custodialism, and if defining them as "ill" but not curable leads eventually to the same undesirable outcome, then how *shall* they be defined, and what kinds of goals are appropriate? It is essentially this problem of client definition that has resulted in a fragmented and uncoordinated structure of services for this category of client and others for whom comprehensive care is thought to be desirable.

Failure of the medical model

Just as the "typical" general hospital is a self-contained delivery unit, in most cases having all the necessary instrumentalities for effecting a cure, so too do the myriad of services dealing with the retarded act "as if" the needs of their clients can be met exclusively from within the limits of each institution or agency. In short, the medical model, effective as it may be when mobilized on behalf of somatic illnesses, seems clearly insufficient—and even counterproductive—when applied to client populations such as the mentally retarded. The point is that the medical model, when applied to the mentally retarded and others, is but a *starting* point in the client service process. But the very nature of the organizational systems derived from this model of service delivery inhibits the kind of interorganizational collaboration that seems to be required in achieving comprehensive care. In sum, the medical model is predicated upon the presence of a viable and effective technology. Where such a technology exists, its favored and at present, most efficient application is through delivery units that are *relatively* self-contained and is embedded in patient catchment systems in which *all* referred patients are likely to receive more or less equal access to treatment.

But in the case of the mentally retarded—and in other types of chronicity—the medical model may be misapplied. On the other hand, the "normalization" model which is predicated upon opposite assumptions, seems more appropriate.

The 'normalization' model

In the case of chronicity, the persistence of the medical model seems to result either in the application of "innovative" or "radical" technologies in the desperate hope of effecting some degree of change or improvement or in the ritualistic application of traditional therapies, which hold out little hope or expectation of recovery. In many cases such as the retarded, the first leads logically to an emphasis on elaborate research and diagnostic programs and the second to custodianship.

Whereas rehabilitative goals emphasize curing the client, either controlling or overcoming the disability, "normalization" goals involve circumventing defects or disabilities and reintegrating the client into as normal a set of social roles as may be permitted by the disability. And whereas rehabilitative goals are pursued through the application of technical therapies *within* institutions, normalization goals are pursued through the application of education and retraining programs and the establishment of supportive social environments often *outside* institutional settings.

To say, however, that rehabilitative services differ sharply in means and ends of "normalization" services, is not to say that one should supplant the other. Ideally, of course, clients should have access to *both* types of service systems so as to maximize the potential benefits from each.

A second element in an ideal and comprehensive array of services involves effective mechanisms of broadly oriented long-term coordination between the constituent units. That is, not only should clients have access to both rehabilitative and normalization services of a *variety* of types, there also should be effective means for transferring clients from one service to another as their needs change, both *within* and *across* rehabilitative and normalization services. Hence a client may benefit by being the object of attention of several agencies and institutions at the same time. In such cases, there is need for "lateral" coordination between services. Similarly, clients may also be in need of multiple services sequentially over time. In these cases a need for "longitudinal" coordination between services exists. Thus an ideally organized system of services is one with capabilities for coordinating various services required at any particular point in time, as well as transferring clients from one service to another as their needs change over time.

What factors and forces prevent an approximation of the kinds of *interorganizational* relationships essential to a closer realization of this kind of comprehensive system of health services? The discussion to follow represents an attempt to determine the service structure for the mentally retarded in one state and to make evaluative statements about it as measured against the ideal system of comprehensive service just described.

SERVICE STRUCTURE AS A MOSAIC

As presently functioning, the structure of services can be best typified by use of the metaphor of a mosaic rather than that of a system. There are *general* and *special medical services, educational services, psychological counseling services, diagnostic and research activities, long-term custodial care, community-based day care centers, family guidance services, welfare agencies, parent-sponsored helping groups,* and others that constitute the *lateral* array of services from which clients might benefit. Among these, moreover are services for *infants, preschoolers, school age populations,* and *adults*—constituting the *longitudinal* components of an ideally conceived comprehensive service system.

Closer inspection, however, reveals gaps and barriers between the individual component units in this service mosaic. Certain services required for the adequate handling of various rehabilitative or normalizing aspects are absent, as are *adequate transitional* services needed to move clients from the condition or status in which they may have been left by one agency and train them to meet the demands of services subsequently entered. In addition to these lacunae in the existing service pattern, *rigid boundaries* exist between separate agencies, analogous to the mortar surrounding the many individual pieces in a mosaic. These barriers constitute impediments to a pattern of comprehensive and coordinated service because they make it difficult for clients to move from agency to agency as required and difficult to penetrate the boundaries of other agencies.

It is important to point out, however, that the problems and inadequacies of interagency structure and coordination *exist totally independent from the adequacy of individual agencies and services.* That is, viewed in isolation, and measured against a standard appropriate to the functions for which they see themselves as responsible, the individual organizations and agencies are service "gems" that could serve as models to be emulated by others concerned with achieving a similar standard of *intraagency* excellence. The excellence of such services, however, is restricted to the limited number of clients who may happen to fall into the catchment area of a particular agency or into one referral network rather than another. A very strong *element of chance* therefore enters into the division of service delivery, not unlike market processes in a laissez-faire economy.

INITIAL DIAGNOSIS AND CLIENT DEFINITION

The first essential of a comprehensive coordinate medical system is a diagnostic process that is capable not only of correctly identifying clients in need but also of referring individuals so identified to the appropriate service-rendering agency. Ideally, this initial definition should be undertaken as *early as possible,* so that the client can benefit from corrective measures as early as possible. Delay in detecting the problem may result in the condition becoming permanently rooted or lead to irreparable social psychological problems, either of which may be avoided if early comprehensive intervention takes place.

In the case of the retarded, for example, surgical intervention for *spina befida* and *hydrocephalus* typify instances in which early application of a rehabilitative mode of intervention *can* be effective. Phenylketonuria (PKU) provides another example of a potentially serious disorder, visible in its early stages but only by competent rehabilitation-oriented diagnostic procedure. Comparable examples are more visible within *appropriately attentive school systems* in which a variety of perceptual and mobility inadequacies can be detected. Thus *delay in proper diagnosis is a first impediment* to generating a client demand for comprehensive care in this sphere of service.

What are some of the reasons underlying delay in the diagnostic process? First, diagnosis at early stages of a disorder requires the detection of *subtle premorbid symptoms* discernible only to those with professional training and specialized technical facilities. Parents, untrained service workers, or professionals with competence in fields marginal to the problem at issue, are not likely to be aware of the nascent disorder. Beyond that, however, is the fact that both lay and professional persons, who may be the first to encounter the intellectually deficient, experience great reluctance to suggest to parents that their child may be mentally retarded. Even at the agency, the word itself is avoided, while a vast number of *alternative universes of discourse* have been created to refer to, describe, and work with clients with the identical behavioral manifestations—failure to act in ways that have come to be regarded as "normally intelligent." Thus, vastly different *organizational languages* have arisen which effectively *harden the lines of division* between the variety of organizations that are attempting to help clients suffering from the same impairment.

While it is understandable that may professional workers, parents, teachers, and social workers experience great reluctance to label a client "mentally retarded," it is of importance to recognize that so long as "organizational languages" about clients differ, it is unlikely that they can be drawn into a comprehensive and coordinated system of service conversation. Hence a general and widespread reluctance and avoidance of common terminology with respect to intellectually deficient clients results in a mosaiclike structure of service in which multiple organizations see themselves as dealing with *different* kinds of client groups.

In association with the reluctance to adopt a commonly accepted label is found the phenomenon that organizational services often seem to be oriented toward providing services to persons and groups *other than the clients* themselves. It is true that in some sense all service organizations deliver services to the "commonwealth" and other second or third parties.

There is a special danger in the case of agencies dealing with the retarded, however, in that indirect service to commonwealth "third parties" may take priority over directing organizational resources and energies to the presumed prime consumers of services—the "clients in contact." That is, once subnormal intellectual capacity has been discovered, typically the child's overt behavioral manifestations and the difficulties this causes for the family or school are largely responsible for the immediate lay definition of the problem and the remedial services sought. Sometimes appropriate services delivered to clients in contact coincide with services delivered to commonwealth third parties. In other cases, treatment of overt behavior problems— largely responsible for precipitating a concern with third-party issues —appears to accomplish little in alleviating the underlying cause of the difficulty. That is, third-party influences may inhibit the effective application of either rehabilitative or normalizing interventions, not to speak of the more global ideal of a coordinated and comprehensive application of services.

CASE FINDING AND REFERRAL

Although technical facilities and trained specialists are present in the community studied, one group privately financed and the other state financed, they do not appear to be linked to a systematic case-finding service. The two agents that most nearly approximate a referral linkage are the District Public Health Association, visiting nurse associations, and private family doctors. The *latter* enter the referral route as a consequence of the otherwise natural transition from prenatal to postnatal care and in cases in which the physician has been invited to provide medical care at the request of parents. The *former* come into play only in the case of newborns originally defined as high risks for possible retardation and then do so only for the first year of life. In either case, *initial detection* is in the hands of the physician attending at birth, with grosser indicators picked up by gatekeepers later in the life course of the person.

Should a candidate for the services here at issue escape initial detection by an obstetrician, pediatrician, or visiting nurse during the first year of life, it is unlikely that a referral will be made until school entrance.

There is therefore a *division of referral,* distributed in time, in organizational setting, and in criteria applied to clients. This division contributes to the difficulties in realizing a comprehensive coordinated network of services. First of all, the individual practicing physician (and his or her hospital-based team) enter the referral process on a one-to-one case basis, but only in the early months of life. Second, the visiting nurse associations later scan high-risk census tract areas— usually centering around those areas of the community with high instances of first and multiple births, which in turn are typically low socioeconomic areas.

Hence the physician referral route favors early detection among high socioeconomic status families while disfavoring those in low socioeconomic status groups. On the other hand, the visiting nurse referral route favors later detection—through routinized area scanning processes—and favors case identification among families of low socioeconomic status. Those who remain undetected through these divisions of referral come next under the purview of the school, which also applies different assessment criteria and standards. Thus time, type of client–referral agent relationship, and standards of evaluation applied differ depending upon the point at which the potential client enters the referral system.

In addition, referral of newborns to the appropriate local nursing association is not entirely adequate and is indicative of the general absence of working interagency linkages. Specifically, names of newborns are not made available to the nursing associations either by physician groups or by hospitals. In the typical case, the individual nurses themselves obtain names of newborns from birth announcements printed in the local newspaper and from word-of-mouth information. Hence the second level of potential client referral involves a primitive case-scanning method.

Moreover, the medically specific orientation of the nurses, combined with the limitation of case contact to the first year of life only, appears to result in frequent failure to diagnose more generalized developmental, perceptual, or learning impairments that may not become evident until well after the first year of life.

The second major obstacle to early diagnosis is through voluntary visits to "well baby clinics" and to private physicians. This mode of detection, however, requires initiative and knowledgeability on the part of parents, and these are least likely to be found among the highest risk populations—those of low socioeconomic status. And in the seeming "free" services such as well baby clinics, there are hidden costs: transportation, child care for children remaining at home, time taken off from employment, and so on. Again, the highest-risk (low socioeconomic status) groups are less likely than are others to enter effectively into this route to early detection. Also, the need for self-motivation eliminates those parents who are lacking in sophistication or are too apathetic to regard routine examinations as useful. The general failure of the well baby clinics to handle acute-care problems and physicians to combine general examinations with acute care precludes a review of those children whose parents bring them in only for acute illnesses. Failure to pick up those children whose parents voluntarily exclude them from diagnostic service eliminates a population that if not overrepresented with cases of physiologically caused retardation does have a preponderance of cases of cultural deprivation.

District nurses following infants are precluded by professional etiquette from usurping the physician's diagnostic function. The *autonomous power* of the private physician means that the district nurse has few means by which to free children for further diagnosis. Somewhat more influence is exerted by the *clinic nurse* inasmuch as nurses and physicians function there more as team members.

Thus private physicians bear the major responsibility for initial referrals and they often delay their diagnosis partly out of their ignorance of new developments in the area of retardation and partly to "protect their patients."

Physicians' reported proclivity to take a wait-and-see attitude is aggravated by two factors. The solo practice of medicine isolates many physicians from professional contact with colleagues and allows individual patients and their families to become the major reference group for these physicians. Diagnosing a child as retarded fails to validate the physician's self-image as a healer. It is easier for the physician if parents resort to the mechanism of self-referral. A second factor influencing physicians to take a wait-and-see attitude evolves from their lack of knowledge concerning medical advances in the field of retardation. District nurses have gone far to overcome this problem by integrating training and continuing education as a regular part of their agency work. Specifically, nurses and social workers from the Division of Retardation have regularly given short courses on such subjects to the various district nurses' associations. However, the *structural isolation* between the profession of medicine and the district nurses' organization largely prevents nurses from effectively utilizing this knowledge.

An important inhibiting factor is that because of the independent and autonomous nature of the vast range of organizations dealing with the retarded, individuals become the clients of *single organizations* rather than of a *system of services*. There is, in short, no systemic case-finding process at the technical, organizational, or interorganizational levels.

These limiting aspects of the diagnostic and referral processes may not, in all cases, be totally dysfunctional for clients. If services that aim to ameliorate the client's problems remain underdeveloped or undercoordinated, then some clients would pass through developmental processes and grow out of their disability, or the moderately handicapped may actually be better served by remaining undetected rather than being defined, labeled, and stigmatized, *but untreated*.

For mild and borderline cases, the label and stigma of retardation may serve as a symbolic barrier resulting in a greater limitation to the individual's normal integration into family, peer group, and school than the impairment may in reality warrant.

However that might be, an integrated system of screening and referral is basic to the development of a comprehensive and coordinated service system. However, diagnosis that results in categorization but not service is a costly and unproductive operation and a potentially damaging one as well.

SPECIALTY DIAGNOSIS AGENCIES

Consistent with the medical model, once gross impairment has been labeled, a "specialist" diagnosis is frequently sought in an attempt to refine and relabel the diagnosis in ways less stigmatizing and seemingly less permanent than the term "mentally retarded." This holds out some hope for the restorative-curative idea, which is the cornerstone of the medical model.

Two diagnostic services exist in the state, one privately sponsored and the other publicly funded. Both receive cases as referrals from first-line medical practitioners.

The diagnostic services offered by specialty services *are* comprehensive in approach. A public clinic operates on a team approach including specialists from a variety of perspectives—medical, educational, psychiatric, and social work. A private specialist develops the same comprehensive approach through relations with two private service agencies and his or her hospital affiliation. The focus of the diagnostic effort, in both cases, centers on determining the nature and cause of the disability. This is aimed to satisfy both the parental preoccupation with the question of "Why isn't my child normal?" and also fits the medical model of the cure depending upon a determination of the cause.

The approach of the diagnostic facilities represents an attempt to *counteract the total pessimism of an earlier era* and to prevent further restriction of the mentally retarded's abilities by allowing them to languish in a custodial environment.

Both these clinics deal with client populations whose members— apparently for morphological or neurological reasons—act at a markedly depressed intellectual level. The generic, and professionally neutral, term by which such persons *might be described* is "intellectually impaired." But for reasons of history and folk language, the commonly understood, but uniformly avoided term is "mentally retarded." In the light of the lack of an acceptable common term to describe and discuss this phenomenon, and both the lay and professional antipathy to the term "mentally retarded," a rich variety of terms have been invented and serve to generate *intraagency* uniqueness and a sense of professional sophistication.

Thus the specialist facilities have developed a terminological lexicon symbolizing their effort to soften the image of the nature of the disorders. Both consciously avoid the labels "mental retardation," "mental defective," and their numerous derivatives because they *connote permanence* and suggest an inability to provide any effective treatment. The private specialists employ labels such as "cerebral dysfunction," "psychoneurological inefficiency," "developmentally retarded," or "developmental lab." The public clinic uses such terms and expressions as "intellectual impairment," "chronological delay," or "compared the behavior of the impaired child with that of younger children." The function of this labeling process is threefold. One is to reorient the efforts toward the provision of ameliorative therapies. The second is to assuage the feeling of parents and counteract their depression. As one private specialist phrased the problem, he avoids the word retardation:[5]

> . . . because of the stigma attached to it. Parents have very strong feelings about the term. They have been hit many times before they see me with the statement that their child is retarded. Retarded has a connotation to them of hopelessness and helplessness. My entire philosophy of management is hopefulness based upon realistic appraisal. If I find clear-cut evidence that the children have malformation of the brain, I have to say to the parent that your child's brain is limited by anatomy. It is hard to tell you how he might grow and develop. He likely will not develop normal intelligence. But he will grow and hopefully find some useful place in society.

However, in the cases where the disability is permanent, where the "child's brain is limited by anatomy," the hopefulness of the medical model cannot be fulfilled, and the frustration and "hopelessness and helplessness" faced by the permanently disabled individual and his parents are merely postponed. Thus, the underlying reality of the condition cannot be totaly ignored or circumvented through symbolic manipulations. In many cases the inescapable fact is that:[6]

> . . . little can be done to help these people. If you have a child with multiple handicaps, that is a child with whom you are never going to be able to do much.

There is a serious problem faced in finding appropriate treatment facilities once an assessment of the extent of the disability has been made. Although private specialists have developed relationships with private voluntary treatment agencies, it is fully recognized that they service a limited clientele.[7]

> It is strictly a private middle class, upper type of service. We do not have clinic services although we again have the affiliations [private voluntary agencies who accept some charity and medicaid cases]. Those people who cannot afford full private care are helped to make necessary transfers [to the publicly financed clinic.] It's [the publically financed

clinic's] function and I feel strongly that that is where this type of case should be filtered. The State has set it up for that.

In addition, the private agencies attempt to limit their attention to clients with "potentially normal intelligence."[8]

Not surprisingly, the private specialist and agencies demand a considerable input of resources on the part of the clients' parents to obtain services. This of course includes money but, even in cases where third-party insurance pays the cost, an input of time is also required. Parental motivation and willingness to participate actively is an essential ingredient to the receipt of service. They thus serve a:[9]

> . . . more select, sophisticated population who are looking for help and are trying to gain some degree of salvageability close to normal functioning.

This often results in truncated services to clients whose parents are neither motivated nor otherwise enabled to enter actively into the existing pattern of coproducerhood.

In sum, the medical model, with its conception of rehabilitation and restoration, seems hardly a workable organizational approach as far as achieving optimum states of interorganizational coordination and the realization of a comprehensive system of care for the intellectually impaired. Movement toward the realization of an effective and operative coordinated system of services is impeded by a number of factors and forces.

First, the impairments are permanent in many cases. In spite of this, however, specialized medical diagnostic facilities continue to employ the language of "possible cure." In the process they may err in the direction of *overoptimism*, thus overlooking the often real and permanent limitations to the client. A further consequence of this is to retain the client as the "property," as it were, of the medically oriented division of labor with regard to the mentally retarded and to impede the referral of clients *outside* the medical sphere and *into* the more socially oriented service division of labor in which the goals of normalization are more likely to be found. Thus, rehabilitative services for clients suffering from such impairments are difficult to organize and coordinate, and useful interagency referrals are difficult to arrange. Badly needed are services and personnel to provide social supports for retarded individuals and to help them and their families achieve as normal as possible an existence in spite of their disabilities. *Rehabilitative efforts alone* are doomed to frequent failure and frustration.

To proceed "as if" handicapped children had "potentially normal" abilities fits a dominant cultural theme of individual independence, and the restriction of services to individuals or children with "potentially normal intelligence" in some private agencies is an attempt to establish an "as-if" mentality among parents and staff. In other agencies it appears to be a mechanism to exclude certain clients permanently from service rather than bring them into service.

In addition, the "as-if-normal" position in cases where the disability is permanent represents a fiction with no basis in reality. However, some cases do not make progress and are "followed through their entire growing period." Others who do not progress have to be transferred to other resources that presumably deal with permanently disabled individuals. Transfers ideally take place, in the classical medical pattern, when the treatment modalities have not been effective in restoring normal functioning.

In sum, the insularity of individual agencies makes *continuity of service* problematic to clients, but no overarching agency exists to ensure continuity of service. Long-term planning and coordination of rehabilitative services and integration with normalization procedures thus are not apparent.

INDIVIDUALIZATION AND AGENCY AUTONOMY

Close to the center of the American ethos rests a commitment to the individual. The individual is regarded as possessing inalienable rights that must be protected, supported, and extended wherever possible. As a corollary, social institutions and political systems ought not interfere with and impede this independence. This leads to a commendable concern with providing individualized services that maximize individual potential.

Most services require clients to be motivated to accept service and point to the futility of providing services to those who lack motivation. The client and—particularly in the case of the retarded—his or her family appear as an autonomous system whose boundaries cannot be penetrated except under the most extreme of circumstances. As discussed later, the *legal authority* for this is closely circumscribed.

Thus in the construction of a health structure the client and family system represent crucial ingredients. They can exercise considerable control and influence in defining and creating appropriate services. This provides some assurance that services meet the felt needs of clients, who are not merely pawns controlled and manipulated by health agencies. Therefore the client and the client's family have the right to refuse to cooperate with services that professionals may perceive as beneficial.

Paradoxically, however, desired societal *and* service goals of maximizing the independence of individuals cannot be accomplished if services are blocked on this basis of citizens' rights. Only if the discrepancies are extreme and the parental reluctance is thought to physically endanger the child can agencies interfere with the autonomy of the family. To cope with this, agencies develop strategies they feel are proper and persuade the child that cooperation is in his or her best interests.

A parallel problem involved is the client or family who not only refuses to accept or seek services but deliberately seek inappropriate ones. Clients, after all, are lay members of the service structure, and their ability to assess needs and prescribe necessary services must by definition be more limited than more knowledgeable persuasive professionals. Leaving the first diagnostic and service decisions largely in the hands of the clients makes the initial link in the structure subject to considerable trial and error. More seriously, the existence of the dual service goal structure alluded to, coupled with the dependent status of retarded children, means families can seek service so as to protect and meet their *own needs* to the potential detriment of the retarded patient. For whatever the cause, intervention into the family system poses a serious dilemma for service deliverers and society.

One of the indirect influences of this normative defense of individual autonomy is to allow a client's own lack of sophistication, motivational strengths, or those of family members to restrict his or her autonomy in seeking service.

Agencies, like clients and parents, have the right to remain autonomous of other actors in the service structure. State or public agencies occupy a special position but the private voluntary agencies are very conscious of their individuality and autonomy. Just as clients have the right to accept or refuse services, so too do the agencies themselves reserve the right to select or control the types of client they service.

NEGOTIATING A DIVISION OF SERVICE

Agencies, then, perceive themselves as autonomous but not as comprehensive. They do not attempt to offer a complete array of services for the full range of client types. They stake out a limited domain and deal with clients who meet *their* service criteria.

The three mainstays of the structure revolve around *professionalism, parental rights,* and *agency voluntarism.* Each has achieved control over its own domain. Professions and professionalizing occupations have, or are striving to gain, control over their area of expertise and responsibility. Among service occupations this entails the power to decide what the nature of their services should be, and how and to whom they should be dispensed. It is the profession, not external agents, that decides their role in the delivery system. Physicians represent the classical case, but *special education teachers* and *psychological testers* occupy a counterpart role in evaluating and placing retarded children. Of course, professions are not totally autonomous, and the consumer still can exercise considerable influence. If one does not like the decision of one professional expert, then one can hire another professional representative who is sympathetic to their position, who is willing to represent it for a fee, and will carry their opinion to the professional body and *negotiate* a resolution.

THE SEARCH FOR COMPREHENSIVE CARE

As a category of clients, the mentally retarded represent something of an archetype of those who might derive great benefit from a coordinated and comprehensive service system combining medical and social components. By "coordinated" is meant a system of interagency referrals that would *maximize* the probability that a client of one agency, in need of the services of another agency, would in fact become a client of the second agency dispensing the desired service. By "comprehensive" is meant a system of services in which both broad and long-term supports would occur. The following constitute the factors underlying the difficulties in reaching these goals.

Delays in client referral

Parents, physicians, and agencies are reluctant to accept or apply the stigmatizing "mentally retarded" label to clients. As a consequence, two overarching definitions of clients are made, within each of which are developed highly specialized organizational definitions of clients. One set of conceptions stresses the neurological-morphological roots of the impairment. The other emphasizes the social and psychological consequences and implications of severe or profound intellectual impairment.

The effect of these two differential views of retardation is to produce two broadly different agency sectors with regard to the condition. The first, modeled on the medical experience, emphasizes cure and rehabilitation and leads to a division of services focused on specialized diagnosis in a search for neurological and/or morphological evidence that might justify a diagnosis other than retardation. The second, which can be called the "normalization" model, takes as a matter of fact the relative permanence of the intellectual impairment, emphasizes the need for social adaptation and readjustment of both the client and significant others, and negates the efficacy of the technically specific interventions of the medical model.

Thus two major sectors exist. One is based on the medical model of cure, leading eventually in the typical case to residential custodial care, the signal benchmark of which is the hope for a "scientific" breakthrough that will permit the realization of a "cure." The other view is that intellectually impaired individuals should be accepted "in their own right," and the probable fact of permanent impairment ought not be a case criterion for long-term clienthood in either a medically specific research/diagnostic setting, or in a long-term custodial circumstance. Thus, the medical sector looks to science, while segregating those to whom the as-yet-undiscovered technology shall be applied. The normalization sector looks to society with the hope and expectation that mentally retarded individuals will be re-integrated into the social order "as if" they were not retarded.

This conflict in belief and ideology—medical versus normaliza-tion—must be set down as the central divisive factor inhibiting move-ment toward coordinated and comprehensive services. Both are utopian and hence contain a significant component of zealotry in the minds of their adherents, a fact that exacerbates the basic ideological conflict between them.

In sum, the widespread repugnance of the label "retarded" serves to delay entrance of clients into the service network and appears to be at the root of the existence of two conflicting sectors.

Clients enter the existing system of services by *four* routes; the individual practicing physician, visiting nurse associations, well baby clinics, and the public schools. Each of these agents and agencies have access to a different potential client population, approach the members of that population with their own particular definitional frame of reference, react to identified cases with a particular service viewpoint, and are likely to encounter a different age group.

Thus a pervading *randomness in the referral process* perpetuates the element of chanciness as to when in the life course case detection will occur, what agent will locate and identify, and what referral alternatives will stem from these circumstances.

Clients as organizational property

There is a sense in which clients constitute valuable resources, sur-rounding which is a mood of reluctance to relinquish them to other organizations. These are all *service* organizations, and as such must retain clients in order to sustain their justification for other resources, monetary and nonmonetary. This seems to be *less* the case in the regional community centers, which are seeking more and more clients, apparently in an effort to secure a more powerful position with respect to long-term policy planning and resource allocation in the field of retardation. Following on the heels of the *division of service* is an in-creasing *division of responsibility,* by which it becomes difficult to determine which organization is in fact responsible for the past, present, and future of the client. Thus, the achievement of a coordinated and comprehensive service system must face the fact that clients may be regarded as resources to be hoarded or at other times as liabilities of which the organization is anxious to rid itself. In response to this, potential referral-receiving organizations exhibit great suspicion concerning the creation of regularized procedures for interagency coordination collaboration, especially when the possible *permanent* exchange of clients might be involved.

There is a very strong set of pressures in this service system to shift the focus of service away from the client in contact and toward a variety of third parties—parents, schools, and some conception of the public good in general.

When human services respond *primarily* to the needs and wishes of parties *other than* the client in contact, then the realization of client-centered services of a coordinated and comprehensive character will be difficult indeed.[10]

The service division of labor and specialization

Specialization, however functional it might be in the individual case, is a major factor inhibiting the creation of coordinated and comprehensive services because it may result in a hardening of boundaries between organizations. Agency specialization seems to create attitudes of distinctiveness and differentiation between organizations that impede the identification of common problems and the achievement of dialogue toward the seeking of common solutions.

There is, in short, an underlying current of competitiveness and individualism between the several agents involved (family members, physicians, and organizations) that produces a system operating very much as a laissez-faire economy, with clients constituting the exchangeables in the system.

For the most part, personnel in the organizations and agencies involved with the retarded are understandably preoccupied with the ongoing and day-to-day routines of their work. They are busy pursuing the work that has been defined as their charge and their obligation. As a result, little attention is paid—and even fewer agency resources allocated—to interagency planning functions or referral alternatives.

Although these problems of comprehensive care are manifold, the concept casts a wide net in terms of its potential impact on all aspects of medical training, administration, financing, and practice.

The scope implied by comprehensive care compels a frame of reference that transcends a parochial interest in the hospital and that relates to conditions and circumstances beyond the walls of the doctor's office.

A major conclusion is that comprehensive care requires a conception of illness emphasizing "early" care and a "reaching out" of the medical care system into the apparently healthy population. What is generally called comprehensive care involves a pragmatic dilemma confronting medicine today—namely, the discrepancy between the *potential* capacity to produce effective health services and the *actual availability* or delivery of such services to those who need them.

SOME ATTEMPTS AT COMPREHENSIVE CARE

The Division of Social Medicine at Montefiore Hospital mainly addresses problems of a chronic type at a point where acute disease has been stabilized and rehabilitation processes begin.[11] Both of these demand family participation, and the outcome is dependent upon patient attitude, family readiness, and general community support.

A major finding was that open access to the hospital did not lead to an abuse of medical services. In fact, group members utilized specialists less frequently than did the control group, and preferred to consult general practitioners.

An important finding was the patient's greater acceptance of the public health nurse in place of the physician, and the warm reception afforded the social worker on the team. However, the image of the social worker as a specialist was found to interfere with a capacity to use the service easily or early. A related discovery was that a "lay referral" system had far-reaching implications for the speed with which a family utilized the new medical service. That is, social and cultural factors in the community milieus of the patients in many instances inhibited the speedy appearance of patients at the hospital.

The Aging Center of Mt. Sinai Hospital represents another attempt to bolster treatment facilities to meet more adequately the goals of comprehensive care.[12] The patients selected for special consideration were persons whose medical needs were intertwined with social and emotional problems. The center was formed to investigate the special problems and needs involved in the aging process and to define comprehensive methods of dealing with them. Under the supervision of a social worker, the service provided patients with a ready reference to community-wide services offered to the aged.

Medical consultations are made available as required through the specialty clinics. The personal physician attends the patient when admitted to the hospital or home care. Special attention is given to group counseling and recreational therapy, recognizing that the aged suffer greatly from loneliness and depression.

The costs of this program are high, but the staff has become more economy oriented as reflected in selectivity in the use of laboratory services. "As physicians in the program have become more familiar with the problems of aging, the costs have come down."

Familiarity with the aged has helped young internists to become more comfortable with their role in chronic and terminal care. Medical residents rotate through the program and are introduced to the underlying philosophy of comprehensive care. Training and education have been expanded to include the encouraging of interests in areas beyond traditional boundaries.

The program has increased a sense of security and confidence on the part of patients to manage more effectively on their own. The drop in referrals to nursing homes and chronic hospitals provides some support for that conclusion.

A further advantage is that interdisciplinary cooperation is learned much more easily. Although staff members are drawn from several disciplines, their allegiance is to a comprehensive service directed at the same patient. The management and medical problems stem from the patient rather than from diverse specialties, and there appears to be less interference from barriers of differential orientation and a greater tendency to draw from each the assistance needed to achieve an overall team aim.

The problem appears to be tied to making home care services as medically significant in the eyes of professional and paramedical personnel as are the traditional and heretofore more glamorous and status-providing aspects of in-hospital work.

The Dean of the University of Michigan Medical School has argued that hospitals, as presently organized, are a contributory factor in rising medical costs. He believes hospitals are usually too large to pinpoint individual responsibility, tend toward unnecessary bureaucratization, and tend to disregard the individual needs of patients. He suggested that a "health complex" concept is needed to rectify these deficiencies.

The proposal is for medical service to be arranged in units according to the requirements of patients rather than in terms of traditional hospital disciplines and services. Such emphasis on patients and their needs would give rise to a series of decentralized and self-contained units.

Usually the medical complex consists of a collection of hospitals characterized by special service orientations (obstetrics, pediatrics, etc.) and is generally bound to a university medical school for educational and consultative needs. As they extend into the wider community with affiliations with community hospitals and other service agencies, the notion becomes more viable. In other words, a group of affiliated hospitals and agencies begins to realize the aims of a health complex as it collectively develops and integrates ambulatory care services, preventive measures, joint education programs, multiphasic diagnostic screening measures, and home care service.

Like the concept of comprehensive care, the idea of a health complex suffers from a lack of clearly defined organizational details. However, a number of concrete developments have been designed to pursue actively what appear to be the manifest aims and objectives of this new and potentially radical style of medical care delivery. The intrinsic features of such health complexes vary considerably, especially in the kinds and scope of patient problems to be served.

In 1965 the Yale University Medical School launched an experimental program designed to develop and study new methods in the provision and teaching of family health maintenance.[14] The emphasis was very much as in the Montefiore demonstration on comprehensive care through treating whole families as "the patient." The scope of the program was extensive, but its patient population small. It was to promote family health maintenance through broad orientations to prevention, treatment, rehabilitation, and assumption of responsibility for coordinating patient use of related community agencies. While physically located on the hospital premises, it is properly viewed as located in the heart of the neighborhood being served.

The educational function of the program is realized by medical students, under preceptors, leading the "health team . . . in place of a solo physician." Continuity is stressed with specialist consultation available. Several external agencies provide personnel for service at the center, such as public health nurses, welfare representatives, and social workers. In principle, all complex medical problems uncovered can be referred to resources of the parent hospital complex.

For the sake of achieving maximum coordination, the planning of the entire program involved a committee of community health agencies as well as a committee from the medical center. Central to the aims was the principle that policy commitment and program support was pledged by the cooperating parties.

The patients and families involved are offered an impressive array of medical care and treatment measures. Since, however, the patients served are few, the concentration of services is not altogether surprising. An important question is whether such a program can be translated directly into large-scale service facilities involving large numbers of individuals.

The St. Paul Medical Center is a nonprofit organization, formed by five hospitals combining their outpatient departments and some ward and teaching services as a nucleus for a special service for indigent patients.[15] In the interest of comprehensive care for these persons, community resources of a wide variety were considered as vitally linked to the program. A program was undertaken to coordinate center activities with those of all other agencies from which and to which patients were referred. This measure involved a concentrated effort at orienting staff to total patient needs, using the policies, programs, and problems of the many health and welfare agencies as auxiliary resources.

A report on the program comments that the coordination problems among the several participating units "have been met vigorously but not with complete success . . . the forces of specialization and apathy remain strong."[16]

These comments on efforts to meet current medical challenges, while obviously failing to provide the substantive materials for purposes of evaluation, do reveal several critical matters relevant to the place of comprehensive care within a total medical care delivery system.

Before taking up human rights and obligations in the health field in the final chapter, it remains to mention two recent delivery system innovations— the *Health Maintenance Organization,* and the *Neighborhood Health Centers*—as additional attempts to achieve comprehensive medical care.

HEALTH MAINTENANCE ORGANIZATIONS

The Health Maintenance Organization is an advanced form of cooperative medical practice based upon morbidity and mortality actuarial probabilities parallel to the economics underlying third-party medical insurance plans. The difference lies in the fact that the insurers (the corporate doctors) are also the providers of health care (the HMO medical staff). Service is usually limited to individuals who join the organization as members of a group, normally as employees of a firm and each pays a monthly premium covering the member and his or her family. In return, the HMO is obligated by contract to provide whatever health services are needed so long as the member adheres to a program of early detection of health problems and adheres assiduously to health care regimens. Care is provided either directly in the facilities owned and operated by the HMO itself (often resembling a small hospital in its own right) or even in medical facilities chosen by the patient. Often, the monthly membership fees are less than what one might normally expect to pay in Blue Cross or other similiar kinds of insurance schemes, and coverage is even more comprehensive. Although they are still too new for final assessments of their effectiveness to be made, these organizations are able to provide this kind of relatively low-cost and comprehensive medical care primarily for three reasons.

First, they rest upon the requirement of a need for active participation in the preventive program as laid down by the medical staff of the HMO. If the relatively low costs are to be maintained, members *must* become active participants in the maintenance of their own good health. The concept of "crisis" care cannot be tolerated in the HMO, and so the threat of revoking one's membership for noncompliance serves as the "stick" in securing patient cooperation, while the "carrot" is comprehensive care at a moderate cost. Second, the HMO must take on many of the characteristics of a bureaucratic organization, especially in the sense that it must have a far larger number of paying members than the number who will actually require the delivery of medical care over any given span of time. The healthy, that is, assist indirectly in paying for the medical care of the ill, as in all forms of insurance. The physician staff, on its part, must relinquish a number of elements of the "autonomy" and "independence" that have served so long as the ideological banner of the free practicing physician, and perhaps a lower lifetime income. In return, the physicians are assured a large pool of clients and the clinical experience they represent and access to a network of free colleague supports and consultations, along with access to a set of day-to-day medical facilities and technologies that they otherwise could not depend upon. Thus, the HMO represents a series of compromises on the part of the patients, who relinquish some element of autonomy and freedom of choice, and the physicians, who give up their claim to independence. Whether in the long haul these patient and professional costs outweigh the respective advantages involved remains to be seen. But for the most part, the HMO seems to offer persons already functioning within the existing medical system the opportunity for a level of care probably of higher caliber than they had heretofore been receiving.

The Neighborhood Health Centers, on the other hand, are designed to link persons with the medical system who heretofore have been *out of it* almost altogether—the urban poor and the otherwise culturally and economically deprived.

NEIGHBORHOOD HEALTH CENTERS—
LAST REMNANT OF THE GREAT SOCIETY

Developed out of the now largely defunct programs of the Office of Economic Opportunity, the Neighborhood Health Centers represent an attempt to bring citizens who are effectively outside the existing medical system into contact with the system in ways that allow the staff of the centers to act as "advocates" for the medically deprived. In the typical case, the centers themselves offer only basic "primary" care—general physical examinations, X rays, laboratory testing, and the like. The major function of the neighborhood centers, however, is to serve as a focus for citizen participation in health care planning and delivery, as a scene for the employment of community lay persons in the health effort, as a referral for clients to existing health services throughout the community, and as a way of seeking the financial resources to secure health care without which community members might simply continue to "go without" in the future as many of them had done in the past.

Emphasis is placed on primary group relationships so as to demystify the medical system, on the employment of neighborhood people to widen the bridge between citizen and medical system, on the presymptomatic phases of illness, and, most important, on the securing of levels of care *short of hospitalization* where possible, including cases of organic as well as functional incapacitation. A strong theme in the Neighborhood Health Centers is that of the democratization of a client-professional relationship that heretofore has been based not so much on negotiation and mutuality as on asymmetry in technology and social power. It remains to be seen whether a fully elaborated "technical democracy" in the health field will eventually evolve out of the *contractual* relationships fostered by the Health Maintenance Organization and the *participatory* relationship seeking to find roots in the Neighborhood Health Centers. There is some indication, however, that the recent movement to seek forms of comprehensive care *outside* of the traditional hospital setting—while well intentioned in a humanistic sense and perhaps both conscious and responsive to patients' negative attitudes toward the "bureaucratic" character of hospital care—have yet to achieve a level of medical efficiency still attributable to the application of hospital-founded "medical model."[17]

These newer forms of medical organization—all arising as a response to the call for comprehensive medical care—alter not only the traditional relationship between separate health organizations but also the standard relationship between medicine and the patient.[18] Each particular innovation—whether it be ambulatory care, home care, or preventive medicine—necessarily limits the *number and kinds* of interagency and medicine-client relationships it can accommodate. Each innovative form may do little more than contribute to the existing segmented pattern that characterizes the American medical scene.

ORGANIZATIONAL INTEGRATION AND THE 'BROKER' ROLE

One option is to accept organizational isolation, program specialization, and separate operational domains. This does not preclude a realization that new needs do exist for broad-based and long-term delivery of service. In fact, the same clients appear again and again for different and specialized services in many different settings. These organizations may be structurally unable to alter either their posture toward the client *or* their relationships with other involved medical organizations. One way to fill the lacunae is through special intermediary or "broker" roles, which span organizational boundaries.

The field of rehabilitation offers an example of this strategy in the form of the "rehabilitation counselor."[19] The dilemma of the broker role of the rehabilitation counselor, and to some extent of the newly envisaged programs of extended care generally, is that an acceptable organizational model is not yet available. Wessen has commented, "There is not yet an organizational pattern for rehabilitation which is typical of human activity in the sense that the school typifies education or the hospital the practice of medicine."[20]

The counselor (who is really the implementer of the new concept of care) must usually function in the context of organizations designed primarily for purposes other than those specifically relevant to rehabilitation. Thus, counselors are found in schools, hospitals, prisons, employment agencies, and departments of welfare.

REHABILITATION

By virtue of a comprehensive client orientation the counselor must continually relate to *other* organizations. These may be formally structured to service patients in terms of perceptions and attitudes not always in accord with the more general objectives and philosophy of the rehabilitation expert.

The development of rehabilitation centers is an effort to free rehabilitation counselors from their basically hostile organizational housing and to provide an institutional anchorage of sufficient bite that rehabilitation (or other innovative experiments in health and welfare) may have an equal chance to compete in the organizational complex with respect to both resource acquisition and client recruitment and conversion. The obvious trap is that in the very process of achieving an organizational home and a lever on the total organizational system, the rehabilitation center may well revert to the very program specialization and interorganizational conflict and divisiveness that originally drove the counselor out of the schools, hospitals, and the welfare agencies.

A solution, of course, is to free such individual emissaries from any identifiable organizational anchorage. That is, to create a genuine broker role to make it possible for new orientations toward patients to be sustained by protecting them from the inroads that are inherently made by full participating membership in a medical organization. Hence, the broker carries the potential of achieving broader-based and longer-term care for patients through mobilizing and integrating the many special services and capabilities of existing isolated—and even antagonistic—organizations. Paradoxically, interorganizational collaboration may be possible in some instances without recourse to the customary strategies of consolidation, cooptation, merger, or program integration, all of which assume prior conditions of lack of conflict and antagonism.

Perhaps a successful use of the broker traveling between specialized institutions stands a reasonable chance of achieving operational comprehensive care (a broad lateral orientation) while sustaining the fundamentally specific orientation of the organizations viewed individually.

CREATING A HEALTH ADVOCACY ROLE

Given the ambiguities and conflicting interests in the existing medical system, patients often are in need of an "advocate," working strictly on their behalf, who is less subject to the constraints and inhibiting factors now active in the structure of services.[21]

A further requirement is that the advocate is sufficiently well grounded in organizational realities that he or she is able to play advocate for the interests of the organizations and agents involved as well. That is, no medical organization totally divested of "valuable" clients will be able to sustain itself and continue its contribution to the coordinated comprehensive service resource. In a parallel sense, no organization can be overburdened with clients who constitute liabilities and at the same time be expected to do very much beyond "protecting" its own interests by isolating itself from other organizations as well as from the advocate.

In addition, the advocacy role would be structurally situated in such a manner that it would be possible to sustain and support the interests of the patient over and above the equally legitimate interests of third parties. For as inevitable and important as third-party commonwealth functions are, a serious pathology arises when the interests and needs of clients in contact are jeopardized by the preeminence of the interests of persons or agents other than the client.

What may be required is an "interorganizational" expert whose allegiance is to the patient rather than to any single medical organization; a *gadfly* for patients whose charge is to *persuade* agencies to relinquish some of their clients when they might prefer not to or *persuade* agencies to accept clients when they might prefer not to. Such a corps of advocates would require some kind of institutional housing, would have to be knowledgeable about the service structure as it presently exists, and would have to have access to these agencies and the key decision makers within those agencies.

Finally, the occupants of such a role would have to be selected with extreme care. In fact, the multiple agencies to be affected by the activities of these individuals should be directly involved in such selection. The "broker role" must be filled with persons capable of deporting themselves persuasively but with a high degree of interpersonal delicacy and skill. Essentially, these brokers do not, and for the foreseeable future probably will not, have institutionalized *authority* behind them, nor can they resort to the use of power themselves to accomplish ends on behalf of their clients.

In short, the broker would assume the advocacy role presently left to the patients, their families, or the special interests and perspectives of individual medical agencies. Thus the advocate role entails assuming wide-ranging responsibility for interagency referral and contact, but without the organizational maintenance needs for ensuring continued support—monetary and nonmonetary—for one's own particular agency or service. It would go far to free the professional from the need continually to protect his or her own agency's autonomy from encroachment by other agencies. Admittedly, should the job be done right, the advocate would continually pass judgment on the appropriateness of services being rendered to patients, and within the system there would *undoubtedly* be a sharp increase in the mood of conflict that is now virtually absent because of the present lack of interagency contact.

SCENARIO II

Patient autonomy: problems of freedom and constraint

Authority is diametrically opposed to the concept which has recently been popular in clinically oriented social work, namely, the right of the individual to self-determination. How far can society allow its members to go in self-destruction, particularly

Janet E. Weindandy, "Techniques of Service," in *Families Under Stress*. Youth Development Center, Syracuse: Syracuse University Press, 1962, pp. 14 passim.

when it endangers the rights and safety of others? The concept of the employment of authority in social work is predicated on the theory that social workers represent sanctioned values of society and as such have an obligation to help their clients internalize these values. I believe that the clients often sense this authority more fully than the social worker does. We have too long bent over backwards being understanding and nonmoralistic and nonjudgmental, which has often served no useful purpose to the client. Other agencies in the community have set certain standards of behavior. The schools have expected children to be regular and prompt in attendance, and to conform to certain standards of cleanliness and behavior. The Welfare expects clients to be honest about their resources, and has set up machinery to punish fraudulent behavior. Public Housing has set minimum standards for housekeeping, behavior, for protection of property and human safety, which are enforced differently depending on the age of the offender.

If he allows his children to truant, he may be charged with neglect; if he fails to provide proper physical care for the children or is abusive to them, they may be taken away from him; if he does not pay his rent or take adequate care of his property, he can be evicted; if he fails to support his family, he will be sent to jail. Call it threatening, if you will. It's a very useful device provided that the threats are not idle ones, but are backed up by substantial enforcement if necessary. And provided, also, that if some anxiety can be aroused in this way, the social worker stands ready to implement whatever program of improvement is agreed upon and sticks with the client long enough to obtain results.

Another fact is that for reasons which are not hard to understand, many adult clients in this group are immature in the psychosocial development; in plain basic English, they are kids themselves. They need and want, sometimes even ask for, controls. The only way I can see to help them emerge from their immaturity is through intelligent use of appropriate controls. . . .

NOTES

1 Public Law 89–749, Congress of the United States.
2 Ibid., p. 2.
3 Ibid., p. 3.
4 William R. Rosengren, *Medical Sectors, Public Health, and Orientations toward Clients*. Report to U.S. National Center for Health Services, 1974 (mimeograph).
5 Quoted in Rosengren, ibid., p. 37.

6   Ibid.
7   Ibid., p. 38.
8   Ibid.
9   Ibid.
10 Peter M. Blau and W. Richard Scott, *Formal Organizations*. San Francisco: Chandler, 1962.
11 George A. Silver, "Social Medicine at the Montefiore Hospital," *American Journal of Public Health*, 48 (June 1958), 724–731.
12 J. C. Matchar, F. F. Furatenberg, and H. P. Kalisch, "Comprehensive Medical Care," *Gerontologist*, 5 (1965), 125–128.
13 William Hubbard, "'Health Complex' Seen Superseding Present Hospital," *Medical News* (May 15, 1967).
14 E. R. Weinerman, R. S. Ratner, A. Robbins, and M. Lavenhar, "Yale Studies in Ambulatory Medical Care," *American Journal of Public Health*, 56 (1966), 1037–1056.
15 I. H. Strantz and W. R. Miller, "Developmental Interagency Coordination in a Program of Comprehensive Medical Care," *American Journal of Public Health*, 56 (May 1966), 785–796.
16 Ibid., p. 795.
17 Stephen Cang, "An Alternative to Hospital," *Lancet* (April 2, 1977), 742–743.
18 William R. Rosengren and Mark Lefton, *Hospitals and Patients*. New York: Atherton Press, 1969.
19 Mark Lefton, "The Role of the Counselor and Agency Structure," unpublished ms. no date.
20 Albert Wessen, "The Apparatus of Rehabilitation," in *Sociology and Rehabilitation*, M. B. Sussman, Ed. Washington: Vocational Rehabilitation Administration, 1966, p. 153.
21 Rosengren, op. cit.

SUGGESTED READINGS

Constance T. Fischer and S. L. Brodsky, Eds., *Client Participation in Human Services*. New Brunswick, N.J.: Trans-Action Books, 1978.
A series of articles dealing with the role of clients in the formulation of agency policy in the fields of health and welfare services.

Eliot Freidson, *Patients' Views of Medical Practice*. New York: Russell Sage, 1961.
A careful study of one of the first and largest attempts to achieve comprehensive patient care, indicating the complexity of the "doctor-patient" relationship when the solo fee-for-service model is abandoned.

William Glaser, *Social Settings in Medical Organizations*. New York: Atherton Press, 1967.
A comparison of how several European countries address the problems of medical care.

Andie L. Knutson, *The Individual, Society, and Health Behavior*. New Brunswick, N.J.: Trans-Action Books, 1969.
A textbook, primarily for health professions students, which is a useful insight into the social and social psychological views of health conveyed to present-day health students.

Charles E. Lewis et al., *A Right to Health*. New York: Wiley-Interscience, 1976.
An interdisciplinary approach to the problems of the extension of access to primary care, covering economic, social, political, legal, and ethical issues.

John B. McKinlay, Ed., *Processing People*. New York: Holt, Rinehart and Winston, 1975.
Nine original review-length articles on various kinds of service organizations and their relationships to their clients.

————~~~————

Established medicine "digs in"

As if to establish their own virtue, many medical leaders obsequiously court the public favor with pronouncement of "Shucks, we don't really care about money and such. All we want is to go on being dedicated doctors."

Baloney! While these image-polishers grovel and fawn, the morale of the working doctors throughout the United States continues to reel and fall under the assaults from politicians, government regulators, and all those who secretly covet a piece of the action in what they perceive as being a lucrative field. . . . Yes, I know all about those doctors who reportedly earn a quarter of a million dollars a year, who cheat on Medicare and Medicaid billings, and who don't seem to give a damn about their patients anymore. But the majority of my colleagues still work more than a 60-hour week, still get up at night to see their sick patients, and still keep the word "care" in Medicare. . . . But it is in the area of working conditions that American doctors experience their greatest dissatisfactions today. Not in fringe benefits, paid vacations, or retirement plans but in the right to do for their patients what their training and conscience demand be done . . . and it is the one that is being the most eroded by a bevy of cost accountants, insurance actuaries, and other sharp-pencil boys whose fiscal decrees are now superseding the medical judgments of the doctors. The eternal enigma, however, is that doctors are traditionally judged by two standards—those of the healthy, who can enjoy the luxury of damning the medical profession in the abstract, and the sick, who want nothing spared in restoring them to the good health to which they are entitled . . . add to these an ever-tightening ring of regulation and restriction, of inspection, and increasing demand for accountability, and you rapidly convert an historically conscientious and trustworthy profession into one that is defensive and protectionistic.

It has been said that the adversary system compels

S. A. Marcus, M.D., president of the Union of American Physicians, *The Providence Sunday Journal*, April 9, 1978, p. C-19. Reprinted with permission.

excellence—this has been the cry of the malpractice attorneys as they nip at our flanks. But as these attorneys, self-seeking politicians, muck-raking authors, and consumerists rock the pedestal that has traditionally been accorded the healing profession, the automatic trade-off of trust for dedication that has always existed in the doctor-patient relationship has also been weakened. . . . We believe that there is indeed a price tag on a good doctor, and that society will get just what it is willing to pay for. . . . What is your opening offer?

CHAPTER 12

Emergent patterns of health care:
the search for moral stability in the midst
of a technological revolution

Any attempt to see emerging patterns within the maze of action and counteraction in the present medical scene is audacious and in one sense destined to failure. The institutions of modern medicine have been subject to so many crosscurrents of change and instability during the past two decades it behooves the members of a society that strives to implement elements of the democratic credo to raise basic questions as citizens and, as the future consumers of medical services, to take whatever participatory role seems appropriate in attempting to shape those changes in progress.

In a sense, the present medical scene simply evolved over a period of time. But there is no mandate that says that the former child—now well into its middle age—should develop into a Leviathan with the resultant public suppression of the "monster" brought about in the Hobbesian imagination. For if the public ceases to be the master of the very institutions which they share responsibility in creating, then Michel's oligarchy, the tyranny of the elite, may well be close at hand. It matters not whether the word "crisis" is used; what does matter is that the established and heretofore hallowed relationship of *asymmetry* between the practitioners of the medical arts and those on whom it is practiced has now been called into serious question. As a result, health and society now stand at a major turning point, and there are certainly possible profound consequences that will overshadow even the great technical advances of the past half-century. For as Daniel Callahan recently said:[1]

> Whether induced by internal or by external circumstances, every major social change in society forces a confrontation with its values. Nowhere is this more evident than in the changes that have been wrought in medicine. In earlier societies, people were necessarily fatalistic about illness; there was little the physician could offer beyond psychological comfort and palliation. Modern medicine, by contrast, commands a powerful arsenal of weapons to forestall death, relieve pain, cure malignancies, and rehabilitate the crippled. But this power, impressive as it is, is nevertheless still less than absolute, and thus it poses particularly

difficult questions of a kind which previous generations had no need to consider.

If death can be forestalled, for how long and in what circumstances should it be? At what point does rehabilitation of the crippled cease to be of benefit to society? If one malignancy can be cured only to set the stage for death by another, just what, if anything, is gained? Medicine has not conquered death, nor is it likely to. But within that limit its power continues to increase, and it is precisely this increase that compels a reexamination of our basic ethical attitudes and premises toward it.

Consider only some of modern medicine's more obvious powers. Effective contraceptives and safe, legal abortions allow a choice in the number of children a couple will bear, while population pressures force another and perhaps different choice. Advances in amniocentesis and prenatal diagnosis are gradually permitting the avoidance of the birth of children with certain defects. The possibility of controlling both the quantity and their genetic quality has obvious and enormous ramifications for traditional sex roles, family life, composition of the work force, and patterns of children rearing.

If one moves from procreation and birth to the other end of the spectrum developments have no less important implications. An ability artificially to sustain life by machines compels newer and more precise definitions of "death" (and, for that matter, "life"). A capacity to transplant organs, to cure the disease of some systems, to keep people alive (but not necessarily happy) demands that one ask what kind of a life is worth living and what kind of death is worth pursuing. That is to ask, in the end, about "death with dignity," about euthanasia, about suicide, about ceasing "useless" medical treatment.

Between the extremes of birth and death, medicine is learning how to manipulate and, in some cases, control human behavior. Psychosurgery, the techniques of depth psychiatry and behavior modification, and psychotropic drugs all offer the promise, and in many cases the reality, of medical intervention in human emotion and cognition. But what could this kind of intervention do to traditional Western notions of autonomy and self-determination? Take aggression in society: Should medicine be made to find alternatives to bankrupt penal systems? Should it become involved in the legal system, for example, by defining "normality" and "deviancy?" In short, what should the role of medical technology be in serving society's broad political and social needs?

FREEDOM VERSUS CONSTRAINT

These are profound questions centering around the enduring issue of the rights of humans vis-à-vis their social order, and are questions previous generations did not have to face. For they crystallize and bring up to date the great American experiments in government by the will of those governed, experiments that intrigued the likes of

Rousseau and the Scottish moralists, who so profoundly influenced the Jeffersonian ideal: If people are born with an "inherent" propensity to live in accord with the canons of "right reason," then logically what kind of political power should they live under? Locke's answer was that it should be a government (or *social order*) of consent. The logic of democratic rationalism was that since men and women are born with a nature for freedom, then when living with others in organization, they will not, if rational, establish an order that makes them less free or equal than they would be in the state of their original nature. Thus, the precursors to the American Declaration of Independence and Constitution envisioned a social order that would restrict only those individuals who do not live according to sound moral reason, but it must be a social order to which all consent. Rousseau took a similar democratic-liberal perspective toward the events of his time. His solution was found in the idea of the "general will"—an overarching agreement among *most* men, the very existence of which gave men a moral claim on their government and therefore on the social institutions to which their consent is freely given, and from which they are obliged to withdraw when the social order becomes no longer "free."

This generalized standard of voluntary participation of citizens, but only in those institutions which are more "free" than "nonfree," has been the vortex around which political debate, formulation, and reformulation has swirled—especially over the past 100 years with regard to the major social institutions of government, education, religion, family, and thought and expression.

But up until the past two decades medicine has evolved and developed into a position of enormous power and influence escaping almost completely unscathed from the maturation processes of freedom and voluntarism that have so importantly shaped all other major social institutions during that same period of time.

But in spite of this, it is only within the past decade that the word "crisis" has been attached to the American system of health care delivery. The term refers to runaway medical care costs; the increasing creation of sophisticated and expensive technologies and hardware; the uneven distribution of medical resources; the absence of a mechanism for ensuring a continuing supply of medical specialists and paraprofessionals in the proper number and in the appropriate places; and the growing awareness of the fact that the gap between the levels of health achieved by middle-class white people and that of minority members (blacks especially) is not significantly narrower than it was a half-century ago. A host of other problems are associated with questions of equality in health care, democratization in decision making in health affairs, and systems of consumer redress in instances in which the quality of health care comes into dispute.

There is a growing feeling that medical schools should be held more accountable for their actions; the extension of the idea that patients ought to have more "treatment-nontreatment" options and alternatives than the organization of medical practice has heretofore made available. There is a developing momentum around the notion that the *most* health care is not necessarily the *best* medical care as well as the attitude that the relationships between patient and medical system ought to be a matter for negotiation and not necessarily one determined by status asymmetry, which has been so typical of the relationship for at least the past half-century.

Most observers—even a reluctant American Medical Association— seem to agree that *somewhere* down the road lies *some kind* of health program of national scope that will be designed to modify these situations and alleviate at least some of the pressure now being put on organized medicine.

In a poignant statement, the present state of stress may have been crystallized in the words of a "radical sociologist" at a recent national meeting of the American Sociological Association:[2]

> The Secretary of HEW is a military officer in the domestic front of the war against the people—the Department of which the man is head is more accurately described as the agency which watches over the inequitable distribution of preventable diseases, oversees the funding of domestic propaganda and indoctrination, the preservations of a cheap and docile labor force. . . . This assembly (of sociologists) here tonight is a conclave of high and low priests, scribes, intellectual valets, and their innocent victims, engaged in the mutual affirmation of a falsehood . . . the (sociological) profession is an outgrowth of nineteenth-century European traditionalism and conservatism, wedded to twentieth-century American Corporate liberalism . . . the professional eyes of the sociologist are on the down people, and the professional palm of the sociologist is stretched toward the up people . . . he is an Uucle Tom not only for this government and ruling class but for any.

HEALTH AS A RIGHT OF CITIZENSHIP

What appears to be occurring is the generalized redefinition of health care from a privilege set aside for those who are especially advantaged in the market forces of society, to a citizen's right possessed merely as a function of holding membership in society. Indeed, the United States stands alone as the only modernized society in which medical care is not regarded, both *de jure* and *de facto* as a *moral* right (which it *is* in the ideology of American society) as well as a *civil* right (which it is not in American reality). And it is this discrepancy between the *ethical morality* of medicine and the civil status it actually occupies that *is* the vortex in which American medicine is now swirling.

The aim of this final chapter is twofold: first, to examine some of the social processes that have brought about this confrontation between morality and rights; second, to suggest some of the *ethical* dilemmas this confrontation recently has brought to the surface.

There is now a growing number of "interested parties" who are increasingly laying claims—based upon rights of citizenship—to have a voice in the determination of medical policy organization and operation. Thus rights of citizenship, rooted in the democratization process, are now meeting rights of medical "expertise" head on. The first is rooted in the traditional association between bureaucracy and democracy; the second, in the link between organizational autonomy and elitism.[3]

All modern formal organizations are increasingly expected to perform commonwealth functions and are increasingly subject to the possible and imminent withdrawal of monetary and nonmonetary resources and other supports as well as to having goals imposed upon them by external agents and publics.

Eliot Freidson has recently written of the ambiguities that all modern professions—especially medicine—will encounter in the near or immediate future as a consequence of the increasing complexity of the larger social environments of which they are but a part.[4]

Critical to the ideas discussed here is that the external agents who are the consumers of organizational products are increasingly also the sources of organizational resources and constitute the publics that view the organization as a general-use resource. It is the social organization of these forces—*commonweal-oriented publics, general resource pressure*, and *resource providers as product consumers*—that has created a "nutcracker" effect on medical institutions.

MEDICAL CHARTERS AND JUSTIFICATIONS

Despite the underlying theme that pervades much thinking, it is axiomatic that medical organizations do not exist *in vacuo*. At the macrolevel they are linked to society and exist as organizations only insofar as they have achieved both a "charter" and "justification." The charter of an organization involves a set of contractual arrangements defining the degree to which it is in control of goal determination with respect both to ends goals and means goals.[5] *Ends goals* are the future states or outcomes the organization is attempting to bring about. In specific cases, these may be the defense of a nation by force in the case of the military, the provision of rehabilitative services for felons in the case of some prisons, supplying certified graduates in the case of colleges and universities, and so on. In large measure it is the chartering circumstances of an organization that determine whether end goals shall fall under the authority of primary organization members (as in the case of some private hospitals) or shall be located in the hands of external others (as is becoming more typically the case in many public medical institutions).

Means goals are those internal structures and procedures by which ends goals are realized. Again, these procedural elements may be dictated through authorities internal to the organization (as is the predominating pattern in most medical practices) or by external agents and publics (as is becoming more typical in medical establishments).

In addition to *charters*, which constitute the main structural environmental link, medical organizations are also linked symbolically to the society as a consequence of their need to be *justified*. That is, whereas the charter determines whether or not an organization will be allowed to determine its goals, the nature of its justification determines whether or not those means and ends will be judged worth pursuing in both a monetary and a nonmonetary sense. Quite aside from the capacity of medicine to determine and produce outcomes, it will not continue to exist unless it is regarded by external interested parties as supplying some *wanted* and *desirable output*. For, as Thompson says:[6]

> The relationship between an organization and its task environment is essentially one of exchange, and unless the organization is judged by those in contact with it as offering something desirable, it will not receive the inputs necessary for survival.

Furthermore, both charter and justification differ markedly depending upon whether the focal organization is in the public or private sphere. The charter of the private organization is grounded in its competitive market position. Should its competitive position be eroded, it must seek ways to shore it up, and in the typical case this involves relinquishing some degree of control of means and ends. This may take the form, for example, of research/training grants in medical schools, reliance on outside public relations firms in the case of some HMOs, or voluntary citizen support groups in the case of hospitals. By way of contrast, the charter of the *public* organization is defined by the scope of its mandate—narrow and specific in the case of the Internal Revenue Service, but broad and extensive in the case of many state departments of health. In either case, however, there is a failure to compete successfully in the private sphere.

In sum, medical organizations exist *qua* organizations within some nexus of charter and justification. Thus, autonomy is always problematic. What is at issue is a struggle for control of organizational means and ends. As a consequence, medicine is now subject to the continuous threat of disequilibrium from these sources, and contemporary pressures on modern formal organizations seem to be more highly diffused now than in the past. It remains to depict a *model of organizations* that lends itself to an understanding of these pressures on medicine, both to indicate the nature of this conflict and to suggest some of its possible effects upon contemporary medical institutions. The basic components of such a model are shown in Figure 12.1.

Modern health organizations must be open enough to outside forces to acquire needed resources, to identify and react to possible criticism from the external environment, and to find places there in which to place their products.

If an organization's mediating technologies are insufficiently open to the environment to serve effectively as buffers and sensors, the organization runs the risk of encountering an accumulated and perhaps overwhelming wave of intrusions upon the operations of its core technologies. On the other hand, if the mediating technologies become too open to the environment, the organization's core technologies may be continually distracted or interrupted. In the extreme circumstance, the organization's goals—and therefore its resources and technologies— may fall under the command of external entities and be turned to totally different uses and purposes. Its "charter" therefore becomes endangered.

Finally, ineffective output technologies are equally threatening to the organization. To the extent that a product unacceptable to society is exported, the organization will lose its market and, in the long run, its resource inputs. On the other hand, if the organization becomes too

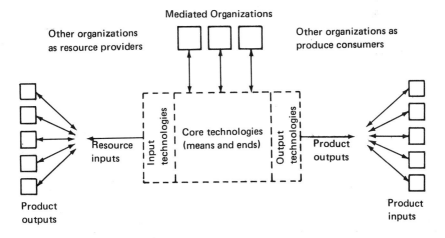

FIGURE 12.1 Organizational nature of inputs and outputs.

Source: Adapted from William R. Rosengren, "A 'Nutcracker' Theory of Modern Organizations," <u>Sociological Focus</u>, 8 (August 1975). By permission.

sensitive to negative feedback from the receiving environment, its core technology may come under the command of agents and entities in the receiving environment, and "justification" may be either undermined or destroyed.

Medical environments consist largely of *other* organizations, each one of which is involved in processes of input, production, mediation, and output identical to those of the focal organization. But medical organization resources are by definition "scarce," as are markets into which organizational products must be placed. Thus a paradoxical situation arises in that organizations are forced to distinguish themselves from *other* similar organizations so as to be able to market their products, thereby sustaining both their charter and their justification. But by the same token, organizations must declare themselves as sufficiently grounded in the mainstream of related organizational activity to secure the necessary resource inputs. Hence there is likely to be considerable strain between the focal organization and those it is attempting to maneuver into a consumer role. *The weaker the organization's control over its means and ends*—that is to say, the *less autonomous its charter and the less persuasive its justification*—the more likely it will be to "take in" unwanted resources and be forced to produce outputs that sustain the goal structures of the consuming organizations rather than its own.

Thus, a situation of *unstable interdependence* typifies the relation between medical organizations, with tenuous autonomy creating the stage for strategies of interorganizational conflict.

In general, therefore, the fact that medical delivery organizations are involved in the production process implies that pressures from the external environment are continually influencing the core technologies of organizations by altering the conditions of resource input and the operation of organizational means and ends during the production processes, as well as through negative feedback aimed to redefine the nature of the organizational product.

Typically, the pressured health organization was heretofore able to counter these efforts at interpenetration by specific buffering units. Hence the near-modern organization might have been able to escape the full implications of the democratization effect insofar as the circumstances producing pressure were for the most part independently conceived and organized—one set of external contingencies at the input end and a second, and quite separate, set at the output end.

In spite of this, recent extensions of concepts of *civil rights* and *participatory democracy* have brought about a transformation of these relationships between medicine and society. The heretofore separate and isolated pressure-inducing external agents are being assembled into an institutionalized array of collectivities and publics now capable of exerting continual and concentrated influence upon the principal structures of health organizations.

This development seems most readily explained by viewing modern medical organizations first as being currently subject to *commonweal expectations,* and second as being regarded as *general resources* that may legitimately be reoriented—by coercion if necessary—to serve the goals and purposes of multiple external publics.

ORGANIZATIONS AS GENERAL RESOURCES AND THE PROBLEM OF MEMBERSHIP

The prototypical cases of organizations as general-use resources are found in the tangible goods sector, where production systems can be "tooled up" to manufacture a wide range of durable or consumable goods. That is, although any one factory may be a single production system at one point in time, a large number of them are adaptable as multiple or alternate production systems. Obviously, decisions to alter these kind of systems are made by those who hold primary membership. Decision-making power, therefore, is held by those who regard the organization as their "property." Such decisions are made as a result of right of ownership. In a parallel sense, the resources taken into such organizations are understood to be the property of the ownership group and may be disposed of in nearly any way that will further the established goals of the organization.

It is equally clear that also in the service sector, such as medicine, organizations possess general resources—elements such as prestige, influence, talent, administrative and policy discretion, planning capabilities and processes, and so on, in addition to more direct monetary components such as budget flexibility, material technologies, staff and support personnel, fixed and consumable equipment, and buildings. These resources also are derived from and are rooted in processes of input from society. But organizational history suggests that until very recently the power to make decisions regarding these service organization resources lay in the hands of the primary memberships groups— that is, those persons regarded as the continuing full-time members, the appointed staff. Thus teachers decided what was to transpire in schools, physicians what took place in hospitals, custodial personnel in psychiatric hospitals, and so on. In the sphere of human service there is a "property-right" parallel that places resource allocation decisions as to organizational means and ends in the hands of those who are counterparts to "owners." In this situation the consumer can only very indirectly influence such processes and decisions through his or her participation in the market.

But profound change is brought about when a public awareness of the general resource capabilities of human service organizations occurs at the same time as a broad extension of the concepts of rights of citizenship and participatory democracy. It is this link between this diffusion of public awareness and citizenship *and* elevated and expanded commonweal definitions and expectations of such organization that creates a new order of tension and conflict for medical organizations that were heretofore subject only to the specific and organizationally isolated sources of conflict and pressure described earlier:[7]

> The issue posed by commonweal organizations is that of external democratic control—the public must possess the means of controlling the ends served by these organizations. . . . The challenge facing these organizations, then, is the maintenance of efficient bureaucratic mechanisms that effectively implement the objectives of the community, which are ideally decided upon, at least in our society, by democratic methods.

The first implication of this is that under commonweal conditions the legitimately *participating membership* includes *all* those with a declared and aroused interest in the organization, not merely the actors directly involved. Second, these same agents and individuals may *also* be *members of the publics* that provide the necessary organizational resources *as well as members of* those publics that are the *required consumers* of organizational products. Hence, when framed in a conflict model, modern health organizations are caught between the dual—and perhaps themselves conflicting—commonweal expectations of multiple resource publics, who may view the organization at the same time as a general resource capable of serving *other* aroused public interests, which are *also* essential to the organization as a consequence of being members of consuming units as well. This effect may be depicted as in Figure 12.2.

Inasmuch as the medical organization may be viewed as both a general-use resource as well as commonweal "property," relevant publics may cease to provide needed resources—*including cooperative participation*—until the organization acquiesces to what may be transitory or momentary expectations of change. Or external agents may refuse to use the organization until such time as its products, material or otherwise, are made more specifically fitted to the goals of the consuming units. Or mediated publics may harass the core technology to such an extent that means and ends become altered in ways that even more fully disarray the ongoing input and output equilibriums.

In short, *publics*, as distinct from specific external social *entities*, have emerged as the most salient elements in the environment of medical organizations. Moreover, when these now publicly expressed external interests take the form of commonweal expectations on the one hand and the form of organizations as general-use resources on the other, then the modern organization falls under the triple threat of withdrawal of resource, interruptions of its activities in the here and now, and the withdrawal of a willingness to consume organizational products. It is for this reason that the "nutcracker" metaphor seems an apt one for these new environmental circumstances of modern organizations. That is to say, such organizations are now exposed to considerable risk of being "crushed" from without.

There is a further exacerbating condition that allows an extension of the metaphor to include the risk of being "exploded" from within. That is the fact that the processes and pressures of commonweal expectations and general resource definitions are not limited to those who are nominally "outside" the organization but extend also to those who are "inside" as well—particularly lower-level and temporary members such as students, clients, recruits, patients, inmates, recipients, workers and others of the rank and file. The active cooperation of the consumer in the production processes of schools, social service agencies, hospitals, prisons, and other "service" systems is absolutely vital to such organizations.[8] Moreover, under the conditions here described, such cooperation can no longer be taken for granted but must be nurtured and sustained by means heretofore not required. When there is public awareness of desired alternatives in the commonweal functions

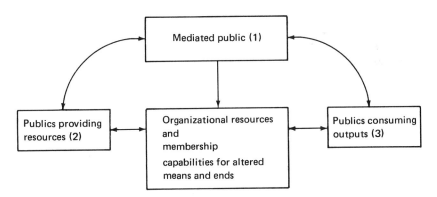

FIGURE 12.2 The "nutcracker" effect on commonweal organizations.

Notes:
Under commonweal conditions, quasi-members constitute publics that provide resources, are also mediated publics, and represent consuming publics.
    Under commonwealth and general resource conditions:
    (1) Mediated publics interrupt the ongoing core technologies.
    (2) Providers of resources withdraw resources.
    (3) Consumers of resources withdraw consumption.

Source: Adapted from William R. Rosengren, "A 'Nutcracker' Theory of Modern Organizations," Sociological Focus, 8 (August 1975). By permission.

of organizations, then the potential for truculence, recalcitrance, sabotage, and even open rebellion is increased.

Without a conception such as this, the recent internal and external turmoil of colleges and universities, the ongoing struggle in the armed services and in their associated training academies with regard to the nonmilitary aspects of military life, the pressures being imposed upon the business community through the "consumerism" movement, the welfare rights movement, the withdrawal of traditional allegiances to religious institutions, and the struggle for control over organizational means and ends in medical systems can be misinterpreted as erratic, isolated, irrational, and violent episodes only vaguely associated with ongoing processes of social change. The approach expressed here is that these events are neither casual nor episodic; nor can they be understood by any other simplistic explanation. They represent more fundamental structural changes in the relationships between citizens and the establishment.

The conflict view set forth here is a self-conscious focus upon conflict rather than upon equilibrium on the medical scene. If it does in fact dramatize some newly developed elements in the contemporary health scene then it should also follow that medical organizations do more than merely "adapt" and "adjust" to external contingencies of strife and contention. Rather, they actively engage in coping with threats from the social environment.

The complexity of the American medical system is so extensive, and the external "interested parties" so numerous, that it is not at all surprising that the competition for control over its elements is so intense. In analyzing this competition for control, Alford writes:[9]

> The *pluralist* or *market perspective* essentially accepts the struggle between interest groups as inevitable and even necessary. This perspective would argue that all of these groups are created and sustained by the technical and organizational requirements of a highly differentiated society and political system. The key professional functions of biomedical research and qualified physician training require that considerable autonomy be given to professional organizations. The key organizational functions of hospital administration, health planning, and the coordination of public health services requires that considerable power and resources be given to those agencies and programs seeking to integrate the various complements of the health delivery system. In this view, the pluralism and seeming "fragmentation" are endemic and even healthy, because they guarantee diversity by maintaining competition between alternative modes of providing health care.

A major point of view which is counterpoint to the pluralist or market framework is what Alford calls the *institutional* or *class perspective:*[10]

. . . the defects in the performance of health institutions are duplicated in many other areas of American society, and that the roots of these defects lie deep in the structure of a class society and create great difficulties for the effective articulation of social needs as political demands and their translation into legislation and subsequent administrative implementation. In this view, professionals and bureaucrats and planners are differentiated sectors of class-based and class-oriented institutions, performing necessary functions within the severe limits imposed by the political and economic privileges held by a relatively small part of the population.

And, as Alford's argument implies, the programs of action implicit in the *pluralistic explanation* are most comfortable with a "medical" model of illness and the *ad hoc* development of palliative programs that would be "additives" to the present mosaiclike medical system. On the other hand, the social action implicit in the *institutional* or *class* perspective seems to fit more closely with a "social model" of illness and leads to far more radical restructuring of the entire pluralistic medical differentiation into a new and more monolithic form.

THE POSITIONS OF ESTABLISHED MEDICINE

But whichever position one wishes to adopt, both acknowledge the conflict of interest that the present polyglot system has generated, and the proponents of neither view express much surprise by the fact that the leading platform for the voice of organized medicine, the American Medical Association, continues to adopt a posture that would preserve the status quo while, in Wilensky and Lebaux's terms, "We move toward the welfare state but we do it with ill grace, carping and complaining all the way."[11]

In spite of the fact that the American Medical Association counts only about 50 percent of the licensed physicians in this country as members, and in spite of the likelihood of further government intervention in the field of health, the AMA remains a powerful force in control of its own house. It resists where possible the establishment of formal peer review processes that would involve citizen participation as well as colleague controls; it has resisted—sometimes successfully and sometimes unsuccessfully—action by the Federal Price Commission on limiting increases in physician's fees; it remains generally opposed to the creation of group practice forms as well as prepayment systems such as the Health Maintenance Organization; it is generally opposed to the establishment of physicians' unions, which would serve as competitors to the AMA's long-standing monopoly of collective physician power. Moreover, it continues to spend a considerable amount of money in public relations activity so as to polish its own public image and therefore soften the cutting edge of its political activities. It continues to do battle with the Internal Revenue Service in the promulgation of final rules concerning the tax-exempt status of revenue received from advertising income derived from AMA publications. It has maintained a strong voice in the actual implementation and control of the Professional Standards Review Organizations, legislated to monitor the quality of medical services paid through Medicare and Medicaid programs, and continues to voice the warning that the proliferation of Health Maintenance Organizations "could lead to a monolithic system" of health care in this country. And, while all of this "political medicine" is taking place, the AMA still possesses enough energy and enthusiasm to throw its surplus weight in areas of public policy connected with affairs that are medical in only the most remote terms.

Quite aside from these, there are a number of specific contemporary issues that fire the points of dissension and conflict in the present ambiguous position occupied by the institutions of medicine—citizens' domain or rights of "ownership." Perhaps the entire issue of patients' rights is most central to the debate.

INDIVIDUAL RIGHTS OR GENERAL WELFARE?

Is the patient to be relegated to a position of total asymmetry, treated as if he or she were an inanimate object, and one whose body belongs to others? The debate over abortion versus the right to life is prototypical of this dispute and centers around the question as to whether the enjoinment in the "sick role" to "obey the doctor's orders" does not have—especially in the case of chronic illness—its pathological form in the license to "do with me what you will." The issue is no longer merely a problem of individual negotiation, but has taken the form of legal precedents as well as established policy. But the issue is complex in that constitutional rights are claimed to be held on both sides—medical establishment as well as patient. Consider the landmark court decision in the State of Maryland in involving *Snyder* v. *Holy Cross Hospital* (352 A.2d 334). The following summarizes the case:

In 1976 Mr. Snyder, who happened to be an Orthodox Jew, sued Holy Cross—a Catholic Hospital—to get an enjoinment against conducting a post mortem examination on the body of his son who had died in the hospital suddenly at the age of 18. The son had died in the ambulance on his way to the hospital, and being so notified the state deputy medical examiner directed the hospital to conduct a post mortem. This was challenged by the father on religious grounds, and the religious prohibition was corroborated by two rabbis. In spite of this, the court ruled that the post mortem had to be performed in the *public interest*. The decision of the court made it clear that the first amendment right of free exercise of religion is a critical part of any patient's "bill of rights," but the rights of society outweigh the rights of the individual when individual rights conflict with those of society. As the court wrote, "Freedom to believe is absolute, but freedom to act is not. Conduct is subject to regulation for the protection of society. The state, by general and nondiscriminatory legislation, may safeguard the peace, good order, and comfort of the community without unconsitutionally invading individual liberties. A person may not, under the color of religion, disturb the good order, peace or safety of the State, infringe the laws of morality, or injure others in their natural civil rights or religious truths."

As the Court summarized:[13]

We find that the religious practices of the father were properly abridged by the State in the application of the Statutes concerning post-mortem examinations. There were compelling State interests which outweigh the interest of the father in his religious tenets. The State has a compelling interest to safeguard the peace, health and good order of the community. To this end it needs to know when a death results from a criminal act or when the cause of death is such that the health and well-being of others may be adversely affected. Here the evidence was legally sufficient to establish that the cause of Neal Snyder's death could not be determined without an autopsy, and the interest of the State in ascertaining the true cause by an autopsy out-weighed the interest of the father in his religious tenets.

It is not in error to conclude that the civil rights of patients is serious business and can in no way now be taken lightly either by courts, patients, or medical administrators and practitioners. What is at issue is the shifting balance between human rights and civil obligations.

If this much can be made on behalf of the civil rights of a dead person, those of living patients are far more intricate, especially involving the critical issue of how much information patients have a right to possess in determining their willingness or unwillingness to subject themselves to medical treatment. In general, it would seem that the "good old days" when the doctor alone could decide how much will be told to patients have now passed. The issue was the subject of a legal decision in 1977 in the case of *Lecher* v. *New York State*:[14]

ROBERT AND LAURA HOWARD, HUSBAND AND WIFE OF EASTERN EUROPEAN BACKGROUND. THEY WERE POTENTIAL CARRIERS OF THE TAY-SACHS DISEASE. The defendant was an Obstetrician and Gynecologist who treated Laura Howard for two pregnancies. This lawsuit was brought with respect to their child Melissa. She was born afflicted with and eventually died of the Tay-

Sachs disease. The plaintiff-parents alleged that the defendant doctor knew or should have known that, being of Eastern European background, they were potential carriers of the disease. They further alleged that tests were available both to determine whether they were Tay-Sachs carriers, and also whether the fetus was afflicted with the disease. It was further alleged that the defendant doctor was negligent in the treatment of the mother and that he failed among other things either to take a proper genealogical history of the plaintiffs or to properly evaluate the history that he did take. Finally, and most importantly, it was alleged that the physician, Dr. Lecher was negligent in that he failed to advise them of the possibility of the taking of tests of them and of the fetus with regard to the disease. According to the plaintiffs, had they been advised that the fetus had Tay-Sachs, they would have terminated the wife's pregnancy by means of a legal abortion. The Supreme Court, Appellate Division, of the State of New York held that the parents could not recover for emotional harm since the injury from which the parents alleged emotional harm stemmed, was not suffered by them but rather was suffered by their child.

The court went on to say, that "if an infant is to endure a life of defects, it must be because that was the moral choice made by his parents and not because they were given no alternative choice to the negligence or private morality of a physician." The principle at stake, so concluded the court, applied equally to any other medical situations involving the life and health of patients; no doctor may hold back any pertinent facts relating to diagnosis, treatment, or prognosis. Even in those instances in which the physician may judge that a patient does not have the emotional stamina to handle bad news, the physician still has the obligation to inform the patient's family. That patients must be given enough information to make intelligent decisions regarding their own health care appears to be the nub of the matter.

Not only is the question of the patient's right to know now a matter for court dispute, it is also the subject of considerable research as what levels of patient knowledgeability opitimize healthful case outcomes.

And this issue of patients' knowledgeability—and therefore willing cooperation in health regimens—has recently been the object of concern for the teaching of self-dialysis for kidney patients in the home,[15] in the appropriateness or inappropriateness of the adoption of the classic sick role for cardiac patients,[16] the role of nurses in conveying useful information to patients to lessen their medical dependency,[17] the patient as a participant in the diagnostic process,[18] the role of patient knowledge and beliefs in securing compliance to medical regimens,[19] the problem of patients' rights in regard to hemodialysis and kidney transplants—including the removal of kidneys from cadavers,[20] and the use of threats and strategies of interpersonal manipulation by medical practitioners in forestalling patient-initiated termination of medical care and regimens.[21] All of these and others hinge around the issue of patients' *right to know*, and its effects upon unbridled professional autonomy on the one hand and individual freedom of choice on the other.

Similar issues are at stake in some of the possible unanticipated consequences of the equal-rights-for-women movement in which role parity for women may in fact increasingly subject women to the life-and-death risks more common to spheres of activity heretofore more or less reserved for men. Do, in fact, human rights supersede the growing conception of "rights to health," or are the relationships between the two still far too new to foretell the final outcome? In any event, it seems clearly the case that the entire issue of patients' rights is a long way from being resolved, and the courts are likely to be busy in this regard for some time to come. A case in point is a suit presently before the New York State Courts in which the father of an 8-year-old victim of cancer charges that his son is being held a "prisoner" at a health spa hospital in New York, against his will and the will of his parents, being forceably subjected to chemotherapy treatments. And this is in spite of the fact that after a period of treatment with laetrile for Hand-Scheuller-Christian disease, the child experienced a spontaneous remission in the Caribbean that his American doctors cannot explain.[22]

A further set of unresolved points of conflict have to do with determining the legitimate boundaries of medical intervention and responsibility, and particularly the increasingly fine lines that must be drawn to distinguish medical research involving human beings and medical treatment as such. Are there special ethical standards that must come into play when the "research" components of medical regimen come to predominate over its "treatment" aspects?

MEDICAL CARE: TREATMENT OR RESEARCH?

An additional consideration, which relies very heavily on Parsons' insight, is that patients in some ways resemble the subjects of research enterprises.[23] Using that parallel, we may take the position that all service organizations are in some sense experimental in nature. The guarantees that they provide are not ironclad. This is similar to Weber's observation that "science" tends to be self-correcting, and by this means it sets forth as a principal societal function performed by medical organizations today.

The essentials of the argument are as follows: Since *no* organization has a completely viable technology, exchanges with clients are to some degree experimental. Experimental activities acquire some of the characteristics of a scientific endeavor. Scientists try to correct and perfect whatever it is they do—to do things more effectively or to do different things that attain a higher level of effectiveness. But since these processes occur against a complex social backdrop, the result can be a very odd mix indeed.

At the initial coming together of patient and practitioner, the practitioner makes an effort to determine just how stable the patient is and to elect the most plausible means of delivering a service that will be durable. The patient tries to make a similar kind of assessment as to the credibility of the practitioner. Hence a "contract" is made, although in fact it may be faulted at a later time. It may turn out, for example, that during the course of treatment either the client or the organization may acquire some additional information about the other that reveals that the original contract, as agreed upon, was a poor one. The patient may decide that he or she agreed to give too much for too little; the organization may make a similar judgment, or decide that the original values brought by the client were too meager, and so on.

Medical organizations, on their side, often contend that patients give them poor histories, fail to make payment when due, and so forth. In spite of this, let us assume that most professionals try to do the very best job for the client of which they feel themselves capable. Given that assumption, as they gain more knowledge about patients during the treatment process, they may often feel obliged to break the original bargain and make a new contract.

Let us take hospitals as a typical case. A patient may enter surgery upon the advice of his or her general practitioner in order to have a hernia corrected. During the course of surgery the doctor might discover some other malady, heretofore unknown. If this is thought to be operable, chances are very good that the contract will be drastically altered while the patient is still under anesthesia. The doctor might, of course, consult first with some of the patient's original cosigners (husband, wife, etc.) in order to gain some validity for changing the rules of the game unbeknownst to the other party. But even if the doctor frankly informs the patient of the desirability of a new contract, it is unlikely that the patient will not agree to it. This is one additional function of professional dominance and client trust in medicine.

This is a pure case wherein the new contract presumably is of equal value to both the patient and the practitioner. The patient gets a larger increment of health than had been bargained for, while the medical profession has performed its self-correcting function properly, and perhaps even provided a valuable learning experience for interns and medical students. The fee may or may not be larger.

More poignant cases, however, are those instances in which the medical or psychiatric staff (mustering whatever professional domi-nance they can) determine that the patient is "not ready" for discharge, and hence void the original agreement in its entirety. The very same forces, it should be said, are at work on individual staff members, too.

In psychiatric hospitals—elite ones especially—renegotiation of patient status is most confused indeed. It is difficult to assess the patient's original worth in the first place, so it is hard to come to an agreement as to the conditions of treatment. And as hospitalization continues, values shift almost daily.

One fact that relates to what has been said is that the medical organization can redefine values and make them stick, whereas the individual patient cannot. The staff members can mobilize more re-sources than can patients, so they can limit the service choices avail-able to potential patients.

It is important now to consider just what is meant by servicing in the generic sense. *The delivery of a medical service constitutes a cor-rection of a perceived defect in values carried by medical clients.*

And it is in this increasingly large area of ambiguity—the mix of medical research with medical treatment—where the human rights of patients may be most at issue and where issues of medical ethics are brought into bold relief.

In large measure, the efficacy and appropriateness of medical treatments of all kinds are founded on a statistical model of probability; that is, the determination to employ a technique is presumably based upon whether or not the patient can expect to benefit from it at a *reasonable* level of probability. And it is at the 50-50 point of prob-ability that such a determination—especially in the case of chronic illness—where "pure" statistics are inadequate, and where questions of the quality of human life and the actual risk of trauma enter the equation. And it is in the "gray" area of research and treatment where the benefits to the practitioners may exceed the possible benefits to clients, especially where quality of life becomes critical. What happens to one's sense of worth and personal integrity to live with a vital organ that was once a part of some other person? Is life as a neutered quadraplegic worth living at all? At what point in the aging process does a patient's *will* take precedence over medical "imperatives"? Is it enough to tell a preoperative patient that, according to "available data" he or she stands only 25 chances out of 100 of dying as a result of the medical procedure to be entered into? How shall medical zeal (and presumably therefore advances in medicine) be balanced against a more holistic view of human life? What shall we do with the informa-tion that recent research in Chicago, in one of the leading centers for the use of hemodialysis, has produced information suggesting that in an undisclosed number of cases the procedure seems to lead to a new form of insanity and death; marked by facial grimacing, muscle spasms, a deterioration of the mental state, and later death? According to one report:[24]

> An important early symptom was a speech disturbance, including slurring, stuttering and hesitancy. Later the patients became confused and disoriented and ultimately lapsed into a vegetative state with death usually between three and nine months after diagnosis. Dunea [a physician in charge and noted as probably the nation's foremost authority on the new disease (labeled "dialysis dementia")] said that at the time the cases were occurring here, few had been reported elsewhere and the outbreak created a moral crisis among staff and patients.

How shall such information be handled in light of the reports that a second doctor claims success in treating some forms of "schizophrenia" through dialysis? How shall further knowledge advance without continued combinations of treatment and research? Who shall make these decisions, and what role in diffusing public information about such matters ought investigative reporting play in these determinations? Is it right that critical decisions concerning the quality and continuation of health and life be based upon medical judgments that are clearly "judgmental" in character and lend themselves to possible abuse of basic human rights?

THE SEARCH FOR ALTERNATIVES

Modern fads and fashion in "countermedicine" also lend themselves to this kind of abuse. Take the current popularity of the analysis of so-called "biorhythms" as a strategy for making critical life and career decisions. In professional sports, for example, whole careers can be strongly influenced by the managerial use of biorhythms. As psychologist Roger Johnson recently reported:[25]

> Sports provide a natural outlet for pop psychology. What better way to account for the mysterious ups and downs that cause victory and defeat? The latest fad is biorhythms. Like astrology, it would have us believe that our behavior is predictable and partly determined from the day of birth.
> Impressive evidence is cited. Arnold Palmer won the British Open in July 1962 when his physical, emotional, and intellectual cycles peaked at about the same time. Several weeks later, his loss in the Professional Golfers' Association championship was explained away because his cycles were in the negative phase. Bobby Fischer's only loss in the 1962 chess championship came on a critical day in his sensitivity cycle. In 1962, Mickey Mantle collapsed on the way to first base for the same reason.

Woody Hayes struck a television cameraman during a recent loss to Michigan, supposedly because he was at a low point of his intellectual and emotional cycles. But if Ohio State had won the football game, the experts surely would have pointed out that Hayes was in the positive phase of his physical cycle.

If coaches and athletes were serious about bodily rhythms, they would throw away their computer printouts and keep a detailed diary of their moods and habits. After many months or years, they might discover personal regularities. As Gay Luce, author of *Body Time* suggests, the formula for biorhythms is childish, but the underlying idea of biological cycles is not.

Biorhythms will surely continue to be sold to the public like toothpaste commercials. We will continue to be told that biorhythms are "endorsed" by Chris Evert, Jim Marshall, the Dallas Cowboys, and even the Las Vegas oddsmakers. This tells us a little about the athletes, but nothing about biorhythms.

Matters such as these relate more to the processes of *authentication* and *credibility* discussed earlier and less to objectively applied criteria of scientific validation. And as the number of "intransigent" medical problems proliferate, it is not reasonable to expect larger and larger number of instances in which the search for cures which weigh heavily in the direction of "miracle" cures will rest their cases on legally established precedents founded on some conception of patients' right to choose. Where authentication shifts to procedures approved through established medical means, the "public interest" is likely to be invoked over the individual's right to choose freely.

UNRAVELING THE PROBLEM OF DISTRIBUTED COSTS

One of the most serious contemporary issues in American medicine is that of costs—how much shall be paid and by whom? And central to this subject, and as yet not fully an issue for public scrutiny and debate, is the matter of how costs are distributed through the entire economic structure and process in the American economy. Direct medical costs can be rather accurately determined in the aggregate and in their per capita implications (see Chapter 3). But hidden costs are much more elusive to detect, and their impact upon inequality in health care costs is less easily revealed.

One issue has to do with how high-cost technologies in hospitals tend to be underused and yet are reflected in the total fees paid even by patients who do not use that technology. It would require close accounting scrutiny to determine to what extent the fees paid by patients with minor ailments actually bear the costs of rarely used diagnostic and treatment facilities; nor do we know much about how the high costs of medical education are in fact subsidized by the paying customer patients who enter such institutions because of the admission policies of a "rock." Nor is it entirely clear whether the "sliding scale" policy that makes it possible for poor people to receive much the same treatment as richer people in fact represents a subsidy for the rich by *disproportionately* charging the poorer patients. Take the following hypothetical case: Supposing the charge for a high-technology procedure for a patient with the capacity to pay is in the magnitude of $15,000 and suppose further that such a paying customer has accumulated $25,000 in surplus money (discretionary funds, we may call it). By this simple arithmetic, the paying customer may receive the needed treatment and still have $10,000 left over to spend for other purposes. The medical costs: high but not disastrous. But compare this situation with that of a poorer patient with a similar malady requiring identical treatment. The *noblesse oblige* principle underlying the "sliding scale" may reduce the direct costs from $15,000 to $5000, thus providing the same care for *one-third the cost;* surely a generous achievement. But perhaps not so strikingly so when the total family economies are taken into account, as in Table 12.1.

Hence, given the long-term deficit that the poor man suffers, the benefits of the largesse accruing from the sliding scale are, as far as he is concerned, largely illusory. More important is the fact that his future is now mortgaged for an untold number of working years, unless he and his family allow themselves to be divested completely of their assets in order to pay the balance—the loss of insurance policies, forfeiture of one's automobile, or even the mortgaging of one's home. In a more general sense, however, given the *disproportionate* money from total income that the poorer man pays, it is not at all difficult to construct any argument that the poorer man is in fact subsidizing the ad-

TABLE 12.1

Health care costs and the "sliding scale": a hypothetical example of a rich and a poor man

	A rich man	A poor man
Payment needed for medical treatment under "sliding scale"	$15,000	$5,000
Available discretionary funds	$25,000	$1,000
Remaining discretionary funds	$10,000	−$4,000 (net deficit)
Amount of future obligation or amount of expropriation	None	$4,000
Total net annual income	$60,000	$8,000
Percent of total annual income for medical treatment	25%	62%

vantaged position enjoyed by the richer man. Thus, in spite of the good intentions of the sliding-scale principle, the entire economic structure surrounding medical care can in fact produce these kinds of multiple inequities.

But what about the fact that very nearly everyone is now covered by some form of health insurance; why should we now worry about such accountings when third parties now pay? The answer to that goes beyond the mere fact that the costs of medical insurance premiums are reflected both in lower real wages paid to workers as well in higher price attached to goods and services purchased by consumers. Virtually every labor union in the country has now negotiated extensive medical insurance coverage for their memberships, and Blue Cross, Blue Shield, Medicare, and Medicaid now cover a vast number of treatment contingencies—even high-cost and long-term services (although the expropriation process is *still* activated at some point so that *one must be impoverished* in order to receive certain benefits).

There are two important dimensions of this type of coverage. First is that no one knows what proportion of the price of a Chevrolet or a suit of clothes in fact represents insurance premiums withheld from the wage structure and paid to insurance companies; it is certainly a significant proportion. More than that, however, is the specter that haunts the future in which the "blank check" principle for third-party payment is no longer honored. That is, medical technology, the medical division of labor, and the health expectations of consumer has reached a level in which it is largely assumed that *no costs* are too high to be borne somehow within the diverse and pluralistic system of payments that now prevails.

What, for example, will take place in the overall health care scene if and when a plan resembling the Kennedy-Korman Bill is passed into law that would provide for an absolute top limit on health care expenditures within the public sector? How will the semiautonomous components of the American medical division for service negotiate with one another for a portion of the total allocation? What services in this new "ecology of games" will undergo restrictions as a result of the negotiative process, and what services will be expanded? How will these new expansions of facilities and service availability be reflected in the number of persons who are drawn into the web of the service complex indicated in previous chapters? Will the process of expropriation proceed at a greater or less pace if service restrictions do occur? Will the growing pressure toward public control of quality of care result in the increased restriction upon "open growth" of medical facilities—including the establishment of offices for private practice, the expansion of existing health facilities, especially in the proprietary sphere, and will a large number of general hospitals that are now "too small" be forced to close? What substitutes for this potential lack of primary care will be made available, and how shall they be controlled? Will issues of quality control and accountability be increasingly subject to lay influences, or shall more centralized and bureaucratized authority systems increasingly take over these functions? In whichever case, what will be the effects of autonomy of the medical division of service on the one hand and freedom of choice of patients on the other.

These and a multitude of other questions will be certain to arise as the confrontation between "technical imperatives and organizational power" on the one hand and citizens' rights on the other matures over the coming decade. In a sense, if the central problems of medicine through the years of World War II were essentially *technical* in nature and those until the last years of the decade of the 1960s were primarily *organizational* in character, it seems clear to many that the central preoccupying questions concerning medicine and society for the foreseeable future will be largely *philosophical and moral* in tone. And as yet neither the medical community, the political community, nor the academic community has demonstrated any special wisdom in this sphere, and it may be precisely because of this lack of moral expertise that the public expression of Mill's "general will" will find new fertile ground in the affairs of health.

And in this sense, the sociology of medicine stands in a uniquely advantaged position in framing the present dilemmas in the public affairs of medicine by pointing to some of the central conflicts and ambiguities brought by the new manifestation of citizens' rights that the recent denouncement of medicine has made possible. In general, the theme seems to be one of *crisis* in the true oriental meaning of the term: an opportunity for newer freedoms along with the danger of new conflict and constraint. Freedom comes in the form of an increasing pluralism and diversity in the availability of medical technologies, organizational forms in which they are delivered, and a diversity of payment mechanisms. Conflict and constraint come in the form of a new tyranny of health in which subjugation to health regimens now has something of the character of a moral imperative and the divestment of some of the more elegant robes of human rights and human dignity and the generalized loss of one's sense of competence to choose and sense of command of one's self-autonomy.

FREEDOM AND OPPORTUNITY IN HEALTH

Freedom is a contradictory element in modern societies, particularly if it involves rights inherent in one's occupying the status of "citizen," and such a status enmeshes persons in a complex network of interdependence that, by its very nature, must involve some loss of freedom. So-called "complete freedom" (the absence of constraint of any kind) is as illusory as the complete absence of social ties and obligations of any kind: the first is a state of bondage that, even in its highly special forms, the courts are increasingly reluctant to sanction; the second is analogous to an ideal state of alienation and is dramatized by the non-human character of feral children. Freedom, therefore, is better seen as a pluralistic opportunity structure that has built-in safeguards against excessive and unwanted commitment to any single binding relationship.

It is this special and tenuous nature of freedom that is crystallized in the concept of citizenship involving rights and obligations inherent in the citizen's status, and this involves the distribution of services and payment therefor on the basis of one's rights or one's needs.

In this sense, where citizenship is binding as both a right and obligation, a person will receive services, in this case medical services, either because of his or her ability to purchase them in the market place, or they are purchased for him or by others because of this individual's claim to status as a person who is entitled to them *because he or she is a person*. Thus far, we have seen that the principle organizational strategies to bring this result about have proved to be less than adequate. The market mechanism of the *private sector of medicine* results in one medical system based upon class differentiations, and the *organizational mechanisms* of the public sector have tended toward pathological forms of bureaucratization as well as to processes of citizen expropriation. The medical system, however, is far more diverse than this simple characterization implies. In fact, potential clients possess *multiple* membership that hinge around differing concepts of rights of citizenship, and multiple groups enhance freedom by allowing one to maneuver in the social-political environment and thereby avoid non-terminable relations with any particular obligation. It is in this sense that the historical movement from situations of *status* (as is implied in the traditional patient-medical system model) to those of *contract* (as is implied in links to the medical system that are negotiated) is movement from less freedom to more freedom. And along these same lines, conflict between patients and the medical system are hardly new for, as Freidson has pointed out, "the struggle between patient and physician seems to have gone on throughout recorded history." The Hippocratic oath attests to this long-standing conflict, because if the behavior railed against therein had never occurred, it would never have been necessary to prescribe for the virtues of the physician.

Moreover, buyers and sellers of medical services, are more closely bound together than buyers and sellers of tangible goods. The closer and more enduring relationship entails a potential for more sustained antagonism than exists in the impersonal and fleeting encounters characteristic of the tangible-goods market.

DIVISION OF LABOR AS SOURCE OF CONFLICT

It has been pointed out that the patient plays a vital part in the division of labor involved in the production of health. "The division of labor," wrote Marx and Engels, "leads to a clash of interests." Where divergent interests arise, antagonism and conflict are generated. While the Marxian theory holds that one of the sources of conflict in the division of labor is the fact that "production and consumption devolve on different individuals," conflict can *also* arise because production and consumption devolve upon the *same* individuals, as in the case of patients who must play an active part in the production of health care. Interests clash because some roles in a division of labor are evaluated as subordinate to others, whatever might be the asymmetry of exchange. At the same time there is a common interest, without which no exploitation and no conflict would be possible. For as Marx and Engels say:[26]

> Division of labor implies the contradiction between the interest of the separate individual or the individual family and the communal interest of all individuals who have intercourse with one another. And indeed, this communal interest . . . [exists] as the mutual interdependence of the individuals among whom the labour is divided.

Of primary importance is the fact that in health care there is an endemic conflict "that arises out of the division of labour, conflict . . . over the terms on which cooperation is to take place."[27] It should be obvious that this is true as much for seller and client in a wide range of services as it is for employer and employee in general.

In addition, as an obverse side to greater productivity, increasing division of labor results in a reduced sense of social responsibility. Merton points out that:[28]

> As professions subdivide, each group of specialists finds it increasingly possible to "pass the buck" for the social consequences of their work. . . . When appalled by resulting social dislocations, each specialist, secure in the knowledge that he has performed his task to the best of his ability, can readily disclaim responsibility for them.

The more specialized purveyors of health service become, the less concerned will they be for the patient "as a whole person." As a result of this, the perception of real or imagined personal indifference is a cause of resentment among patients and thus a source of the potential, and frequently real, conflict to which we are now witness.

But this process can be interpreted in another way. For example, increasing specialization leads to a decline in responsibility, which is resented by the patient. A scarcity of patients induces the specialist to assume greater responsibility—and control, which may also be resented by the patient. In either case an inescapable potential for conflict arises in the relationship between patients and practitioners in the field.

One root of conflict arises from attempts of the patient to become privy to the esoteric knowledge of the practitioner, while the latter tries to prevent the erosion of his or her privileged position by shielding the "mysteries of the trade." This can be viewed as a conflict over inequalities of privilege. The specialist's position may be endangered by the patient becoming his or her own physician. However, keeping the patient in the dark creates both resentment and unrealistic expectations, both of which generate conflict. Hughes points out that:[29]

> In the hearts of many laymen there burns a certain aggressive suspicion of all professionals, whether plumbers or physicians. In some people it flares up into a raging and fanatical anger . . .

This antagonism stems in part from a sense of powerlessness on the part of the patient, whose dependence is based on lack of knowledge. This antagonism may be reciprocated in the form of contempt for the ignorant layman on the part of the professional.

One becomes a patient on the assumption that the seller of health possesses the requisite knowledge for rendering a specialized service, and thus the patient falls under the generalized authority of the practitioner.

Antagonism and resentment between patients and those to whom they are subordinated in various medical organizations is a subject of increasing relevance because of the rapid growth of the medical establishment.

After patients enter the medical division of service for the production of a medical treatment, their status is generally subordinate to the status of *staff* personnel. Szasz's discussions of the major general who was demoted to psychiatric patient and of the governor who refused to be so demoted are classic illustrations. However, where patients come into the service organization from a social stratum markedly lower than that of the staff, an added element of resentment and contempt contributes to the potential for conflict. Where the participants in medical service come from different class subcultures, their interaction is often marred by divergent definitions of the situation. The strains between middle-class teachers, hospital personnel, and lower-class clinic patients, and between staffs and clients of welfare organizations are well known.

The relationship of patron *and client* was the essence of the manorial system and, in the words of Marc Bloch:[30]

Protection, oppression—between these two poles every system of clientage oscillates; and it was as one of the principal elements in a system of this sort that serfdom was originally constituted.

While the feudal analogy should not be pushed too far, many services, especially those of a medical nature directed toward problem-fraught populations, lead to highly dependent clients—another source of antagonism.

Where medical organizations have a broad and long-term social interest in the lives of the patients they serve, clienthood involves an element of servitude, especially for low-status recipients of service. In a servile condition, a person lacks independence of action and a sense of real self-identity. In this sense subordination of the *whole person* rather than performance of a specific *subordinate role* is the essence of servitude. Many poor and powerless patients are incorporated into the division of labor in medicine in ways that tend to degrade them in this way.

Thus induction of the patient into the division of labor opens new arenas of conflict as the medical sector grows in size and complexity and the element of *adversary* relationship obtrudes into it.

Conflict is elaborated in a number of directions in medicine. Not only are there conflicts between patients and health care agents, but there are also conflicts between patients and health care agents acting on behalf of third parties. The nature and outcome of treatment as well as the size of the fee are focal points in the struggle between patients and therapeutic services:[31]

> When a patient presents himself to a physician for medical care and the physician proceeds to render that care, the law implies that a contract has arisen between the parties. It is from this contractual relationship that the duty of a physician to his patient arises.

Contracts entail divergent interests and potential conflict. Malpractice suits by patients and legal action by physicians and hospitals to collect unpaid bills are expressions of overt conflict, but there need not be a court case for conflict to be present and troublesome. Conflict may arise from the failure of physician or hospital as well as from unrealistic expectations of the patient. If the patient believes that he or she has received bad, wrong, or injurious treatment, this belief can be real in its consequences. In court the burden of proof is on the patient, who must find, in most cases, an expert witness to substantiate any claim of malpractice. An exception is made for cases under the principle of *res ipsa loquitur* (the thing speaks for itself), where the laws of simple assault and abandonment apply. This principle applies to foreign bodies left in the patient after surgery, X-ray burns, unauthorized procedures, and such unusual outcomes as the loss of a tooth during tonsillectomy or the fracture of a leg during childbirth.

There are an estimated 9000 malpractice claims each year in the United States, with total settlements of about $50 million. Dismissal of a majority of complaints does not lessen the intensity of conflict, nor does the number of formal complaints indicate its extent.

Under a free-for-service system, conflict over payment is endemic. "Deadbeats" and "gougers" are not the only ones involved in conflict over medical bills. "The best doctor-patient relationship will fail if the doctor is too greedy," writes Blum.[32] And there is no consensus as to the line between "too greedy" and "just greedy enough." In addition, the fee-for-service system, and surely the HMO system, may also lead to conflict because there are incentives for physicians to strive for high-volume practice, which may result in lower quality of service, particularly unnecessary operations.

For these and other reasons, a simple "democratization" of health care institutions and practices is not likely to eradicate the sources of conflict, inequality, and instabilities in health care. Part of this is due to the fact that processes of democratization and lay participation increases rather than decreases the role complexities of effective patienthood, which obviously must increasingly acquire both political and economic overtones.

PATIENTS AS OCCUPANTS OF MULTIPLE STATUSES

As has been already implied, the growing democratization of medicine has created a new arena for the expansion of human freedom as well as a potential for greater constraint and coercion.

Much of the uncertainty here is a result of the fact that the modern society has transformed the patient into buyer, worker, client, and resource all in one. The buyer role implies a voluntaristic relationship. The worker role calls for a negotiated, contractual inequality. The client role implies subordination to the possessors of an esoteric body of knowledge. Finally, the characteristic of being a human resource for the agencies delivering medical services implies further potential for the exploitation and alienation of the consumer.

The person who sets out to obtain a service in the medical sector is *first of all a buyer*. He or she is getting something for which either the buyer or a third party must pay. Thus, the buyer and seller stand in a symmetrical relationship in the context of a market situation.

However, the relationship is not a simple one because the medical consumer is not only in a symmetrical market relationship but at the same time in a number of asymmetrical relationships with elements of subordination. As a coproducer, the patient gives time and effort with-

out which the service could not be produced and thus is aiding and
abetting in the exercise of dominance over him or her. To some extent
the patient is a party to sustaining the conflict between buyer and client
roles. Parsons and Smelser point out that this is a fundamental distinction between the tangible-goods area and service areas such as health
care:[33]

> The market for consumer's *goods*, we have noted, is likely to be less
> imperfect economically than any of the variants of the labour market.
> The fundamental reason underlying this proposition is that the control
> of a physical commodity can be transformed completely from its "pro-
> ducer" to its "consumer," . . . But a *service* is inseparable from the
> performer's person; his other role-involvements inevitably impinge upon
> the situation in which the service is performed.

Workers in many fields have responded to the contingencies of
protracted role involvements in the labor market by forming unions
and similar organizations to develop peer support. Organizations of
patients for coping with analogous contingencies are not highly developed. Such organizations may become more prominent in the future
as institutional means for resolving conflicts in medicine. The reasons
for this may be that the aspects of the worker role in the condition of
patienthood will be better understood and structures analogous to
trade unions may serve to lessen the asymmetry in the relationships
between consumers and purveyors of services. This development holds
forth a potential for realization of greater equity on the part of the
consumers of medical services.

Consumers enter a quasi-professional system in which they are cast
in the role of ignorant laymen, subservient to those who are privy to
esoteric medical knowledge. Given the continuing drift toward professionalization, it is not surprising that such a trend toward subservience
is found in even the most menial of medical services. Even the rhetoric
of professional-client relationship promotes dominance over the client.
Freidson has described medicine as a prototype of this pattern:[34]

> It [medicine as a service system] has the authority to direct and evaluate
> the work of others without in turn being subject to formal direction and
> evaluation by them. Paradoxically, its autonomy is sustained by the
> *dominance* of its expertise in the division of labor.

Thus, the client status—in contrast to the buyer status—introduced a
large asymmetry into the relationship sometimes approaching a servile
status. The more the organization is also to legitimize its claim to
expertise and therefore expand its sphere of dominance, the more
asymmetrical the relation becomes. Again, with medicine as the prototype, Freidson says:[35]

Clearly, many complaints about the depersonalization of the client in the medical organization are complaints about what some technical ostensibly therapeutic procedures do to people. Simply to be strapped on a rolling table and wheeled down corridors, into and out of elevators, and, finally, out into an operating room for the scrutiny of all is to be treated like an object, not a person. To be anesthetized is to become literally an object without the consciousness of a person. And to be palpated, poked, dosed, purged, cut into, probed, and sewed is to find oneself an object. In such cases, it is the technical work of the profession, not "bureaucracy," which is responsible for some of the unpleasantness that the client experiences in health organizations.

Hence, consumers are subordinate to the influence and power of the organization precisely to the extent that the organization is able to exercise persuasive dominance over them. As a result, the buyer and client roles are in direct conflict with one another, producing a dilemma for the patient. The buyer role renders the consumer a free agent presumably working on his or her own behalf. But the client role renders the consumer a powerless object.

Finally, the consumer is *also a resource* for the organization, and this tends toward a new dimension of alienation in society. First of all, the consumer is a vital and necessary input; hospitals must have patients. But a more basic factor is that even though consumers may enter the organization voluntarily and on the basis of a contractual arrangement, they may later find themselves in an *involuntary* relationship for which they have *not* contracted.

Paradoxically, a process of medical coproducership, which may have begun as a service to the patient, may well be suspected of turning out later to be more a service for the health organization, as in the case of the numerous quasi-experiment/research procedures that appear under the guise of "treatment."

In Marx's terms:[36]

> . . . the alienated character of work for the worker appears in the fact that it is not his work but work for someone else, that in work he does not belong to himself but to another person.

This, then, leads to the question of how the patient's participation can be secured in the light of the conflicts and incongruities connected with the mix of the patient's buyer-worker-client-resource roles now present in modern medicine.

INDUCEMENTS AND TRUST IN MEDICAL CARE

The successful completion of a surgical procedure or a medical regimen requires that both the *prime* producer and the *prime* consumer interact long enough for the process to be completed. The entrance of a person into a health organization constitutes a relationship—not necessarily *legally* binding—in which the patient is committed to "stick it out to the end" and the health organization promises to come through as best it can on its promise. The drawing of a "contract," even one of problematic binding power, proves some lack of trust between client and organization. This fact announces to each party that a situation of potential conflict has been entered.

Almost exclusively in the private sector, the tentative agreement reached between patient and health organization involves the exchange of *money*. When buyers give money to the organization, that serves as an enormous incentive for them to follow through in a coproducer capacity. However, at this stage the exchange seems very one-sided. The buyer has given money and the producer has only promised to assist in the production of health.

It is not until there has been, in Anthony Downs's term, "the exchange of non-monetary" values, that the question of asymmetry can be resolved.[37] It is in this sense that the individual patient has "power" inducement as a principal strategy for making the organization's obligation binding.

But, in spite of conflict and alienation, social relations in the medical sector are not characterized by a "war of all men against all men." This implies the presence of some mechanisms for the abatement of conflict and alienation, as well as the strains caused by conditions of mutual mistrust and self-interest.

The contingent nature of mutual trust is not due merely to the contractual relationship and the functional interdependency characterizing the coproducer process, but mainly to processes of exchange. Clearly, the inputs in this exchange are both monetary and nonmonetary from both the patient's and practitioner's points of view. Each would therefore like to make certain that a "fair" exchange is made, which in turn generates feelings of trust and solidarity. On the other hand, the fact of exchange in the pure economic sense causes the relationship to tend toward asymmetry in that there is a probability of "unfair" advantages being taken. This, in its turn, generates feelings of mistrust and conflict between patients and the medical system.

The link between the situation of interdependence and tenuous trust has been put by Parsons as follows:[38]

> Every such organization is, to use our special jargon, justified by providing something which is valuable, but not provided for in the otherwise life-circumstances of the beneficiaries—something for their futures, whether it be recovery from illness, improvement of the educational level, reconciliation with "the law," and so on. The question, then is how these interests on both sides of the [client-organization] differentiation, can be reconciled with the needs of the participants to

live in the "here and now," and somehow maintain their equilibrium. For instance, we are frequently told these days that the new generation will have none of the "deferred gratification" but insist that every aspect of their current mode of life should be intrinsically gratifying, as of the "here and now."

With these dilemmas in mind, a prime issue has to do with how symmetry and asymmetry, trust and mistrust, fairness and unfairness, conflict and solidarity are in fact worked through in the process of coproducing services in medicine.

THE PATIENT AS 'CLIENT'

As implied in the previous chapter, deliberate focus on the client in an effort to achieve comprehensive care involves an important change in the customary relationships between the medical system and patients, namely the distinction between the patient as "client" on the one hand and as "customer" on the other.

When patients are defined as clients, they logically must seek medical care on their own. An implicit and correlate assumption is that patients can effectively conduct a self-diagnosis and enter rationally into the suitable referral system, which then will route them to the proper care-giving practitioners or organizations. A functional correlate, of course, is the medical ethic prescribing that neither the physician nor the hospital may actively *seek out* those persons for whom the potential services are regarded as especially suitable and proper. All of this is consistent with the medical model of illness.

In general, the restrictions against the medical doctor's right to "advertise" has its organizational equivalent in the reluctance of hospitals to reach out into the population and differentially select their patients. The implication is that clients need not choose invidiously or otherwise between doctors and services, and that medical organizations need not select judiciously among the great reservoir of potential clients. Such a perspective assumes also that the referral system by which patients are routed to institutions is efficient in its function. Hence, efforts to impose blanket integration plans—to integrate indiscriminately all medical facilities in a city, a region, or an area—are consistent with the traditional tenets of professional conduct and with the underlying conception of the patient as client.

As Scott and Volkart have said, "To the extent that there is today a 'crisis in American medicine,' as many of our leading periodicals are fond of asserting from time to time, it is not a crisis centering around the quality of medical services as such, but concerns chiefly the organization and distribution of those service."[39]

The specifically focused and short-term institution—the typical general hospital, for example—epitomizes the organizational embodiment of the patient seen as client.

The conception of the patient as "customer," however, implies a different set of relationships between the medical system and the populations served. It assumes, first of all, that the patient is in no position to select among unequal and different alternatives in medical care. Second, it assumes that all medical facilities are not equally appropriate for all members of the population. Out of these two assumptions springs the compelling conclusion that different constituent elements in the medical complex must seek ways to *define* their relevant publics and to make their relevance publicly known. Hence, medical organizations that view patients as *customers* must reach out to the population —to capture segments of it is perhaps too strong a term—in order to deliver the chosen medical service to the appropriate people.

The newly emerging conception of the patient as customer means also that hospitals incorporating such a view must logically denounce a commitment to the classic "magical hand" referral system. One unexplored clue to the possible enhancement of interagency collaboration in the health field is precisely this newer conception of the patient as a customer, especially when the customers are those of the population who have but loose ties with the extant referral system or are in those communities with an uncodified local medical power structure or one in the interim period of internal change.

THE ETHICAL PROBLEM OF PATIENT CONTROL

It is hardly possible to predict what predominant organization form is likely to emerge to supplant the traditional highly focused and short-term hospital. To the extent that one does predict, however, there will be profound changes in the prevailing conception of the patient as a client and considerable pressures exerted upon the existing "informal organization of medicine" at the community level. Dissatisfaction with the prevailing patient referral system and greater numbers of experiments in comprehensive care involving interagency collaboration are likely to appear.

It might be fair to predict at this point that whatever alterations might occur along the contemporary life-space axis of our scheme as far as hospitals are concerned, a more elongated time orientation toward patients is a real probability. This is so not only because of the changing age shape of the population and the nature of chronic diseases, which call for long-term care, but also because of the numerous pressures toward the expansion of public health responsibilities and the ethic of humanism the increasingly demands effective care in *both* the long and the short run.

In sum, hospitals, whether they attempt to address the total patient or merely some specifically selected aspect of him or her, are likely to attempt to maintain their domain over a longer period of time. My final argument, then is that a drift from a short-term toward a long-term orientation carries with it profound ethical implications that cannot be ignored.

As pointed out, the medical system has both technical and humanistic themes in its traditional underpinning. And the drift toward a broad and comprehensive orientation appears to have very close ideological linkages to the demand for less depersonalized and more humane concern for the total person. The paradox, of course, is that hospitals that attempt to intervene broadly in the patient's life must devise a wide range of control strategies over patients in order to maintain their compliance with regard to as many of those aspects of the patient's life space that the medical agent chooses to address.

The comprehensive concept has similar implications for the exercise of coercion, but of a quite different order because of the period over which the threat of its use persists. The drift toward extended long-term intervention also has ideological components. Where this occurs in the *public* sphere, the interorganizational conspiracy of elongated control and coercion may take the form of statutory right to control. At the same time, the public sphere normally includes prescribed mechanisms by which clients may legitimately counter organizational controls, or at least state appeals exempting them from such controls and terminating the organization's grasp.

Where it occurs in the *private* sphere, the exercise of long-term control and coercion more likely takes the form of a conspiracy of persuasion that hardly permits clients to exempt themselves effectively. One might suspect, therefore, that one outcome of comprehensive care may ultimately come to be directed toward those *least likely to resist* effectively: the uninformed, the acquiescent, and other "powerless" segments of the population who see as their only options living with organizational controls, and "colonizing" to the extent of carving out some modicum of personal autonomy in the interstitial areas of life to which some medical organization has not as yet laid a claim.

For example, in discussing the implications of the all-out effort against mental illness among the poor, Warren Haggstrom argues that the fundamental source of poor peoples' disadvantages in health and *rapprochement* with health institutions is their lack of power—an inability to "define the situation" and an inability to erect countercontrols and barriers to inhibit violations of privacy and personal autonomy. For if there is an identifiable integrating theme in these new and intense treatment approaches for the poor, it is that agencies can best attack problems of mental illness among the poverty-stricken by exploiting the fact of their powerlessness. The psychiatric worker can approach lower-class potential patients in their homes, the poolroom, the local tavern, or their places of work, and they can be otherwise enticed into health system's orbit without being informed as to what is happening to them.

The adoption of a broad and long-term orientation toward patients seems likely to enhance the potentials for interagency contact and collaboration. It may lead also to a more efficient utilization and comprehensive distribution of available medical resources to a wider population base.

The patient however, may be in danger of being engulfed by a bondage brought about by an awesome organizational and ideological revolution to an extent to which civil rights have a way of being transformed into citizens' obligations, compliance to which often take the form of strict legal restraints phrased in the judiciary terms of the "public interest."

Dating perhaps from the turbulent years of the mid-1960s, is a growing differentiation between those who hold to the patterns of the past (which, in the context of a discussion of industrial development, can be best described as an adherence to Western bureaucratic conceptions) and those who embrace an as yet not fully defined ideological position of involving an extension of citizens' rights (which has been described as an essentially "Maoist" conception).[40] The principle differences between these two *Weltanschauungs* are summarized in Table 12.2.

In their discussion of these changes, Katz and Kahn write:[41]

> Social experience as well as theory suggests the need for change in the classical bureaucratic model, and modifications, real and alleged, are being propagated in many parts of the world. For example, the kibbutz communities of Israel violate many of the assumptions of eastern bureaucracy in their rotation of personnal in official positions, their group decision making, their equality of rewards, and their departure from universalistic criteria in personnel selection. Nevertheless, they compete very effectively with the private sector . . .

In some sense, health as a general and commonweal resource has produced a new array of patient rights and medical system prerogatives, which are necessarily in conflict at several points. And to the degree that this is true, a central question has to do with whether it is possible to achieve a maximum expression of "technical health" at the same time as one maximizes political prerogatives, economic justice, and human rights of autonomy and personal dignity. As Becker has written:[42]

> The great philosopher Henri Bergson wrote that the continuation of evolution was accomplished by geniuses who broke out of the automatic

TABLE 12.2
'Western' and 'Maoist' concepts of organization

Western conceptions	Maoist conceptions
1. Use criteria of technical competence in personnel allocation	1. Use both political purity and technical competence
2. Promote organizational autonomy	2. Politics takes command, and openness to outside political demands
3. Legal-rational authority	3. Mass line participative-charismatic authority
4. Informal social groups unavoidably occur	4. Informal groups can and should be fully coopted
5. Differentiated rewards to office and performance encouraged	5. Differentiated rewards to office and performance deemphasized
6. Varied compliance strategies needed, depending on the organization	6. Normative and social compliance should play the main role everywhere
7. Formalistic impersonality	7. Comradeship
8. Unemotionality	8. Political zeal encouraged
9. Partial inclusion and limited contractual obligations of officeholders	9. Near total inclusion and theoretically unlimited obligations
10. Job security encouraged	10. Job security not valued, and career orientations not encouraged
11. Calculability through rules and established procedures	11. Flexibility and rapid change valued, rules and procedures looked on with suspicion
12. Unity of command and strict hierarchy of communications	12. Collective leadership and flexible consultation

SOURCE: Adapted from Daniel Katz and Robert L. Kahn, *The Social Psychology of Organizations*, 2nd Ed. New York: John Wiley, 1978, p. 274.

cultural patterns of perception and renewed the life surge in a forward direction. The challenge of the modern theory of democracy is that more people than just the geniuses or gifted leaders will have to free themselves from cultural constraint in order for sufficient new energies to emerge from nature. And the religious geniuses themselves already knew that their own small numbers were not enough, that large masses of people will have to turn from narrowness and illustion to a more universal development . . . a large part of the evil that man unleashes on himself and his world stems not from a wickedness in his heart, but from the way he was conditioned to see the world and to seek satisfaction in it. . . . He follows orders, keeps his nose clean, and gets whatever satisfactions his character structure has equipped him to seek. . . . Today we realize . . . that the renewing forces alive in nature have to break through the crust of character armor that the frightened and obedient Homo sapiens has bottled himself into.

All the signs and symptoms point to the fact that medicine is slowly entering a new era in which health—along with its associated agencies, institutions, and occupations—has become an object of public debate and it will eventually find a public solution, not one generated strictly out of the imperatives of medical technology. In the field of health the question is no longer "What can be done?" but rather "What *ought* to be done?"

SCENARIO II

A.D. *2000: death, where is thy sting?*

It's the year 2000. Americans have a life expectancy to age 90, euthanasia is legal, and individuals have come a long way toward accepting death calmly, without fear or pain.

In this scenario, the average retirement age is 76, and many people begin new careers in their 50s, causing massive shifts in the labor market. A popular career for an older person is "lifestyle engineer," a professional who counsels through personal experience on work, leisure, and health.

And the dying no longer experience pain in most cases—except by choice. If people perceive the risk of premature death to be decreasing, they may buy less life insurance and place more of their money in other financial vehicles. Author Romma Klingenber's scenario of A.D. 2000 sees space colonies reserved for people over 70, and terminal patients allowed to program their own deaths any way they see fit. Most people choose painless death with ample use of heroin and mind control techniques. . . . Some dying persons choose the "adventure death" offered by travel agents, a series of history-inspired suicides in various settings.

For persons of lesser means, city governments provide right-to-die service centers where it is possible to die and be cremated at low cost.

Middle-income Americans frequently sell the right to use parts

The Providence Evening Bulletin, Providence, Rhode Island, Monday, April 10, 1978, p. 1. Reprinted with permission.

from their bodies if they become "neomorts" or brain-dead cadavers kept functioning by machines.

. . . Estate taxes consume almost all of any estate transfer, since opposition to such measures died out after people started living to 90 and worrying less about their children—age 70.

NOTES

1   Daniel Callahan, "Health and Society," in *Doing Better and Feeling Worse*. John H. Knowles, Ed. New York: Norton, 1977, pp. 23–24. By permission.

2   William R. Rosengren, "Some Sociological Impediments to Health Care Delivery," quoted in *National Congress on Health Manpower*. American Medical Association, Chicago, 1970. By permission.

3   H. H. Gerth and C. Wright Mills, Eds., *From Max Weber: Essays in Sociology*. New York: Oxford, 1958.

4   Eliot Freidson, "The Futures of Professionalization," in *Health and the Division of Labor*, M. Stacey et al., Eds. London: Croom Kelm, 1977, pp. 14–38.

5   William R. Rosengren, "A 'Nutcracker' Theory of Modern Organizations," *Sociological Focus*, 8 (August 1975), 271–282.

6   James D. Thompson, *Organizations in Action*. New York: McGraw-Hill, 1967.

7   Peter M. Blau and W. Richard Scott, *Formal Organizations*. San Francisco: Chandler, 1962.

8   C. Gersuny and W. R. Rosengren, *The Service Society*. Boston: Schenkman Publishing Company, 1973.

9   Robert R. Alford, *Health Care Politics: Ideological and Interest Group Barriers to Reform*. Chicago: University of Chicago Press, 1975, p. 262.

10   Ibid., pp. 263–264.

11   Harold L. Wilensky and Charles N. Lebaux, *Industrial Society and Social Welfare*. New York: Russell Sage, 1958, p. xvii.

12   Charles Perrow, "Members as Resources in Voluntary Organization," in *Organizations and Clients*, William R. Rosengren and Mark Lefton, Eds. Columbus, Ohio: Merrill, 1970, pp. 108–109.

13   *The Regan Report: On Hospital Law*, W. A. Regan, Ed., No. 17 (January 1977).

14   New York State (386 NYS2d46).

15   Janice Flegle, "Teaching Self Dialysis to Adults in a Hospital," *American Journal of Nursing*, 77 (February 1977), 270–272.

16   Julia S. Brown and May E. Rawlinson, "Sex Differences in Sick Role Rejection and in Work Performance Following Cardiac Surgery," *Journal of Health and Social Behavior*, 18 (September 1977), 276–291.

17   David E. Hayes-Bavtista, "Termination of the Patient-Practitioner Relationship: Divorce, Patient Style," *Journal of Health and Social Behavior*, 17 (March 1976), 12–21.

18   Josephine Kasteller, Robert L. Kane, Donna M. Olsen, and Constance Thetford, "Issues Underlying Prevalence of Doctor-Shopping Behaviors," *Journal of Health and Social Behavior*, 17 (December 1976), 328–339.

19   Vida Francis, Barbara Korsch, and Marie J. Morris, "Gaps in Doctor-Patient Communications," *New England Journal of Medicine*, 280 (1969), 535–540.

20   Roberta G. Simmons and Richard L. Simmons, "Organ Transplantation: A Societal Problem," *Social Problems*, 19 (1971–72), 36–56.

21   James A. Burdette, John C. Cassel, Barbara S. Hulka, and Lawrence L. Kup-

per, "Communication, Compliance, and Concordance between Physicians and Patients with Prescribed Medications," *American Journal of Public Health,* 6 (September 1976), 847–843.

22 *Providence Evening Bulletin* (Friday, December 2, 1977), p. 6.
23 William R. Rosengren, "The Social Economics of Membership," in *Organizations and Clients,* Rosengren and Lefton, Eds., op. cit., pp. 205–222.
24 *Providence Evening Bulletin* (Thursday, April 13, 1978), p. 34.
25 Roger Johnson, "Biorhythms: Fact or Fiction?" *New York Times,* December 25, 1977, p. 2, section 5. © 1977 by the New York Times Company. Reprinted by permission.
26 Karl Marx and F. Engels, *The German Ideology.* New York: International Publishers, 1947, p. 22.
27 T. H. Marshall, *Class, Citizenship, and Social Development.* New York: Doubleday, 1965, p. 182.
28 Robert K. Merton, *Social Theory and Social Structure.* New York: Free Press, 1957, p. 568.
29 Everett C. Hughes, *Men and Their Work.* New York: Free Press, 1958, p. 82.
30 Marc Bloch, *Feudal Society.* Chicago: University of Chicago Press, 1961, p. 265.
31 Joseph Stetler and A. R. Moritz, *Doctor, Patient, and the Law.* St. Louis: Mosby, 1962, p. 306.
32 Richard H. Blum, *The Management of the Doctor-Patient Relationship.* New York: McGraw-Hill, 1960, p. 136.
33 Talcott Parsons and Neil Smelser, *Economy and Society.* New York: Free Press, 1956, p. 57.
34 Eliot Freidson, *Profession of Medicine.* New York: Dodd, Mead, 1970, p. 77.
35 Ibid., p. 78.
36 Karl Marx, *Selective Writings in Sociology and Social Philosophy.* T. B. Bottomore, Ed. New York: McGraw-Hill, 1954, p. 93.
37 Anthony Downs, *Inside Bureaucracy.* Boston: Little, Brown, 1967.
38 Talcott Parsons, "How Are Clients Integrated into Service Organizations?" in *Organizations and Clients,* Rosengren and Lefton, Eds., op. cit., pp. 1–16.
39 W. Richard Scott and E. Volkart, Eds., *Medical Care.* New York: Wiley, 1966, p. 1.
40 Daniel Katz and Robert Kahn, *The Social Psychology of Organizations,* 2d ed. New York: Wiley, 1978.
41 Ibid., p. 273.
42 Ernest K. Becker, *The Birth and Death of Meaning.* New York: The Free Press, 1962, pp. 184–185.

SUGGESTED READINGS

Orville G. Brim, Jr., Ed., *The Dying Patient.* New Brunswick, N.J.: Trans-Action Books, 1979.
A collection of original essays on the problems encountered, at the value level, of the dilemmas involved in dying under medical surveillance.

Rick Carlson, *The End of Medicine.* New York: Wiley, 1976.
A "futuristic" view of the probability contours of the health scene by the beginning of the twenty-first century.

Jay Katz, *Catastrophic Disease: Who Decides What?* New Brunswick, N.J.: Trans-Action Books, 1979.

The conflict between technological capabilities and human rights and values in the use of extraordinary medical technologies.

Eliot A. Krause, *Power and Illness.* New York: Elsevier, 1977.

An "explicitly left wing" critique of the American medical establishment, with an attempt to analyze current problems from a perspective of differential power.

Charles E. Lewis et al., *A Right to Health.* New York: Wiley-Interscience, 1976.

An interdisciplinary analysis of the factors that prevent persons from securing access to primary medical care.

Richard A. Rettig, *Cancer Crusade.* Princeton, N.J.: Princeton University Press, 1978.

A history of the use of the "moon-shot" fever of the late 1960s that sparked the political activity generating the "war against cancer," as set forth in the National Cancer Act of 1971.

Index

ethnic similarity between physicians and, 165–166
expectations of normal course of events, 301–302
as occupants of multiple statuses, 421–423
power structure of hospital and, 20
residential status in hospitals, 20
responsibility and prognosis in definition of clienthood, 293–295
rhythmic patterns of behavior in hospitals, 299–300
rights of. *See* Medical ethics
sick role. *See* Sick role
socialization to role of, 285
subservience in the place of treatment, 295–299
Paxton, H., 118–119
Peer rebukes, 250
Pennsylvania, University of, 120, 146
Pepper, Max, 139
Perkins, Elisha, 216
Perrow, Charles, 139, 318–319
Personal well-being, feelings of, 6, 7
Ph.D. (nursing), 258
Phenylketonuria (PKU), 366
Physical integrity, 6, 7
Physicians
  authority of, 244–249
  autonomy of, limits on, 251–255
  conflict with patients, 418–421
  decision to become, 120–126
  ethnicity as factor in hospital sponsorship, 161–167
  fees of. *See* Physicians' fees
  hospital affiliation, importance of, 19–20
  hospitalization and, 70–71
  income of, 73, 79–82
  "informal" recruitment of, 137–138
  organization and cooperation with other physicians, 18–20
  percentages in various forms of practice, 72

pool of, 73–76
relations with sociologists, 88–94
reliance on nurses, 259
securing a practice, 150–153
social types of, 89–90
task delegation to paraprofessionals, 272–273
Physician's assistants, 270–277
Physician's associate, 275
Physicians' fees, 80
  allocation of health dollar to, 69
  paid with federal money, 77–78
  specialization and, 71
Pinel, Philippe, 333
Pluralist perspective, 23–24, 404, 405
Pneumonia, 31, 43, 45, 49
Poland, infant death rate in, 43
Polio vaccine, 32
Pop psychology, 412
Population base, changes in, 34–38
Powell, Francis D., 352
Practical nurse, 257
Pregnancy, sick role in, 264–270
Prepaid practice, 19
Prep room, 296–297, 302, 303
Preventive medicine, 19, 32
Private hospitals, 64–68, 171
Professional charter, 174, 175, 176
Professional organization
  defined, 8
  diversity in, 17–22
  labor force, changes in, 72–74
  in 1900, 33–34
  paraprofessionals. *See* Paraprofessionals
Proprietary hospitals, 64–68
Pseudopsychiatry, 219–223
Psychiatric patients. *See* Functional disorders
Psychiatric realm, marginal medicine in, 219–223
Psychic surgery, 235–236
Psychoanalysis, 340
Psychological testers, 376
Psychomedications, 322–323, 331, 349–352
Psychorelaxation exercises, 235